Intelligentsia
and
Revolution

INTELLIGENTSIA

AND

REVOLUTION

Russian Views of Bolshevism
1917–1922

Jane Burbank

New York   Oxford
OXFORD UNIVERSITY PRESS
1986

Oxford University Press

Oxford   New York   Toronto
Delhi   Bombay   Calcutta   Madras   Karachi
Petaling Jaya   Singapore   Hong Kong   Tokyo
Nairobi   Dar es Salaam   Cape Town
Melbourne   Auckland

and associated companies in
Beirut   Berlin   Ibadan   Nicosia

Copyright © 1986 by Oxford University Press, Inc.

Published by Oxford University Press, Inc.
200 Madison Avenue, New York, New York 10016

Library of Congress Cataloging-in-Publication Data
Burbank, Jane.
Intelligentsia and revolution.
Bibliography: p.
Includes index.
1. Communism and intellectuals—Soviet Union.
2. Soviet Union—History—Revolution, 1917–1921.
3. Intellectuals—Soviet Union—Political activity.
I. Title.
HX528.B87   1986   320.5′322   85-32096
ISBN 0-19-504061-9

1 3 5 7 9 8 6 4 2

Printed in the United States of America
on acid-free paper

Acknowledgments

The people who have helped me write this book have, perhaps, as divergent points of view as the Russian intellectuals who are my subjects. This is for the better and I am grateful to them all. First, I wish to thank Richard Pipes, Edward L. Keenan, and James D. Wilkinson for their advice and careful reading when this project was a dissertation. As the thesis became a book, Paul Avrich, Elizabeth Wood, and Ronald Mercier read entire drafts and gave me the great benefit of their suggestions. Frederick Cooper, Marc Jansen, and André Liebich offered very helpful comments on sections of the manuscript.

Several people who lived during the revolution or in the early emigration shared their memories and ideas with me. Olga Chernov Andreyev and Natasha Chernov Reznikova, Vera Broido-Cohn, Valentina Maximovna Crémer, Tatiana Sergeevna Frank, George Garvy, Anya Gourevitch, and Sylvia Gourevitch helped to shape my image of their parents', or husbands', generation. Tamara Klépinine, Igor Aleksandrovich Krivoshein, Wladimir Weidlé, and Sergei Pavlovich Zhaba generously described their early lives and their experiences of the revolution and civil war. Pierre Pascal discussed his lengthy stay in Russia, and Boris Sapir, scholar and activist in the best intelligentsia tradition, offered not only a glimpse into his past, but also valuable guidance for my archival searches.

Without archives and libraries, the past itself could not speak, and I was fortunate to be able to use many excellent and accommodating facilities. I am grateful to the librarians and other workers at the following institutions: the International Institute of Social History in Amsterdam; the archive and library of the Hoover Institution on War, Revolution and Peace at Stanford University, especially Hilya Kukk; the Bibliothèque de documentation internationale contemporaine at Nanterre, in particular Mme. Kaplan; the Bayerische Staatsbibliothek and the Osteuropa-Institut in Munich; the library of the Eberhard-Karls-Universität in Tubingen; the Bakhmeteff Archive at Columbia University and its former curator Stephen Corrsin; the Bibliothèque nationale, the Archives nationales, and the Turgenev Library in Paris; the British Museum in London; the Public Record Office at Kew; the Graduate Library of the University of Michigan, in particular Joseph Placek; at Harvard University— the Houghton Library, the Russian Research Center and its administrator Mary Towle and librarian Susan Gardos, and Sheila Hart and my other friends and former co-workers in Widener Library.

To reach these far-flung collections and to use them I needed material resources. My research on this project was supported by fellowships from the American Council of Learned Societies, the Krupp Foundation, and the Whiting Foundation, and by faculty research grants from Harvard University.

As this project reached its final stages, new people joined it. I was privileged to work with Nancy Lane of Oxford University Press, and I am grateful to Kate Schecter, who painstakingly reviewed the entire text and notes. I also wish to thank the editors of the *Cahiers du monde russe et soviétique*, in which material from the first two chapters appeared in a different form.

Although it may seem that this book has had a history as peripatetic as that of the Russian intellectuals after 1917, in fact it had only three homes. One was Paris, in 1977 and 1978, when I first conceptualized the project and where I was sheltered and encouraged by two very kind and very different representatives of the St. Petersburg intelligentsia, both born in 1895—Wladimir Weidlé and Valentina Maximovna Crémer, née Vinaver. The second home was Adams House at Harvard, where Robert and Jana Kiely provided me with both company and a quiet place to write my dissertation and begin a book. Most of the work on the book was completed in a third home, Ann Arbor, where I found intellectual community a reality and not a myth. Two groups in particular enlivened my year's leave in Ann Arbor in 1983–84. William Rosenberg and Ronald Suny and other members of the University of Michigan's Center for Russian and East European Studies offered a warm and scholarly welcome, and the members of the Community Action/Social History group who gathered in Charles and Louise Tilly's living room on Sunday evenings showed what seminars should be.

Many friends in many places have made my life pleasant while I was working on this project. I am very grateful to them. Above all, I thank Fred Cooper for our companionship, with its happy past and its promise for the future.

Ann Arbor, Mich.   J.B.
September 1985

Contents

Intelligentsia
and
Revolution

The anniversary of the Decembrist uprising. They, too, almost one hundred years ago, were here in these cells. . . . They died believing in their cause. Our generation lives, losing faith in what it has done. What lesson is there for our successors, even if we ourselves are unable to make use of it? When people ask me, ''Was it worth making a revolution, when it led to such results?'' I answer with two considerations:

1. It is naive and shortsighted to think that it's possible to *make or not make* a revolution: it arises and begins beyond the will of individuals. How many times have people tried to ''make'' it and then faltered due to the indifference of the circumstances and the persecution of enemies. . . . To hold back the revolution is the same kind of dream as to continue or to intensify it. Who holds back a storm and who stops it? . . . This is not fate or determinism. This is the logical development of events on a grand scale under the influence of an enormous mass of moving forces. Regret, repentance, reproaches, and accusations are interesting and, perhaps, appropriate in individual life, concerning personal characteristics or personal experiences. Concerning the revolution, they mean nothing. . . .

2. If I were asked to . . . begin everything again or to stop it, I would not hesitate for one minute to begin again, regardless of all the horrors the country has gone through. And here is why. The revolution was inescapable for the old had outlived itself. The balance had been destroyed long ago, and at the foundation of the Russian state system, which not long ago we called a colossus on feet of clay, lay the dark popular masses, deprived of a link to the state, of an understanding of society and of the ideals of the intelligentsia, deprived even of simple patriotism. The striking lack of correspondence between the top of society and its foundation, between the leaders of the state in its past forms—and the leaders of the future as well—and the mass of the population—this struck me in my youth, in my first years of university life. . . .

Since then, the long years have shown me how hard it is to do anything on the path I chose, and how the old regime with thousands of obstacles obstructed that path, along which even without its direct and idiotic opposition it was possible to move only very slowly and with great difficulty. . . . Now, when the revolution has come on a scale and in a direction that no one was able to foresee, I still say, better that it has happened! Better, that the avalanche hanging over the state has rolled down and ceased to threaten it. Better, that the abyss between the people and the intelligentsia has opened up to the bottom and has finally begun to be filled up with the debris of the old regime. Better, that the trigger has already been released and the shot made, than to wait for it any second. Better, because it is only now that real constructive work, replacing the clay legs of the Russian colossus with a worthy and safe foundation, can begin. . . . I do not fear these experiments [of the socialists, based on] turbulent youthful thought and lack of knowledge of the people themselves and foreign history. Foreign experience is always badly used; the best science is our own mistakes. Louis Blanc was right when he said that "society has not just a head, but also a soul, and when the soul has changed, then the body will be transformed as well." For me this reconciling accord now has a primary significance. The soul of our people has changed little so far, but it has changed, and most important it has opened up and state life has come to it, seized it or demanded an answer from it. Sooner or later the building of a new state system will begin on the only possible and stable foundation. This is why I accept the revolution and not only accept it, but welcome it, and not only welcome it, but affirm it. If I were asked to start it all over, now without hesitation I would say: "Let us begin!"

A. I. Shingarev,
Member of the Central Committee of the Kadet Party
Imprisoned in the Petropavlovsk Fortress
December 14, 1917

Introduction

The Intelligentsia Tradition

The interpretation of the Russian revolution began in its midst, as Russian intellectuals tried to explain the vast crisis that engulfed them. From its earliest days, the revolution gave new urgency and meaning to issues that had concerned the intelligentsia in the past—socialism and its possibilities in Russia, the relationship between Russia and the West, the values of the Russian people, and the power of the state. The rude shock of a social upheaval radically at odds with most intellectuals' ideas of change and progress challenged them to understand the revolution, its causes, and its meaning for the future.

In 1917 and for the next five years, the intelligentsia's theories were shaped and tested in rapidly shifting circumstances. Caught with the people for whom they claimed to speak in the collapse of the imperial system, theorists and critics were confronted with the disintegration of life as it had been and the harsh struggles for survival and control that in time shaped a new nation. At first, the existence of the state itself was threatened by the end of the old political and economic organization, the rebellions of nationalist and local movements, and the long civil war between many armies. Later, after the Bolsheviks' expulsion of the last White troops in November 1920 and their victories over the massive peasant revolts and the Kronstadt insurgents the following year, a settlement became perceptible. The introduction of the New Economic Policy appeared to change the relationship between the ruling party and the population, and the great famine of 1921 and 1922 made rebuilding a national imperative. The ideas and commentaries of Russian intellectuals reflect this gradual development, from the uncertainties of 1917 to the consolidation of Bolshevik power.

5

By the end of this critical period, anarchists, socialists, liberals, monarchists, and cultural nationalists had formulated a broad array of perspectives on the revolution, viewpoints that defined debates within the intelligentsia for many years and anticipated the arguments of other, later, commentators. These theories offer a complex image of the revolution seen from within, a multi-faceted picture that does not support the outworn conventional interpretations—the triumphant march of Bolshevism and its opposing pole, the accidental interruption of Western-style development—and should inform and provoke further historical study. Moreover, Russian intellectuals in these years confronted dilemmas that still perplex critically thinking people. How should socialists respond to governments that claim their cause, but whose practices undermine their goals? What could social theory contribute to politics? What was the role of an intelligentsia in the revolutionary crisis and after?

To these questions, Russian observers brought the skills of a particular culture—the divided, critical, and politicized world of the intelligentsia in the early twentieth century. Their views of revolution reflect back the consciousness of this self-designated class, with its explicit political and philosophical commitments, its unspoken assumptions and values, its strengths and weaknesses. This group portrait belongs in the history of the revolution, a time when both action and inaction counted and when tactical and institutional choices made by the intelligentsia were critical for the future.

The subjects of this study were, for the most part, leading figures in the prerevolutionary intelligentsia—social and political theorists who sought to articulate national interests and who continued to pursue this goal after 1917. From the myriad of commentators on the revolution, I have selected individuals whose situations captured the dilemmas facing the various factions within the intelligentsia and whose analyses expressed the wide range of ideological perspectives on the revolution. The first chapters of this book focus on theorists of the revolutionary left—Martov, Axelrod, Potresov, and other oustanding figures in Russian social democracy; Chernov and Vishniak, representatives of two different tactics and analyses within the broad span of the Socialist Revolutionary party; and Kropotkin, the gentle patriarch of Russian anarchism. Another section examines the odysseys of two Russian liberals, Miliukov, the leader of the Kadet party, and Struve, the former Marxist and idiosyncratic proponent of religious nationalism. The slim chapter on postrevolutionary monarchism is anomalous; in addition to the historian Ol'denburg, it includes an anti-Semite and his cohorts, enemies of the intelligentsia but important contributors to the revolution's image in both Russia and the West. The last part of this study concerns three major figures—Berdiaev, N. S. Trubetskoi, and Ustrialov—who stood outside the conventional political alignments and stressed instead the primacy of culture, race, and nationality.[1]

For a number of reasons, Bolshevik theory is not a major subject of this book. First, the concerns and possibilities of the leaders of the revolutionary state differed fundamentally from those of other intellectuals. For the Bolsheviks from 1917 to 1922, the most important questions were practical: how to build socialism, not what was being built. Second, the revolution altered radically the context of Bolshevik analysis. One part of the revolutionary movement had now become the government, and this meant that even the new leaders' most speculative writings were imbedded in the politics of power. Third, the Bolsheviks' tactical and theoretical statements have been examined by many scholars, whose work should be complemented by a study of other views.[2]

My focus on the intelligentsia outside the government does not, however, exclude the Bolsheviks from the text. They are everywhere, both in the theories and in the experiences of the intelligentsia after 1917. For many intellectuals, especially socialists and liberals, the new government was the main target of their criticism and the culprit for what, in their opinion, had gone wrong with the revolution. For others, Bolshevism was a symptom of more profound, long-term processes that had shaped the revolutionary crisis and its outcome. Most important, the fact of Bolshevik government and its apparent power to reform the state put the Bolsheviks at the center of the intelligentsia's analyses and defined the terms of renewed confrontation between the governors and their opponents.

To the hostility of the "anti-Bolshevik" intelligentsia, as it now could be identified, the Bolshevik authorities responded in different ways at different times. For the first years covered in this book, the issue for the new state was survival, and its approach to intellectuals who did not support the government was correspondingly harsh. Besieged, the Bolshevik leadership did not hesitate to attack the dissidents and their organizations, although during the civil war some brief concessions were made to the moderate socialist parties. But after the war was over, security still did not seem to be at hand, and the government stepped up its efforts to eliminate a domestic opposition. The state's rigorous campaign against potentially threatening ideologies in this period overwhelmed any possibility for serious public debate or for a well-developed "Bolshevik" response to the theories of the outsider intellectuals. In accord with this lopsided relationship between power and ideas, the Bolsheviks' engagement with their critics' arguments has been given only intermittent attention in this study.

As this summary account suggests, the Bolsheviks' step into government in 1917 had a crucial impact on the future of the intelligentsia in Russia, one that suggests the defining characteristics of this group. The new state made no place for the intelligentsia of the past, with its functions of political criticism and articulation of alternative ideals. By 1922, many of the intellectuals who tried to pursue the old oppositionist culture had been expelled from Russia; in this physical sense, the prerevolutionary intelligentsia was defeated by the revolution. But in these same five years, the experience of the revolution, and in particular the success of Bolshevik institutions, inspired a brilliant outburst of theory and criticism from thoughtful, informed observers. Faced with an explicit challenge, believers in the intelligentsia tradition resumed with new vigor their role of speaking for the nation against the state.

For the revolution, despite its hardships, revived the intelligentsia's sense of purpose. This had been eroded in the preceding decade when the old simplicities of nineteenth-century politics—the single ethical polarity between state and people, the notion of the "people's will" and of the intelligentsia as its expression, confidence in reason as a means to progress—lost meaning in a complex and changing polity. The intelligentsia, which had defined itself through moral commitments, was threatened by the loss of these absolutes.[3]

One everyday challenge to the self-conception of the intelligentsia was the rapid expansion of the professional class in the early twentieth century.[4] While this group provided the market for much of what the political opposition wrote, and although many of the radical intellectuals were themselves products of the Russian educational system, the new opportunities presented by the burgeoning economy undermined the idea of the intelligentsia as a small, embattled group struggling against oppression. Many of those who would formerly have been hounded into full-time opposition to the state now chose to become doctors, teachers, or agronomists instead, not to mention those who entered industry or the civil service.[5]

The increase in the numbers of educated people, of "society" in the vocabulary of the time, was matched by the exuberant growth of elite culture in the same period. Fueled by the opening up of opportunity, the creation of new institutions, and the wealth of a sympathetic bourgeoisie, the outburst of creativity in literature, painting, dance, and design at this time was unique and splendid. In addition, Russian scholars made major contributions to the sciences and the humanities and were active participants in their international communities.[6] This ferment in cultural life was not apolitical. Symbolists, suprematists, and futurists rebelled against the present and created visions of the future in their works; many artists and academics were eager to escape the autocracy's controls.[7] But the actions and interests of the cultural and professional elite were diverse, and the various functions of the "broad intelligentsia," as this group was sometimes labeled, contradicted the traditional notion of the intelligentsia as the servant of the exploited.

The most concrete negation of this imagery was the revolution of 1905. What seemed at first an affirmation of the intelligentsia's ideology—a vast popular rebellion, uniting peasants, urban workers, and "society" against the state—proved deceptive. The united opposition was never a reality; the people's revolution was defeated; and the autocracy, not the intelligentsia, set the terms for national politics. The deep disappointment with the outcome of the revolution, felt by both revolutionaries and reformists, cast a long shadow over the debates of the next years.

One expression of the pervasive demoralization in this period was the intelligentsia's interest in its own history. P. N. Miliukov, the leading spokesman for liberal reform, followed his three-volume study of Russian culture with a fourth tome on the great intellectual debates of the nineteenth century.[8] Iulii O. Martov, the Menshevik theorist, turned toward the past as well, chronicling the decline of the populist movement and the expansion of socialism and liberalism from a Marxist standpoint.[9] In 1906 appeared the first edition of R. V. Ivanov-Razumnik's *History of Russian Social Thought*, a grand and explicit effort through intellectual history to shore up the ideology of the intelligentsia as the bearer of progressive ideas. Ivanov-Razumnik's definition—"the intelligentsia is an esthetically anti-Philistine [*anti-meshchanskaia*], sociologically non-estate and non-class, historically continuous [*preemstvennaia*] group, characterized by the creation of new forms and ideals and the active introduction of them into life in the tendency toward physical and mental, social and individual, liberation of the personality"[10]— expressed the defensive self-consciousness of people who believed in their collectivity and defined this collectivity by their beliefs.

This cultivation of the intelligentsia idea was facilitated by the removal of most restrictions on the press in 1905 and 1906.[11] But even the possibility of freer public speech—a major achievement of the first revolution—exposed the changes in the intelligentsia's position, the fragmentation of its interest and the intensification of its internal battles. Disputes were nothing new, of course, since ideological controversy had always been the sustenance and substance of intelligentsia politics. Yet in the past the factions and schools within the opposition had at least agreed that their major target was the autocracy, while after 1905 a part of the intelligentsia turned its weapons against itself.

This offensive took a familiar form—a collection of articles on the Russian intelligentsia published in 1909. But *Vekhi* [*Landmarks*],[12] as the book was titled, was not another retrospective reconstruction, but a scathing repudiation of the intelligentsia's basic principle—the idea that revolutionary politics would liberate the Russian people. Against the materialist, sociological assumptions of the radical movement, the contributors to the collection—Petr Struve, N. A. Berdiaev, and five other prominent intellectuals—set the world view of philosophical idealism. From this high perch, they accused the intelligentsia of ignorance and immorality; the left's disregard for spiritual values, for the absolutes of state, law, and religion, meant that it was incapable of national advocacy and ethical leadership. The revolution of 1905, they felt, showed that the propagation of socialist ideas had led to disaster. The *vekhovtsy* insisted that true reform could come only from a moral rebirth and called upon the intelligentsia to turn inward and to discover new, constructive principles.[13]

Vekhi's assault on the primary values of the intelligentsia, with its implication that the whole opposition movement had been misguided, provoked an indignant, voluminous response. For two years both reformers and radicals—Kadets, Mensheviks, Bolsheviks, and Socialist Revolutionaries—devoted time and talent to the counterattack, to the defense of their political orientations and the defamation of the idealist renegades. But for all this effort, the debates over *Vekhi* led to no resolution, and the intelligentsia remained deeply divided between the advocates of moral renewal and their opponents, who attributed Russia's problems to its social organization.[14]

This failure to come to a consensus on the nature of the goals of the intelligentsia was one more indicator of the new society of twentieth-century Russia, with its erosion of the intelligentsia's self-image. The expanding economy and partial liberalization had opened up new possibilities for consciousness and thought, possibilities expressed in alternative and competing moral systems. The spread of idealist philosophy and of religious mysticism, which penetrated even Marxist circles,[15] was a logical response to these conditions, a reassuring answer to many who, confronted with the specificity of values, still wanted to believe in absolutes. Similarly, the paper scramble for the nineteenth-century heritage—with mainstream oppositionists claiming descent from the Decembrists, the martyrs of the People's Will, and theorists of Russian and European socialism, while idealists recalled the legacy of Chaadaev and Tolstoy—was another way for intellectuals to legitimize themselves in circumstances that called their ideology of service to the people into question. Both the new faith in absolute principles and the older progressivist and Eurocentric determinism of the left were self-affirming statements for Russian intellectuals, statements that defined and appealed to history, but whose validation lay ahead.

In the years between 1905 and 1917, the intelligentsia had little success in bringing its visions—new and old—to life. After their initial strident call for different and positive ideas, the *vekhovtsy* failed to produce a concrete program for moral transformation. Their opponents among the overtly political intellectuals did no better. The organizations that were intended to promote the intelligentsia's various causes suffered major setbacks in the Duma period. Thwarted by the autocracy's stubborn hold on power and their own inability to create a national consensus, the liberals could not convert their representation of the professional elite into a significant voice in government. The Socialist Revolutionary party was gutted when the police infiltrated and exploited its terrorist organization. Many leaders of Russian Marxism spent these years in European exile, where ideological, organizational, and personal battles consumed their energies. While these advocates of representative government, popular sovereignty, and socialism persevered in their attacks upon the government and upon each other, national politics seemed to come to a demoralizing stalemate.[16]

In this time of discontent, some felt that the intelligentsia was simply obsolete. This was the view of Aleksandr Blok, the foremost poet of the Silver Age. Speaking at the Religious Philosophical Society in St. Petersburg in 1908, Blok challenged the intelligentsia's assumption of community with the Russian people. This was a dangerous illusion, Blok argued; the intelligentsia and the people were separated by an unbridgeable divide. There was no possibility that the partisans of progress, science, and culture could enter the elemental world of the Russian peasants, and the intellectuals' efforts in this direction were only hastening their own ruin. Blok felt that an immense "earthquake" awaited Russia, a disaster that society was unable to prevent. The intelligentsia sensed the threat to its culture, Blok asserted—this accounted for the pervasive "feeling of sickness, anxiety, catastrophe, explosion"—but few admitted their fears.

> It's as if today's people had found a bomb in their midst; each conducts himself according to the commands of his temperament; some expose the pin in an attempt to unload the charge; others only look on, their eyes wide with fear, and think, will it begin to spin or won't it, will it explode or not; still others pretend that nothing has happened, that the big round thing lying on the table is not a bomb at all but just a big orange and that everything that is happening is only somebody's little joke; others, finally, save themselves by running away, all the time trying to arrange things so that they won't be reproached for a breach of the proprieties or accused of cowardice.[17]

This sense of helplessness and calamity, the underside of the sparkling, cosmopolitan high culture, was exacerbated six years later by the war. The international conflict only increased the fragmentation of the intelligentsia. Socialists and liberals were divided among themselves over the military effort and whether to attack the state in wartime. Patriots who chose to support the government were outraged by its incompetence. Although the gloomy and apocalyptic mood of these years was broken in February 1917 when the old regime fell without a struggle, this triumph was short lived. The flurry of political activity that followed the disappearance of the monarchy disguised the weakness and isolation of the moderate reformers who first took charge. Nothing in the ideological struggles of the past had prepared them to govern the country; nor could they prevent the explosion of class warfare. Nonetheless, many intellectuals did not, as Blok had advocated, surrender their culture to the "elements." After the October coup, their old task of moral criticism and of articulating national ideals acquired a new vitality in opposition to the Bolsheviks' emerging power.

1

Revolutionaries in the Revolution: The Search for Democratic Socialism

Menshevik Prospects

On December 3, 1917, a majority of the delegates to the Extraordinary Congress of the Russian Social Democratic Labor Party (RSDRP-Menshevik) voted for a resolution describing Bolshevik rule as a "regime of permanent anarchy," condemned to rely upon "terror and arbitrary rule, the suppression of civil liberties, and the democratic unleashing of base egoistic instincts." Russia was not ready for a "socialist transformation," the Menshevik resolution insisted, and the "social-demagogic undertakings" of the "Bolshevik dictatorship" would only spread civil war throughout the country, destroy the economy, and lead to the "collapse of the state." Nonetheless, the October "coup" was progressive in one respect. The seizure of power from the Provisional Government had dislodged the possessing classes from government, a positive development in the eyes of Martov, the Menshevik leader and author of the resolution. Freed from the constraints of coalition with the bourgeoisie, while rejecting the "utopianism" of the Bolsheviks, the social democratic party could now begin to put the revolution back on course.[1]

The first, essential step was to reestablish unity in the revolutionary movement—unity between workers and peasants, among the socialist parties, and, most important, within the proletariat. The "backward proletarian masses" had fallen prey to the "anarcho-syndicalist policy of Bolshevism," Martov's resolution noted, and the Mensheviks were to guide the "conscious elements of the proletariat" back to the correct route of "independent class tactics.'' This, the party's most important goal, was to be accomplished without force:

> No matter how fatal in their consequences the deviations of the proletariat from the path of class struggle may be, the social democratic party, leading in its [the proletariat's] midst the struggle for its return to that path, repudiates the methods of violent suppression of spontaneous upsurges toward social liberation.[2]

The ambiguities of this party pronouncement—its simultaneous charges of anarchy and dictatorship; its insistence on the impossibility of socialism in Russia and its rejection of bourgeois government; its commitment to an ideal of class struggle apparently at odds with the actions of the proletariat; its willingness to tolerate a "fatal" outcome to the revolution rather than resort to violence—might seem a testimonial to the confusion of the times. But in fact Martov spoke in terms long familiar to the Menshevik leaders,[3] and his carefully constructed analysis reflected the Mensheviks' commitment to basing their tactics on Marxist principles. The tensions of the declaration expressed two fundamental problems that had faced Russian socialists since the 1890s—the multiplicity of interpretations that could be drawn from Marx's work and the difficulties of applying Marxist theory in a country whose economic and social development lagged behind that of the Western capitalist states. The Bolsheviks' seizure of power did not create these challenges, but it intensified them and gave their resolution new urgency and significance.

The Mensheviks' search for a Marxist understanding of the Russian revolution has meaning for later anti-capitalist movements in the third world, and, in many respects, their situation seems contemporary and familiar. Yet they came to their decisions and made their choices in a radically different context. For them, there were no precedents—no socialist revolution in any nation; none expected in a "backward" country; no models or counter-examples against which they could measure the Bolsheviks' aims and possibilities. This absence of a historical socialism made Marxist theory all the more important to the Mensheviks; it was the only science Russian socialists could use.

Marxism, too, was different in 1917, unreconstructed by the confrontation with revolution, but nonetheless a complex array of theory, interpretation, and controversy. As participants in the lively and cosmopolitan debates of the late nineteenth and early twentieth centuries, the Russian social democrats were firm anti-revisionists, advocates of revolution as the route to socialism. At the same time, their views had been shaped by the determinism of European theory: the revolutionary transition to socialism could occur only after capitalism had prepared the economic and social conditions for a new stage of life. This understanding of historical development, based on Marx's analysis of capitalism, was the socialist orthodoxy of its time, adhered to until 1917 by most Marxist theorists, including Lenin.[4] A second mainstay of Menshevik ideology, based on Marxist theory and organization in the West, was the party's reliance upon the proletariat as the agent of progress and, connected with this, upon class conflict as the means of historical advance. The Mensheviks had tried since the 1890s to promote working class organization on the Western model in Russia. As indicated in its name, the party's raison d'être was the defense of working class interests, while the working class itself was expected to make the revolution.

But which revolution? The Menshevik's answer was provided by historical materialism: since Russian social and economic development was still fettered by autocratic rule, the first task was the bourgeois revolution that would release the rival forces of capital and labor for the next stage of struggle and advance. This much of Menshevik theory was a straightforward projection of Marx's description of capitalism in Europe onto Russia's future, a transference that satisfied both the nationalist and the Europhilic sentiments of the Russian left.[5]

What accorded less well with this wholesale application of Western lessons was the Mensheviks' reluctance to take the bourgeoisie with the bourgeois revolution. As defenders of the proletariat in its class struggles, the Mensheviks regarded the capitalists as the enemy. In Russia, the RSDRP had always insisted, revolution would be made by the proletariat. This idea was expressed most dramatically in the party's first program, written in 1898:

> The further east in Europe one proceeds, the weaker, more cowardly, and baser in the political sense becomes the bourgeoisie and the greater are the cultural and political tasks that devolve on the proletariat. The Russian working class must and will carry on its powerful shoulders the cause of political liberation.[6]

For the Menshevik intellectuals, this confidence in the proletariat and its values outlasted the disappointments of the 1905 revolution, the protracted controversies with their Bolshevik rivals in the RSDRP, and the outbreak of the world war. The first serious challenge to the Mensheviks' idea of Russia's future came with the revolution in February 1917. Although in theory the Russian social democrats should have found themselves the leaders of a working-class opposition to the victorious bourgeoisie, the fall of the monarchy thrust the leaders of the party into government. From the earliest days of the new Russia, Mensheviks in the capital were prominent in the Petrograd Soviet of Workers' and Soldiers' Deputies and, later, they shared responsibility with other socialists and liberals in the Provisional Governments.[7]

This experience in power was brief and disappointing. The erosion of support for the policies of the moderate left, the successes of the Bolsheviks in the army and factory organizations, and the Mensheviks' electoral losses in the Petrograd Soviet in the fall seemed to undermine the party's theories. But for the outstanding figure of Russian social democracy, Iulii Osipovich Martov (Tserderbaum), the development of the revolution between February and

October only reinforced the Mensheviks' fundamental conviction that the revolution was to be bourgeois and that the working class would be the agent of liberation.

Iulii Martov: Principled Protest Against the Commissarocracy

Martov, with his passionate devotion to democratic socialism and his reluctance to use violence in this cause, was as representative of Menshevik dilemmas after 1917 as Lenin was of Bolshevik solutions. Martov's writings in the next years of war and reconstruction trace his long and tortuous struggle to describe the revolution from a Marxist perspective and to establish party policy accordingly. His analyses, recommendations, protests, and predictions are of more than theoretical interest. As the only individual who could unite and guide the Menshevik party after its devastating experience in 1917, Martov was, potentially, a significant actor in the reformation of Russia.

Even before the revolution, Martov was first among equals in the leadership of the Menshevik faction. His authority derived in part from his central role in the formation of the RSDRP and its evolution into Bolshevik and Menshevik organizations.[8] An adroit theoretician and a master of ironic polemic, Martov shone in the spheres of party politics and Marxist controversies. But beyond his quick, complex intelligence, Martov's personality held a particular appeal. Frail, awkward, *célibataire*, he charmed his comrades with his total dedication to his principles. His incessant search for the correct, progressive position, his disregard for personal political gain, his impeccable and demanding revolutionary ethics, made him the "beautiful soul" of Russian social democracy.[9]

Martov returned to Russia from his wartime retreat in Switzerland in May 1917, after having first requested, then refused, and finally, after a month's delay, accepted the passage through Germany that Lenin had seized upon immediately.[10] In Petrograd Martov, like Lenin, found the leaders of his party defending positions he opposed. The Menshevik Central Committee favored "defensism"—the continuation of the war against the Central powers—and it was supporting the coalition of socialists and liberals in the Provisional Government. Martov, an "internationalist" on the war, wanted socialists to act for an immediate and universal peace. Moreover, he could not tolerate the notion of socialists' sharing power with the bourgeoisie; from July he advocated the formation of an all-socialist government that would exclude the "bourgeois" ministers.[11] Failing to convince the Menshevik Central Committee to change its policies, he led his Internationalist faction of the RSDRP in a campaign of protest against the party leadership.[12] Martov's opposition to the Mensheviks' support for the Provisional Government meant that when it fell, he was free from the stigma of defeat, at least in the eyes of his party.

Although Martov's call for an all-socialist government during the summer and fall of 1917 might seem a contradiction to the notion of a bourgeois revolution, it was a logical development of Menshevik theory. Just as in the past, Martov relied upon the proletariat, not the bourgeoisie, to guide Russia forward through the required stages of development. He explained his position most clearly in an article from mid-October 1917 entitled "How to Deal with the Bourgeois Revolution."[13] The bourgeoisie, he argued, was incapable of accomplishing the "tasks" set before it by the revolution. Thus, the time had come for a "dictatorship of all democracy" to take charge. Only a government of what Martov called "revolutionary democracy"—a government representing workers and peasants—would be able to achieve the revolution's goals: land reform, the formation of a democratic republic, and the rescue of the country from the imperialist war. "Don't worry," Martov assured his readers, the "bourgeois revolution carried out without the bourgeoisie" would take the course of the English and French revolutions before it. There was no "danger" that the revolution would "jump off the bourgeois tracks."[14]

This confidence in the possibility of bourgeois revolution directed by a socialist government was the conventional wisdom of Russian social democracy, with an important addition. Martov, citing Marx's analysis of 1848, emphasized the importance of securing the support of the peasantry—"petty-bourgeois democracy"—for the alliance against the possessing classes. While the conditions of Russian agriculture had prepared the peasants to side with the revolution, the future depended in large measure on the consciousness of "petty-bourgeois village and town democracy," on the peasants' and small tradespeople's understanding that their interests would be served by a break with the "capitalist bourgeoisie."[15]

There was another condition essential to the success of Martov's "dictatorship of democracy." The proletariat in its turn had to "be capable of understanding the real limits of the bourgeois revolution." Here Martov acknowledged the spread of what he called "Bolshevik maximalist illusions." The Bolsheviks were winning popularity by promising the impossible—a "leap" into the socialist future. Despite the attraction of Bolshevik slogans, Martov refused to condone this violation of Marx. The task of social democrats was to defend the standpoint of scientific socialism and "to explain to the proletariat the limits of its class struggle in the present stage of historical development." With the proper conception of the historical situation, the proletariat could replace the bourgeoisie as the governing class and the revolution would still "go according to plan."[16]

Thus, shortly before the Bolsheviks took power Martov spoke for values traditional to Russian social democracy—hostility to the bourgeoisie and reliance on the force and consciousness of the working class. This orthodoxy was challenged by the "utopian illusions" of the proletariat, but these, too, could be surmounted by an appeal to Marxist principles. The solution to the revolution's ills lay in the future with the enlightened guidance of a socialist government. These days before the October insurrection were the last in which

Martov, and socialists throughout the world, could measure the deficiencies of the present against the abstract socialism of ideas. They were soon confronted with a state that claimed the socialist mantle and declared itself the representative of the working class.

Martov's first response to the October seizure of power was anguish, confusion, and paralysis. The "worst" has happened, he wrote to Axelrod on November 19, "Lenin and Trotsky have seized power when better men might make mistakes." What was even more "terrible," he confessed to his old comrade who had been caught abroad by the coup, was that his "conscience" did not allow him to do his duty as a Marxist—to "stand by the proletariat even when it is mistaken."

> After agonizing vacillations and doubts I decided that . . . to "wash one's hands" and step aside for the time being was a more correct outcome [iskhod] than to remain in the role of an opposition in that camp where Lenin and Trotsky decide the fate of the revolution.[17]

This withdrawal from the political fray was based in part upon the failure of Martov's initiatives in the first weeks after the coup. In accord with his call for a "dictatorship of democracy," Martov had tried to replace the Bolshevik Council of People's Commissars with a temporary government, composed of ministers from several socialist parties and responsible to both the Soviets and the labor unions. At the insistence of *Vikzhel*, the All-Russian Executive Committee of the Railroad Workers' Union, talks directed toward forming such a government began in the days of uncertainty after the fall of the Provisional Government and collapsed as the Bolsheviks secured their hold on the capitals. In Martov's eyes, the *Vikzhel* negotiations had had only one positive result— the appearance of a short-lived opposition within the Bolshevik Central Committee. [18] And where the masses were concerned, the Mensheviks' efforts went almost entirely unrewarded. Martov did not spare Axelrod the early returns from the Constituent Assembly elections; these indicated a severe defeat for the Menshevik slates—5 to 10 percent of the vote in the towns, less than this in Petrograd, nothing in the countryside.[19] Apart from the Caucasus, Martov commented, "We, generally, do not exist as a mass party."[20]

But the electoral defeat alone was not decisive in Martov's decision to forego state politics. As his candid letter to his old comrade showed, there had been other ways to "stand by the proletariat," and other reasons for standing back. According to the arrangement worked out by the Left SRs and the Bolsheviks, the Mensheviks were invited to send representatives to the new Central Executive Committee (CEC) of the Soviet, reformed to include peasant, labor, military, and party delegates. Although this was a step supported by "our workers," Martov declined to participate. "We decided," he explained to Axelrod, "that to enter under the circumstances would mean to cover up a masquerade, for already real power is not in the hands of the CEC, but of Lenin and Trotsky who are calling their own parliament to play the role of the Bulygin Duma."[21]

This jab at the autocratic behavior of Lenin and Trotsky was a formalized expression of Martov's intense moral revulsion at Bolshevik tactics. Elsewhere in his lengthy letter, he was more emotional. The "form" of the Bolshevik coup was so "disgusting," he confessed, that he sympathized with the socialists who had immediately walked out of the Second Congress of Soviets in protest.[22] He despised the Bolsheviks for resorting to "terror" to enforce their decrees—for shutting down the press, for beating up and arresting other socialists, and especially for openly inciting "lynchings and pogroms." It was not violence alone that repulsed Martov, but what he regarded as a crude and deceptive exploitation of class hatred. Convinced that an immediate transition to socialism was impossible, he considered the Bolsheviks' declarations of "workers' control," "equalizing land usage," and other promises of immediate equity so much "social demagogy." Everything was done "ungrammatically, irresponsibly, and senselessly," he observed to Axelrod, and served only to inflame the "ordinary masses' hatred of all socialism and the workers."[23]

Martov's letter to Axelrod revealed the intricate tangle of values and relationships behind his self-imposed retreat. First, he was honest about the lack of popular backing for his party and refused to act against a government with mass support in Petrograd. Yet, despite the urgings of the workers in his own party, Martov could not bring himself to join the Bolshevik leaders. This would have been a betrayal of his own ethics, principles, and convictions. To him, participation in the government would mean approval of the politics of terror, collaboration with the dictatorship by providing it with a facade of representation, and, worst, further deception of the proletariat through the acceptance of the impossible program of implementing socialism.

But in addition to these political considerations, Martov was held back by his visceral repugnance at the new "forms" Russian socialism had assumed. Six weeks later, when he had recovered from the first shock of the Bolsheviks' success, he could assess his earlier reaction. Writing to a friend abroad he explained that his opposition to the new regime stemmed not only from his belief that it was a "senseless utopia" to try to "implant socialism in an economically and culturally backward country," but also from his "organic inability" to come to terms with an "Arakcheevan conception of socialism" and a "Pugachevian conception of class struggle."[24] "For me," Martov elaborated,

> socialism was never the denial of individual liberty and individualism, but on the contrary its highest embodiment. . . . No one brought up on Marx and European socialism had thought differently. But here there is flourishing such "trench army" quasi-socialism based on the general "simplification" of the whole of life, on the cult not even of the "calloused kulak," but simply of the kulak, that you feel yourself somehow guilty in front of any cultured bourgeois. . . . Under the guise of "proletarian power" . . . the most

> reprehensible vulgarity [*meshchanstvo*] is let loose . . . with all its specifically
> Russian vices of *nekul'turnost'* [lack of culture], base careerism, bribery,
> parasitism, dissoluteness, irresponsibility, and so on.[25]

This degradation, Martov thought, would ultimately discredit socialism in the
eyes of the people and undermine their confidence in themselves. "We are
moving, through anarchy, . . . toward some kind of Caesarism, based on the
whole people's loss of faith in the possibility of self-government," he
predicted.[26]

These qualms, hesitations, and fears plagued Martov constantly in the first
months after October. But despite his refusal to join the government, he was
an adamant defender of the revolution against its enemies. From the first days
after the coup, his major strategic concern had not been the Bolsheviks, but
how to prevent a "counterrevolution." In November and December, he
inveighed against the anti-Bolshevik strikes in the capital, blaming the civil
servants' boycott for the terror[27] and calling on all workers to stay on the
job.[28] As before October, he was vehemently opposed to any alliance with the
bourgeoisie and committed to serving his ideals as a spokesman for the
Russian working class.

But how was this to be done? Events since October had called Martov's
earlier strategy into question. Neither the leaders of the government nor its
followers seemed capable of carrying out the bourgeois revolution he had
predicted. Yet within the RSDRP Martov now enjoyed a position of authority—a consequence of the Bolshevik takeover that had shattered the fractured
Menshevik leadership, destroyed the policy of "coalition," and left his
Internationalists in a majority in the new Central Committee. Secure within the
world of Menshevik politics, his task was to find a new strategy that
corresponded to "objective" conditions. Thus, in the last months of 1917, he
began a long struggle to come to terms with a revolution that had gone so far
off course.

In his first attempts at analysis, Martov fell back upon historical precedent
and the example of the French revolution. He compared the terror to the reign
of Robespierre: Lenin's followers were the Russian *sans-culottes*—"a motley
[*rasnosherstnyi*] mass of armed soldiers, 'Red Guards,' and sailors who are
more and more, as it was with the French *sans-culottes*, turning into pensioners
of the state"—and, more ominously, the premature attempt at class dictatorship was preparing the way for "every kind of Bonapartism"[29] Here Martov's
argumentation took a characteristic and moralistic turn. Before the Bolshevik
takeover, he had argued that the Russian revolution would follow the pattern of
the bourgeois revolutions in the West, and that this was both necessary and
progressive. Now he held the Bolsheviks at fault for repeating history too
closely.

A second and more substantive theme of Martov's commentary at this time
was Russia's "backwardness," a convention of nineteenth-century Marxism

given new life by the revolution. Like the analogy with the French revolution, the concept of the backward country served a double purpose. The idea that Russia was following behind the European countries on the single road from feudalism to capitalism to socialism both condemned the Bolsheviks' "communist experiments"[30] to failure and, at the same time, explained why the revolution had taken such a perverse, un-European form. It was the attempt "to plant a European ideal on Asiatic soil"[31] that Martov held accountable for the distortions of socialism and class struggle in Russia.

Although Martov incorporated the concept of Russia's backwardness into his resolutions presented to the Mensheviks' Extraordinary Congress,[32] he gave these initial impressions of Bolshevism no coherent theoretical expression in 1917. Moreover, these appeals to historical materialism, while useful as explanations of why the Bolshevik program would fail, were of little help in defining a positive strategy for the Mensheviks. Martov's declarations to the Menshevik congress, in session from November 30 through December 7, 1917, showed that where practice was concerned he had hardly moved from where he stood before the seizure of power. As before, the party was to work for the essential alliance between the peasants—"petty-bourgeois democracy"—and the working class. Once again, the party was to support a government uniting all the socialist parties, although now this goal was to be reached through the formation of a socialist coalition within the Constituent Assembly. Once more, the party was to struggle both against Bolshevik terror and anarchy and against "counterrevolutionary tendencies" within democracy. And as always, the means of this struggle were to be exemplary. The RSDRP, concentrating all efforts on its primary goal of "establishing the unity of the proletarian movement on the basis of independent class politics and its liberation from anarchistic and utopian adulterations [*primesi*]," would accomplish this task by "rallying the conscious elements of the proletariat for systematic influence on the backward proletarian masses in all worker organizations and in all arenas of revolutionary struggle."[33]

Combined with the Congress's injunctions against violence, this meant that the Menshevik leadership relied, as before, on the power of the word and the agency of the working class. The party's function was to "rally" class-conscious workers who would enlighten more workers—the "masses"—who would then act to save the revolution. This conception of party activism—of "rallying [*splochenie*]," closing ranks around correct ideas articulated by the party but preexisting in the consciousness of the proletariat—appealed to the deepest convictions and self-imagery of the Menshevik intellectuals, people who saw themselves as explicators of ideas.[34] Their task was to engage not the Bolsheviks, but the workers, who would in turn convince the rulers to change their ways.

In this pacific struggle one heavy weapon was the party press. Responding to the censorship and closures of socialist papers in the first weeks of Bolshevik rule, the Mensheviks employed tactics they had practiced under the old regime.

Martov revived the guise of "Aesopian language," in his "Fable for Children of a Certain Age," a bitter condemnation of the assault on freedom of the press.[35] Menshevik papers shut down after October were reopened under different names. *Rabochaia gazeta* (The Workers' Paper), the central organ of the RSDRP, closed on November 18, 1917, by the Military Revolutionary Committee, reappeared intermittently in the next weeks as *Luch*, *Zaria*, *Klich*, *Plamia*, *Fakel*, *Molniia*, *Molot*, *Shchit*, and, finally, *Novyi luch* (The Ray, The Dawn, The Call, The Flame, The Torch, The Bolt of Lightening, The Hammer, The Shield, The New Ray).[36]

In accord with the party's efforts to act through the proletariat, these papers contained news, analyses, and directives to their readers. The paradigm for Menshevik journalism was the political instruction to the working class, frequently a request not to abet or tolerate the pernicious actions of the government. "Comrades, don't give evidence to the Bolshevik Secret Police," a headline in *Shchit* (The Shield) beseeched. Calling on workers to protest against the outlawing of the Kadet (liberal) party, the editors expounded: "The Kadets are your enemies. But if you permit trampling on the rights of your enemies, then in this way you justify those enemies when they trample on your rights."[37]

A second arm in the Menshevik arsenal was agitation and organization through local party organizations. In his search for a policy that conformed to social democratic ideals, Martov found a model in the Menshevik party at Rostov. The struggles in this city on the Don prefigured those in all of Russia, he wrote late in December 1917. First, the Bolsheviks had ousted the city Duma and declared "Soviet power"; then, the new government had in its turn been defeated by the forces of General Kaledin.[38] Through all of this, the local SDs had defended a consistent, class-based position. First, they had protested the establishment of a "Bolshevik dictatorship," and later, when the military took over the city, they had defended Bolshevik and other workers against the new authorities. As leaders in the reformed Soviet, they helped organize a mass funeral procession honoring the working-class victims of repression and protesting the policies of the military government. The results of these efforts were encouraging to Martov. The slogans and forms of the Rostov movement showed that the Rostov workers had "sobered up" after the "anarcho-Bolshevik spree," and that this "sobering up . . . had deepened their democratic self-consciousness." The moral seemed to be that the working class had learned from its experience with Bolshevik leadership and from the example set by the Mensheviks. The "role of the party of the proletariat," Martov concluded, was that followed by the Rostov SDs: to protest against "Bolshevik adventurism" and to side demonstratively with the proletariat against the right.[39]

The strategies of exhortation, demonstration, and moral example were employed by the Menshevik Central Committee to defend the Constituent Assembly in January 1918. Despite the RSDRP's abysmal showing in the elections, the Mensheviks championed the Constituent Assembly as an institutional alternative to Soviet government, a last chance to put together an inclusive socialist coalition, and a bulwark against the impending counterrevolution. As the year drew to a close, the Assembly took on iconographic qualities in the Menshevik press. Only the Constituent Assembly could "save the Russian revolution," declared *Novyi luch*. If supported by the "whole people," it could "end the civil war, stop the disintegration of the state, secure land for the peasants, achieve a rapid and lasting peace, regularize industry and supply and stop the avalanche of poverty and unemployment that is moving forward to engulf the masses."[40]

Worker support for the Assembly was to be expressed in a mass demonstration on January 5, 1918, the day of the opening session. Since the Bolsheviks had made no secret of their hostility to the Constituent Assembly,[41] this show of enthusiasm was intended as a vital sign of political loyalties. Against the demands of some pro-Assembly factory organizations, the Menshevik Central Committee renounced the carrying of arms and made party participation contingent upon the nonviolent character of the manifestation. "Our party," Martov intoned in *Novyi luch*, "would never put its hand to any conspiratorial attempt to overthrow the government of Leninists by Leninist methods."[42]

With this boast Martov issued a clear moral challenge to Lenin. In "Fear is a Poor Counselor," Martov's last article before the convening of the Assembly, he drew two historical parallels. The first likened the opening of the Constituent Assembly to the convocation of the first Duma, in 1906. Then, as now, Martov asserted, Russia's rulers feared the enthusiasm of the masses in support of a new state institution. In closing, he drew a more ominous comparison. Calling up the specter of Bloody Sunday, when tsarist troops had fired into a peaceful demonstration, he linked Lenin to the autocratic past:

On January 9, 1905, Nikolai Romanov shot down the Russian people's faith in tsarism. Does Vladimir Ulianov have enough Romanov cowardice to shoot down today with his own hand the people's faith in socialism and democracy?[43]

Lenin's response was unambiguous. Soldiers massed for the purpose shot into the demonstration, leaving the Mensheviks to organize another funeral procession of honor and protest.[44] "Everything is as under the tsar," mourned *Novyi luch* on January 6:

Shame on the government that compels workers to shed workers' blood!
Workers! Protest against those guilty of the criminal slaughter!
Glory to those fallen at the hands of the oppressors for the defense of the conquests of the revolution!
Long live the sovereign Constituent Assembly!
Down with civil war![45]

The Menshevik print shop was vandalized after this issue was printed, forestalling further commentary on the breakup of the Constituent Assembly itself.[46]

Soon after the failure of this attempt at moral suasion, the First All-Russian Congress of Trade Unions gave Martov a chance to appeal directly to the constituency for which he claimed to speak.[47] The major issue before the congress—the role of the Soviets and labor unions in the new state—revealed clearly the fundamental divisions within the Russian left. Zinoviev, the Bolshevik spokesman, used these differences to rhetorical effect, denouncing all criticisms as attacks on the socialist revolution [48] and setting them against his glowing vision of Russia's future. In his speeches, the Soviets were the "soul," the "temple," of the socialist revolution, while the trade unions were but "an element [chastitsa] of power," whose primary role was the organization of the economy. Now that the bourgeoisie had been overthrown, the independence of the unions was irrelevant. In socialist Russia, freedom to strike and to form alliances meant only "freedom of sabotage."[49]

To Zinoviev's stirring rhetoric, Martov replied with speeches that exemplified his virtues as a theoretician and his defects as an orator. He began, in contrast to Zinoviev's zealous factionalism, with an appeal to unity—past unity around *his* party's goals. Speaking on January 9, the anniversary of Bloody Sunday, Martov again recalled the heroic struggles of 1905, a time "when not one socialist, not one conscious worker in Russia doubted that the way . . . to socialism lay through the democratic revolution" and when the Constituent Assembly was the slogan of the working class. For Martov, the contrast between this hallowed memory and Zinoviev's celebration of the demise of the Constituent Assembly as the "beginning of the socialist era" was in itself an "all too obvious" demonstration of the "underlying falsehood" of the new, rival "communist" conception of revolution.[50]

But in the best traditions of enlightenment, Martov based his arguments before the union and Soviet delegates not on sentiment, but on the principles of orthodox Marxism.[51] The notion that the mere existence of the Soviets meant the beginning of socialism he rejected as the "purest nonsense."[52] To construct socialism it was not enough to know what was wrong with capitalism; it was not enough to seize the banks;[53] it was not enough even to have political power, to have a "party that sincerely, subjectively, wishes to introduce socialism"; it was wrong to succumb to the tempting thought that socialist production could be introduced by political force.[54] These shortcuts were impossible. A socialist society required a particular economic structure, and the preconditions for a socialist economy—the concentration of industry, the predominance of a conscious, highly skilled, and numerous proletariat, a peasantry that supported socialist production—were missing in Russia. As Marxists had always responded to their bourgeois critics, socialism did not depend upon idealism and personal sacrifice, but instead upon conditions of plenty, under which "no one would have to purchase an improvement in his life at the price of another's."[55]

The absence of these conditions was extremely significant for the future of the working class in Russia, Martov noted. In a country with a proletarian minority, the state's policies would be dictated not by the proletariat, but by the economy. Workers would be the "cogs" of the new state machine, and their interests would clash with the interests of this "state socialism."[56] Moreover, should the Bolshevik state collapse, workers who had lost their autonomous organizations would find themselves at the mercy of "bourgeois counterrevolution."[57] For the unions to relinquish their independence now, to give up their role as defenders of the particular interests of the working class, would amount to "suicide" for the labor movement.[58]

With his speeches at the Congress of Trade Unions, Martov fulfilled the rigorous standards of Menshevik politics. He addressed himself to the working class alone; he based his position squarely on Marx—"there was never anything the matter with Marx and scientific socialism," he responded to the left SRs, only with those who "betrayed Marxism" and turned away from the "single ideology that is able to express the interests of the working class"[59]; he did not gloss over the severe problems facing Russian workers; he eschewed rhetorical indulgences and rosy prospects. His approach was to put the facts into the framework of Marxist theory and thus to help the proletariat judge for itself. But the judgment at the Trade Union Congress went against the Mensheviks. Martov's reasoned appeal to Marxist theory, to tradition, to gradual progress through democracy and capitalist production paled beside the new logic of class rule. The Bolshevik resolution on the "current situation" received 182 votes to the Mensheviks' 84.[60]

This defeat is hardly surprising when examined in the faint light of the Menshevik alternative to merging the unions with the state. Martov's speeches at the Congress of Trade Unions showed little confidence in any kind of working class rule. He explicitly portrayed labor unions as class-based organizations that were not to be drawn into government, and were instead to perform the functions they had in bourgeois societies—the defense of working-class interests against both state and bourgeoisie:

> The tasks of the labor movement are not to give itself up to the service of state power [*vlast'*] as a dependent institution, but to take part in all economic life only in so far as elements of realism, Marxism, and scientific socialism and an estimation of real forces permit the labor union as an independent organization to introduce corrections into the plans of the state power [*vlast'*].[61]

This description of union activism, with its assumption of class independence within and against the larger society, suggests the extent to which Martov's conceptions of politics were shaped by bourgeois structures. His notions of social organization and possibilities were founded on the theory of class conflict, on the creative force of opposition, and did not permit the working class to govern a divided, pre-socialist state.

Martov's strict separation of political and economic spheres in January

1918, as well as his support for the Constituent Assembly and his opposition to Soviet rule, indicated that he had stepped back from his advocacy of an all-socialist government to guide the bourgeois revolution. Or at least he seemed to have drawn back from the working class and his confidence in political liberation through proletarian rule. His experience since October had not only fulfilled his worst suspicions about the Bolsheviks, it had shattered his empowering image of the proletariat. In the first months of 1918 two themes recurred in Martov's analyses—the despotism of the revolutionary government and the anarchism of the revolutionary masses.

Before the October revolution, Martov had been concerned about the "utopian illusions" of the masses; after the seizure of power he witnessed the realization of some of these "illusions" with dismay. The Mensheviks' resolution on workers' control at the Extraordinary Congress condemned the Bolshevik "experiment in workers' control"[62] for its destructive effects on Russian industry. From the centralist perspective of the RSDRP, workers' control produced "anarcho-syndicalist" illusions, "factory patriotism," and "bourgeois property values," and made it impossible for the government to regulate industry in the interests of all.[63] Later, in January 1918, Martov discarded the protective notion that Bolshevik policy had engendered these particularistic attitudes. Instead, he suggested—reversing his earlier view—that it was the localized consciousness of at least part of the working population that accounted for the popularity of the Bolshevik program. Writing in *Novyi luch*, revived once again after the Constituent Assembly debacle, he commented:

> the fascination that the slogan "All power to the Soviets" possesses in the eyes of the peasant[ry] and the backward part of the working masses is explained to a significant degree by the fact that they invest this slogan with the primitive idea of the rule of local workers or local peasants over a particular territory, just as the slogan of workers' control is invested with the idea of the seizure of a particular factory, and the slogan of agrarian revolution with the seizure by a particular village of a particular estate.[64]

Martov objected as well to the decentralization envisioned in the draft constitution passed by the Third Congress of Soviets on January 15. Against Stalin's objections, the Left SR commissar Trutovskii had introduced a clause giving local Soviets exclusive authority over local affairs, and assigning higher Soviets only mediating functions.[65] Martov poked fun at a proposal that seemed to him a sop to the "naiveté" of the Left SRs. Trutovskii's ideas, he scoffed, amounted to a

> new system of state organization which, happily combining the most daring ideas of Stepan Timofeevich Razin, Mikhail Aleksandrovich Bakunin and the frugal fishermen—the apostles of our lord Jesus Christ—would with one stroke of the pen, divide Russia into several hundred thousand independent communes to the great confusion of the telegraph poles, which proudly

imagined that they linked . . . all these [backward places] into one indissolubly unified organism.

The Bolsheviks had prepared the way for this perversion of federalist principles with their cultivation of the anarchistic sentiments of the "dark masses."[67]

The socialist readers of *Novyi luch*, materialists well versed in the struggles of Marx against Bakunin, were presumably sympathetic to Martov's ironies and to the notion that Bolshevism was tainted by association with anarchy.[68] But for the future, Martov assured his followers, they had nothing to fear from the clauses of the draft constitution. Its centrifugal vision would remain on paper. In reality, Bolshevik anarchism would amount to control and exploitation of the villages by the army and the commissars:

> In practice primitive anarchistic freedom will be reduced to a common denominator by combat detachments that will "self-determine" disobedient villages and settlements, attaching them to the fulfillment of the plans of the commissarocrats [*komissaroderzhavtsy*] on an all-Russian scale. . . . [T]he full self-determination of individual towns and villages will turn out to be as empty as the full self-determination of the individual nationalities.[69]

This reference to the false freedom of the new regime and its reliance on force to subdue the population was the other side of Martov's criticism in 1918. During the first half of the year he developed his comparison of Lenin with Nicholas II into a full-blown analogy between Bolshevik rule and the tsarist regime. His articles in the Menshevik press were filled with bitter denunciations of what he dubbed the "commissarocracy,"[70] and its restoration of repressive and bureaucratic rule. Like the tsarist ministers, he noted, "our dictators" claimed the right to control the movements of the people, denying dissident socialists the right to leave the country and retaining the internal passport system.[71] The new regime, following the traditions of the old, had taken away the freedoms of the press and of assembly,[72] suppressed the voices of its opponents in elected institutions,[73] and resorted to the expedient of government by "temporary measures."[74]

With this barrage of moral criticism, Martov himself resumed the political role he had played under the autocracy. In April 1918 his excoriation of the personal failings of the new leadership embroiled him in a tangle with Stalin. Martov's offense was an article, published in *Vpered* on March 31, that referred to a prerevolutionary party trial of Stalin for his part in a robbery in Baku. Stalin responded with a charge of slander. In court, Martov insisted upon calling witnesses and this, apparently, convinced the Revolutionary Tribunal to drop its inquiry into the truth of the allegations about Stalin's past. Nonetheless, the court found Martov guilty of "an insult to the power of the government, . . . capable of arousing sediton and disorder in the broad laboring masses" and rebuked him for "criminal usage of the press."[75]

This ordeal was for Martov another example of the abuse of power by the

Bolshevik leaders for whom personal and national interests were identical. In an article entitled "The People—It Is I," he denounced "Lenin, Trotsky, Stalin and their brotherhood" for "regarding themselves as the people and state and treating any offense to themselves as a state crime." The interpretation of an insult to Stalin as a "crime against the people" was worthy of Louis XIV and demonstrated that Russia now had a "genuine multi-headed monarchy."[76] Later he noted that the procedures of the trial showed that the Bolsheviks viewed state power as a source of private profit:

> Every Sosnovskii, every Sverdlov, Steklov, Krasikov, and Kozlovskii looks on power as common booty [and] considers himself obliged to violate his own decrees, his own human dignity, and all principles in order to help a crony when it is necessary to put some varnish over a dark spot on his past or present.[77]

At the end of April 1918 the decision against Martov was annulled[78]—an indication both of Martov's moral authority with the leaders of the state and of the weakness of Bolshevik power in the spring of 1918.[79] The drastic deterioration of the economy and an extensive, amorphous political crisis presented severe threats to the government, and offered the Menshevik opposition new opportunities. Carried forward by the tide of discontent, moderate socialists—both Mensheviks and Socialist Revolutionaries—won significant victories in elections to provincial Soviets.[80] In addition, a new organization of the proletariat, the Assemblies of Factory and Plant Representatives, had been formed outside the Soviets in Moscow and Petrograd and several towns in the central industrial region.[81]

The Mensheviks' possibilities were further strengthened by shifts in the tactics of the party leadership. In March, differences between former "defensists" and "internationalists" in the Central Committee had been allayed by common outrage at the Brest-Litovsk peace and the real costs of ending the war. Martov, the former advocate of peace, now led the Menshevik Central Committee in united protest against the "cabal" with Germany.[82] Moreover, the Menshevik Central Committee had followed the Bolshevik government in its move to Moscow, and, his initial refusal to join the "masquerade" of Soviet rule notwithstanding, Martov became an outspoken participant in the sessions of the Central Executive Committee of the Soviets (CEC).[83] Martov's standing within his party combined with the widespread dissatisfaction with the government gave him at last a chance to act against the "commissarocracy."

But despite this improvement in Menshevik prospects, Martov remained a passive, moral critic in the spring of 1918. He held back from developing the Soviets or the Workers' Assemblies as alternatives to Bolshevik power, and refused to lead or even to condone violent opposition to the government. Forced to choose between his fears of anarchy and his hatred of despotism, he sided in effect with order.[84]

The reasoning behind Martov's caution was expressed most directly and cogently in an article tersely entitled "Workers and State Power." Published in an ephemeral Menshevik journal *Novaia zaria* (The New Dawn) in April, this analysis presented a bleak picture of revolutionary Russia—"torn to pieces, hungry, crippled by the Brest peace," in a "state of complete economic disorganization, bloody civil strife, the absence of law and order and security of life." In these circumstances, Martov asserted, "the most urgent task" was the "creation of state power." Workers should recognize this vital necessity for two reasons. First, the "popular masses," or, later in the text, "the dark masses of the city and village poor," could sustain these anarchic conditions for only a short time. A revolution that remained too long in this stage would become "hateful" to the people and would perish. Second, present conditions threatened the "complete destruction of Russian industry" and thus the "destruction of the working class itself." What Russia needed to save the revolution and the working class was a "united government," able to organize the country.[85]

The basis for this united government could not be the Soviets in Martov's view. "There is no Soviet power in Russia and no power of the proletariat," he insisted. Soviet power was a fiction because the Council of People's Commissars was not responsible to the Central Executive Committee of the Soviets and in fact ruled autocratically through its bureaucrats and armed agents. Here, however, Martov gave his familiar old-regime analogy a new twist. The Council of People's Commissars, although autocratic, was not omnipotent. Like the tsarist ministers, the commissars were unable to control their subordinates—the feuding regional, city, and provincial Soviets and the various armed groups and individuals who exercised authority in the country. Real power in contemporary Russia belonged to "anyone with a machine gun."[86]

While the suggestion that the Bolsheviks could not enforce their will was new, Martov's answer to the problem of state power was old—the Constituent Assembly. Only a popularly elected Constituent Assembly could, he argued, "work out laws binding on the whole country that would put an end to today's ruin, decline, and anarchy and establish the institutions and regulations for . . . ongoing popular control over all central and local authorities." The working class would be in a minority in such a body, Martov acknowledged, because the "huge majority of the Russian people does not consist of the conscious proletariat." But the earlier elections had shown that the majority of the delegates to the Constituent Assembly were committed to democracy and that they had supported a democratic republic, political liberties, and land reform. Moreover, the alternative of Soviet rule had been tried, and it had turned into the "irresponsible, uncontrolled, unjust, tyrannical and costly power of commissars, committees, staffs, and armed bands." This demonstrated that a minority could only rule through violence and was incapable of building a "stable" government. To reject the power of the Soviets in favor of a democratic republic was, in Martov's view, to exchange "imaginary" power for a "share" of "real influence on the politics of the state."[87]

Where was this democratic republic to come from? Martov gave no hints, other than the fact of his conventional appeal to workers to support his recommendations. Moreover, the chaos and destruction he described seemed to explode the fundamental postulate of Menshevik theory—the idea that the Russian working class would make a bourgeois revolution. The Constituent Assembly was imaginary in April 1918, and Martov's abstract and pacific defense of this phantom demonstrated only his own loyalty to the ideals of social democracy. He remained faithful to the forms of the political life he recommended—speaking out at meetings of the Central Executive Committee of the Soviets, publishing critiques of the governors in the party press, writing position papers for the Menshevik leadership. Confronted by the threat of anarchy, he refused to set one "part" of the working class against another. Ultimately, he assumed the position he had initially rejected and chose to strike at Bolshevik despotism as a member of the loyal opposition.

But this was not bourgeois society. Martov's demands that the opposition be allowed to speak at the Central Executive Committee were frequently ignored, and his ironic comparisons of the CEC's procedures with those of bourgeois parliaments—observations usually unfavorable to the CEC—were not appreciated.[88] Yet some of Martov's speeches in the CEC—his castigation of the government for its secret diplomacy,[89] its refusal to "trust" the judgment of the workers,[90] its establishment of "the dictatorship of individuals,"[91] its declaration of martial law in Moscow late in May[92]—hit their mark all too well, especially at a time when the Bolshevik government was threatened by disturbances in the capitals and revolts in outlying regions. On June 14, 1918, the Mensheviks, with the Socialist Revolutionaries, were expelled from the CEC for their "counterrevolutionary" actions.[93] Soviets throughout the country were instructed to exclude representatives of these parties, and the newspapers of the moderate left were once again shut down, in most cases this time, for good.[94]

Even in the face of this explicit and physical attack on the idea and institutions of loyal opposition,[95] Martov continued, as best he could, his policy of moral criticism. In late June he badgered the Soviet authorities with his pamphlet "Down with Capital Punishment," a protest against the government's public violation of its own prohibition on the death penalty[96] and against the pervasive, unofficial use of political execution. "As soon as they came to power, . . . they began to kill," wrote Martov. The "party of executioners" was responsible for the murder of tens of thousands of people without trial—of prisoners of war, of long lists of so-called counterrevolutionaries, of villagers and townspeople shot by the Cheka and the Military-Revolutionary Committees. Once more Martov harked back to the tactics of the old regime: the Revolutionary Tribunals were the equivalent of Stolypin's courts-martial of 1906. The Bolsheviks had "borrowed from tsarism the bloody religion of legalized murder—in the name of the interests of the state."[97]

Yet against this state and its organized violence, Martov still would not condone the use of force. The RSDRP had never advocated terror in the past,[98] and he exhorted workers to refrain from bloodshed now. "Don't take the lives of your enemies, be content with taking back from them that power, which you yourselves gave them," he advised in "Down with Capital Punishment," and, as for means, suggested that they "take the cannibal-executioners to a people's court."[99] These pathetic declarations accorded with the temperate tactics Martov recommended and tried to enforce in the summer of 1918. Mensheviks who joined the various armed uprisings against the government were expelled from the party,[100] and when the Constituent Assembly became a slogan of the anti-Bolshevik forces in the Volga area, the Central Committee dropped its support for the institution.[101] For Martov the expansion of the civil war in the summer of 1918 simplified the dilemmas posed by the amorphous disintegration of authority in the spring. The struggle against counterrevolution took precedence over other goals, and the Menshevik Central Committee supported the Bolshevik government as before—not for what it was, but for what it was against.

At first, the civil war had little effect upon Martov's views of Bolshevism and its prospects. His qualified approval of the revolution, expressed in the Central Committee's resolutions in October 1918, was essentially a repetition of his position at the Extraordinary Congress a year earlier:

> The Bolshevik overturn of October 1917 was historically necessary, for in breaking the ties between labor and capital it expressed the urge of the laboring masses to subordinate the course of the revolution entirely to their own interests.[102]

Here, as in December 1917, Martov's modulated text indicated his struggle to describe a revolution that did not fit Marxist orthodoxy and yet had, by virtue of its break with capitalism, to be judged progressive. And here, too, Martov's ambivalence about the "laboring masses" was in evidence. They—not the proletariat—had tried to put their interests above the "course of the revolution." This meant the "overturn" had been mass based and therefore necessary, but had it perhaps been fatally diverted?

Throughout 1918 Martov was unable to confront this question. His writings returned again and again to the theme of democratic revolution, as if to remind his readers of what should have been done. In his essay on "Marx and the Problem of the Dictatorship of the Proletariat," for example, he argued that Marx and Engels after the failures of 1848 had "freed themselves from the influence of the Jacobin tradition," and recognized that a revolution could be successful only with the support of a majority of the population—the proletariat and other "healthy elements of the nation." Only a state representing the "conscious will of the majority" would be able to resist an "economically powerful minority," and thus, he insisted, the true dictatorship of the proletariat "could exist only in the framework of democracy, . . . only with the establishment of full political equality for all citizens."[103] At the end of the year he began to work on his memoirs, a monument to the struggle for democracy before 1905,[104] and, when given an opportunity, he continued to agitate for a democratic republic, for independent trade unions, for legalization of the opposition, and to condemn Bolshevik terror.[105]

But the fantasy of loyal, legal opposition was difficult to fulfill. In January 1919 the Menshevik party was allowed to reopen their Moscow newspaper, but after only fifteen issues of critical journalism, the party press was closed again.[106] In March of the same year the Central Committee was arrested and the party's headquarters temporarily closed.[107] Throughout these trials, Martov oscillated between hope that the government would "reform" and cynical contempt for the hypocrisy and ruthlessness of the Bolshevik leadership.[108] It was only in the spring of 1919 that he began to form a new theoretical perspective on the events since October 1917 and to accommodate his analysis to the Bolsheviks' success.

In *World Bolshevism*, a series of essays printed on a Menshevik press in Kharkov,[109] Martov at last treated Bolshevism as a reality, rather than a perverse "expression" of the more authentic historical process.[110] In these studies he attempted both to explain the powerful, international appeal of Bolshevik ideas and to expose the fictions on which these ideas rested. His conclusions about the development of the postrevolutionary state were critical and pessimistic. The "formula of 'All power to the Soviets' " had simply masked the contradictions in the masses' efforts both to create a mechanism that would suppress the exploiting class and, at the same time, to "free themselves from any state machine."[111] In the end, the Soviet state had turned into a "machine based on exactly the same divisions between the . . . 'administration of people' and the 'administration of things,' the same oppositions between 'management' and 'self-management,' the same contrasts between the bureaucrat and the citizen that characterized the capitalist class state."[112] None of the goals of Lenin's *State and Revolution* had been fulfilled.[113] The revolution, despite its claim to have broken with the past, had followed the political pattern of the bourgeois revolutions before it—"power had been transferred from one conscious minority . . . to another."[114]

Even more penetrating than Martov's assessment of Russian reality were his explanations of why Bolshevik ideas were so popular, especially in Western Europe. The idea of "world Bolshevism" had seemed absurd to Russian socialists only a year ago; how could primitive Russia have become a model for the West? The answer, Martov felt, lay not in the real possibilities of the Bolshevik system, but in the psychological appeal of Bolshevik ideology.

The "psychology of Bolshevism," Martov explained, relied first of all upon a maximalist disposition, a "naive social optimism" that believes that ultimate social goals can be achieved at any time, regardless of "objective conditions."[115] In addition, this "psychology" ignored the requirements of production. The focus of Bolshevik ideas was upon the needs of the user, not upon the producer and the productive process. Finally, Bolshevik supporters were inclined to confront all problems politically—with the struggle for power, with armed force, and with scepticism toward democratic methods.[116] According to Martov, all these "atavistic" characteristics were more closely related to "Bakuninism," to Lassalle's socialism, or to the movements of the *sans-culottes* in the French revolution than to scientific socialism.[117]

Who was to blame for this regression in mass values? Behind the Bolshevik success Martov saw old foes—the bourgeoisie and the imperialist war. It was capitalism that had prepared the way for Lenin.

Workers, Martov argued in *World Bolshevism*, were susceptible to Bolshevik ideas because the war had destroyed the guiding tradition of the European labor movement. Once the International had broken apart, the proletariat lost its faith in the "old moral political values" and split into antagonistic factions. Destruction rather than production became the factor determining proletarian existence. Workers' ignorance of the importance of increasing labor productivity, their disdain for work itself, their faith in promises of immediate gratification—these were the legacy of the capitalists' war. Just as the bourgeoisie had hoped that military victory would resolve its crises, workers had learned to look to a proletarian triumph as a total solution.[118] Thus, the pro-Bolshevism of the European proletariat was a consequence of the "sickness" of capitalist society.[119] Imperialism had driven Western Europe back to the economic and cultural level of Eastern Europe, and "world Bolshevism" was, "perhaps," the "first blow of revenge" from the destroyed and exploited East.[120]

From a theoretical perspective, Martov's *World Bolshevism* was a perceptive analysis of post war politics. His emphasis on the power of the war to shape proletarian consciousness, on the helplessness of the labor movement against the world crisis, was impeccably materialist. The triumph of corrupting circumstance over the values of the working class was, to him, a demonstration of the fundamental significance of the economic structure:

> the superior triumph of Marxism as the "materialist view" of history is expressed in its very "defeat" as the practical leadership of the [labor] movement. The fact that it [Marxism] evolved under the influence of historical circumstances into "social-patriotism" in the consciousness of one part of the working class and into primitive anarcho-Jacobin "communism" in the consciousness of another part expresses that same *mastery of "being" over "consciousness"* . . . taught by Marx and Engels.[121]

But where was the way forward from this "defeat"?

Martov's essays made it plain that he no longer expected a European revolution to correct the course of Bolshevism,[122] and of course he rejected any notion that the bourgeoisie, Russian or European, could exert a positive influence.[123] He saw only two prospects for the future—"either a victory of reason over spontaneity in the proletarian revolution, or economic and cultural regression for a relatively long period."[124] This put Martov right back into the dilemma he had described so well. Bolshevik minority rule did not offer the proletariat the chance for active political struggle, the chance to make its own choices, educate itself and thus escape from the oppression of the past and present.[125] And without this opportunity of what use were the Mensheviks' lessons? Martov's own analysis suggested the limits of "reason."

Throughout the civil war, the Menshevik Central Committee remained caught in the failed abstractions on which it had based its policies. The program of Russian social democracy remained the critical defense of the government against its enemies.[126] The Mensheviks' limited possibilities for agitation varied inversely with the fortunes of the Bolsheviks in the war, and in the summer of 1920, with the end in sight, the government began to eliminate the RSDRP entirely from political life.[127] At this time the Central Committee decided to send Martov, who was in poor health, abroad. At the end of September, he left Russia on a Bolshevik passport.[128]

In Europe Martov embarked on a new, more feasible, project; he was to inform Western socialists about the Russian revolution. This was a mission born of many defeats—the decimation of the party organization, the lack of any democratization of Bolshevik rule, the failure of the revolution to conform to Menshevik theory. There was, in addition, the total ineffectuality of the Mensheviks' delicate program of defending the revolution while criticizing the Bolsheviks. One of Martov's letters, written in December 1920 to his comrade Fedor Dan imprisoned in Moscow, captures the tensions, doubts, and surviving certainties of the past three years:

> The question of in what proportion, *practically*, a party desiring to remain Marxist must connect the striving to "rationalize" the historical process with the accommodation of its tactics to a given spontaneity can hardly have a *theoretical* answer.
>
> I fear that here the problem moves from the realm of "science" into the realm of "art," . . . that it's impossible to find a theoretical formula that would cover all situations, and that in fact what is decisive is the political intuition and the psychology of the vanguard, in which fortunately are combined elements of rationalism and the pathos of spontaneity. . . . All the same, it is comforting that firmness of position at a time when the poles of the dialectical process are changing won't remain without results, in the sense of introducing stable ideological values into the consciousness of the working class coming out of the crisis. And in this sense . . . we ought to work, mainly, for our own future, so that in the consciousness of the masses, when it again begins to form, we will be "clean" from responsibility for the present outcome of the crisis of the revolution.[129]

Menshevik Dissenters: Plekhanov, Potresov, Zasulich

Martov did not speak for all of Russian social democracy. There were Menshevik intellectuals who did not accept the defensive pacifism of the party leadership. These dissenters, like Martov, looked at events from a Marxist perspective. Their ultimate goals, like his, were the building of a socialist society and the liberation of the working class, and they, too, were committed to progress, to the fight against reaction, and to defense of the proletariat. But these values, the dissenters felt, put them on the other side of the barricades. For them, from the beginning, Bolshevism was the counterrevolution.

Within the RSDRP, Mensheviks who took the course of uncompromising hostility to Bolshevik rule became known as "rightists."[130] The realignment of Russian social democracy began immediately after the October insurrection, when eleven of the twenty-three members of the Menshevik Central Committee resigned over the majority's decision to work for a coalition government inclusive of the Bolsheviks. The conflict between Martov's faction and the opponents of cooperation continued at the Extraordinary Congress, where Mark Liber declared that the Bolshevik regime had "nothing in common with the class dictatorship of the proletariat" and called on the party to support "the right to insurrection" against it.[131] The Extraordinary Congress was the last, and its decision, by a vote of 50 to 31 with eight abstaining, to accept Martov's ambiguous and cautious resolution left the rightists permanently outside the party leadership.[132]

In the coming months, the old differences between defensists and internationalists paled beside this new split between the Central Committee and its "rightist" opponents. The fundamental division was not so much over tactics, but, as befit a party of enlightenment, over the party line and its implications for action. To the rightists, Martov's complex assessments, his notion that the coup had been progressive while its "forms" were backward, was nonsense. The revolution was a disaster for the labor movement and therefore should be opposed. To Martov, on the other hand, the rightists' total condemnation of Bolshevism and their support of militant opposition showed a dangerous ignorance of the relationship of social forces and threatened to tip the balance toward "reaction." Fearful of the consequences of rebellion, he used his authority in the Central Committee to invoke party discipline against the dissenters of the right.[133]

Martov's efforts to enforce the Central Committee's policies, as well as the restricting circumstances of Menshevik politics after 1917, obscure the extent of "rightist" sentiment within the RSDRP. The vote at the Extraordinary Congress was not overwhelming, and by the spring of 1918, rightists could point to the emergence of a working-class opposition to Bolshevism. In contrast to the intellectuals at the party center, many of the leaders of Right Menshevism—such as P. A. Garvi, M. S. Kefali, and A. N. Smirnov—were "*praktiki*," labor organizers who spent their lives closer to the factory than to the party leadership.[134] Because of this activism, few rightists survived to speak up in the emigration; they are less conspicuous in the histories of Menshevism than their ideas and numbers warrant.

In addition to organizers in the unions, right Mensheviks could count among their number four of the six major founders of Russian social democracy. Plekhanov, Potresov, Zasulich, and Axelrod were all unbending opponents of Bolshevik power.[135]

Georgii Valentinovich Plekhanov returned to Russia in March 1917 after thirty-seven years in exile. The "father" of Russian Marxism, Plekhanov was given a hero's welcome upon his arrival in Petrograd. By the time of the October seizure of power, however, he was a broken man—rejected by his own party for his support of the war, fearful of the radicalization of the revolution, and physically destroyed. At sixty-one, he was dying of tuberculosis.[136] A few days after the October coup, a group of soldiers and sailors broke into Plekhanov's apartment in Tsarskoe Selo and, seeing only a class enemy before them, threatened Plekhanov and his wife. After this disconcerting episode, the bedridden man was taken into Petrograd and the shelter of a hospital. In January 1918, when two leaders of the Kadet party—Shingarev and Kokoshkin—were murdered by their Bolshevik "guards" in the hospital where he was staying, Plekhanov was moved a last time across the border into Finland.[137]

During these trials, Plekhanov campaigned against Bolshevism in the pages of *Edinstvo* (Unity), a newspaper he had revived after his return to Russia.[138] The "father" of Russian Marxism founded his views of the revolution on the materialist orthodoxy of nineteenth-century socialism. Three days after the October coup—and three before the break-in at his home—he recalled Engels' statement that there could be no greater historical tragedy for the working class than a premature seizure of political power. This, Plekhanov argued in *Edinstvo*, was exactly what the Bolsheviks had accomplished. Their regime would end in catastrophe because the proletariat was in a minority in Russia. While the peasant majority might support the working class temporarily, its interests were essentially proprietary and capitalistic. Eventually, the peasant economy would defeat a proletarian government.[139]

A corollary of Plekhanov's analysis was that, should the working class or a "single party" pursue its dictatorship against the will of the majority, it would have to use terror to remain in power. In his last article, published on January 13, 1918, Plekhanov insisted that the Bolshevik dictatorship was deceptive, dangerous, and un-Marxist:

> Their dictatorship represents not the dictatorship of the toiling population, but the dictatorship of one part of it, the dictatorship of a group. And precisely because of this they have to make more and more frequent use of terroristic means.

The use of these means is the sign of the precariousness of the situation, and not at all a sign of strength. And in any case neither socialism in general nor Marxism in particular has anything to do with it.[140]

This last comment suggests the extent to which the Marxist legacy had become a weapon in the ideological struggle for the revolution. Plekhanov was responding in part to an affront from *Pravda*, where his authority had been invoked in the Bolsheviks' attack on the Constituent Assembly. Under the heading "Plekhanov for Terror," an anonymous article cited Plekhanov's well-known speech at the 1903 RSDRP party congress in which he had defended, hypothetically, the right to overturn an elected parliament in the interests of the revolution. "This is what Plekhanov thought when he was a socialist," the *Pravda* writer jabbed.[141] Plekhanov's answer to this insult showed that his experience in the year of revolution had not budged him from his commitment to Marxism as he saw it. While supporting the Constituent Assembly, he refused to be associated with the defense of the rights of parliaments. He stood by his 1903 statement, he insisted in *Nashe edinstvo*; he still put the goal of the "good of the people" above all others and above any "unconditional principles" concerning means.[142] The problem was not that the Bolsheviks had dismissed an elected institution, but that they had dismissed it for the wrong goal—their own political power, not the "success of the revolution." Plekhanov still spoke for "scientific socialism," while the dispersal of the Constituent Assembly was an example of a minority dictatorship's need to use to Bakuninist methods. "It is impossible to hold me, as a theoretician of Russian Marxism, responsible for every absurd or criminal act of every Russian 'Marxling' [*Marksenok*] or every group of 'Marxlings,'" Plekhanov sniffed.[143]

So much for the Bolsheviks. As for the working class, here, too, Plekhanov held fast to his past glories and self-image. In the December 19 issue of *Nashe edinstvo* he called attention to his election as the honorary chairman of the social-democratic club "Workers' Banner," and thanked the "worker groups and organizations" who sent him letters of consolation after the raid on his apartment. To Plekhanov, these were signs that at least the "workers' intelligentsia" was still loyal to social democracy. Recent events—the "days of the crazy nightmare," as one worker's letter put it—had not revealed any shortfalls in the "treasure house of scientific socialism," only that the ideas and methods of social democracy had not spread far enough into the working class. The task of social democrats was to raise proletarian consciousness, to overcome the disabling inheritance of the old regime. Those who took this course could expect "more thorns than applause," Plekhanov cautioned: "But we will remember what is most important—that no matter with what distrust we are regarded by unconscious workers—and these are still, alas!, too many in number—they were and remain our brothers, whose enlightenment each of us is obliged to serve to his last breath."[144]

Plekhanov's death on May 30, 1918, served to illuminate, if not enlighten, the rapidly changing politics of revolutionary Russia. His body was brought back from Finland to Petrograd, where the funeral of Russia's first Marxist theoretician became a symbol of labor opposition to the government.[145] The burial, arranged jointly by Plekhanov's *Edinstvo* group and the Petrograd bureau of the Assemblies of Factory and Plant Representatives,[146] was boycotted by the Petrograd Soviet,[147] while in Moscow at the CEC Trotsky praised Plekhanov for providing "sharp-barbed arrows" to the revolution in the past and promised to redirect these "weapons" against his present followers.[148] It was easier, for both sides, to deal with Plekhanov's memory than with his embittered, arrogant intransigence. A martyr for the workers' intelligentsia, a lesson in both wisdom and folly for the Bolsheviks, Plekhanov entered into the nascent iconography of the revolution.[149]

One of the speakers at Plekhanov's funeral was Aleksandr Nikolaevich Potresov, another veteran of the revolutionary movement. Like Plekhanov, Potresov was an intransigent opponent of Bolshevik power and an outcast from the RSDRP leadership. His differences with the Menshevik majority developed before October and were rooted in his fear of German domination and his ardent support for the war against the Central Powers.[150]

For Potresov, the war had provoked a radical restructuring of priorities and a revised perspective upon class politics in Russia. Well before Martov's call for "state power" in April 1918, Potresov put the cause of national salvation first. Social democrats had to remember, he argued at a party conference in August 1917, that the revolution was taking place in their country, a country facing conquest. If the nation were destroyed, the revolution would perish with it.[151] Fearing for Russia's survival, Potresov was appalled by the weakness of the national leadership and the amorphous rebellion of the population. The wartime crisis opened his eyes to the deficiency of national feeling in both the intelligentsia and the masses.[152]

The only class that had risen to meet the test of war, wrote Potresov in an article entitled "Fatal Contradictions of the Russian Revolution," was the bourgeoisie. The Russian bourgeoisie, so maligned by social democracy, was the force that in 1915 had mobilized the defense effort and, in so doing, had begun the liquidation of the old regime. Awakened at last by the challenge of war, the bourgeoisie had risen above its own class interests and taken up the tasks of national reconstruction. In both economic and political affairs, the bourgeoisie had acted, and acted with energy, while the socialists simply followed after events.[153]

The war experience changed Potresov's opinion of the working class as well. The other "contradiction" of the Russian revolution was the poor showing of the proletariat. The workers upon whom social democrats had pinned their hopes had not provided a national leadership. The war and the German threat to the nation awoke nothing in the masses of the proletariat. It did not find in those masses a response worthy of the most revolutionary class of contemporary society. The impression of a common national [*obshchenarodnaia*] disaster slid, one might say, over the surface of the proletarian consciousness, did not touch its depths, did not produce any fundamental shocks, did not turn into a motivating force of proletarian mobilization.[154]

The activity of a few workers in the Military Industrial Committees, a "minority even of the conscious part" of the proletariat, was only the exception that proved the rule.[155]

The explanation for this lack of patriotism among the workers was to be found, Potresov thought, in Russia's dreary national heritage. The Muscovite spirit lived on in the present, in a society divided into "Ivans and Ivashkas"— the Ivans of the tsarist government and the Ivashkas who crawled before the authorities. The so-called revolutionary tradition born of this oppression was not socialism, but slave revolt. Pent-up hatred of government was the only political sentiment native to Russians; it explained the population's "deepest indifference" to the fate of the nation as well as the appeal of internationalism among the intellectuals.[156]

Potresov became more critical and fearful of mass rebellion as the months went by. The Bolsheviks, he wrote on September 10, were like bubbles on the surface of the dark, anarchistic depths. He was afraid for Russia when he realized that

> the increase in the number of bubbles reflected the growth of the process of blind seething, that the Russian proletarian, and half-proletarian, half-peasant mass, having never known the discipline of political organization, nor the tasks of the professional movement . . . is prepared to permit its ideologues, that is, its scum, its bubbles, to decide those complex, endlessly difficult, almost unresolvable problems that are posed now before a huge country by the international catastrophe as well as the imminent economic collapse.[157]

From this gloomy vantage Potresov witnessed the October insurrection and its aftermath. The Bolsheviks' peace initiatives fulfilled his worst suspicions. Lenin was handing Russia over to Germany and betraying both the country and the revolution.[158] Within Russia, peasant rebellion, not Marxism, had triumphed. The revolution had revealed the "rural, peasant" quality of the Russian proletariat. It was the "village," he wrote in February 1918, that had "murdered the revolution of 1917" and that threatened with its "ceaseless soldier-peasant anarchy" to bring the nation down as well.[159]

These two concepts—Bolshevik treachery and peasant anarchy—were central to Potresov's analysis of the revolution. His outrage and his recommendations were voiced in *Den'* (Day), a newspaper reconstituted in May 1917 by a group of social-democratic defensists critical of the Menshevik leadership. After October, Potresov's unrelenting campaign against the "Bolshevik sickness" and the government's concessions to German "imperialism"[160] brought *Den'* repeatedly into conflict with the authorities, a losing battle reflected in the paper's changing masthead. Shut down for three weeks after the Bolshevik takeover, *Den'* reappeared in November first under its original name, a few days later as *Novyi den'* (The New Day), and subsequently as *Noch'*, *Polnoch'*, *V glukhuiu noch'*, *V temnuiu noch'*, *Griadushchii den'* (Night, Midnight, In the Dead of the Night, In Darkest Night, Dawning Day), and, alternately and intermittently, from December 1917 until its demise in May 1918 as *Den'* and *Novyi den'* once again.[161]

Potresov's articles in *Den'* and its successors were addressed not to the government or the "village," but to his present and erstwhile comrades in social democracy. Part of the fault for the collapse of the nation lay with the socialist intellectuals themselves, Potresov averred, and he held the left intelligentsia, unlike the Bolsheviks or the peasants, responsible for their choices. The brunt of his criticism was directed at the socialists' inability to cast off their ideological blinders. Where their relationship to the proletariat was concerned, the Mensheviks lived in a Gogolian world of "dead souls," Potresov complained;[162] they preferred their "party fetishism" to a confrontation with life as it was.[163] Indeed, he commented after the Extraordinary Congress,

> it turns out that life is one thing and the atmosphere of the party circles, the organizational cells, is something completely different, and the processes that develop in one and the other can . . . go in diametrically opposed directions.[164]

The party was blind even to its own fate; it could not see that its *de facto* acceptance of the Bolshevik leadership would lead to political suicide.[165]

Potresov's attack on "party fetishism" went beyond the pale of Menshevik politics; it turned one of the party's most treasured self-representations— loyalty to its own past and principles—into mere narrow-mindedness. Moreover, Potresov claimed that the Menshevik leaders were "half-Marxists," who refused to base their tactics on an objective evaluation of social conditions. Reason, he insisted, required socialists to face up to the character of the revolution and to make a choice consistent with reality. Either one accepted the Bolshevik premise that Russia was now establishing socialism as the prologue to world revolution, or one "descend[ed] from the Bolshevik heaven to the sinful ground of sad Russian reality" and recognized that Russia suffered not from excessive but from insufficient capitalist development. In the latter case— here Potresov's wartime reevaluation of class behavior helped him to break an old taboo—one had to recognize that as far as Russian development was concerned, the interests of the proletariat and the bourgeoisie were bound together. There were only two courses—for or against the Bolsheviks, and no "wise man from *Luch*" could think up a third.[166]

Potresov remained true to this analysis as the crises of 1918 broke upon each other. Throughout February, March, and April he continued to castigate the RSDRP leadership for its illusions about the future. In accord with his perspective on the economy, he called, without apology, for the building of capitalism; the national task was to make "poor, indigent, backward Russia rich," he wrote in March.[167] As for politics, Potresov's program was the formation of an "all-national" movement against both the Bolshevik government and the German invaders.[168]

Potresov's summoning of "all Russian citizens" to save the nation, echoed later in Martov's call for "state power" in April 1918, suggests the extent to which the question of the state had been forced upon the socialist intellectuals during the war and revolution. Despite their differences, both Martov and Potresov came sooner or later to perceive the revolution as eroding and possibly annihilating state organization on the territory of the vanished Russian empire. One element of this threat was the prospect of German conquest and exploitation, a danger that at first loomed large for defensists only, but was more commonly perceived after the Brest-Litovsk peace awakened the dormant nationalist commitments of other social democrats. But even more ominous was the socialists' discovery that the people for whom they thought they spoke had little, or no, national allegiance. This fact, faced directly by Potresov, disguised in Martov's allusions to the "dark masses," threatened to undermine the entire structure of social democratic politics, based upon the vision of a centralized state supported by the people.

Potresov's tactical response to this debilitating reality served to exacerbate his differences with official Menshevism. Disappointed with the "half-peasant" proletariat and impressed by the actions of the bourgeoisie in the last years of the war, he called upon socialists to build a "bridge" to bourgeois society. As in the struggle against the autocracy, leftists and liberals were to cooperate in the fight against Bolshevism; their platform would be the sovereignty of the Constituent Assembly.[169] The denunciations that this proposal elicited from the Menshevik leadership illustrate the nature of the ideological divisions within social democracy. While Martov supported Potresov's goal—the replacement of the Bolshevik regime with a democratic republic—he could not tolerate the means. From the orthodox Menshevik perspective, no good could come from the class enemy. Martov's own call for support of the Constituent Assembly was in effect a prescription for bourgeois structures, but, true to the principle of a workers' revolution, he addressed his appeal, like all others, to the proletariat alone. To him and to the Menshevik Central Committee, Potresov's open advocacy of cooperation with the bourgeoisie was anathema.

But to Potresov, rejection by the Menshevik leadership was nothing new. The official party's criticism only confirmed his view that "the party milieu was impossibly conservative even in our revolutionary times."[170] He continued to return *Luch*'s barbs in kind, attacking the socialist intelligentsia for its "clannishness [*kruzhkovshchina*]" and "party-circle cretinism."[171] What angered him most was the left intellectuals' lack of realism, their refusal to take sides against the Bolsheviks, and their passive expectation that a "democratic revolution" would emerge of its own accord.[172]

Although Potresov's arguments expressed a theoretical consistency absent from the considerations of the Menshevik Central Committee, he, too, was unable to bring his politics to life. What was Potresov's journalistic campaign, if not a different kind of "clannishness"? He spoke, like Martov, to other intellectuals, and his efforts for a revolution in a Western image were equally unsuccessful. The spring of 1918 brought no national revival; instead the state disintegrated further under the impact of the German annexations, the formation of anti-Bolshevik armies, and the localization of the economy.

Confronting the failure of his hopes and the fulfillment of his fears, Potresov began to question the philosophy on which his life's work was based. On May Day 1918 he was still defending the cause of socialism against historical contamination. Drawing a line between Marxist tradition and Bolshevism, he condemned the "Bonaparte-Communists' " celebration of May first as a desecration of the true aims of the international labor movement.[173] But writing on the one hundredth anniversary of Marx's birth a few days later, Potresov revised this brittle and abstract dichotomy. He now acknowledged the transforming interaction between Russian history and Marxist theory. From his new perspective, the old quarrel between Marx and Bakunin, the antagonism that Martov had exploited emblematically to debunk the Bolshevik success, seemed after fifty years to have taken a different turn. Bakunin had won. Or, even more disturbing to the social democratic ethos, Bakunin's ideas had entered into Marxism as it entered into life. That Marx's name was now used to sanctify an "objectively reactionary . . . revolt of the country against the city, [an] all-Russian partition [in the] spirit of Stenka Razin"[174] was Bakunin's vengeance. That Plekhanov, Marx's most brilliant pupil and spokesman in Russia, now lay unrecognized and forgotten in a sanatorium, was another sign of the radical redefinition of his legacy. Alluding to Griboedov's nineteenth-century comedy, Potresov confessed that this modern Russian version of "Woe from Wit" prevented an "objective" evaluation of Marx. Too much pain had been sanctioned with his genius.[175]

After Plekhanov's death, Potresov's slide into pessimism and iconoclasm became even more pronounced. By then he had come to see Plekhanov's life as a losing and misguided battle for the Europeanization of Russia. Plekhanov's attempt to mediate between "so-called 'scientific socialism' and ill-fated Russian reality" had been defeated by "practical life." The war and two revolutions had put an end to the illusion that Russia would follow a Western path, an illusion based on the misguiding constructs of socialist theory. Plekhanov, Potresov suggested, had "made the same mistake as Marx had made in his time . . . the mistake of all people who see the distant future so well that they are inclined by their farsightedness to underestimate that which is near at hand." If the social democrats had looked about them they would have seen that the Russian past

permeated even the processes of change: capitalist development took noncapital-
ist form; Russian Marxism resembled the older populist tradition. The best
dreams had been destroyed by the "inertia of life."[176]

While critical of Russian social democracy, Potresov did not reject the
wider intelligentsia tradition. This was the one aspect of the past of which
Russians could still be proud, he insisted. The greater the threat of barbarism,
the greater the need to hold on to the "accumulated cultural capital" of earlier
struggles. After the revolution, Potresov reached out not only to the bourgeoisie
but also to the Russian Marxists' political rivals, the populists, in appreciation
of their common "intelligentsia democratic culture." In February 1918, on the
occasion of the twenty-fifth anniversary of the populist journal *Russkoe
bogatstvo* (Russian Wealth), he recalled the words of Mikhailovsky, the
journal's former editor and populism's major nineteenth-century theorist:

> Remember his remarkable, truly historical words: "If life with all its everyday
> [*bytovye*] features breaks into my room and smashes my bust of Belinsky and
> burns my books, I will not resign myself even to [the will of] the people of the
> village. I will fight."[177]

As if anticipating the defeat ahead, Potresov paid homage to the values shared
by the intellectuals in their heroic years, "those ideas of truth and justice,
which had been crystallized in the process of the long suffering growth of the
Russian democratic social consciousness."[178] No matter in whose name these
ideas were threatened, they were worth fighting for.

Potresov's efforts to save the intelligentsia's ideals were as extensive as his
fragile health permitted. Following his recommmendations in *Den'*, he built his
own "bridge" to the bourgeoisie by joining the Union for the Regeneration of
Russia, a coalition of anti-Bolshevik liberals and moderate socialists.[179] In
addition, he continued his work in Petrograd with the "workers' intelligentsia," former members of the Military Industrial Committees, now active in the
"Workers' Banner" club, and with the Petrograd Group of Social Democrats,
an organization of dissident Mensheviks.[180] He wrote frequently in *Den'* and
other non-Menshevik publications—the party press remained closed to him—
until the opposition papers were systematically eradicated in June 1918. After
this Potresov lived underground, agitating against both the Bolsheviks and the
conciliatory tactic of the RSDRP.[181] He was arrested by the Cheka and
imprisoned for three months in 1919, arrested again and imprisoned briefly the
following year. The harsh conditions of this life—hunger, cold, prison, severe
illnesses, enforced silence, the painful, bitter disputes within social democracy—destroyed him physically. In 1924, when he was bedridden for life, the
authorities permitted him to go abroad.[182]

One of Potresov's old comrades in the "Workers' Banner" club was Vera
Ivanovna Zasulich, a founder with Plekhanov of the Emancipation of Labor
Group, Russia's first Marxist organization, and a heroic figure of the

revolutionary movement. On April 13, 1918, the "Workers' Banner" club celebrated the fortieth anniversary of Zasulich's acquital for shooting F. Trepov, the unpopular and brutal governor of St. Petersburg. As Potresov noted at this ceremony, Zasulich's name was a "common banner" for the Russian intelligentsia, a symbol of self-sacrifice and protest against injustice.[183]

Like Potresov and Plekhanov, Zasulich had been active in the defensist cause during the war. Despite her poor health, she worked with Plekhanov's *Edinstvo* organization throughout 1917. Sixty-eight years old at the time of the coup, Zasulich was bitterly hostile to the Bolshevik revolution. In February 1918, she published a short analysis of the new government in *Nachalo*, an ephemeral newspaper of the Petrograd defensists. Her article, "The socialism of Smol'nyi,"[184] summed up the "rightist" case against the Bolsheviks.

The Bolsheviks, Zasulich noted, claimed to be establishing socialism, but exactly what this meant had not been explained. First, the party had declared that the seizure of power was intended to give the people "peace, bread, and freedom," and to hasten the meeting of the Constituent Assembly. But when the "quality of . . . peace and freedom and the quantity of bread" proved disappointing, the Bolsheviks turned from these "too concrete things" to "socialism" as a goal. Socialism was a "big thing," not to be handed over on a platter; for it you needed "terror" and "chaos" and the presence of these was obvious to everyone. As for the Constituent Assembly, here, too, socialism came in handy. Since socialism was being established, we must have "already lived through the period of bourgeois government; our bourgeois republic was already an outmoded stage of development." The Constituent Assembly was therefore an "anachronism, a vestige of the past." The "wheel of history" took care of the socialist opposition as well. The socialists had fulfilled their role in the bourgeois era, but now the "socialist revolution" turned them into "simple bourgeois counterrevolutionaries."[185]

This was Smol'nyi's version. But Zasulich measured Russian history against different standards. "In fact," she insisted,

> we had never experienced a bourgeois period, our political revolution had not been completed, our new institutions were only beginning to be outlined, the country was preparing for elections to the Constituent Assembly when suddenly it was overtaken by a counterrevolutionary coup.[186]

The Bolsheviks were "usurpers," and with their violence and abolition of civil liberties they had provoked the opposition of all "conscious citizens" who valued the achievements of the revolution.[187]

Of all the Bolsheviks' enemies, none had better reason to oppose the "new autocracy" than the socialists, Zasulich continued. The Bolsheviks were not turning the capitalist means of production into socialist ones, but instead "eradicating capital" and "destroying large . . . industry." The Germans would see to it that Russian production did not revive. These actions against capital were not only, as Lenin would have it, strikes against the bourgeoisie, but blows against the proletariat as well. All those who had left the natural economy and depended on wage labor would be harmed by this attack on industry. Bolshevik policies, whether "[workers'] control" or different forms of violence, had sealed the fate of the Russian economy. Factory production would vanish and with it the industrial proletariat.[188]

This catastrophe for socialism was not confined to Russia. From Zasulich's perspective in February 1918, Russia's loss was Germany's gain. She concluded her article with a prediction of worldwide conflict and a defeat for the hopes of the left: "Renewing the power of German militarism, doubling its strength, our fate will lead to such an outburst of militarism the world over that any possibility of socialism will be pushed into the distant haze."[189]

This was Zasulich's last article. *Nachalo* disappeared after a few issues.[190] Sometime in the winter of 1918–1919, Zasulich was evicted from the Writers' Home, a shelter for intellectuals in Petrograd. Disheartened, she died of pneumonia in May 1919 and was buried beside Plekhanov.[191]

The "rightists' " arguments did not disappear, but emerged repeatedly in various opposition movements against the Bolshevik regime. The Assemblies of Factory and Plant Representatives of 1918, the Iaroslavl' uprising in July 1918, the massive revolts in the Volga-Ural area throughout the summer of 1918—all these gave substance to the rightists' charge that the Bolshevik revolution did not represent the interests of labor.[192] Despite the suppression of opposition organizations and the defeat of popular rebellions, the slogans and demands of the "workers' intelligentsia" continued to appear in newspapers from the non-Bolshevik regions and in the broadsides and small-format publications of the underground press.[193] Potresov's organization, the Petrograd Group of SDs, agitated through 1922 for the Constituent Assembly, the eight-hour day, open elections to the Soviets, freedom of speech, press, assembly, the release of political prisoners, the rights of the "real revolution" against the "counterrevolutionary" oppressors.[194] "All manifestation of independence among the workers, as in the people [*narod*], meets with one terrible reply: 'Up against the wall and shoot!',' declared a broadside from May Day 1919.[195] Even in November 1922, after the systematic repression of left-wing opposition, a Moscow SD organization recirculated Zasulich's "The Socialism of Smol'nyi" in an illegal mimeographed journal.[196]

In accord with Martov's view of the revolution, the Menshevik Central Committee rejected outright both militant rebellion and abstract repudiations of the revolution. Despite the popularity of the anti-Bolshevik position—as Martov complained to Axelrod in 1920, the "public was always more right than we" and "took in from our sermons only . . . the . . . critique of Bolshevism"[197]—the party leadership expelled individuals and entire party organizations for taking a stand against the government and kept at a distance from even the most pacific of these endeavors. But from the perspective of the dissidents, it was the party leaders who were outsiders.[198] In the words of two factory representatives of the metal industry in the Urals, the "exclusion from the party of whole regions, like the Urals, Siberia, the Don, and Petrograd" meant, "logically, . . . not that the members are being excluded from the party, but that the party is excluding itself from the Central Committee."[199]

Like these labor activists, Plekhanov, Potresov, and Zasulich rejected the Central Committee's exclusive claim to the social democratic cause. The party stood for goals they would not renounce, and they issued their statements, despite Martov's maledictions, under the banner of social democracy.[200] The essence of this intraparty struggle, in which both sides spoke the language of the left, was a conflict over the interpretation of old ideals in a new context. For Russian socialists, the revolution was not so much a test of ideas against reality, but a discovery of what these ideas might mean. To both sides, party theory counted tremendously. Like other opponents of the imperial regime, the socialists were used to losing and did not measure their principles according to political utility. What mattered was knowing what was right, what course should be followed, even if the struggle would be long and costly.

In several respects, the revolution had revealed agreements among the theorists of social democracy. Plekhanov's description of the premature revolution, Potresov's observation of the lack of nationalist values, Zasulich's condemnation of the destruction of industry—all these echoed or were echoed in Martov's writings. Where this consensus broke down was over the meaning of the Bolshevik revolution for socialism. And here different responses revealed different conceptions of that cause. For Martov, whose fundamental commitment was to class struggle, the break with the bourgeoisie came first, and thus, despite its distortions of socialist goals, the Bolshevik government was better than the alternatives and a step forward in history. For Plekhanov, Zasulich, and Potresov, who gave priority to Marxist economics, to advancement through the development of capitalism and bourgeois society, the Bolshevik "counterrevolution" was a devastating setback, if not the end, for the expansive hopes of prerevolutionary socialism.

Pavel Axelrod: "A Dictatorship over the Proletariat"

Another of the heroes of Russian Marxism who opposed the Bolshevik revolution was Pavel Borisovich Axelrod. Axelrod, in his late sixties in 1917, was a grandfather of Russian social democracy in a political and a personal sense. A founder with Plekhanov and Zasulich of the Emancipation of Labor Group in 1883, in 1917 he still enjoyed the affection and respect of all his fractious comrades.[201] Like the other revolutionary leaders, Axelrod returned to Russia after the February revolution, but at the time of the October insurrection he was in Stockholm as a delegate to a peace conference of socialist parties. Although he initially wanted to return home to work against the Bolshevik government, he was convinced by Martov's urgings, his son's warnings, and, especially, his own observation of European politics, that he could better serve the cause of social democracy by remaining in the West.[202] Appalled by the European socialists' enthusiasm for Bolshevik rule, Axelrod took it upon himself to correct their views. His goal, which he pursued with great energy for the next four years, was to destroy Western illusions about the revolution.[203]

Axelrod's efforts were directed not at the Western public at large nor at Western governments, but toward the European proletariat and its representatives in socialist politics. By means of speeches, pamphlets, letters, and journalism, he tried to make his voice heard by international social democracy. In 1918 he published two periodicals—*Les Echos de Russie* and *Stimmen aus Russland*—in an attempt to reach readers of French and German; his major theoretical statements on Bolshevism also appeared in English in *The Russian Commonwealth*. While keeping up his long-standing correspondence with Kautsky, Bernstein, and other friends,[204] Axelrod carried his campaign against Bolshevism into the formal apparatus of European socialism. He attempted repeatedly to influence socialist opinion at the conferences and congresses that met after the war to reconstruct the international labor movement.[205]

This focus on socialist organizations and in particular upon the opinion of the European proletariat was consistent with Axelrod's lifetime belief in the liberating power of the mature working class. It had been a book of Lassalle's speeches that had first astounded Axelrod in 1871 with the "grand perspective" that the proletariat could become a force for its own liberation and for the freedom of all people.[206] When Axelrod first visited Europe in 1874 as a refugee and a veteran of the revolutionary movement, he was profoundly impressed by a mass meeting of German workers and, especially, by a courage and dignity that he had never seen in Russia.[207] This vision of a powerful, educated, and self-confident proletariat inspired his efforts to introduce Marxism to Russia and remained a touchstone of his political work and theoretical writing until his death in 1928.[208]

Unlike most of the social democratic intellectuals, Axelrod was truly, in his friend Binshtok's words, an "intellectual of the people [*narodnyi intelligent*]."[209] The eldest child in a poor, uneducated Jewish family, he made his own way to political awareness and leadership. Lacking the economic and social resources of his comrades in the radical intelligentsia, Axelrod and his wife struggled to support themselves.[210] He did not accept party subsidies until he was old and very ill.

For Axelrod, personal experience and Marxist commitment were mutually reinforcing; his own life showed that oppression led to self-reliance and solidarity—the values of a liberating proletarian revolution. In accord with this perspective, he advocated that the social democratic movement in Russia be based upon an educated, self-directed working class. This conviction led him in 1903 to denounce Lenin's notion of a party of professional revolutionaries, to oppose three years later the tactic of conspiratorial revolution,[211] and, in 1917, to reject the Bolshevik revolution. In his opinion, the Bolshevik regime was "not a dictatorship of the proletariat but a dictatorship over the proletariat."[212]

Especially painful to Axelrod was the realization that the Bolsheviks were destroying the working-class movement that Russian socialists had been building since the 1890s. Informed of the failure of the *Vikzhel* negotiations, the dismissal of the Constituent Assembly, and the destruction of the independence of the unions, Axelrod wrote in *Les Echos de Russie* that "in the name of communism, they [the Bolsheviks] are opposing and doing violence to the best and the most intelligent among the Russian workers and destroying their organizations."[213] This destruction of the proletariat's achievements in the past was compounded by the new regime's corruption of its supporters. The Bolsheviks, Axelrod came to believe, relied upon the "dregs [*lumpeny*]" of the population—some were turned into their "Praetorian Guard," while others were "corrupted and formed into a privileged class which is as much bound up with the Bolshevik dictatorship as the old landowners, civil service, and officer class were with the tsarist regime." Thus, the members of the laboring classes under the dictatorship were either the objects or the subjects of a new oppression. In both cases, Bolshevism meant the demoralization of the Russian proletariat. [214]

How had Russian socialism produced such a perversion of its own ideals? Axelrod attempted to answer this question in an essay from 1919 entitled *Who Betrayed Socialism? Bolshevism and Social Democracy in Russia.*[215] The fault, he argued, lay with both Lenin and the Russian revolutionary past, or, more precisely, in Lenin's rejection—even before 1905—of the principles of European socialism in favor of the conspiratorial traditions of the Russian intelligentsia. Axelrod considered Lenin's ideas critical for the outcome of the revolution. At the same time, he regarded Lenin's approach to politics not as an innovation in Marxist theory, but as a regression to a primitive state of the Russian revolutionary movement.

In *Who Betrayed Socialism?* Axelrod characterized the pre-Marxist movement, in which he as a young man had participated, as utopian and anticonstitutional. It was utopian in its ignorance of the historical process. The Russian radicals of the 1860s and 1870s had believed that socialism could be brought about at any time—"at any historical moment, in any country, completely independently of the stage of its economic, political, and cultural development." Aware of their country's backwardness, the revolutionaries cultivated the notion of Russia's "special path"—her ability to bypass capitalism altogether and to achieve socialism without the agony of bourgeois development. The means to this end was thus straigthforward, and appealing to its proponents—the heroic efforts of the intelligentsia rebels would suffice to bring about the revolution.[216]

With this enticing prospect before them, the revolutionaries were free to ignore or disparage Western ideals of political freedom, democracy, constitutionalism, and parliamentary institutions. These concepts, like the rest of the bourgeois order, they considered beneficial only to the possessing classes, Axelrod noted. The struggle for political rights, liberties, and structures was regarded as a waste of effort, when revolutionaries could devote their energies instead toward the achievement of socialism. It was these predispositions to revolutionary voluntarism and antiparliamentarianism that Lenin had exploited and exemplified.[217]

Axelrod pointed to two tactical developments of the 1870s that had anticipated Lenin's political methods. The first of these was Bakuninism. Like other social democrats in the aftermath of 1917, Axelrod associated Lenin with Bakunin, but with an emphasis on Bakunin's corruption of the intelligentsia. According to Axelrod, who had himself once been an enthusiast of Bakunin's ideas,[218] Bakunin had introduced Russian intellectuals to the idea that mass destructive action was a means to liberation. While social democracy had subsequently tried to channel mass action through the organized labor movement, Bolshevism returned to the negative side of the Bakuninist legacy—to the strategy of destruction. In this sense, Bolshevism was "Bakuninism resurrected."[219]

A second prototype for Bolshevik tactics was the strategy of conspiratorial revolution—Russian "Blanquiism" in Axelrod's words. The revolutionary intelligentsia of the late 1870s and early 1880s had been too impatient to wait for the masses to educate themselves and lead the liberation movement. They chose instead to work for an immediate seizure of power by the intelligentsia elite alone, Axelrod observed. Only after they had gained control of the state would they call for the people's support. Conspiracy became the means by which the revolutionaries could proceed immediately to solve Russia's problems.[220]

Although anarchist and conspiratorial strategies had suffered a severe setback after the assassination of Alexander II in 1881, Lenin had revived them both. His behavior in the RSDRP, his tactics during the post-1905 opposition to the autocracy, and, especially, his concerted attempt from the moment of the February revolution to seize power for his own faction were in the tradition of Bakunin and Blanqui. The essence of Lenin's program, according to Axelrod, was the total destruction of bourgeois society by the masses and the conspiratorial seizure of power by the radical intelligentsia. Masquerading as Marxism, Bolshevism was in both its assumptions and its tactics a return to the utopian socialism of the 1870s, an elitist, destructive, undemocratic force.[221]

Thus, the answer to *Who Betrayed Socialism?* was clear: it was Lenin who had diverted the Russian revolution away from the course prepared by European social democracy. Axelrod remained firmly committed to this explanation, which emphasized the role of a single directive individual and his culture.[222] He never went further to analyze the basis of Lenin's success, but instead addressed the revolution's failures, as measured against the standards of

Marxist orthodoxy. To Axelrod the revolution was not socialist, and this was its most salient and significant quality.

Like Plekhanov, Axelrod predicted that Bolshevik rule was leading the Russian proletariat toward the tragic outcome Marx and Engels had predicted for premature seizures of power. That the historical conditions for a proletarian revolution were absent in Russia was obvious: the consciousness of Russian workers was even further behind that of their European peers than Russian capitalism was behind its European model, he declared in *Who Betrayed Socialism?* "Even more important," he continued, was the fact that "our industrial proletariat comprises a minute part of the whole population of Russia and is completely lost in the mass of more than a hundred million peasants, the vast majority of whom have only begun to emerge from a half-barbarian condition." A seizure of power based on the destructive self-interest of these masses did not and could not constitute a socialist revolution.[223]

Appalled by the conditions and prospects of revolutionary Russia, Axelrod turned again for help to European socialism. As a counterforce to Bolshevism, he proposed an "international socialist intervention" in Russia. Acknowledging the inability of Russian social democracy to displace the Bolsheviks, yet hostile to military action by the Whites or the Allies, Axelrod wanted a socialist solution. The moral pressure of European proletarian opinion would, he hoped, persuade the Bolsheviks to make concessions to the socialist oppostition and raise the spirits of the exhausted and disheartened Russian workers as well.[224]

The major obstacle to Axelrod's proposed socialist intervention was the pro-Bolshevik attitude of socialist leaders and workers in the West. To Axelrod, with his confidence in reason, these sentiments had to be the products of insufficient and misleading information. The socialist press itself was at fault, he claimed, in that it, for the most part, refused to report news damaging to the Bolsheviks' revolutionary image. "It is profoundly sad, fatal, and humiliating for the socialists," Axelrod stated to the conference of the Second International at Berne in February 1919, "that it is the bourgeois press and not the socialist press that publishes, generally, truthful reports on what is happening in Russia."[225]

In this context Axelrod realized that his word alone, and even the testimony of other socialists who remained in Russia or who had only recently arrived abroad, would not suffice to bring about the proletarian intervention he had advocated. Convinced in any case that the best education was self-education, he proposed instead that an international socialist investigatory commission be sent to Russia to see Bolshevik repression at first hand. Then the Europeans would understand that service to the cause of socialism, both Russian and international, demanded not simply "platonic" denunciations of Allied intervention, but action against a regime that was "anti-proletarian and counterrevolutionary."[226]

Although Axelrod pleaded for an investigatory commission in his journals, in correspondence, in newspapers willing to publish his articles, and in the congresses of the International,[227] nothing came of his idea. A commission of inquiry chosen by the Berne conference in February 1919 did not reach Russia because its French and English members were denied passports by their governments, and the International failed to make good any alternative plan.[228] At no time were the European socialist leaders wholeheartedly behind Axelrod's project. Their attention was focused on their own followers, who, in the words of a French socialist, "dream of a dictatorship in the Moscow style."[229]

While Axelrod's rejection of Bolshevism was unmixed with Martov's ambiguous allegiance to the revolution, his proposal for "socialist intervention" revealed his own intransigent loyalty to ideological constructions. If the Bolsheviks were the hypocrites he had described, willing to destroy socialism for the sake of their own monopoly on power, why would they be swayed by the reproaches of the international proletariat? Axelrod never asked for an army of the Western proletariat, and his writings became more explicitly antimilitarist with time.[230] For him, the effectiveness of anti-Bolshevism was less important than its socialist integrity.

In Axelrod's moral vision, even the collapse of Bolshevism would take the form of a lesson in socialist ethics. It would be a fitting end to the regime, he suggested, if it were to "break its own neck" in the conflict over the democratization of the Soviets—a struggle into which he believed European socialists could breathe new life.[231] This concern for the appropriate action, one that would tell morally upon the pseudo-revolutionaries, overrode Axelrod's appraisal of the Bolsheviks' bad faith. He underestimated, too, the reluctance of European socialists to interfere in a situation that could be exploited at home for their own purposes. As his friend Tsereteli noted, Axelrod recognized the Europeans' internal considerations, but he preferred, nonetheless, to appeal to "impractical" ideals.[232]

Underlying Axelrod's hopes for Russia was his transcendent confidence in the working class. His abiding faith in the organized proletariat's power to perceive and reject oppression blinded him to the political significance of an apparently successful revolution. Like the Menshevik Central Committee, who counted on the Russian proletariat to reform the revolution, Axelrod relied upon European laborers—the inspiration for his life's work—to reach beyond their immediate concerns to take up the Russian cause. He was on firm ground in arguing that developments in Russia would affect the entire socialist movement, but he expected the working class to do too much.

Martov's Battles

Axelrod's campaign in the West after 1917 was one expression of the internationalist—or, more precisely, pan-European—conceptions of the Rus-

sian social democrats. From his perspective, a socialist investigation of
Bolshevik Russia could be a two-way street: the Bolsheviks might be pressured
to reform by the Western left, and an exposure to Russian reality would sober
up the Europeans. Even if the Bolsheviks failed to change their ways, Axelrod
hoped at least to clear the air in Europe: "to show the workers of the whole
world in plain daylight the true character of the Bolshevik dictatorship and . . .
to forestall that ideological chaos that has reigned in the ranks of the socialist
proletariat under the influence of its blind worship of Bolshevism."[233] For
Axelrod, changing the minds of Europeans was an important goal in its own
right, not only because Western socialists had opportunities for organization
and expression denied to Russian labor,[234] but also because the "idealization of
Bolshevism" could destroy the "whole international revolutionary movement"
as he had known it.[235] Therefore, even in the wake of many disappointments,
he continued to struggle against the "illusions" of the European left.

Axelrod's efforts to influence Western opinion were complicated by those
of other Mensheviks in Europe. In September 1920, Martov arrived abroad
with his mandate from the Menshevik Central Committee.[236] The Menshevik
leadership's turn toward Western Europe was consistent with its revised
analysis of the historical moment. In the spring of 1920 the Central Committee
slid slightly to the left and declared in its platform that the world was now ready
for the socialist era, a pronouncement accompanied by a reassertion of the
principles of majoritarian and democratic class rule.[237] In a practical sense, the
Mensheviks' new focus on Europe was facilitated by the resumption of the
mails and renewed contacts with European socialists.[238] But most important
was the lack of possibilities at home after another Bolshevik crackdown in the
summmer of 1920. A Menshevik party conference scheduled for August had to
be cancelled after most of the delegates were arrested, and by September many
of the SD leaders had been in jail or internal exile for months.[239] Under these
conditions, the party shifted its endeavors to the West.

Although Martov's journey abroad was conceived as a short-term project,
this was the beginning of a permanent resettlement for the Menshevik
leadership. Within five months of his arrival in the West, Martov with R. A.
Abramovich had established both a new party headquarters in Berlin, styled the
Foreign Delegation of the RSDRP, and a new Menshevik periodical.[240] After
more than three years of press censorship, the Mensheviks were able to resume
their preferred mode of action—critical journalism.

Martov's émigré publication, *Sotsialisticheskii vestnik* (The Socialist Mes-
senger) began as a temporary expedient.[241] It set forth two goals:

> Service to the needs of the socialist democratic labor movement in Russia,
> deprived at present, thanks to the policy of the Bolshevik government, of its
> own printed organ, and information of the public opinion of Western
> European socialism concerning the growth and problems of the revolution and
> the proletarian movement in Russia.[242]

Despite this plan to reach a Western audience, *Sotsialisticheskii vestnik* was published in Russian. Its perspective upon events and its selection of material reflected exclusively the viewpoints and needs of the Menshevik leaders in Berlin.[243]

Martov's first goal on his European mission was not journalism, but participation in a conference of the German Independent Socialist Party (USPD), the Western party with which the Menshevik leadership felt the greatest affinity. The issue facing the German Independents at the conference in Halle in October 1920 was whether or not to join the Comintern. Martov had been invited to attend by leaders of the party minority, who wanted to give their opposition to the Third International more substance.[244] It was the Menshevik leadership's first chance to present Western socialists with opinions based on three years' experience of Bolshevik rule.

In accord with his earlier pronouncements, Martov's speech at Halle on October 15, 1920, combined stern, detailed criticism of Bolshevik inequity with a defense of the revolution against its non-socialist enemies. His charges against the Bolshevik government were severe: Bolshevik foreign policy—the military campaign into Poland, the call for revolutionary war in Europe, and the ideologically compromising alliances with bourgeois nationalists in Asia—displayed the regime's hypocritical disregard of international socialism and its desire to use the Third International for its own self-serving ends.[245] The Bolsheviks never asked their foreign partners' advice before acting, Martov pointed out:

> The fact is that, regardless of its enormous significance for the fate of the proletarian movement of all countries, it [Bolshevik policy] is made autonomously—or, to be precise, autocratically—by the Russian Bolsheviks, who confront the whole proletariat with accomplished facts.[246]

As for the internal policies of Bolshevism, here Martov indicted the Bolsheviks for their rule by terror. The taking and killing of hostages, the mass reprisals directed against people who had nothing to do with alleged crimes,[247] the persecution of socialists who spoke out against the regime—these could not simply be dismissed as consequences of the war. They were deliberate actions taken by the Bolshevik leaders, who had intentionally "cultivated the animal instincts and demoralization sown by the war" with their propaganda. Was terror—"the policy of frightening hostile classes and parties with wholesale murder of the guilty and the innocent"—permissible for a socialist party? And mass arrests, the closing of the press and the prevention of political meetings, the imprisonment of strikers without trial, the exclusion of certain parties from the Soviets, the sending of Communist oppositionists to the battlefront, were these the methods of a "socialist system of government"? Rejecting the notion that these tactics, while inappropriate for Europe, were "necessary in backward, uncivilized Russia," Martov called on the international socialist movement to condemn Bolshevik terror and to help the Russian proletariat escape from party despotism.[248] The evidence showed that

> the Russian revolution is sick and by its own means cannot heal itself. It needs the healing influence of the organized international socialist proletariat; only under this influence will the Russian proletariat find a way out of the dead end in which it finds itself.[249]

While this perspective seems not unlike Axelrod's, Martov's address carried a fundamentally different message. First, although his opposition to the Comintern was clear, he never called directly for a rejection of the twenty-one points. And neither did he ask for an intervention of any kind in Soviet affairs. His emphasis was instead upon external and forward-looking solutions. Martov wanted a *new* International, one that would reject the dual illusions of Bolshevism and reformism and, at the same time, defend the Russian revolution against the threat of imperialism.[250]

In some respects, Martov's appearance at Halle was a poignant replay of earlier confrontations. His mission to the West had not only returned him to the arena of free assembly, strikes, and demonstrations, it had brought him back into verbal battle with his old foe Zinoviev—the spokesman for the Third International at Halle. The contrast between their persons was even more striking than in 1917. Zinoviev gave his usual block-busting speech,[251] while Martov's voice was by now so ruined that, after a few words, his paper was read for him by another delegate.[252] But although Zinoviev, the representative of a victorious revolution, spoke to enthusiastic applause in a hall bedecked with Soviet flags,[253] he did not hold all the cards at Halle. Martov's speech about Bolshevik terror fell on some sympathetic ears, inspiring demonstrations against *"der Menschewistenschlächter Zinowieff* [Zinoviev, butcher of the Mensheviks]."[254] As in the past, however, Martov lost the vote. His defensive critique of Bolshevism failed to convince the USPD of the dangers of Comintern membership. The final vote was 237 for joining, 156 against.[255] Still, Martov was pleased by the plan of the defeated delegates to reorganize the party rump on a non-Comintern basis.[256] As in Russia, he saw the decision of the minority to go its own way as a victory for principle.

Martov's proposals at the Halle conference point to the major differences that had arisen between Axelrod and the Menshevik Central Committee over the previous three years. While Axelrod had worked to influence socialist opinion through the Second International, the Menshevik leaders in Russia had decided to break their ties to this organization and to work through a new, but non-communist grouping of socialist parties. This reformed socialist alliance would, the Menshevik Central Committee hoped, set itself free from the evils of the bourgeois past represented by the Second International and, simultaneously, help the RSDRP in its campaign against the Bolsheviks. The RSDRP's idea of an International in its own image extended beyond these basic principles to specific programs. Since counterrevolution was a greater evil than Bolshevism, the actions of international socialism were to be directed against the revolution's external foes. European socialists were to work for recognition of the Soviet government and for ending the trade blockade of Russia. Martov expected Western Marxists to make the same distinctions between the revolution and Bolshevism as he had and to act accordingly. Commenting on his speech at Halle, he denied that his criticism of Bolshevik policy hurt the cause of the Russian revolution:

> Oh, no! The Russian revolution must be defended with tenfold energy against international imperialism and Russian counterrevolution, *independent of the evaluation that the proletariat of other countries makes of the correctness of Bolshevik policies from the socialist point of view.*[257]

Unlike Axelrod who considered Bolshevism the imminent evil, Martov as before put defense of the revolution first.

These differences were apparent in the organizational allegiances of the Mensheviks in emigration. Immediately upon hearing of the Central Committee's decision to leave the Second International, Axelrod resigned his position as the representative of the RSDRP abroad.[258] He continued to promote socialist intervention through his contacts with Western socialists and to try to change the Central Committee's position. Other Mensheviks, like Tsereteli, participated in the Second International. Martov and the Foreign Delegation sought to achieve their anti-Bolshevik, anti-reformist goals through the activities of the International Union of Socialist Parties, the so-called Vienna or Second-and-a-Half International, founded in February 1921.[259]

Like his quest for correct class tactics in Russia after 1917, Martov's search for an ideologically sound International took him down an ever narrowing path that finally disappeared. Throughout 1921 and 1922 he continued to advocate the formation of a "real" International, free from the "illusions of national reformism and anarcho-Bolshevism."[260] Although he had castigated the Bolsheviks at Halle for failing to consult other socialist parties about Comintern policy, Martov, too, advocated a strong International that could overrule member organizations on questions of national policy.[261] He persisted in this suit even after the collapse of unity talks between the Second, Second-and-a-Half, and Third Internationals in April 1922, calling for more work, not at the bargaining table, but in healthy isolation from the corrupting influence of the current socialist alliances.[262]

This intransigence left the RSDRP with few allies among the European parties, especially after the German Independents merged with the German Socialist Party in September 1922 and the Vienna Union with the Second International formed the Labor and Socialist International (LSI). Martov's response to these developments was to contrast the "mechanical" unity of the LSI with the authentic socialism he espoused. "As revolutonary Marxists," he wrote in November 1922,

we naturally thought and continue to think that these conditions of real unity
can be created only on the basis of the practical return of the movement to
revolutionary-class positions, by means of surmounting or overcoming, on the
one hand, reformist-nationalist illusions and, on the other, Blanquiist-
Bolshevik illusions and superstitions.[263]

What was this but a repetition of the slogans of 1917—the rejection of both the
bourgeois path and Bolshevik "illusions"—on a new international scale? By
refusing to compromise with either moderate socialists or communists in
Europe, the Menshevik Foreign Delegation once again ensured the party's
impotence.

The Foreign Delegation's exigency with regard to European socialists went
hand in hand with its intolerance of pluralism in Russian émigré politics and of
dissent within the Menshevik party. Access to the press in Western Europe had
once again exposed the deep divisions over the revolution within Russian social
democracy, and intensified Martov's concern for party unity. The most vicious
attacks in *Sotsialisticheskii vestnik* were made not on the Bolsheviks but on
Russian liberals and, especially, leftists who were not in full accord with the
Foreign Delegation's theoretical or tactical propositions.

This struggle against wrong ideas strained even the close ties between
Martov and Axelrod. When the postal service between Europe and Russia was
reestablished in the beginning of 1920, Martov had resumed his correspondence with Axelrod, explaining party policy and sending personal news with
the irony and openness of their long-standing comradeship.[264] But once Martov
reached the West and consultation with Axelrod became a possibility, he shied
away from Axelrod's request to meet[265] and took care to remind Axelrod in
November that it would be "better if he had no formal responsibilities to the
party."[266] When their reunion took place the next month, it was unsettling for
both sides. Martov complained of his "disappointment" that all had not been
said,[267] while Axelrod concluded that the differences between them would
never be resolved.[268] He had no "illusions" about having any influence on the
party, he wrote to his friend S. D. Shchupak, but felt it necessary before his
"political conscience" to draw up "some kind of parting document" that
would explain his position since October 1917.[269] In April and May 1921, after
negotiation, a long letter from Axelrod explaining his position was published in
Sotsialisticheskii vestnik, accompanied by Martov's response.[270] But this
display of differences was exceptional. Axelrod, with his refusal to defend the
revolution, was not allowed back into the party center. Ill and politically
isolated, he nonetheless maintained personal ties with Martov, sending him
money, encouragement, and affection from his own despair.[271]

Martov's most exasperating enemies in the emigration were those connected with right Menshevism in Russia—a resilient foe. In 1920 several
"rightist" SDs appeared in London, intent upon providing an "objective
illumination" of the "facts of Russian life" to their "European comrades."

The self-styled "London Group of Social Democrats" included a number of veteran *praktiki*, as well as I. Upovalov and G. Strumilo, representatives from two metalworkers' unions in the Urals. Having begun "discussions" with contacts in the British Labour party, the London group wrote to Martov in September 1920, asking the Central Committee to "sanction the official existence" of their organization.[272]

To this request for recognition and guidance, Martov responded coldly. The London Group's idea that social democratic policy toward Russia should be predicated upon a critical examination of the Bolsheviks' internal policies differed "radically" from the Menshevik party's "tactical" position, he noted. According to Martov's letter,

> in the struggles against Denikin and Wrangel and against Poland and against the intervention and the blockade, . . . [the party] defends the same position that the Soviet government defends *without any conditions*, that is, independent of the policies the Soviet authorities carry out inside Russia at that time.[273]

He castigated the London group for calling the Bolsheviks "executioners of the Russian proletariat," because the epithet did not reflect the party's view of the "*social nature* of Bolshevism." He also objected to the "parliamentarianism" of their call for "general, equal, direct, etc. elections to the Soviets." Such differences of interpretation meant that his correspondents could not present themselves as repesentatives of the RSDRP. Especially when in Russia "a large majority of former members of party organizations" were taking positions contrary to those of the Central Committee, necessitating a "series of disassociating declarations and disciplinary measures," the party could not allow any declarations in its name abroad, except those of its special delegates. "The delegates of the Central Committee for the representation of the RSDRP abroad at present are myself and R. Abramovich," Martov continued. As for others,

> I would recommend to those comrades who still pursue the path of defining their own political line, whether due to being cut off from Russia for a long time or because of previous differences with the party, that they form *Russian social democratic clubs*, not bearing the character of party cells, for the purpose of reworking their stated position.[274]

Much to Martov's annoyance, the London Group ignored this tutelary reprimand and persisted in its independent tactics. When, in January 1921, the group declared its support of the Conference of Members of the Constituent Assembly, held in Paris at the initiative of Socialist Revolutionaries and liberals, Martov had had enough. "To the London 'Group of SDs,'" he wrote on February 5,

> Your letter of 22 January arrived after we learned of your first political address as a "Group of Russian SDs" in the form of a greeting to the Assembly of Members of the Constituent Assembly. . . .

It was impossible that you did not know that this would be taken by the party as a demonstration *against is policy*. It was impossible that you did not know that, for the party, a private conference of the KDs and SRs who had participated in the Constituent Assembly is nothing else than a conference on mutual action against the Bolsheviks, and that the party from the end of 1917 has repeatedly expressed its negative attitude on principle toward socialists' collaboration with bourgeois parties especially on these grounds. . . . Appearing publicly with this greeting you throw down a challenge to the party. The inescapable result of this was the attached declaration, through which we withdraw party responsibility for the action of your group and counteract its attempts . . . to give the impression that it has something in common with the RSDRP.

This declaration is printed in the first number of *Sotsialisticheskii vestnik*, the organ of the Foreign Delegation of the RSDRP. . . . It will be forwarded for the information of the activists of the English labor movement.

Members of your group must know that only those who leave the group, if in Russia they were members of the RSDRP, can remain members of the latter. . . .

The question of party discipline has nothing to do with the question of freedom of opinion. Everyone is free not to share the opinions of the party majority and to express this, as long as the matter does not concern action. But in action a member of the party must behave as a soldier in a united army. You are not obliged to consider the party's decisions to fight for the recognition of Soviet Russia correct and you can criticize this decision. But outside, appearing before the European proletariat or the European bourgeoisie on the Russian question you must defend the party opinion in its entirety; if you can't, you don't have to speak on the question. This is . . . elementary.

The resolutions of the "Menshevik" meetings that you saw in Petrograd in the fall of 1920 were probably made at meetings of the Petersburg "activists"—social-patriotic fanatics of coalition. . . . The party does not consider them socialists, or even proper democrats.

L. Martov[275]

This was Martov's democratic centralism. Dissidents were defined out of the movement. Martov had himself employed the rhetoric and promoted the cause of the London SDs—labeling the Bolsheviks "cannibal executioners" in "Down with Capital Punishment," defending the Constituent Assembly based on universal suffrage—but that had been in the first half of 1918. Since then these tactics had become incompatible with his overriding goal, the defense of the revolution against its enemies. The most vital issue dividing Martov from the London group was that of cooperation with the bourgeoisie, symbolized by the London SDs' declaration in support of a meeting that included both socialists and liberals. This was a strategy Martov could not permit, even in the gestural politics of the émigré intelligentsia. The foundation of Martov's politics was class struggle: Only the working class could make the Russian revolution and only the working class could put it back on course.

Martov's faith in a revolution according to Menshevik plan began to revive in March 1921 with the announcement of NEP. The turn to the "new course," as the policy was first known, seemed to be an admission of the failure of "utopian" socialism and a belated resort to the RSDRP's own economic program. The Menshevik Central Committee had, after all, consistently advocated the denationalization of internal trade and small industry. Their 1919 platform, "What Is To Be Done," was a plan for partial decentralization.[276] Martov, however, did not regard Lenin's decision as a concession to Menshevik wisdom. Although in private he accused the Bolsheviks of stealing his party's program,[277] in public he interpreted NEP as going too far toward capitalism.

NEP, in Martov's view, was not so much a bow to the Mensheviks' superior economic planning as it was a vindication of the party's theories. Our party, he insisted, had always seen that the Bolsheviks' ruinous policies would lead ultimately to an "economic regression." This prophecy had been fulfilled. After the factories had ceased to run, the peasants had reverted to a natural economy, and the supply of the cities had become impossible, the Bolsheviks had been forced, under the pressure of mass revolt, to reject their program of "immediate communism" and to "capitulate to capitalism to a greater degree than that recommended by our party platform of 1919."[278] When the Mensheviks had recommended an economy based on a mixture of state ownership and free trade, there had at least been hope for a socialist revolution in the West and help from friendly countries. But now that the proletariat in the West had been reduced to a "defensive" position, Russia had to face the prospect of "capitalist encirclement," and that the "reconstruction of the Russian economy, unthinkable without the immediate aid of the West, must take place in close cooperation with European and American capitalism." The failure of the European revolution could not be blamed upon the Bolsheviks, but their party could be held at fault for destroying socialist alternatives within Russia: "Having bureaucratized its whole economic apparatus, enserfed the unions, factory committees, and cooperatives, and stifled all rudiments of initiative in the people, 'war communism' itself killed all possibilities for socialism."[279]

This analysis of NEP was another turn of the screw of historical materialism, à la Martov. His discussion suggested that had the Bolsheviks earlier acted in accord with history as he and his party had perceived it—socialist revolution in Europe, bourgeois revolution in Russia—the resort to capitalism could have been productive. But they instead had violated the rules of progress, and now historical forces were against them.

NEP also inspired Martov to expand his earlier comparison of the Russian revolution with the French. Like the *sans-culottes*, the Bolsheviks had tried to push too far, going beyond their economic possibilities in the first years of the revolution, he wrote in the fall of 1921. This "utopianism" was the "ultimate reason behind the terrorist regime and the party dictatorship." The Bolsheviks had lasted longer than the *sans-culottes*, but this could be attributed, first, to the weakness of international capitalism in a time of crisis and, second, to the resort to NEP as a last-ditch attempt to maintain themselves in power. Nonetheless, this strategy was doomed to fail. The "political form" of Bolshevism was in contradiction with its economic program, Martov asserted. Ultimately, "the political superstructure will have to accommodate itself to those economic forces that, with their passive resistance, will lead the utopia to a crash."[280]

But despite Martov's opposition to Bolshevism, this predicted collapse was not for him a happy prospect. The familiar contest between Bolshevik "forms" and economic forces would be played out, he thought, at the expense of the Russian proletariat. The adoption of NEP, he argued, deprived the dictatorship of its ideological justification.[281] The Bolsheviks were now state capitalists, whose only goal was increased production, who cooperated with the imperialists, and who—with their piece-work rates and commercial accounting and starvation of the unemployed—treated the proletariat no differently than did governments in the capitalist countries.[282] If Bolshevism had earlier "expressed the utopian strivings of a significant part of the proletariat for the immediate establishment of social equality," it now guarded the interests of the bourgeoisie. The "proletarian masses," who had "forgiven" the Bolsheviks for their errors as long as the dictatorship had been directed against other classes—the bourgeoisie, the intelligentsia, and the peasantry—would now break with the party only to find themselves defenseless against its "social reincarnation" in the corrupt, "supra-class bureaucracy." Thus, with *Schadenfreude* Martov saw his predictions of a Bonapartist reaction fulfilled.[283]

But perhaps there was another way. Martov saw in the Bolsheviks' reversion to capitalism new possibilities for the Menshevik party, possibilities calling for a "complete reevaluation" of its economic program and modifications in its tactics. With the ruling party clearly on the side of the capitalist policies the Mensheviks had deemed "necessary" for Russia's development, the RSDRP could take up its old role—the defense of working-class interests against the state. The Mensheviks' goals would be "freedom of class organizations," social security, better working conditions, and the formation of a democratic republic, as "the political form through which the real power of the working classes is realizable." As in the past, however, opposition did not mean armed struggle. Any attempt to encourage the peasant rebellions that threatened the state would be considered "objectively counterrevolutionary."[284] The struggle for workers' rights and for political liberties would be carried on by traditional tactics:

> Rejecting the means of overthrowing Bolshevism through the route of the revolutionary uprising, the party as before will strive by means of the

organized pressure of the masses to extract political concessions from the existing government, which will allow them [the masses] to strive for and to achieve the triumph of their will over the arbitrary rule of the dictators.[285]

Although Martov's fears of a "Bonapartist conclusion to the red dictatorship"[286] undercut the optimism of these plans, the tactical significance of NEP to the Menshevik leadership abroad was that the party could resume its opposition to the Bolshevik government without compromising its commitment to socialism.

It was too late. Lenin also had recognized the possibilities for political organization under NEP and was intent upon denying them to the moderate socialists. A major element in the "new course" was the containment of the opposition. Lenin made this clear in April 1921 in his brochure *On the Tax in Kind (The Meaning of the New Policy and its Conditions)*:

> Let anyone who wants to play at parliamentarism, at Constituent Assemblies [*v uchredil'ki*], at nonparty conferences, go abroad to Martov, you're welcome to it. . . . But we aren't playing "opposition" at "conferences". . . . We are going to keep the Mensheviks and SRs, both the open ones and those disguised as "nonparty," in jail.[287]

This was not an idle threat. Within a year the Menshevik leadership was in jail, or camp, or exile. And there was no free choice of emigration. Only after an embarrassing hunger strike in Moscow's Butyrki prison in January 1922, were some of the Menshevik leaders allowed to leave the country.[288] In September of that year the Central Committee of the RSDRP decided to withdraw from all elections to the Soviets, since each list of candidates only led to new arrests.[289]

This was a persecution far worse than that of 1918, but it was a situation familiar from the past and one that fit the self-conceptions of Russian social democracy. To Martov, the terror was a sign of the weakness of the dictatorship,[290] while persecution was evidence of his party's strength. Even the first, February 1921, issue of *Sotsialisticheskii vestnik* concluded its three-column list of party members arrested in Russia with the following declaration:

> Such is the (incomplete) chronicle of the persecution of our party. It speaks not only for the senseless police spirit that saturates the whole politics of Soviet power. It is also an eloquent witness to the fact that this RSDRP, victimized over the past three years and daily declared a "staff without an army," remains, despite all persecutions, an organized force, which neither terror nor slander have it in their power to deprive of influence on the working class.[291]

The party "awaits the next steps of the crusade by Lenin against the socialists," wrote Martov in June 1921 upon hearing of the beatings of political prisoners in Moscow. "It is in the crucible of persecution that our influence over the masses of the socialist *avant-garde* of the proletariat will be forged and tempered."[292]

In his response to NEP, Martov had come full circle back to the theories and tactics he had expressed in the fall of 1917. His prediction that immediate socialism was impossible, that it would lead to a bourgeois reaction, seemed to have come true with Lenin's concessions to the peasantry. Moreover, Russia, as he had feared, now depended upon foreign capitalism for its economic reconstruction. In Martov's view, Western imperialism was behind Bolshevik policy under NEP. The abolition of the Cheka in February 1922 was not simply duplicitous—its personnel and operations were transferred to the new State Political Administration (GPU)—it was also a matter of bourgeois decorum. The Bolsheviks were preening for the upcoming Genoa Conference of the European powers.[293] The Bolsheviks' efforts to obtain European loans were further indications that the regime was becoming "the gendarme guarding the interests of international capital against the helpless Russian people."[294] Martov knew that borrowing from Europe was necessary—in 1919 he had even advocated paying back the imperial debt[295]—but this did not stop him from debunking the Bolshevik policy as a sellout to the imperialists.

From Martov's perspective in 1922, capitalism could now be seen behind all the unexpected twists and turns of recent history. As he had argued earlier in *World Bolshevism*, it was capitalism that had infected the proletarian movement with "philistine nationalism and opportunism" and caused the world war. The war had prepared the way for Bolshevism, and Bolshevism had in turn reinforced the reformist—pro-capitalist—forces in the proletarian movement. "Reformism gave birth to Bolshevism; Bolshevism strengthened reformism," he observed in the fall of 1922. No break into "revolutionary realism" had ever been achieved.[296]

Martov's focus on the capitalist threat recalls the fundamental choice he had made and remained true to throughout the revolutionary period. To him, class struggle meant being against the bourgeoisie. Even in his moments of greatest panic in the spring of 1918, he had not counted on the class enemy. Instead, with his pacific call for the nonexistent Constituent Assembly he had aided the nascent Soviet state. Fear of "reaction" had determined the Central Committee's decisions in Russia. Fear of the international bourgeoisie predominated in the emigration. With the Foreign Delegation, the primary enemy had moved abroad.

Because Martov took the course of nonviolence in the years of revolution, he enjoyed the moralist's luxury of not choosing between evils. He was against them all—against war, against dictatorship, against capitalism, and, in his own terms, he was an internationalist, a democrat, and a Marxist all at once. The more charges that could be brought against the enemy the better, regardless of conflicting assumptions. That NEP was a capitalist plan was bad; that the Bolsheviks had not adopted it sooner was bad as well.

One obvious contradiction in Martov's strategy was his support for a regime that he condemned as dictatorial and that gave every indication of its will to destroy the Menshevik party and the workers' liberation for which it spoke. But every time this anomaly was put before him—by Axelrod in his letters, by Potresov's articles, or by the various rightist dissidents—Martov used the criterion of party traditions to deny his critics' integrity. The nonviolent policy adopted after the October coup acquired a kind of moral momentum. "Remaining true to our tactics, accepted in the October days," "preserving immutable loyalty to our program," "we have always interpreted . . . "—these declarations of fidelity and consistency became more, not less, important over time.[297]

Mortally ill with tuberculosis, Martov was confined to sanatoria for the summer of 1921 and then again from June 1922 until his death in April 1923.[298] During his two and a half years in Europe, he turned more frequently in his articles to the defense of Marxism, reaffirming the validity of the theory that had guided his life's work. It was true, he noted in May 1922, that recent developments in the history of capitalism demanded "new scientific study," but

> the methods of study as well as the basic *theoretical* assumptions . . . must remain Marxist, if we want this analysis to move us forward. . . . We have no reason to doubt historical materialism, the theory of value, or the class basis of socialist ideals, for the upheavals of the war and revolutionary crises have so far only confirmed, and not disproved these bases of Marxism.[299]

At the end of 1922 Martov was once again provoked by his archenemy—the social democratic "right." This time the efforts of the rightists were spearheaded by Potresov's followers. While Potresov remained in Russia, two of his protégés, Stepan Ivanovich (Portugeis) and S. Zagorskii, emerged in the emigration. To make matters worse, several of the London SDs joined them in producing a new émigré journal. *Zaria* (Dawn), first issued in Berlin in April 1922, reopened old wounds.[300]

If there were any doubts about Martov's primary loyalty to class struggle and his fundamental opposition to the bourgeoisie, these were clarified by his response to the social democratic dissidents. His long article "Liberal Socialism," published on January 1, 1923, was an attack on Stepan Ivanovich's "fetishism of democracy."[301] Socialism, Martov argued, was not hostile to democracy, as Ivanovich had claimed. Instead, democracy had become part of socialism's program in the nineteenth century. What socialism rejected was the "democratic illusion"—the "lie of existing democratic republics and monarchies" that limited class struggle in the name of the "sovereignty of the people." True socialists had learned that democratic institutions should be used by the organized proletariat, but they did not fall for the fiction of "pure" democracy.[302] According to Martov, Ivanovich's whole argument about the ends and means of socialism had missed the point.

> Marxism could not be less concerned with the relative . . . value of abstract categories [such as] "freedom," "democracy," "national economy," and so

on. . . . Not because democracy is the "means" and socialism the "end," or
because the ideal of political equality is less "high" than the ideal of social
equality, but for one reason only—that the real base of the historical process—
the class struggle of the unpropertied against the propertied—leads through the
first to the second.[303]

Marxism did not postulate a "final goal" for humanity or for individuals, it
only stated "the very real fact that the historical movement of a *specific class*
must *end* with the establishment of a specific goal—the introduction of a
socialist economy."[304]

From Martov's perspective at the beginning of 1923, the end seemed far
away. Conditions in Europe—the machinations of the governments, Mus-
solini's "Bolshevism of the right," the militarization of society, and the
inevitability of a new imperialist war—not only shattered the impossible dream
of peaceful progress through democracy, they also made the correct course of
class struggle long.[305] But as in 1917 Martov insisted that the way forward was
with the working class, and he concluded his article with this subdued
prediction:

After, perhaps, both the long ideological crisis and the disorder created by the
bankruptcy of Bolshevism, which has dirtied and spat on all the slogans of
revolutionary Marxism, the proletariat will be obliged by the experience of its
class movement to return to the socialism of class struggle, to the socialism of
Marx and Engels.[306]

Trust in the ability of the working class to learn from its experience—this
was the touchstone of Martov's politics even after years of disappointments.
Had he learned as well? His bitter words about Bolshevism suggested his
despair, but his answer was the same as ever. Standing by the proletariat meant
waiting for it to appear.

The proletariat that had appeared so far had not lived up to Martov's
standards. In Russia, a "part"—a big part—had fallen prey to Bolshevik
"utopianism." Another part resisted, but these workers Martov, for "objective" reasons, could not support. In Strumilo and Upovalov's words, the
RSDRP "put a knife in the back of the democratic proletariat fighting against
the arbitrariness of Lenin and Co."[307] But Martov could explain these
aberrations of class consciousness in Russia. "Backwardness," "Asiatic
soil," "Bakuninism"—although obscured by formalized appeals to workers as
the good conscience and active subjects of constructive change—these conceptions accounted for the failure of the working class to take the course the
Mensheviks had plotted. Moreover, NEP had confirmed what Martov predicted
in *World Bolshevism*—the dictatorship would preserve the Russian proletariat
in its backward state. As for Europe, here, too, Martov had been let down, by
both the socialist leadership and the working class. The European proletariat
seemed infected by the same diseases he had seen in Russia—Bolshevism and
reformism, feeding on each other.

But these observations did not budge Martov from his view of history nor from his tactics. There was an overarching explanation for all these developments—that "real base" of class struggle and the "very real fact" that the working class movement would end in socialism. In his own terms, Martov had advanced this struggle—by supporting the Bolsheviks' "break" with the old order, by opposing "reaction" in all its forms, by consistently defending the "socialism of Marx and Engels." He was still on the side of progress; the proletariat would still make the revolution; and when it did, he and his party would be clean.

2

Revolutionaries in the Revolution: Populist Perspectives

The Revival of Russian Populism

Like the Mensheviks, Socialist Revolutionaries and anarchists in Russia hoped for a revolution that would liberate and benefit the exploited. These intellectuals spoke from socialist traditions that had developed in the mid-nineteenth century—the communitarian, anti-state conceptions of Herzen, Bakunin, Lavrov, and Mikhailovskii, and the voluntaristic activism of the People's Will conspiracy and the "Going to the People" campaign. After the failure of this first wave of revolutionary effort, populism was reborn as a theory of political economy in the 1880s and 1890s. In response to the state's policy of capitalist industrialization, the economists V. Vorontsov and N. F. Danielson elaborated the older notion of Russia's separate path into compelling arguments against the expansion of capitalism and for a direct, national transition to socialism instead. Despite the strengths of these theories, by the mid-1890s they had been outmoded. Influenced by the growth of Russian industry, the promise of proletarian liberation, and a brilliant generation of Marxist intellectuals, the tide of radical opinion turned toward Marxism and the model of European social democracy.[1] Nonetheless, within a decade of this ideological defeat, Russian populism—the phoenix of the intelligentsia—revived once more, this time in the form of the Socialist Revolutionary party (PSR).[2]

This political rebirth was in large part the work of Viktor Chernov.[3] As a student in Moscow in the 1890s Chernov had been a witness to the intelligentsia's debates over Russia's future and a member of a circle that idolized

66

the populists of the 1870s. His participation in this group led to his arrest in 1894, and to administrative exile in Tambov province, where he came in contact with a number of populist organizations.[4] Alienated by Russian Marxism,[5] and attracted by the ideas and possibilities of a movement based upon the peasantry, Chernov made it his mission to unify the populists on the basis of a "serious scientific-philosophical synthesis." In 1899, at the age of 26, he left "stagnant, autocratic, Orthodox Rus'" for the "noisy seething centers of European culture" on his quest for theory.[6]

Within three years Chernov, with other émigrés and activists at home, had constituted the nucleus of the Socialist Revolutionary party (PSR), with a Central Committee, a party newspaper *Revoliutsionnaia Rossiia* (Revolutionary Russia), and a theoretical journal—*Vestnik russkoi revoliutsii* (Herald of the Russian Revolution).[7] Most important, Chernov's experience abroad had helped him produce the synthetic vision that seemed to describe the conditions and possibilities of modern Russia. His analysis, circulated to party organizations and adopted by the PSR at its first congress on January 2, 1906,[8] was an amalgam of Marxism and the notion of Russia's separate path.

In the SR program, both Russia and the "forward countries of the civilized world" were seen as participants in the progress of "international revolutionary socialism" toward "social solidarity" and the "all-sided harmonic growth of the human personality," based on the "growth of man's power over the natural forces of nature." But this forward movement would take different forms in Russia from those experienced by the "countries of classical capitalism." In Russia, capitalism had not brought progress toward the collective forms of production and of labor characteristic of the West; instead it had intensified Russia's economic and political crisis, paralyzing production in the village, creating a vast "reserve labor army," and heightening the reactionary politics of the "patriarchal-police regime," the gentry, and the village kulaks. To Chernov, this intensification of the "contradictions" of development meant that the "proletariat," the "laboring peasantry," and the "revolutionary-socialist intelligentsia" could unite in a revolutionary struggle against the autocracy.[9]

The critical factor in this revolutionary movement was the consciousness of the working class—by which Chernov meant both peasants and industrial workers. Ultimately, the working class, organized in a "social-revolutionary party," and, if necessary, in a "temporary revolutionary dictatorship, would expropriate the capitalists and reorganize production and society on socialist principles. This was the Socialist Revolutionary party's maximum program. At present, however, the working class was only a "revolutionary minority," and therefore able to force only "partial" changes in the system.[10] The party's role under these conditions was to assist the formation of consciousness in the working class and thus to help it become the agent of the future revolution:

> The Party of Socialist-Revolutionaries will strive so that the policy of partial
> conquests will not screen from the working class its final, basic goal, so that
> through revolutionary struggle it will achieve in this period only those changes
> that will develop and strengthen its cohesion and capacity for liberating
> struggle, facilitating the raising of the level of its intellectual development and
> cultural needs, strengthening its fighting positions and removing obstacles on
> the path to its organization.[11]

In accord with this goal, the party was to "defend, support, or seize with its
revolutionary struggle" a long list of social and economic reforms, among
them civil liberties, electoral rights, the establishment of a federated democratic
republic, a progressive labor policy and land reform.[12]

In its progressivism, its commitment to class struggle, and its notion of the
party's role, the SR program of 1906 was similar to the self-defining
conceptions of the Mensheviks. This was no coincidence, since Chernov had
borrowed much of his construction directly—without attribution, as was his
habit—from contemporary Marxism. But in several respects Chernov's synthesis diverged from social democratic theory. First, the SR platform made
more room for the intelligentsia. Both the "growth of impersonal class
antagonisms" and "the intervention of conscious fighters for truth and justice"
were essential for social progress, declared the program's theoretical introduction.[13] How these two elements were to interact was suggested by the party's
"minimum" program: the intelligentsia "fighters" were to help the revolutionary consciousness of workers and peasants to emerge. Thus, while Chernov
did not conceive of the intelligentsia as the makers or leaders of the revolution,
their guidance was essential to put and keep the working classes on the
revolutionary path.

Second, in sharp contrast to the Mensheviks, the SRs considered peasants
and urban workers equal partners in the "working class." Peasants who
labored for themselves or others were not classified as "petty bourgeois," but
instead as workers who had been or would be radicalized by the expansion of
capitalism in Russia.[14] Labor, not property, was the defining factor. Connected
with this significant shift in social theory was the SRs' land policy. The key
provision of the SR "minimum" program was a radical land reform. The SRs
were not alone in advocating land redistribution in 1905–1906—at this time
even the liberal party supported the compulsory transference of gentry and state
holdings to the peasants, with compensation. What was unique about the SR
program was its extension of the idea of the peasant commune to the entire
country. Chernov advocated the "socialization" of the land, by which he
meant taking land out of the market economy and out of ownership and turning
it into an "all-national possession [*obshchenarodnoe dostoianoe*]," controlled
by "central and local organs of popular self-government." Land usage was to
be based on the repartitional commune's tradition of "equal-labor usage"; rent
was to be allocated to general social needs; lands with wide-reaching social

value, such as forests and lakes, were to be controlled by popular organizations of broad scope; mineral rights would belong to the state.[15]

These proposals—which amounted to a revolution—had a deceptive aura of specificity and legalism, as if they could be enacted as a "partial reform." But here, as with other parts of the party program, there was little indication of how the SRs intended to turn their platform into politics. The 1906 program concluded with a commitment to "agitate" for a Constituent Assembly based on general electoral rights. There, it was assumed, the people's representatives would act to establish "free popular government, essential civil liberties, and the defense of labor's interests." The Socialist Revolutionary party would both "defend" its program in the Constituent Assembly and "strive to implement [it] directly in a revolutionary period."[16]

This ambiguous formulation, like the land reform itself, blurred the distinction between gradual and radical transformations of society and ignored entirely the question of mass support for Chernov's broad vision. Such neglect was characteristic of the PSR throughout its existence. The party's theoretical pronouncements served less as appeals to others than as affirmations of the intellectuals' own views. This populist mentality—confident, righteous, and abstract—was self-preserving in the revolutionary period and, like Martov's Marxist orthodoxy, proved impervious to political defeats.[17]

In the decade before the revolution, the Socialist Revolutionary party suffered major setbacks. Its terrorist campaign against the state resulted in the penetration and destruction of the party's conspiratorial apparatus, an accomplishment of Azef, one of the most successful double agents of modern times.[18] After 1914 the PSR like the RSDRP was divided over the war effort. The February revolution brought the SRs with the Mensheviks into the Petrograd Soviet and the Provisional Governments, but only exacerbated the differences between defensists and defeatists in the party. Not surprisingly, Chernov, who served as Minister of Agriculture from May to September 1917, failed to put through the party's land reform.[19]

But despite the dissension within the party and its ineffectiveness, the SR intellectuals remained convinced by their own assertions in 1917. They still believed that the Consitutuent Assembly would establish "*narodovlastie*"—popular sovereignty—and bring social justice and national community to Russia. One of the most undaunted was Chernov, who in August resigned his government post to serve the people better through his party.

Viktor Chernov: "The Dictatorship of the City over the Country"

Chernov left Petrograd two days before the Bolsheviks seized power. Like Martov, he supported the program of an all-socialist government in the fall of

1917, a position contrary to that held by a majority in the Central Commitee of the PSR. Chernov decided to tour Russia for a month in order to bring the party leaders in the capital back in touch with the countryside.[20] This behavior was typical of Chernov in the revolutionary period. Always searching for a popular solution to the revolution's ills, he was never in the right place at the right time.

Despite Chernov's ineptitude, he stood out among the SR intellectuals as the personification of the populist spirit. He enjoyed the reputation of being acclaimed by peasant audiences and was adroit at cultivating his role as founder and chief ideologue of the party. Even when the SR organization did not support Chernov's position, it could not dispense with his mystique. His incompetence as an administrator and his indecisiveness in action had not diminished his status in a party dedicated to the future authority of the whole people.[21]

Chernov returned to Petrograd in time for the PSR's Fourth Congress, held concurrently with the Second Congress of the All-Russian Soviet of Peasant Deputies, from November 26 to December 5, 1917. At the party congress, the first and last to take place after the October revolution, Chernov regained his primacy in the leadership of the PSR. He was reelected to the Central Committee, chosen as its presiding officer, and later delegated unanimously by the Central Committee to the editorial board of the party's paper, *Delo naroda* (The People's Cause).[22] Like Martov at the Mensheviks' Extraordinary Congress, Chernov returned to authority on the wave of recrimination and radicalism that swept the moderate left after the Bolshevik success. One earlier consequence of this swing to the left had been a schism in the PSR, formalized in November with the organization of the Left Socialist Revolutionary party.[23] But this defection and the main party's unsuccessful attempts to oust the Bolsheviks in the immediate aftermath of the October insurrection[24] were conveniently forgotten as the party regrouped on the side of progress. This was a personal triumph for Chernov, who now led the congress through its analyses of the current situation, past mistakes, and future possibilities.

The Socialist Revolutionaries' assessment of the Bolshevik government at the Fourth Congress was unequivocally negative. The new regime was condemned for its failure to meet the needs of the peasants and workers for whom the SRs claimed to speak. Bolshevik policies were not creating the conditions for a "truly socialist organization of production," but only spreading "economic ruin." The ruling party lived by exhausting the meagre resources accumulated in the past and, with its "clumsy interference," prevented any improvements in the provisioning of the country. The separate peace with Germany was characterized as a "dangerous adventure," through which Russia stood to lose more than any other country. In one of Chernov's favorite expressions, the Bolshevik party was "incapable of constructive national work."[25]

The SRs denounced Bolshevik tactics with equal vehemence. Lacking positive programs and thus the support of the "majority of the laboring population of Russia," the Bolsheviks had to rely upon "crude force" and "party terror." "Soviet" power was only a "screen" for the party's "oligarchic domination" over the Soviets themselves. The Bolsheviks had proclaimed two dictatorships—"the dictatorship of the city over the country" and "the dictatorship of the least conscious part of the soldiery and the most excitable [*vzvinchennaia*] part of the proletariat over the city"—and were "sowing the seeds of discord between the city and the country."[26]

In the resolutions of the SR congress, this criticism of Bolshevik rule was juxtaposed with a harsh and unequivocal condemnation of the Socialist Revolutionaries' policies before the October coup. The Provisional Government, too, had proven incapable of meeting the requirements of "our revolution," especially in the area of land reform. According to the party's revised perspective, the experience of 1917 had proved that coalitions with the bourgeoisie were incompatible with the pursuit of SR goals. The "healthy part of socialist democracy" had not shown "sufficient resolve," had not taken power for itself, and had let the weak Provisional Government fall prey to the "first conspiracy." Now, the party had to go a better way, the way of "unity" and "democratic discipline" around a policy that was "strictly consistent with the spirit of the party's understanding of the nature and tasks of the Russian revolution."[27]

Chernov set forth this party "understanding" at the congress. According to his formulation, the Russian revolution was neither bourgeois, as the Mensheviks would have it, nor "maximalist-socialist"—the Bolshevik interpretation. Instead, Russia was experiencing a "popular-laboring [*narodno-trudovaia*]" revolution, the first, in Chernov's phrase, to "breach the fortress of bourgeois property and bourgeois law." The revolution had "opened the transitional, historically intermediate period between the epoch of the full flowering of the bourgeois system and the epoch of socialist reconstruction." Since this "truth" had not been sufficiently appreciated, the revolution had not yet found its proper course. (Chernov's image was that of a river not following its own channel.) But now that the "popular-laboring" essence of the revolution had been made clear, the mistakes of the past could be overcome.[28]

As these resolutions at the Fourth Party Congress indicated, Chernov felt that the Bolshevik seizure of power affirmed his own policy—the repudiation of coalition government—and offered an opportunity to set his party and the country on the correct political course. Although he did not, like the Mensheviks, have to struggle to fit the Bolshevik takeover into a Marxist historical framework, Chernov's response to October was at least equally abstract. The two administrations of 1917—first the several Provisional Governments and now the Bolshevik one—were condemned for not accomplishing a hypothetical "Russian revolution." Since Chernov measured reality against his theoretical postulates, he was not alarmed by the Bolsheviks' "risky, not well-considered, and frivolous measures." These were simply "experiments," while the SR pronouncements met "real needs."[29]

In December 1917 the SRs still had one relatively concrete goal in which to trust. This was the Constituent Assembly, embodying the aim of Russian populism—that the people would themselves determine the structure of the national government.[30] In accord with Chernov's view that the revolution was now free to take its proper path, the resolutions of the party congress displayed little concern about the assembly's viability. The party was to "concentrate sufficient organized forces around the defense of all the Constituent Assembly's rights," but its overriding concern was to oppose any "counterrevolutionary ventures." Neither were there any preparations for the formation of a government on the basis of the Assembly. The SR fraction in the Constituent Assembly was expressly instructed not to take the course of "negotiations and compromises with other parties" in order to gain a majority at the meeting. Instead the party resolved to prepare a series of legislative projects on ending the war, land reform, control of production, and the rebuilding of the Russian state on a federal basis.[31] This approach accorded with the SRs' unquestioning identification of their party's program as the popular will and with their assumed role as facilitators of the people's ascension to power.

The issues raised and methods chosen at the SR party congress suggested that nothing of substance had changed since the days of the Provisional Government. Six weeks after the October insurrection, Chernov was still fighting the theoretical battles of the *status quo ante*. From the party resolutions, it appeared that Russia would soon be a federal republic on the way to a just peace and an orderly socialization of the land, while the Bolshevik dictatorship would be a misguided episode of the past.

The first major challenge to the SR vision of the future was the destruction of the Constituent Assembly. Although its demise could have been predicted from the Bolsheviks' public statements, the SRs carried on until the last as if their plans were about to be accomplished.[32] Both the party's confidence in its own wisdom and its reluctance to assume political responsibility were in evidence at the Assembly's convocation on the night of January 5–6, 1918. Chernov, elected president by a wide margin,[33] pointed to the burdensome nature of his duties in his opening remarks:

> I am very aware of all the responsibility and difficulty of the duty conferred upon me. Please believe, citizens and comrades, believe that I will use all my capacity for impartiality in order to direct the debates of this assembly so that they will correspond to the seriousness, the worthiness of the present assembly, and the greatness of the duties conferred upon it.[34]

Even as the elected leader of an assembly chosen by the broadest franchise in Russia's history, Chernov was unwilling to assume an active part in governance. The "duty" conferred upon him merged with the "duties" conferred upon the assembly; he was only the moderator of the people's will.

Chernov's circumstances may in part explain this modesty. As he spoke guns were trained upon him by pro-Bolshevik soldiers and sailors in the galleries of the Tauride Palace.[35] It took courage to stand up to the abuse and threats that constantly interrupted the proceedings, and it took determination to see the people's will embodied not in the rifles and the catcalls but in the legislation adopted by the Assembly's SR majority. Deserted first by the Bolsheviks and then by the Left SRs, the Assembly continued its discussions until dawn, when a sailor, citing instructions from "a commissar," insisted that the delegates leave the hall.[36] Under pressure from the Assembly's armed "guard," Chernov held rapid votes on proposals concerning land reform, the means to end the war, and the structure of the Russian state. Thus, in the last minutes of the Constituent Assembly's existence, the SRs' central concerns— the national redistribution of the land, the negotiation of a general, not a separate, peace, and the establishment of a democratic federal republic—were ratified by the nation's elected representatives.[37]

The lockout of the Constituent Assembly the next day did not shake the SRs' faith in the "popular-laboring" revolution, but only confirmed the party's claim that Bolshevism was a "deeply counterrevolutionary movement."[38] From the Socialist Revolutionaries' perspective, the meeting and the activity of the Assembly had given more substance to the concept of *narodovlastie*. Endowed with the legitimacy of martyrdom, the Constituent Assembly remained throughout the next years the central icon of SR politics.

But if the SR leaders did not change their views, the events of January 6 forced them to find new tactics. The Constituent Assembly would not reappear of its own accord. The party's response was once again based on its confidence in the popular will: Bolshevism was to fall at the hands of the people themselves. "The fate of the country and the degree of consolidation of the conquests of the revolution depend upon how soon the laboring masses overcome Bolshevism," declared the Central Committee's *Theses . . . for Party Agitators and Propagandists*. The party's role was to "unmask Bolshevism" and to organize the people for an "open mass struggle against Bolshevik anarchy." An "open" campaign meant legal action: the SRs were to strive for majorities in the Soviets and prepare the masses to support the Constituent Assembly—the only basis of "genuine popular authority." In no case was this struggle to take a "conspiratorial" form.[39] Like the Mensheviks, the SR Central Committee followed a two-stage strategy: the party's leaders would awaken the people to the dangers of Bolshevism, but the people would accomplish the necessary changes. After the Bolshevik coup, the SRs waited for the Constituent Assembly; after the Constituent Assembly, they waited for the people.

In the Central Committee's literature, this renunciation of force was based on the same fear of "splitting the masses" that had characterized the Mensheviks' response to October. The party's *Theses* referred to the "still blinded soldier and worker masses who have not yet lost their faith in . . .

[Bolshevism] and do not see all its fatality for the working class.'' The problems that had plagued the social democrats were also central to the SR analyses—the state of "civil war . . . between the separate regions of Russia, the city and the country, between adjacent villages, soldiers, and the Red Guard, and . . . workers of separate factories,'' the disintegration of the economy caused by the "disorderly division of lands and wasteful sales of livestock and equipment,'' and the absence of national values—''the fragmented masses do their private will and fulfill their private interests outside of any forms of subordination of their interests to the interests of the nation as a whole.''[40]

From these observations it would appear that the SRs' confidence in the masses had been misplaced. But Chernov and the other party leaders had an explanation for the selfish misbehavior of Russian workers and peasants. The popular consciousness was being ''corrupted'' by Bolshevik demagogy. For this reason, the party's first task was educational. The ''merciless unmasking of Bolshevism,'' it was assumed, would lead the population back to the course that corresponded to its true interests, which were those of the nation as a whole.[41] Manifestations of the people's ''private'' concerns were attributed to Bolshevik contamination, and thus presented no challenge to populist conceptions. This reasoning strengthened the SRs' case against the Bolsheviks and, at the same time, reduced the tension between the party's commitment to the people and its fear of them.

The Central Commitee's 1918 *Theses* elaborated upon earlier denunciations of the Bolsheviks's social policies. The new government had not only contaminated the people's values, it had also distorted the SRs's own programs. As Minister of Agriculture in the Provisional Government, Chernov had pursued the chimera of a legal, nationwide, egalitarian land policy without success and blamed the bourgeoisie for his difficulties; now he criticized the Bolsheviks for their failure to accomplish an orderly and just reform. He was similarly contemptuous of the Bolsheviks's industrial policies. The concept of control over production, which he claimed was first proposed by the PSR, had been perverted by the ruling party into the ''simplistic demagogic slogan of workers' control.'' By handing over individual factories to their workers, the Bolsheviks were ignoring the need for commercial and industrial planning. Their attempts to blame their industrial difficulties on bourgeois sabotage were absurd; the problem was that no one was performing the necessary managerial functions. Only the state could act to coordinate the interests of workers and consumers, use the skills of technical personnel, and work out a ''higher system of planning'' to replace the capitalist system. But with Bolshevik ''workers' control,'' production was simply running down. The result would be mass unemployment and, eventually, the ''complete discrediting of socialism, turning it into crass equalization at the level of general poverty, accompanied by a fall in productivity, and degenerating into the socialization of backwardness [*oproshchenie*] and starvation.''[42]

The near collapse of the economy in 1917 and 1918 had dampened the SRs' confidence in the imminence of socialism. This was expressed in Chernov's definition of the revolution at the Fourth Party Congress. The notion that the revolution was "popular-laboring" not "maximalist-socialist" had reincorporated the idea of stages into SR theory. After October, the SRs, like the Mensheviks, began to stress Russia's backwardness. The country did not possess the "material or social-psychological preconditions" for socialism; Russia was "impoverished and uncivilized [*nekul'turnaia*]."[43] This harsh judgment would seem to contradict the PSR's confidence in the wisdom of the nation, but the Socialist Revolutionary *intelligenty* continued to believe in salvation by the masses. The country was too backward for socialism, but the people were expected to save it from the Bolsheviks. This was the Socialist Revolutionary perspective when, late in the spring of 1918, the civil war began.

Although the Central Committee of the PSR opposed military action for most of the war, there was an initial period during which some SR leaders sought to join an armed opposition in the name of the Constituent Assembly. The failure of this effort, like the failure of the Provisional Government, only reinforced the SR leadership's hostility to "coalition" and its commitment to a purely popular struggle.

Chernov was always unenthusiastic about military opposition to the Bolshevik government. While other prominent SRs—N. D. Avksent'ev and V. M. Zenzinov among them—searched for allies in the anti-Bolshevik cause, Chernov's major concern was that the reputation of the Constituent Assembly not be harmed by compromising strategies. Although he cautiously sanctioned the formation of an opposition government in the Volga area, he refused to approve the efforts of other party members to construct a united military front. Chernov left Moscow in June 1918 for the Volga region, but arrived too late to witness the anti-Bolshevik uprisings at Samara, Saratov, and Izhevsk, and managed to miss the State Conference at Ufa as well.[44]

In Ufa, a town in the Urals, Russian socialists, liberals, and military officers had met to form a temporary government that would preside over the war against the Bolsheviks and subsequently cede its authority to a reconvened Constituent Assembly. The five-member "Directory" was a major achievement for these activists, who had been working through such groups as the Union for the Regeneration of Russia and the National Center to coordinate and consolidate the opposition.[45] To Chernov, however, the Directory represented a fatal coalition with the bourgeoisie. He preferred the sectarian deliberations of the "Committee of Members of the Constituent Assembly" (*Komuch*), a feeble SR organization located in Ekaterinburg. Likening the Kadets to the Girondists in the French revolution, Chernov warned against the dangers of a reactionary provincial revolt.[46]

Chernov had a constitutional argument against the Directory as well. The Ufa Conference had no right to choose a government, he argued, because this privilege belonged to the Constituent Assembly. Only the presidium of the

Assembly—and Chernov was its president—could establish the procedures for such essentials as convening the delegates, setting a quorum, drawing up an agenda. Everything at Ufa had been done without concern for the legitimate devolution of authority. Arguing on the bases of both counterrevolutionary analogy and constitutional succession, Chernov convinced the majority of the SR Central Committee to demand the dissolution of the Ufa conference and to call for vigilance against the forces of reaction associated with the anti-Bolshevik campaign. As if to underline the purely symbolic essence of these party declarations, Chernov's "Ufa Charter" was issued *after* the conference had been adjourned.[47]

In November 1918, when the Directory was overthrown by military officers at Omsk, Chernov's prognosis was confirmed. Once again, it seemed, participation in a coalition had led to disaster. For Chernov and other Socialist Revolutionaries, the fall of the Directory was as significant as the Bolshevik seizure of power. Admiral Kolchak, who took command of the Siberian anti-Bolshevik front, was held responsible for a reactionary coup d'état against the people's will.[48] The defeat of the Constituent Assembly had reinforced the SRs' belief in *narodovlastie*; the "betrayal at Omsk" heightened their fear of reaction. Chernov described the situation as follows:

> The battle begun in the name of democracy had been for a long time degenerating into a battle between two minorities, both equally alien to any idea of democracy and fighting only for dictatorial and arbitrary power over the nation.[49]

The Socialist Revolutionary slogan became "Neither Lenin nor Kolchak."[50]

For Chernov opposition to the forces of reaction was more imperative than the fight against the Bolsheviks. On the run from both Red and White authorities, he left the erstwhile "territory of the Constituent Assembly" in an unsuccessful attempt to organize an "armed force" against Kolchak. His proposed strategy was a "two-front" battle against both enemies, an approach that effectively put an end to the SR military effort. The PSR ceased to support the fight against the Bolsheviks because, in Chernov's words, "to maintain [our] troops on the front would indicate making them fight for Kolchak and the political and social restoration."[51] Afraid of aiding the counterrevolution, the SRs renounced armed combat for the duration of the civil war. Again, failure counseled patience.

But this withdrawal from the war did not mean acceptance of Bolshevik authority. After the Red Army had recaptured Ufa, Chernov was invited by representatives of the government to "recognize Soviet power" and return legally to Moscow. Suspicious of such "favors," he traveled in disguise to the capital, arriving in March 1919. The government's radio announcement of a reconciliation with the PSR and Sverdlov's declaration in the Central Executive Committee that Chernov was on his way to Moscow to sign an accord with the state confirmed Chernov's fear that these "negotiations" were only a ruse with which to impress the Western powers at the impending Prinkipo conference. After the PSR was "legalized" by a declaration of the CEC, Chernov advised his comrades to take advantage of the opportunity to organize but to keep the party apparat secret. This perspective was given credibility when, after only ten days of publication, *Delo naroda* was shut down again, and the arrests of party members resumed.[52]

The "legalization" episode pointed up the differences between Menshevik and Socialist Revolutionary attitudes toward the state. Writing in *Vsegda vpered*, Martov encouraged Chernov to negotiate with the government. For the Menshevik leader, the SRs' support of armed opposition represented the strategy he had tried so hard to suppress within his own party. Put down your arms, Martov told Chernov, "in order to have the possibility of struggle against those who used our sacrifices and our blood for . . . a reactionary coup."[53] Struggle, in Martov's mind, was something that happened within society; he and his party were in revolutionary society, struggling against its wrong-headed government and, at the same time, fighting the reactionaries who wanted to destroy the revolution. This was not Chernov's perspective. Although he shared Martov's fear of reaction and gave up military opposition for this reason, he did not believe that the PSR had to choose between two sides. Instead the party could reject them both and pursue its independent course at the people's side. This would lead, ultimately, to the triumph of another, better, revolution.

Chernov's viewpoint was adopted by an SR party council in June 1919. Attended by over thirty representatives from two-thirds of the party organizations on Soviet territory, the council voted that its task was to prepare for a future struggle "in the name of *narodovlastie*, freedom, and socialism." Like the Mensheviks' pronouncements in this period, the SR platform shifted to the left. Since the war had created the conditions for a "socialist revolution," it was time to go over to the transitional stage of "laboring democracy [*trudovaia demokratiia*]." In the language of the Russian left, this change from a "popular-laboring" transformation to "laboring democracy" was significant. The SRs were now defending a class, and not a national, revolution. The creators of this new revolution would not be the Bolsheviks—they, according to the party resolution, had "repudiated the fundamental principles of socialism"—nor, of course, the supporters of restoration, but the people themselves, the "third force" of "laboring democracy." While the SR leaders had shifted to a new class position in 1919, dropping the nation in favor of the peasants and workers, they still upheld the populist tradition that the people would make the revolution. The party's role was "ideological work among the laboring"; the people's revival as the "third force" was "inevitable."[54]

In addition to setting forth the party program for the future, the SR council of 1919 developed the party's earlier schematic assessment of Bolshevism into a more perceptive statement on the revolution in Russia. The most significant aspect of this analysis was the Socialist Revolutionaries' view of the revolution in the countryside. According to the party resolutions, the "major characteristic of the present phase of . . . the Bolshevik dictatorship" was the "colossal contradiction" between the peasantry's vital economic role and its political insignificance. The peasants were now more than ever the major productive force in Russia, the SRs stated. With the elimination of the gentry and the disruption of industry, the peasants alone had to support the government, the army, and the "nonproducing consumers of the city," in addition to themselves. The Bolsheviks understood this economic fact, but refused to accord the peasants a political voice that would correspond to their role as producers. For the "city dictatorship," the peasantry was not the "subject," but the "passive object of politics."[55]

The peasants, however, could not even perform their economic function because of Bolshevik tactics. As the new government tried to establish its control, the peasants had been subjected to a series of "measures of direct expropriation" by the authorities. Their grain requisitions, "contributions," and extraordinary taxes were made more severe by the flood of paper money that destroyed peasant earnings and made a rational economy impossible. In response to these practices, the peasants had slaughtered their livestock and reduced their cultivation to a "suicidal" minimum. Thus the Bolsheviks had succeeded in setting the city and the country against each other, as the SRs had predicted in 1917. But the government's "terror and repression" could not contain these contradictions forever; the Bolsheviks' violence against the peasants was only postponing greater bloodshed that was yet to come.[56]

The SRs' critique of Bolshevik tactics in the countryside was connected with their continued defense of democracy as the only basis of socialist government. The state's treatment of the peasants demonstrated the destructive potential of the Bolshevik's "barracks-bureaucratic [kazarmenno-biurokraticheskii]" perversion of socialism. Because of the dictatorship, the peasants had no voice in their own affairs. A democratic policy toward the peasants would, the party program noted, liquidate the Committees of the Poor, the appointed regional executive committees, the "whole bureaucratic net" of village commissars appointed from outside, and give the peasants the decisive voice in politics that their numbers and their "real and relative weight" in the national economy merited.[57]

The forcefulness of these arguments was not matched by any significant action by the SR leadership. After the brief "legalization" of March 1919, the party was pushed underground again. Chernov remained in Moscow, and like Martov, began to write his memoirs.[58] This was a life that demanded Chernov's talent for conspiracy and indulged his sense of revolutionary heroism. He boasted that he worked daily in a Soviet institution under the noses of the police, without being recognized.[59] His wife and children were not so lucky. They were arrested in January 1920 and held hostage in an effort to catch Chernov.[60]

Chernov's most spectacular feat during this underground period was a public appearance in May 1920, at a meeting organized by the obstreperous Moscow

Printers' Union[61] in honor of the visiting British Labour Delegation. Having requested the floor in the name of the PSR, Chernov, unrecognizable with a long beard, gave a fifteen-minute speech condemning Bolshevism.[62] His oration compared the development of Russian communism to that of Christianity. In both cases, a group of ascetic zealots had turned into a corrupt hierarchy "drunk" on power and privilege and their faith had become a symbol of oppression. Under Bolshevik rule, socialism had turned into a "living corpse." Bolshevism meant a return to the bureaucratic and militaristic methods of the old regime. In one of Chernov's favorite analogies, the ruling party had evolved from the stage of "Lenin-Pugachev" to "Lenin-Arakcheev."[63] Having exploited mass rebellion, the regime now relied upon regimentation. The revolution had become, in a characteristic pile-up of labels,

> a party absolutism, some kind of peculiar guardian-type [*opekunskii*] socialism, oligarchic-bureaucratic in its administrative structure, with the methods of the barracks and forced-labor [*kazarmennyi i voenno-katorzhnyi po metodam*], in a word [!] Arakcheevan communism.[64]

In his speech Chernov thanked the British Delegation for coming to Russia and for making this "mass workers' meeting" possible, a "meeting not of the bureaucratic upper crust [*verkhi*] . . . but of the worker depths [*nizy*] themselves." He praised the printers for their "example," and reminded "all workers" that "freedom of expression, the press, assembly, and . . . general election . . . belonged to them by right."[65] Chernov took this opportunity to exhort workers to defend these rights:

> Make use of them on the spur of the moment, without asking permission from anyone. Seize them as I seize here the right to speak before you from this rostrum; I, whose comrades on the Central Committee of the SR party were arrested yesterday, are being arrested and will be arrested and thrown into jail.[66]

This was hardly an inducement to speak up. But it was a bravura performance, filled with the fantasy of SR politics. Once again, Chernov denied the force of established power by suggesting that people could act for themselves and by themselves bring abstract principles to life.

At the end of his discourse, Chernov announced his name and in the ensuing commotion managed to slip out of the hall. He got away with his free speech, but for others his tactics led straight to prison. The leaders of the Printers' Union were arrested, along with several of his friends. This put ten members of the PSR Central Committee in jail; two others had been shot earlier in Siberia.[67]

Chernov's emphasis on free elections and civil rights at the Printers' Union meeting became a major element in the Socialist Revolutionary critique of Bolshevism. In September 1920, another party conference declared that only democracy could guarantee the success of socialist construction. The experiences of the past three years had shown that the dictatorship would not correct its own faults: "The logic of any minority dictatorship leads to a situation in which offering the people the freedom to express their will undermines the bases of the dictatorial government's power." Thus, the transition to socialism required not only "objective economic preconditions," but also "majority rule."[68] The party program stressed the importance of civil liberties for the individual as well:

> Narodovlastie signifies not only the rule of the majority, but also the protection of the rights of the minority. Putting forward as political demands the establishment of freedom of speech, press, assembly, unions, and the inviolability of the individual, the PSR proceeds not only from the conception of the protection of the rights of "man and the citizen," but also from the concrete needs of the movement of the laboring masses.[69]

As for the means to transform the revolution, the PSR now took a shaky stand on the side of armed struggle against the government. With the defeat of the White leaders Denikin and Kolchak earlier in the year, there was no longer any danger of aiding the "landlord-bourgeois" reaction. In view of the Bolsheviks' destructive policies, the threat from foreign imperialism, and the "existence of a village insurrectionary movement of the popular masses to overthrow the communist dictatorship," the SRs announced "the inevitability" of a "revival by the party of the armed struggle with Bolshevik power." But this would be a "future" battle. For the present the party was to work on the "organization of the popular active forces," while carrying on a "most decisive struggle against any kind of counterrevolutionary endeavors, no matter what [their] slogans."[70]

The PSR's 1920 program, like the Menshevik platform of the same period, introduced a new focus on the Western labor movement. The class struggle in Europe promised to provide that majoritarian, democratic revolution that eluded the moderate left at home. Moreover, the Western workers, whom the SRs thanked for their campaigns against the blockade and intervention, were needed to counter the "imperialistic, self-serving Entente tactics" toward war-torn Russia. In this cause, the PSR took up the task of "unmasking" before a different public. The party was to expose these dangerous designs to the "working classes of the West."[71]

In accord with this international perspective, Chernov slipped over the Estonian border in the fall of 1920.[72] Outside Russia, he seized his rights in the émigré press. He first published in Narodnoe delo (The Popular Cause), a party newspaper in Reval, and later, in December 1920, revived the SRs' prerevolutionary journal, Revoliutsionnaia Rossiia (Revolutionary Russia). Not one to miss an opportunity for legendry, Chernov's lead article in the first issue of Revoliutsionnaia Rossiia spelled out this pedigree:

> Resuming publication of the party organ abroad, we give it an old name— Revolutionary Russia. In this there is a certain amount of distinctive political

symbolism. For again, as before, revolutionary Russia is driven into the underground. Once again, as before, it is necessary to seek abroad for a place to publish socialist party organs, "out of reach." Once again, as before, revolutionary Russia is pursued and crucified at home. . . . [73]

For Chernov, as for Martov, persecution was evidence of his party's strength. Time had tested the party; the weak had fallen by the wayside; and the struggle for real freedom had just begun. With the end of the civil war, "revolutionary Russia" could now renew its battle "on all fronts against the Bolshevik despots." Workers could fight "against the militarization of labor, against bureaucratization and dictatorship" in the production process, for free labor unions, against the "new privileged estates—the Soviet bourgeoisie and Soviet bureaucracy," against all the distortions of the "authoritarian, barrackschaingang parody of communism." Peasants could resume their struggle against the "new Soviet labor services [*barshchina*], against Bolshevik serfdom," against the elimination of the peasantry from politics, against the "petty tyranny of the commissarocracy [*komissarokratiia*] in the village." Despite this battle rhetoric, Chernov was still opposed to violent tactics. Repudiating the "mythical immediate peasant [armed] crusade," he predicted that the struggle for freedom could now take the form of a "rational system, with a . . . *crescendo*"—from mass organization, resolutions, negotiations, demonstrations, strikes, to a "general strike" that would include the "laboring intelligentsia." As for the Socialist Revolutionary party, it had never occupied itself with "putschism," or the "fantastic plans of ordering the completion of the national anti-Bolshevik revolution." The popular revolution would "give birth to itself," he insisted.[74] The PSR would contribute organization skills in order to prevent "blind elemental excesses" and to give form to

the same revolutionary Russia that had lost itself in the chaos and darkness of the days before October, that with a heavy heart had temporized during the bloody haze of the crazy duel between the white and red dictatorships, and that once again is finding itself today, in order that it may find its rights in struggle.[75]

Chernov's contribution to the "crescendo" was a torrent of critical journalism in the émigré press. His articles from this period elaborated all the underlying themes of PSR's view of Bolshevism—the exploitation of the peasantry,[76] the destruction of democratic government and civil rights,[77] and the perversion of socialist ideals.[78] At the same time, he joined the internecine conflicts of the intelligentsia abroad. One of his first targets was Martov. Since the summer of 1918 the Menshevik leader had accused the PSR of aiding reaction,[79] a charge to which Chernov was acutely sensitive.

From an outsider's viewpoint, it might appear that Chernov and Martov had little over which to quarrel. Both leaders of the moderate left had drawn back from the violent struggles of revolutionary Russia and tried to take their parties with them. Their fears of "anarchy" and "reaction" prevented them from aiding both "elemental" uprisings and military efforts against the state, while their commitments to democratic revolution precluded cooperation with the Bolshevik "dictatorship." There was only one period in the civil war when Chernov's and Martov's tactics were at odds. This was the summer and fall of 1918, when Chernov supported the authority of the "Committee of the Constituent Assembly" and armed rebellion against the Bolsheviks, while Martov dropped the Constituent Assembly slogan and became a defender of the Soviet government. In several respects, their analyses of Bolshevism were alike. Both Martov and Chernov regarded the Bolsheviks as exploiters of the people, not as their representatives; both condemned the terror; and both rejected party dictatorship in favor of more democratic rule. These shared criticisms, however, did not preclude one underlying difference in perspective, one that was significant for the revolutionary intelligentsia. Martov defended the Bolshevik revolution as a step forward in history, but for Chernov Bolshevism was regressive.

Chernov attacked the RSDRP's defense of the Bolshevik government in an article written for the third anniversary of the October seizure of power and entitled "Revolution or Counterrevolution." There was an "objective" answer to this question, Chernov felt. One could avoid the deceptions of terminology and of declared intent by looking at what the revolution had accomplished, not at what the historical actors thought of themselves, nor at their stated goals, but at what—in Chernov's phrase—"they add to the capital of history." Mensheviks "of the Martov type" defended the Bolsheviks for their achievements in five areas: they had ended the war, solved the land problem, replaced the old bureaucracy with a new proletarian apparatus, expropriated the capitalists, and revolutionized the foreign proletariat. These were the strongest arguments in the Bolsheviks' defense, Chernov felt, but he proposed to show that all of them were specious.[80]

The Bolsheviks had not ended the war, Chernov argued, but brought it home. Their "peace" had put Russia at the mercy of the other combatants. Moreover, "tens of new fronts" had opened up as the Bolsheviks, as if repeating the "whole history of our national wars," tried to reconquer the vast non-Muscovite territories. As for land reform, Chernov was still an advocate of the national and equalizing distribution he had failed to enact as Minister of Agriculture. From his perspective, the Bolshevik coup had ended efforts to achieve a lasting land reform by sanctioning a vast land-grab. This was a "step backward from a well-considered *socialization of the land* to a primitive *black repartition*, the disorderly anarchistic seizure of the land reserves by the peasants in closest proximity to them" with devastating results for agriculture. The "objective task" of the revolution was to "replace the gentry economy with a laboring one, on principles capable of increasing the productivity of the land." But the Bolsheviks' policies, as they themselves admitted, had led instead to a "regression in the village economy."[81]

The reform of the state apparatus was illusory as well, Chernov argued. It was true that a flood of new people from the masses had acquired status and privilege as state officials. But was this "plebeianization of the personal composition of the bureaucracy" to the public good? The "objective historical task" was the democratization of government, which meant changing not only the governors, but also the process of governing itself. The Bolsheviks had "substituted plebeianization for democratization," and had "liquidated" democracy in the government's procedures. They had destroyed the local organs of self-administration, the cooperatives, and the trade unions, and proceeded to the "monstrous universalized bureaucratization of everything—of the state, the national, and the popular economy." Of what use was it to peasants and workers to be ruled by ex-workers, ex-sailors, ex-peasants who had acquired the position and psychology of their predecessors in the tsarist bureaucracy? Chernov, who was partial to classical ornament, insisted that there was a difference between the people and the mob, between "demos" and "ochlos." What "history" required was the rule of the "demos," the people "educated through democracy, and for democracy, for self-rule." What the Bolsheviks had accomplished was "ochlocracy"—mob rule through the bureaucracy, with its "natural adjunct, the dictatorship of an organized clique." And this "terroristic" dictatorship destroyed " 'with blood and iron' every wish even to think about self-government."[82]

It was easy to make a case against the Bolsheviks' economic policies, although Chernov was unfair in citing this as a basis for the Mensheviks' support of the regime. As elsewhere, he ignored their criticism while adducing his own. In his view, the war had been a critical factor in Russia's industrial condition. Wartime pressures had forced Russian industry into "higher," more collective forms, into a "military socialism" of a despotic type. According to Chernov, the revolution should have freed this socializing process from its "militaristic" perversion, while continuing toward the goals of nationalization and regulation. The Bolsheviks, he claimed, had moved in the opposite direction—increasing the militarization of labor and destroying the productive capacity of what had already been achieved.[83]

As for the need to defend Bolshevism because of its radicalizing impact upon the foreign proletariat, Chernov dismissed this argument out of hand. The European image of the revolution, in any case, was not based on the views of Russian observers, since the Western proletariat had created its own "romantic revolutionary legend" out of the "purest misunderstanding of our Bolsheviks." And in Central Asia, the Bolsheviks' major concern was not the working class, but England. There as elsewhere they were indifferent to the social composition and goals of the movements they encouraged. The people of the East were only pawns in the Bolsheviks' effort to gain diplomatic recognition from the Europeans.[84]

None of the arguments for the accomplishments of Bolshevik rule held up, Chernov concluded. The Bolshevik leaders had not met his "elementary demand" that a revolution create a higher stage of human development. Therefore, October had been not a "revolution" but a "coup" that resulted in a severe setback for Russia.

> Here there cannot be two opinions; the overall result will be economic and political regression and not progress, and objectively Bolshevism is not a revolutionary, but a reactionary or counterrevolutionary force.[85]

Without creative possibilities, Bolshevism was a "deadend" in revolutionary history. It was high time to move on.[86]

How? As Chernov's program in *Revoliutsionnaia Rossiia* indicated, he was confident that the people would make a democratic revolution. Other SR intellectuals took a different approach and made one more effort to revive the PSR's old panacea—the Constituent Assembly. After the defeat of the last White army in November 1920, moderate Socialist Revolutionaries in Paris called for a meeting of "members of the Constituent Assembly" to form a united democratic opposition to the Bolsheviks.[87] Chernov refused to partici-pate in this conference. To him, a meeting that would include both liberals and socialists was another example of that infamy, "coalition." "Russia cannot take up anything that resembles a coalition with census elements," he insisted. Perhaps more to the point, the meeting, which included both Kerensky and Miliukov, threatened Chernov's internalized identity as the symbolic represen-tative of Russian democracy. He wrote to the SR Central Committee in Russia that, as the president of the Constituent Assembly, he could not engage in any "private conferences of its members."[88]

Chernov need not have worried. While the conference of thirty-three of the fifty-six deputies to the Constituent Assembly alive outside Russia produced a semantic conciliation between right SRs and left Kadets, this "coalition," like so many other SR projects, had no results for revolutionary Russia.[89]

Chernov's hositility to the Paris convocation was an indication of the fissures within the PSR abroad. Since 1917 he, like Martov, had been struggling to enforce party discipline around his own program,[90] only to find the conflicts among party activists intensified by the revolutionary situation. Still, Chernov's notion that he led the PSR was more easily sustained in Russia where there could be no public meetings and no dissident journalism. In Europe, the splits within the PSR were on display for all who cared. Chernov tried to use his authority as the Central Committee's representative to reunite the wayward, but to no avail. Not only did the fragmentation of the party proceed more rapidly when the various factions could once again attack each other in print, but in addition, these differences of opinion were reinforced by geographic separation. Among the several SR colonies,[91] Chernov gravitated toward Prague, where the Czech government had offered the émigrés assis-tance. Here, as a leader of the party "left-center" and with a subsidy from the government for *Revoliutsionnaia Rossiia*, he continued his struggles for the people's cause.[92]

As Chernov's inaugural editorial in *Revoliutsionnaia Rossia* indicated, he regarded this removal from Russia as a temporary setback. It had, after all, been only three years since his last stint in European exile. The fact that he had left illegally in flight from the police only confirmed Chernov's sense of his own importance, as did his differences of opinion with other SR leaders. In his 1921 publication, appropriately titled *Mes tribulations en Russie soviétique*, he commented:

> I have always considered it a blessing and also an honor for me to be the principal target of these different attacks. They are, it seems to me, the best evidence that I, too, could do something for my party, for Russia, and for the revolution.[93]

This statement testifies not only to Chernov's egoism, but also to the focus on the state that was typical of SR politics. Despite Chernov's self-assigned role as representative of the masses, and despite his manifest aversion to real, as opposed to symbolic, leadership, it was the attacks of the rulers or of other intellectuals that affirmed the value of his efforts. Perhaps there were no attacks from the people, or perhaps these were not remembered. In Chernov's memoirs, there is no mention of the remark, allegedly shouted at him by a sailor during the July Days of 1917: "Take power, you son of a bitch, when it's handed to you."[94]

Mark Vishniak: Constitutional Illusions

Among Chernov's opponents within the Socialist Revolutionary diaspora was Mark Veniaminovich Vishniak, a member of the party "right" in Paris. Unlike the SR group in Prague, which focused its political activity on the Russian émigrés, the Parisian Socialist Revolutionaries had a European orientation. Most of these intellectuals had been supporters of the war and the Provisional Government before October and of the Constituent Assembly and the Directory until Kolchak took over in Siberia. They did not count on the Russian masses to liberate themselves and turned instead to the Allied governments and to European opinion. Paris offered them a chance, it seemed, to have an impact on foreign powers and parties—at the Peace Conference, in the formation of the League of Nations, through contacts with French socialists.[95] In addition, Socialist Revolutionaries in Paris had been the first after the revolution to revive the Russian press abroad. Beginning in January 1918 they issued a number of French-language publications directed, like Axelrod's *Les Echos de Russie*, both at Russians in the West and at European socialists.[96] It was natural that Vishniak, who believed that his commitment to democratic revolution was shared by European intellectuals, should join this cosmopolitan community.[97]

Vishniak's commitment to revolution was a product of Russian autocratic politics. Born in 1883, the son of a Jewish merchant, Vishniak encountered "not a whiff of revolution" in his Moscow gymnasium, and he was not temperamentally inclined to radicalism.[98] Nevertheless, he was converted to the revolutionary cause in the winter of 1904–1905, when he was arrested and jailed for attending a student demonstration. Released on the eve of Bloody Sunday, Vishniak became an agitator, organizer, and propagandist for the PSR in Moscow, writing for the party newspaper *Revoliutsionnaia Rossiia* and later for the Moscow Soviet's *Izvestiia*. Within a year, this student of Kantian philosophy and jurisprudence was drawn into the underground life of arrests, escapes, illegal propaganda, exile, and comradeship with the Socialist Revolutionary intelligentsia. This recommitment seemed to preclude a law practice in Russia. But Vishniak had never had much sympathy for the Russian bar; in any case, his formal training in jurisprudence in Germany and Russia became useful at a later date. After the February revolution, he acted as a special counsel to the PSR, working on a constitutional plan and on the Provisional Government's commission to prepare the elections for the Constituent Assembly.[99]

As a member of the Electoral Commission, Vishniak was arrested on November 23, 1917. He was released from prison in time to attend the single session of the Constituent Assembly on January 5–6, 1918. Elected secretary of the assembly, Vishniak recorded its proceedings amid the uproar, abuse, and threats from the Bolshevik section.[100]

The next day the Constituent Assembly was locked out, and Vishniak was an "enemy of the people" and back in the underground.[101] He first tried to publish an account of the events of January 5 and 6 and to promote the cause of the Constituent Assembly in Petrograd and Moscow, only to have several publications closed by the censorship. Sought by the Cheka, he decided to leave the capitals to join the anti-Bolshevik forces in the Urals. Following several mishaps and detours, including six weeks spent in a Kiev prison, Vishniak eventually reached Odessa after the Siberian effort to defend the Constituent Assembly had failed. Here he worked with a coalition of liberals and socialists on *Griadushchii den'* (The Future Day), yet another incarnation of Potresov's *Den'* run by its former editors, S. Zagorskii and V. Kantorovich. In April 1919, after the fall of the liberals' Crimean Regional Government to the Bolsheviks, Vishniak left Russia aboard a Greek ship.[102]

Once in Paris, Vishniak took up the work for which he was best suited— political analysis. He played only a secondary role in the right SRs' efforts at high politics, in part because the older members of the SR intelligentsia— Avksent'ev, Rudnev, Fondaminskii, and Zenzinov—took the lead in representing the party faction abroad, in part because he preferred writing to "orating" on political questions.[103] He was now free from the institutional and self-imposed constraints of opposition politics, but he concerned himself with an old problem—the fate of democracy in Russia.

His first approach to this subject was to expose the anti-democratic ideology of the Bolshevik leadership. In his 1919 essay *Bolshevism and Democracy*,[104]

Vishniak emphasized that the Bolshevik leaders had explicitly attacked and discarded democratic principles. Unlike Axelrod and Martov, Vishniak did not regard this as a regression to conspiratorial and Bakuninist traditions, but rather as a product of Russian social democracy itself. In his essay he recalled the RSDRP's debates on party organization in 1903, when Plekhanov had defended a stand against universal suffrage as "hypothetically conceivable" and when Trotsky, supporting Martov's exclusion of proportional representation from the party's considerations, had elaborated, "*all* democratic principles must be *subordinated* exclusively to the interests of our party." In Vishniak's opinion, the Bolsheviks had simply drawn the "practical conclusions from the blunders, gaps, and one-sidedness of orthodox Marxism" in Russia.[105]

Nowhere was this cynicism about democracy clearer than in Lenin's shifting position on the Constituent Assembly. Vishniak reminded his readers that Lenin had begun to attack the Constituent Assembly as soon as he returned to Russia; his April theses had condemned a parliamentary republic as a "step backward" from government by the Soviets.[106] Yet this statement of principle had not prevented the Bolshevik party from using the cause of the Constituent Assembly as a tactical weapon against the Provisional Government. The immediate convocation of the assembly was one of the slogans of the October seizure of power. When victory was in sight, however, Lenin renewed his attack on democratic principles, identifying the "root of evil" in the "will of the majority." Relying upon the "people's will" was worthy of only the "stupidest petty bourgeois," wrote Lenin in the Bolshevik paper *Rabochii put'* (The Worker's Way) a few weeks before the coup:

> How many times has it happened in revolutions that a small but well-organized, armed, and centralized force of the commanding classes has crushed to pieces the force of the "majority of the people," badly organized, badly armed, fragmented?[107]

Revolutionaries should learn from this past, Lenin had insisted. The "people's will" and the "idea of the majority" were simply the debilitating "bourgeois prejudices" of that "mean petty bourgeois, cowardly democracy that has not escaped from slavery."[108]

Vishniak pointed out that Lenin's strictures were not only designed to overcome the hesitations of would-be revolutionaries, they had been elevated into principles of Bolshevik rule after the party had taken power. Once it became clear that the Constituent Assembly was not going to have a Bolshevik majority, the party leadership began to attack the institution in whose name it had claimed to fight. Lenin's nineteen theses on the Constituent Assembly, published in *Pravda* in December 1917, renewed his old charge that the Constituent Assembly as an "ordinary bourgeois republic" had been outmoded by Soviet power.[109] When the Constituent Assembly had been suppressed, the Bolsheviks returned to the principles of the April theses. The party's congress in March 1918 decreed "liberty and democracy not for all, but only for the

laboring, exploited masses in the name of their liberation from exploitation"
and the "destruction of parliamentarism, as the separation of legislative from
executive functions, and [in its place] the merger of administration with
legislation."[110]

Vishniak devoted the rest of *Bolshevism and Democracy* to an analysis of
the "republic of Soviets" that was supposed to supersede and surpass
bourgeois democracy. In reality, Vishniak claimed after his experience in
Russia, "Soviet democracy" was a

> chaotic pile-up [*nagromozhdenie*] of organs [of authority]—the new on top of
> the old, over the highest even higher ("extraordinary"), the overlapping of
> their responsibilities, the constant conflict of the innumerable multitudes of
> their agents with the "extraordinary commissions" and with the natural desire
> of each of them to be higher than all the rest. . . . Everyone gives orders, and
> no one carries any orders out.[111]

The Bolshevik leaders' attempts to reconstruct authority had only centralized
control in the hands of the Council of People's Commissars, and ended up by
denying rights to all, both exploited and exploiters. The "highest form of
democracy" had turned into a "dictatorship of a minority over the majority."[112]

One of Vishniak's major concerns in *Bolshevism and Democracy* was, as
the title suggests, to place the blame for the failure of democracy in Russia on
the Marxist—not the populist—left, on the Bolshevik party and, especially, on
Lenin. From this point of view, it was Lenin who had taken democracy out of
socialism.[113] But with time Vishniak's writings on this subject became more
reflective. Why had the Constituent Assembly been so easily defeated? For
most Socialist Revolutionaries, the Bolsheviks' dismissal of the Constituent
Assembly had only enhanced the symbolic value of the institution, endowing it
in retrospect with an aura of national legitimacy. Vishniak, however, began to
question the strength of constitutionalism in Russia's broader political traditions and to see the defeat of the Constituent Assembly in a larger historical
context. In fact, he argued, Russian intellectuals had never been thoroughly
committed to popular rule through representative institutions.

Vishniak developed this analysis in "The Idea of the Constituent Assembly," two essays published in January and February 1920 in *Griadushchaia
Rossiia* (The Future Russia), a short-lived periodical of the émigré intelligentsia
in Paris.[114] In these articles, Vishniak looked back at the nineteenth-century
intelligentsia and observed that while the *intelligenty* had on many occasions
been willing to sacrifice themselves *for* the people, they had never concerned
themselves with the people's right to determine their own government. Even
for the patriotic Decembrists, changes in state institutions were to be enacted by
the rulers, not the ruled. Later in the century, when the intelligentsia had turned
against the idea of the state, the question of political forms became superfluous.
Representative institutions on the European model stood in the way of Russian
goals—revolution and spontaneous, immediate socialism. It was a terrorist

organization—*Narodnaia volia* (The People's Will)—that first publicized the concept of the Constituent Assembly. But in this group's plans, the proposal for a national assembly was subordinated to other, more radical, goals. The *narodovol'tsy* made it clear that if the people failed to show sufficient initiative, their own revolutionary government would enact the necessary changes in its stead. In *Narodnaia volia*'s 1882 program Vishniak found the hierarchy of values that had persisted in the political culture of the intelligentsia: revolution was more important than securing the free expression of the people's will.[115]

This willingness to bypass democracy for the sake of the intellectuals' own political goals later permeated Russian Marxism as well, Vishniak contended. Formally, the social democrats' program had supported both the Constituent Assembly and the seizure of power by the working class.[116] But the theoretical pronouncements of the Russian Marxists had not endorsed the principle of popular legislation. Vishniak turned to Plekhanov's 1903 speech to support his point:

> Every particular democratic principle must be examined not in and of itself in its own abstract sense, but in relationship to that principle, which can be called the basic principle of democracy, namely, to the principle that says "*salus populi suprema lex.*" Translated into the language of a revolutionary this means that the success of the revolution is the highest law. . . . A circumstance in which we, social democrats, would come out against general electoral rights is hypothetically conceivable. . . . And from this point of view we must view the question of the length of parliaments. If in an outburst of revolutionary enthusiasm the people chose a very good parliament, then we would have to try to make it a long parliament, and if the elections were unsuccessful, then we would have to try to dismiss it not in two years, but, if possible, in two weeks.[117]

Vishniak did not hesitate to charge his own party with this same lack of concern for the institutions of representative government. The PSR's call for a Constituent Assembly had been accompanied in the party platform by support, "in case of necessity," for a "temporary revolutionary dictatorship." In Vishniak's opinion, the SRs had never escaped this maximalist disposition. They, too, put revolutionary goals above democratic means.[118]

Even during the 1905 liberation movement, none of the three parties of change had been solidly behind the demand for a Constituent Assembly, Vishniak asserted. The social democrats considered socialism more important than democracy; the SRs wanted revolution first, as a means to democracy and socialism; and the liberals could not unite on the principle of popular sovereignty. Vishniak concluded that the Constituent Assembly had been only an "idol" for the "freedom-loving but rootless and doctrinaire Russian intelligentsia." It gave them a visionary alternative to autocratic rule, but it had never acquired absolute and unconditional value in Russian political thought.[119]

In "The Idea of the Constituent Assembly," Vishniak went beyond his earlier arguments in *Bolshevism and Democracy* and outside the limits Axelrod had set in *Who Betrayed Socialism?* The blame for the failure of democratic institutions in Russia had to be shared; the present catastrophe for democracy had historical roots in the traditions of the entire intelligentsia. Vishniak's main concern, however, remained Russia's present, not the past. If the Russian intelligentsia as a whole had never fully understood or appreciated representative institutions, Lenin's party had exploited the emotional appeal of democracy, while at the same time eliminating it as a political reality. Fascinated and appalled by the distance between the image and the facts of Soviet government, Vishniak set out to examine the actual structure of authority in Russia in his pioneering study, *Le régime soviétiste*, published in Paris in 1920.[120]

In this work, subtitled "Etude juridique et politique," Vishniak attempted to explain to the Western public, especially Western socialists, the reality behind the Bolsheviks' "highest form of democracy." As a participant in the Parisian SRs' effort to influence the international socialist movement,[121] Vishniak, like Axelrod, had been disappointed by the European socialists' desire to remain noncommittal on Russian affairs or, worse, to regard Bolshevism as the incarnation of socialist revolution. *Le régime soviétiste* was intended to open Western eyes to Bolshevism in practice. Firm in his commitment to the democratic and rationalist heritage of the Enlightenment, Vishniak appealed to his Western comrades on the basis of these values.

Building on his earlier Russian language study, *Bolshevism and Democracy*, Vishniak began *Le régime soviétiste* with a description of how the Bolsheviks had arrived at the "negation of democracy."[122] He cited the party's makeshift policies on the Constituent Assembly as well as its "new methods" designed to secure a Bolshevik majority at the meeting once it was clear that the vote had gone against them—the outlawing of the Kadet (liberal) party, the delay in allowing the Assembly to meet, the arrest of several SR leaders before the convention, Bolshevik control over registration and entry at the hall.[123] Most important, the alternative principles of Bolshevik government had been articulated in the ideological struggle against the Constituent Assembly, and it was these to which a major part of Vishniak's study was devoted.

After the Constituent Assembly had been destroyed, Lenin's ideas on Soviet power had been affirmed at the party's congress in March 1918.[124] Here, as Vishniak had noted earlier, the party gave its approval to the idea of limited democracy: freedom and democracy were for the exploited alone; the "exploiters" and "former exploiters" were without rights. "Parliamentarism" was rejected in favor of the fusion of executive and legislative powers in the new Soviet government.[125] These conceptions of authority were subsequently embodied in the Soviet Constitution of July 1918. Thus the pronouncements of the winter, products of Lenin's struggle against the "miserable bourgeois and parliamentarian republic," were turned into the founding premises of the new Soviet state.[126]

That the Bolshevik government had decided to issue a constitution at all was a tribute of sorts to "bourgeois prejudice," Vishniak commented astutely. In form, this constitution seemed like any other: it comprised a declaration of rights and six sections, subdivided into chapters and articles. But Vishniak's examination of this document showed not only, as might have been expected, that the Soviet Constitution differed fundamentally from European law, but also, and this was new and significant, that these differences did not express a new or "higher" kind of justice. What was new in "Soviet democracy" was old, in Vishniak's view—it was a regression to absolutist government based on distinctions between social estates.[127]

From Vishniak's perspective, the outstanding feature of the new Soviet absolutism was the denial of the principle of universal rights and duties. The Soviet Constitution prescribed instead the unequal distribution of privilege. Formally, legal distinctions were made on a class basis. The working class alone was granted freedom of conscience, speech, assembly, and access to education; while the "exploiters" retained only duties. But in reality, the system depended upon more complex divisions and a different principle of organization. Some "rights" were denied to everyone—there was no mention of a court system or of a right to strike—and, within classes, "there were the privileged among the privileged." Ration cards, to take a material example affecting the "right to food," were distributed hierarchically.[128] Red Army soldiers and members of the Communist Party were entitled to one to one-and-a-half pounds of bread a day, workers and lesser functionaries to three-quarters of a pound a day, nonparty people who accepted the Soviet platform to one-half pound a day, and the fourth and last category of all other citizens was to receive only one-quarter pound of bread daily. To Vishniak this meant that the hallmark of the new regime was the differential allocation of material rewards according to their recipients' "utility to the Soviet government."[129]

Electoral rights were also assigned according to this principle. The constitution had not simply disenfranchised those who did not engage in "productive and socially useful work," it had also established in law the differentiation between the city and the country that the Socialist Revolutionaries had feared from the first days of the revolution. According to Soviet electoral procedures, one deputy to the Congress of Soviets was elected by each 25,000 urban Soviet electors, while rural voters returned one deputy for each 125,000 peasants. This proportion—one worker's vote equalled five peasant votes—held true for regional and local Soviets as well. In addition, peasant representatives were chosen through a four-tiered series of elections, while the urban deputies participated in a two-stage system. These principles of Soviet democracy—the denial of all rights to some "categories" of the population and the unequal distribution of both electoral and material privileges among the rest—represented, in Vishniak's opinion, a repudiation of individualism and a return to the feudal system.[130]

In *Le régime soviétiste* Vishniak distinguished between Bolshevik principle and practice. While the Soviet Constitution displayed the hierarchical and absolutist values of its makers, it was still, he felt, no guide to the actual workings of the regime. After his examination of Soviet law, Vishniak went on to analyze how the government functioned.[131]

Vishniak's study showed that although the Soviet Constitution declared power to be vested in the Soviets, real authority in the country belonged to the Bolshevik party. By replacing the "parliamentary" separation of powers with a unified executive and administration—and by ignoring the judiciary altogether—the Bolsheviks had established the basis of an unchallengeable central command. Moreover, power did not flow, as Lenin had promised, "from the bottom to the top." While in theory the government—the Council of People's Commissars—was responsible before the Congress and the Executive Committee of the Soviets, in fact the opposite was the case. The Soviet deputies at both national and local levels had been transformed into functionaries dependent upon their superiors. Control over the central authorities from below was nonexistent.[132]

The history of Bolshevik government provided ample proof of the impotence of the Congress of Soviets, Vishniak informed his readers. All major decisions had been made by the Bolshevik leaders *before* the convocation of Soviet representatives. The October coup took place on the eve of the Second Congress of Soviets, the dissolution of the Constituent Assembly shortly before the Third. In both cases, the congresses had to ratify faits accomplis. Nothing had changed in this respect since the formal adoption of the Soviet Constitution. The government continued to announce its decisions after the fact to the Soviets or to bypass them altogether.[133]

Nowhere was this inversion of political responsibility more apparent than in the electoral procedures of the regime. The members of the real government were self-selecting. The method was "auto-designation by the members of the Central Committee of the Bolshevik party" and *post factum*, automatic ratification by the Central Executive Committee of the Congress of Soviets. Since the beginning of Bolshevik rule, the government had never been elected or replaced by a representative body, Vishniak pointed out. The right of instant recall, so admired in the West, was used by the government to reward or punish delegates to the Soviets, not by the Soviets against the government.[134]

Elections to the Soviets also served a function different from that imagined by Western democrats, Vishniak observed. Rather than ensuring the possibility of change, elections maintained the status quo. In theory, the unequal distribution of voting rights should have guaranteed elections favorable to the Bolsheviks. But in fact, the government acted outside the law to eliminate possible challenges to its rule, as in its exclusion of Socialist Revolutionaries and Mensheviks from the Soviets in June 1918. The government set the date for elections at its convenience; not once had they been held within the three-month period established by the constitution. Unfavorable elections were annulled;

desired results were obtained by extralegal means. "When necessary," Vishniak noted, "the dead reappear among the living for the duration of the elections." The elimination of the "bourgeois prejudice" of the secret ballot was important to the government—elections to the Soviets were made public and thus more accessible to influence. Nonetheless, the highest authorities preserved the right of secrecy for themselves. Their votes in the Council of People's Commissars and the Bolshevik Central Committee were protected from public scrutiny.[135]

In its manipulation of elections, the government was unhampered by inconvenient regulations; no general electoral law had been enacted.[136] But in other areas, the Bolsheviks had shown that they did not hesitate to violate both the spirit and the letter of their own laws. Capital punishment was Vishniak's case in point. Despite the abolition of the death penalty at the Second Congress of Soviets, execution was used systematically throughout the country by the Extraordinary Commissions (the Chekas). No provision had been made for the Chekas in the constitution; yet these commissions, established by special decrees and executive instructions, had "reestablished" the death penalty on an unprecedented scale in the capitals, cities, villages, the army, and the countryside and exercised unlimited power over the lives, liberties, and material goods of the population.[137]

Vishniak emphasized in *Le régime soviétiste* that this restoration of the secret police was only one of many tsarist practices revived by the Bolsheviks in power. They had also reverted to the "normal" procedures of autocratic rule. Limitations on freedom of movement, the internal passport system, prohibition of strikes and demonstrations, the creation of honorific titles—such as "honorary hereditary proletarian"—and awards, the centralization and bureaucratization of all social and economic life, nepotism and peculation—all these familiar characteristics of the imperial regime were now part of Bolshevik practice. In Vishniak's view, this was not an accident, but a deliberate use of the old centralist structures. In support of his analysis, he quoted Zinoviev's judgment: "The autocracy pursued bad ends, but the state mechanism of tsarism was good."[138]

Although it was too soon for the regime to have achieved the hereditary transmission of authority, Vishniak noted that family and personal connections already determined appointment to high state office. At the top of this pyramid was Lenin, with his small band of long-term companions in the Central Committee of the Bolshevik party. The personal dictatorship of this group was the real source of power in the Soviet system. Vishniak pointed out that Lenin himself had defended this form of government at the Fourth Congress of Soviets: "There is absolutely no contradiction in principle between Soviet democracy, that is to say, socialism, and dictatorial power exercised by certain individuals."[139]

The cynicism of this proclamation was typical of Lenin's attitude toward government, Vishniak suggested. It was this mentality, rather than the articles of the Soviet Constitution, that determined the methods of rule in Russia. As in the past, liberty and democracy were of no consequence to the people who controlled the state.[140] The Bolsheviks' testimony made this clear, Vishniak emphasized; not one of the new leaders pretended to defend democracy for its own sake. He cited Trotsky to this effect: "We have trampled down the principle of democracy in the name of the higher principle of the social revolution,"[141] and Bukharin:

> If the working class wrote on its banner "Long live individual liberty! Long
> live freedom of coalition! Long live the right to vote!" this is explained by one
> simple reason—the working class was too weak.[142]

For the benefit of his European readers, Vishniak noted the similarity between the Bolshevik perspective on democracy and that of the French reactionary Louis Veuillot: "When I am weak, I ask you for freedom because it is your principle. When I am strong, I deny it to you because that is mine."[143]

This total disregard for individual rights and its significance for life in Russia were exceedingly difficult for Westerners to comprehend, Vishniak felt. "The regime of Soviet violence and the regime of relative liberty in . . . Western Europe . . . , even under the domination of the democratic bourgeoisie, are organically too different," he commented. He recognized that war and revolution had produced an "epidemic" of enthusiasm for "soviet" government among Western socialists, and was irritated by the fact that every "*snob radicalisant*" considered it his "strict duty to express his esteem and admiration for this new form of State."[144] Nonetheless, Vishniak concluded his study by calling Western socialists to confront the facts of Russian life and to recognize the Soviet government not as a new and promising social system, but as a regime that united the faults of democratic states with those of despotism. Bolshevism combined the representation of interests with the denial of majority rule. Its only principle of governance was dictatorship, extracted from its meaning in socialist ideology and elevated into a "juridical norm of state."[145] As such, Bolshevism offered no theoretical novelty; the justifications for subjecting a population to the dictates of enlightened rulers were at least as old as Plato.[146]

With *Le régime soviétiste* Vishniak had gone beyond "unmasking" to disrobing; he had tried to educate the Western public by putting both the constitutional garments and the living body of the Soviet system on display. In his study, a precursor of modern Sovietology, Vishniak had to confront a problem that plagued all such investigations. How could one prove anything with certainty about the Bolsheviks' attitudes, if, as he suggested, secrecy and hypocrisy were endemic to their politics? Vishniak's approach was simply to juxtapose word and deed. The Bolsheviks' repudiation of democracy could be believed because their actions corresponded to their declarations. But as a rule the Bolsheviks were not to be taken at their word. Their constitution, while indicative of the party's absolutist mentality, did not represent the true structure of authority. Despite its facade of "Soviet democracy," the practices of the regime showed that real power lay with the Bolshevik party leadership.

The evidence of the facts, however, was still vulnerable to wishful interpretation. Where Western impressions of Russia were concerned, it seemed to Vishniak that distance exaggerated and intensified ideas. "The thousands of kilometers that separate Russian Bolshevism from the Western countries . . . have given it features of sublimity and grandeur," he commented.[147] To him and to other Russians who had lived under Bolshevik rule, Western notions of Soviet government seemed stupid and morally repulsive. How could one disabuse Europeans, especially socialists, of their illusions when they seemed so intent upon remaining ignorant of reality? Visniak refrained from the self-defeating temptation to resign himself to Western blindness and naiveté. Instead he appealed to values he thought both Russian and Western intellectuals shared—truth and, especially, democracy.

Democracy was the ultimate question of government, Vishniak insisted. There could be no socialism without it. And, in Vishniak's view, democracy meant one thing: the rule of the majority. Here there was no possibility for compromise. You were either for or against majority rule. If you were for it, you had to be against the Bolshevik system.[148]

Here Vishniak, unlike so many of the Russian intellectuals, made his terms explicit. By democracy, he meant a form of government, and, in particular, government through universal suffrage. While the Bolshevik leadership specifically rejected this conception as "bourgeois," and while socialists like Martov and Chernov used "democracy" in protean fashion, referring sometimes to a class or a presumed constituency—"revolutionary democracy" or "laboring democracy"—and sometimes to representative procedures, Vishniak had taken his stand in defense of rules—majority rule. There was a kind of historical irony in this Russian revolutionary's defense of majority rule before his Western peers. He was defending a principle the Russian intelligentsia had borrowed from the West during its struggle against the autocracy. But by now the cycle of ideological influence had come full circle; Europeans wanted a new word from the East. Few Western intellectuals were inclined to recognize a connection between democracy and representative, elected institutions.

In the aftermath of revolution, Vishniak, like Potresov, turned back to the older intelligentsia tradition. In 1920, with four other Socialist Revolutionaries, he founded a new "thick journal" in Paris. *Sovremennye zapiski* (Contemporary Notes) commemorated in its title two revered Russian journals, *Sovremennik* (The Contemporary) and *Otechestvennye zapiski* (Notes of the Fatherland), hefty and compulsory reading for the nineteenth-century intelligentsia; like these publications, it was divided into two sections—political and cultural.[149] The editors, in their statement of principle, declared *Sovremennye zapiski* to be "nonparty," but at the same time asserted their support for the democracy of the February revolution, for a Russian federal republic, based on civil rights, and for economic reform, including the transfer of the land to those who worked it.[150] Contributors to the political section included right Socialist Revolutionaries, right Mensheviks (among them Martov's nemesis Stepan Ivanovich), and left liberals. This ecumenical approach irritated the enemies of "coalition." Chernov wrote home to the PSR Central Committee in Russia that he considered *Sovremennye zapiski* "positively harmful for the party."[151] More important in the longer run was the journal's cultural section. Here for twenty years, *Sovremennye zapiski* provided a forum free of censorship to a number of outstanding Russian writers—Aldanov, Belyi, Nabokov, and Tsvetaeva among them—and to Russian scholars and philosophers, including M. Rostovtsev, P. Vinogradov, K. Mochulskii, and Lev Shestov.

Vishniak's major contribution to the journal was his regular commentary on Russian affairs, "In the Homeland" (*Na rodine*). These lengthy articles provided him with an opportunity to discuss issues and events in contemporary Russian life. He discovered to his regret that the experience of the revolution, far from demonstrating the merits of civil liberty, universal rights, and representative government, had made these—his—goals the more remote. Although Vishniak could not bring himself to believe that a "twentieth-century nation of 130 million" could remain unfree, the antidemocratic legacy of Bolshevism was, he felt, pernicious and profound.[152]

In his articles in *Sovremmenye zapiski* Vishniak emphasized the psychological impact of the Bolshevik regime. Nowhere was this more evident than in the Kronstadt uprising of March 1921.[153] The spontaneous rebellion of thousands of sailors at Kronstadt against Bolshevik tyranny raised Vishniak's hopes for the eventual liberation of the Russian people. But at the same time he saw in Kronstadt manifestations of the "mental slavery" imposed on Russia in the preceding three and a half years. Both the tactics and the goals of the insurgents showed, he felt, that Bolshevism had "corrupted" the people's "minds and souls."[154]

Vishniak admired the courage and the ethical intransigence of the Kronstadt rebels. The revolt, based upon the sailors' judgment that "life under the yoke of the Communist dictatorship has become more terrible than death,"[155] had his full sympathy. In his article on Kronstadt, Vishniak pointed out the idealism of the rebels—their generous treatment of Bolshevik prisoners, their request for moral, not military, support, their refusal to take the offensive, and their willingness to rely instead upon the justice of their cause. This course of moral sacrifice for the collective good was, in Vishniak's opinion, the opposite of Lenin's call for selfishness in his infamous slogan, "Steal what was stolen!"[156]

Nonetheless, Vishniak admitted, the Kronstadters' methods provided evidence of Lenin's influence. The sailors, for example, refused the assistance of the Red Cross or any "non-left-socialist party." This need to rely only upon the like-minded was also expressed in the decision of the Kronstadt Temporary Revolutionary Committee not to extend its operations to the mainland, a resolution that significantly weakened the revolt. In Vishniak's opinion, these actions showed the extent to which Bolshevik ideology had permeated popular consciousness. A moral method was by definition uniquely lower class and "left-socialist."[157]

The same association of morality with class and political persuasion was evident in the positive goals of the rebellion, Vishniak wrote. The Kronstadt Revolutionary Committee, while clearly speaking out for freedom, wanted liberty for workers and peasants, not for others. Point two of the Kronstadt program reflected the interests of some radical intellectuals, with its demands for "freedom of speech and press for workers and peasants, anarchists, and left-socialist parties," but the idea of general, universal rights was alien to the rebels. Their program was *trudovlastie*—workers' power—not *narodovlastie*. They accepted the superiority of the Soviets over the Constituent Assembly as governing institutions. The Kronstadters' political demands, Vishniak observed, "did not go beyond the limits of Soviet ideas and the class basis of state authority." However sound their criticism of the Bolshevik dictatorship, the Kronstadt sailors had come to believe in class rule and to reject democracy.[158]

In these conceptions of legitimacy Vishniak saw an enduring and tragic legacy of Bolshevism. Over the past three years, the Bolsheviks had succeeded in putting democracy on the defensive and even in changing its meaning for Russia. Before the revolution, Vishniak wrote, democracy had meant defending justice and liberty for all, but especially for workers and peasants whose rights had been limited by property qualifications, place of residence, or lack of education. But after the Bolshevik success, a commitment to democracy meant defending the rights of the bourgeoisie, disenfranchised on the basis of their class. The Bolshevik government had not hesitated to exploit this association.[159]

It was this psychological influence—the separation of democracy from socialism—that Vishniak feared most of all. Like Martov and Chernov, with their complaints that socialism was being "discredited," Vishniak's major concern was for his ideals. He believed, as did other intellectuals both in and out of government, that principles and values were important and that they could be changed. Thus, although Vishniak thought that the Bolsheviks would one day fall from power, he was afraid of the new attitudes they had implanted. "The past rules the future not only in the world of things, but in the world of ideas and images," he wrote in his article on Kronstadt. The Bolsheviks would die, but the idea of the Soviets and of class-based power would live in popular memory. To him, this was in the long term the most serious setback for democracy in Russia.[160]

Vishniak's indictment of Bolshevism for "corrupting" the popular mind bore witness to his own idea of health. He never asked whether the "people" might have had their own reasons for opposing democracy on his terms. Many aspects of the popular mentality escaped him. He noted, for example, that the rebels at Kronstadt regarded Trotsky and Zinoviev as models of Bolshevik perfidy, while they imagined that Lenin in his innocence had been prevented from knowing the truth. Vishniak surmised that these attitudes might reflect the old device of displacing blame onto the "bad advisors," but he could not bring himself to ask why the Kronstadters accepted this idea.[161] Although he criticized the Russian intellectuals for their lack of commitment to popular sovereignty, it did not occur to him that the people might be similarly unenthusiastic. In this, Vishniak, for all his constitutionalism, was typical of the SR intelligentsia. He assumed that the people of Russia supported democracy and democratic institutions and that the creation of a Constituent Assembly was their goal as well. Their particularistic choices after 1917 he blamed upon the Bolsheviks alone.

Despite Vishniak's illusions, his post revolutionary writings offered a perceptive analysis of the mental world of Russia's political leaders. He knew the ideological habits of the intelligentsia well and was able to step outside their culture to criticize their vague and omnibus conceptions. For the *intelligenty* who opposed the old regime, the institutions of democracy were of little value when juxtaposed against their grander goals of freedom and socialism. After the revolution, Russia had suffered from this lack of interest in institutional reform, Vishniak pointed out. Lenin's government had exploited the longing for change, without giving the country a new means of government. Instead, under the guise of socialism and workers' democracy, the Bolsheviks were pushing Russia back into the past.

As a non-Marxist, Vishniak regarded the Bolsheviks' rejection of individualism and the representative institutions of bourgeois society, not as a step forward but as a regression into feudalism. Having discredited the ideals of the bourgeois-democratic revolution—liberty, equality, and brotherhood—they had revived monarchism, national oppression, and personal enserfment as principles of state. *Raison d'état*, not Marxism, determined Bolshevik policy, wrote Vishniak in December 1921. NEP, with its seventeen categories of labor and its enormous range of administratively determined salaries, had overfulfilled his analysis in *Le régime soviétiste*. Society was once again divided into separate groups with different duties and different rewards allocated by the state. There was neither "economic equality," nor "'formal' liberty." Bolshevism meant instead a return to eighteenth-century absolutism, to the "ladder of . . . ranks and titles," and a state based upon the administration of unequal social estates.[162]

The only answer to this grand hypocrisy, Vishniak felt, was not more rhetoric about new forms of government, but the recognition of a fundamental incompatibility between democracy and the exclusive political power of a group. Here he agreed with Lenin: democracy and proletarian power were distinct. One did have to choose between the Soviet system, where power was assigned in theory to a class and exercised in practice by a party, and democracy, which meant the equal authority of all people, without social or political distinctions.[163] Although the difference was clear enough, Vishniak feared that there were few in Russia committed to majority rule. The Bolshevik appeal to particular and divisive interests had been too successful.

Petr Kropotkin: "How Communism Cannot Be Introduced"

On February 13, 1921, two weeks before the rebellion at Kronstadt, Petr Alekseevich Kropotkin was buried in Moscow. His funeral—organized privately and in defiance of the Bolshevik authorities—was attended by tens of thousands of mourners who marched five miles in the winter afternoon to take Kropotkin's body to his family's ancient plot in the Novodevichii Monastery. When the procession passed the Butyrki prison, anarchists and other sympathizers inside pounded on the bars and sang in honor of Russia's most venerated spokesman for liberty.[164] It was the last time that the anarchists' black flags were displayed in the capital. Within the year, most proponents of anarchism in Russia were dead, in prison, or in exile.[165]

Kropotkin had returned to Russia on May 30, 1917, after forty years abroad.[166] Greeted with overwhelming enthusiasm by a large crowd in Petrograd, the seventy-four-year-old veteran was offered a post in the Provisional Government. This, on anarchist principle, he declined.[167] He was nonetheless overjoyed by the February revolution and regarded the Soviets as the nuclei of the free, self-governing communism that he had advocated for so many years. Throughout the summer and fall of 1917, Kropotkin called on Russians to unite to save their country and its revolution. Like Plekhanov, Potresov, and Zasulich, and to the surprise of many of his friends, he supported the prosecution of the war. From his perspective, German militarism presented an immediate and grave threat to human progress, a danger sufficient to justify the state-based effort required for its defeat.[168] Like Potresov, he reached out in the national cause to the bourgeoisie, calling for cooperation among industrialists, workers, and peasants.[169]

After the Bolsheviks took power, Kropotkin's presence and his opinions were less welcome. Unhappy from the start about the course of events, Kropotkin "saved" himself with work.[170] He prepared several of his early writings for publication and participated in two organizations that concerned themselves with Russia's political future. One of these, the Society for Rapprochement with England, published a single issue of a journal on European culture in February 1918, only to be shut down by the authorities. Kropotkin's major project at this time was the Federalist League, a group devoted to planning the reconstruction of Russia on a federal basis. But this scholarly endeavor was also obliterated by Soviet power. In the spring of 1918, when the first of five volumes of federalist studies had been prepared for publication, the government broke up the league and confiscated its material.[171] The revolution did not treat its veterans kindly. Like Zasulich and

Potresov, Kropotkin was harassed and outcast by the new regime. Twice the quarters assigned to him in Moscow were requisitioned and he and his wife were forced to move. Finally, in the summer of 1918, they left the capital for the town of Dmitrov, to live in a cottage offered them by Count Olsuf'ev.[172]

In Dmitrov, forty miles north of Moscow, Kropotkin and his wife subsisted on the produce of their garden and the aid offered by Kropotkin's many admirers.[173] He was helped in his old age by anarchist friends from Russia and abroad and by the local peasants, who revered their new neighbor.[174] Isolated from Russian politics and contacts with the West, Kropotkin devoted his time to writing and to activity in his new community. Life in Dmitrov offered him a chance to take part in the local communal organizations. He became a member of the Dmitrov Union of Cooperatives, the town's self-organized government, and defended it against the encroachments of Soviet authorities until the destruction of the union and the arrest of all its leaders in November 1920.[175]

For Kropotkin, the cooperative movement in Russia embodied the principles of communal anarchism. It confirmed his belief in mutual aid as the natural and necessary basis of social life. In contrast to the aggressive individualism of many nineteenth-century anarchists, Kropotkin had given his attention to the life of individuals *in society*. He had tried to provide anarchism with a constructive social theory, based on scientific evidence. Rejecting the right of the state to control people's lives, Kropotkin wanted to demonstrate the possibility of an alternative basis for human organization.

Kropotkin's prognosis of an anarchist future rested upon two arguments: first, that the principles of mutual aid, justice, and self-sacrifice were innate in nature and in people as part of the natural world, and, second, that history demonstrated progress toward greater mutuality in social life. These judgments were founded on his studies of altruism in animal populations, investigations that antedate modern evolutionary biology by a century. Kropotkin had been convinced by his observations in Siberia and elsewhere that life was not, as the distorters of Darwin would have it, simply the "war of each against all," but rather that survival depended upon the ability of the individuals in a species to cooperate.[176] This condition applied to people as well; Kropotkin believed that the most enduring human institutions were cooperative. The village community and the voluntary associations of city dwellers were his favorite examples of mutual aid in history. The modern state, however, founded upon compulsion and competitive capitalism, was a monstrous perversion of human nature. From Kropotkin's perspective, it was doomed to extinction.[177]

So, too, was the Soviet government. Kropotkin's reaction to Bolshevism was consistent with his lifetime commitment to a society based on free and constructive cooperation. The Bolshevik state was an example to the world of "how communism cannot be introduced."[178]

To Kropotkin the Bolshevik regime represented not "communism" but "state communism," a critical distinction. Throughout his long life in political philosophy, he had always been hostile to Marxism, as a centralist and authoritarian movement. He had reiterated this position on the eve of the October revolution in his pamphlet *Communism and Anarchy*.[179] Here he contrasted "state communism" or "bossist [*nachal'nicheskii*] communism" with "anarchist communism." State communism could never succeed, he argued, because it was a contradiction in terms. The state through its ability to punish and compel deprived the individual of freedom, and without freedom the whole structure of cooperation would collapse. The best evidence that state communism was "impossible" was the mentality of its advocates: they wanted power, not liberation.[180]

From this perspective, the Bolshevik seizure of power was an attempt at the impossible. Writing to British workers in June 1920, Kropotkin testified, "in my opinion, the attempt to build up a Communist Republic on the lines of strongly centralized State Communism, under the iron rule of the Dictatorship of a Party, is ending in a failure." Moreover, the government, using the excuses of the war and foreign intervention, had increased the "natural evils of State Communism . . . tenfold." While the idea that the Soviets would control the economic and political life of the country was excellent, in fact the "Party Dictatorship" had reduced the Soviets to the "passive role played in times past by States General and Parliaments, when they were convoked by the King" to support his own power. The destruction of the free press meant that a workers' council could not be a "free and valuable adviser," and the elimination of free elections passed "a death sentence on . . . new construction."[181]

Despite his pessimistic analyses and observations, Kropotkin did not simply resign himself to the failure of the Bolshevik state. In addition to his work with the cooperative at Dmitrov, he made several efforts to sway one individual who might have altered the government's course. On three occasions—in the fall of 1918, May 1919, and August 1920—he met with Lenin in person and alone.[182] In addition, he sent Lenin a series of letters, protesting both specific and general abuses.[183]

In March 1920, Kropotkin wrote to Lenin on behalf of the employees of the post and telegraph commissariat in Dmitrov. "You know, of course," he commented,

> that to live in the Dmitrov district on the two-to-three-thousand-rouble salary which these employees receive is *absolutely impossible*. For 2,000 roubles you cannot buy even a bushel of potatoes, and I know this from my own experience. In exchange you are asked for soap and salt, of which there is none. Since the price of flour has risen to 9,000 roubles a pood [thirty-six pounds], even if you manage to find some you cannot buy enough for eight pounds of bread, or enough wheat for five pounds. Without receiving provisions the employees, in a word, are doomed to actual starvation.
>
> Meanwhile, along with such prices, the meagre provisions which the post and telegraph employees have been receiving from the Moscow . . . supply depot . . . *have not been delivered for two months*. Local food agencies cannot release any of their own supplies, and the appeal of the employees . . . to

Moscow remains unanswered. A month ago one of the employees wrote to you personally, but so far has received no answer.

I consider it my duty to testify that the situation of these employees is truly desperate. The majority are *literally starving*.[184]

To Kropotkin, the plight of the Dmitrov employees was symptomatic of "whole categories" of Soviet workers in the countryside. He pleaded with Lenin to look outside the capital and at how people had to live in revolutionary Russia:

Living in a great centre, in Moscow, you cannot know the true situation in the country. To learn the truth about existing conditions you must live in the provinces, in close touch with daily life, with its needs and calamities, with the starving—adults and children—and with the scurrying from office to office to secure permission to buy a cheap kerosene lamp, and so on.[185]

What everyday life showed so blatantly was the tragedy of bureaucracy and "bossism." "Wherever one turns," Kropotkin continued, "there are people who have never known anything of real life committing the most flagrant errors, errors paid for in thousands of lives and in the devastation of whole regions." These party bosses and committees had destroyed the creative potential of the Soviets and stymied the "construction from below" Russia needed to survive. The experience of "real life" made "one thing certain": "Even if a party dictatorship were the proper means to strike a blow at the capitalist system (which I strongly doubt), *it is positively harmful for the building of a new socialist system.*" If the new state did not turn to the "creativity of local forces," he concluded, "the very word 'socialism' will become a curse."[186]

In December 1920, after the defeat of the White Armies and after the Dmitrov cooperative had been destroyed, Kropotkin wrote Lenin another bitter letter. This time he protested the state's decision to hold SR and other prisoners hostage to the good behavior of the members of their parties and alliances who were at liberty. To Kropotkin, this was a return to the policies of the Middle Ages. The threat to execute these prisoners "without mercy" in the event of an attack on Soviet leaders was a "revival of torture for the hostages and their families" and "unworthy" of men who were working for the "future of communism." Of course the life of men in power was difficult, Kropotkin added, but "even kings and popes have rejected such barbarous means of defense as the taking of hostages." The revolution was supposed to be a great move forward toward equality; then why put it "onto a road leading to its downfall, owing mainly to defects which have nothing in common with socialism or communism but which are survivals of the old order and old deformities, of unlimited and omnivorous authority?"[187]

Kropotkin's criticism was directed at Bolshevik methods, not at the revolution itself. Like other socialists, he accepted the overturn of the old regime as a positive, irreversible achievement and viewed events since then as part of a larger historical process. The Russian revolution, he wrote in an unfinished essay from 1918, was the third in a series of great popular upheavals, each of which had improved the condition of humanity. The English revolution had left a legacy of religious tolerance, local authority, and constitutional rule; the French revolution in turn had influenced the whole nineteenth century with the ideal of equality before the law, the establishment of representative government, and the destruction of the feudal structure. Russia was to accomplish what the last revolution had left undone—to spread the rights of man farther to the East and to solve the social question left unanswered in France.[188]

Kropotkin never renounced this belief in the progressive nature of the Russian revolution; to do so would have called into question the entire positivist foundation of his philosophical system. He did, however, point to a specific flaw in the revolution that lay deeper than the abuses perpetrated by the Bolshevik state. The revolution, he continued in his 1918 essay, lacked a "lofty, inspiring ideal," and it was this spiritual lack that accounted for the fundamental difference between this revolution and its predecessors. In place of the French vision of freedom, equality, and brotherhood, the ruling idea of the Russian revolution was economic materialism. This doctrine, moreover, had come to Russia from Germany in its crudest form. The libertarian traditions of French communism had been displaced by a conception of social revolution as the "unleashing of individual desires."[189] In this image of a revolution without ideals, Kropotkin's allegiance to the traditions of French socialism, his Germanophobia, and his repudiation of Marxism coalesced.

But once again, discouraging thoughts did not cause Kropotkin to reject his goals or to withdraw from the struggle for them. At Dmitrov, he returned to his earlier philosophical investigations and decided to write a two-volume work on the origins and purpose of moral standards.[190] This project grew in importance with time. In a letter to Alexander Berkman from May 1920, Kropotkin commented that human thought was "struggling . . . between Nietzscheanism and Christianity"—conceptions that were anathema to his notion that morality was both communal and of this world. It was therefore all the more essential to demonstrate to people their own worth.[191] "I have resumed my works on questions of morality," he wrote to Berkman,

> because I consider this work absolutely necessary. I know that it is not books that create intellectual currents, but rather that it is the other way round. I also know that to explain this idea, the help of books is indispensable.[192]

Kropotkin completed the first volume of this project. In it he attempted once more to demonstrate the empirical basis of cooperative ethics by tracing the development of moral principles, historically, from origins in the natural world through the end of the nineteenth century. But he could go no farther, and the work remained unfinished. The last sentence of volume one pointed inward: "While customs are determined by the history of the development of a given society, conscience, on the other hand, as I shall endeavor to prove, has a much deeper origin—namely, *in the consciousness of equity* which physiologically develops in man as in all social animals."[193]

As Kropotkin's letter to Berkman indicates, he did not regard his work on ethics as a retreat from the revolution, but as a contribution to a better future. True to his principles, he never lost his faith that a new cooperative life would arise after the tumult of the revolutionary crisis. The syndicalist organizations and the Russian peasant cooperatives would form the basis of a true communism within fifty years, he predicted. The task of "impressing these two movements with living strength . . . of giving them form, developing them, preparing a solid base for them and helping them transform themselves from weapons of self-defense into a powerful means of reorganizing society on the principles of communism" required people younger than he and, especially, "cooperation from the workers' and peasants' milieu." The forces to build this life existed in the workers' and the peasants' movements, but they had not yet "recognized their own mission." They did not understand that they were not yet "imbued with the communist ideal." Kropotkin, it seemed, was writing for them.[194]

Kropotkin's view of the revolutionary process was, as a Soviet biographer expressed it, "complicated."[195] He was a harsh critic of the Bolshevik "party dictatorship" and convinced that communism could not be introduced from above. He was acutely sensitive to the real hardships of daily life and to what they meant for communism and its future. Like others on the left, he cared for the purity of his goals, and could not stand to see them violated in practice. Like Martov, he found himself caught in the dilemma of how to bring forth the values he believed were *in* mass movements. In the end, he, too, defended intellectual endeavors as necessary to eliciting this morality from others. Always, he was loyal to historical progress.

Kropotkin's remarks to visitors at Dmitrov revealed the shifts of mood characteristic of other intellectuals in these years.[196] In March 1920 he commented to Emma Goldman, "We have always pointed out the effects of Marxism in action. Why be surprised now?" Seven months later he advised her, "There is no reason whatever to lose faith."[197] Both these pronouncements indicated the emphasis on progressive and evolutionary forces that was so vital in Kropotkin's thought. Because he viewed the revolution as a collective and historical movement, Kropotkin felt that there was little an individual or a party could do to influence it. The revolution, he wrote shortly before his death, was "a natural phenomenon, independent of the human will," which "thousands of causes" had combined to create. At the same time, it was a product of "all of us," as well as of earlier revolutions, socialist writings, and advances in science and industry. But, like a great storm, the revolution had chosen its own course, "not along those ways we had prepared for it," and individuals were powerless to redirect its force. One could only gather together people *"who will be capable of undertaking constructive work in each and every party after the revolution has worn itself out."*[198]

Kropotkin's modest perspective on his own life and his grand view of progress helped him bear the physical and psychological tribulations of the years at Dmitrov.[199] From 1917 to 1921 he met with a series of defeats—the closing of his cultural and federalist organizations, his inability to make any constructive impression on the Bolshevik authorities, and most immediately the destruction of the Dmitrov commune—yet he did not lose hope. The revolution's challenges to Kropotkin's empirically based ethics were deflected by his confidence in a future, better, collectivity. The state and the superhuman forces of a vast upheaval accounted for the evils he observed, while his faith in the innate morality of the human species and the forward movement of history remained intact.

Populism in Defeat

In cooperative anarchism, Russian populism took a most appealing form. Who could not want to believe in Kropotkin's vision of voluntary mutual aid? Moreover, Kropotkin's insistence upon freedom from state oppression came closer to the desires of the Russian peasantry than did the Socialist Revolutionaries' projects for a democratic state. Kropotkin was as well a more consistent populist. His "anarchist communism" did not rely upon the Constituent Assembly or the party to embody the people's will, and, without these structures, there was no need for the complex self-deceptions, the rhetoric of representation, or the myth-making of the SR intellectuals. To Kropotkin, communism was an explicitly *moral* endeavor that would be built from below or not at all. When the revolution proved to lack a "lofty inspiring ideal" and to be warped by "old deformities," he acknowledged these deficiencies. His revolution would not be complete until people understood and acted on their own goodness.

For SRs like Chernov, such a literal, straightforward populism was impossible. In Chernov's commentaries on the revolution, the "people" served only in the abstract, as a legitimation of his own ideals. This transference was conspicuous in Chernov's analysis of the Kronstadt rebellion. For Vishniak, Kronstadt had been a breaking point—an illustration that the "people" were not fighting for his kind of democracy. Not so Chernov. His article "Kronstadt and Democracy," published in April 1921, exhibited his addiction to pathetic fallacy.[200] Citing the Kronstadters' declaration—"We are fighting now for the overthrow of the party yoke, for the real power of the Soviets, but there let the free will of the people [*narod*] decide how they want to be ruled"—Chernov blithely interpreted:

> Whoever talks about the free all-national [*vsenarodnaia*] will, is talking about general, direct, secret, and equal all-national suffrage, is talking about *narodovlastie*, is speaking against any substitution for it, not only Commissar-sovereignty [*komissarovlastie*], but even "Soviet-sovereignty [*sovetovlastie*]."[201]

According to Chernov, the Kronstadt sailors had seen the "necessity" for returning to the slogans of January 1917, "repeating in almost the same phrases the summons of the president of the Constituent Assembly."[202] In another article on the "lessons of Kronstadt," Chernov drew three conclusions. The defeat of the rebellion meant, first, that the Kronstadters had put too much trust in the Bolshevik authorities; second, that they were wrong to omit the Constituent Assembly slogan; and, third, that they lost by failing to take the military offensive.[203]

Kronstadt, it seems, was Chernov's ideal event—a spontaneous, popular rebellion, for almost the right values, that failed, and left its lessons for the future. There were not many such opportunities after 1920. For the most part, Chernov turned his attention to more lofty topics, of which the Bolshevik state was one. *Revoliutsionnaia Rossiia*, formally designated the central organ of the PSR in August 1921,[204] took up one of the functions of the prerevolutionary exile press by publishing government documents smuggled out of Russia. With its section "From Behind the Curtains of the Government Machine," filled with Bolshevik memoranda and policy statements,[205] *Revoliutsionnaia Rossiia* followed the tradition set by Herzen's *Kolokol* (The Bell) and Struve's *Osvobozhdenie* (Liberation). In addition, Chernov continued his two-front journalistic battles with other émigrés, defending SR tactics against Martov's rigorous criticism in *Sotsialisticheskii vestnik*[206] and lashing out at "coalitions," both past and present.[207] But the major focus of Chernov's efforts in the emigration was theory—the articulation of what he called "constructive socialism."

There was much to be said for the principles underlying Chernov's new project. What he described in a series of articles under the rubric of "Programmatic Questions" was the need for a new socialist theory that would integrate industrial and agricultural economies. In this respect, "constructive socialism" was to go beyond the limits of both "utopian" and "scientific" socialism; it would be "synthetic"—uniting proletarians and farmers of the world against capitalism,[208] giving people authority as both consumers and producers, avoiding the extremes of anarcho-syndicalism and state-dictatorship,[209] combining the "democratic character [*demokratichnost'*]" of the Second International with the "revolutionary initiative" of the Third.[210] Many of the strongest elements of Chernov's critique of Bolshevism were incorporated in this vision. Constructive socialism would undo the injustices of the "dictatorship of the city over the country," of bureaucratic domination, and of the abolition of civil liberties and democratic procedures. But the weakest aspects of Chernov's personal politics were also present—his precious and pretentious language, for one, and his ethereal notions of causality. What was the new "synthetic, universal, constructive socialism,"[211] if not another one-man declaration, repeating Chernov's harmonic notions on a global scale?[212] The "third force" for this socialism was somewhere in the stratosphere.

Meanwhile, in Russia, the people had spoken and been defeated. Soon after Chernov's departure in the fall of 1920, the "Green" rebellion in central Russia had taken hold and grown into a vast peasant war against the state.[213] But even at a time when Lenin acknowledged that "the large masses of the peasantry . . . were against us,"[214] the PSR held back. While local SRs and Left SRs participated in the so-called "Antonov" rebellion, Chernov and the Central Committee counseled against this "half-bandit" enterprise.[215] The PSR's tenth party council, held in August 1921, adopted the following resolution on tactics in the village:

> Steadfastly to continue the party's earlier line of conduct on insistent explanation to the peasantry of the total futility and danger of incidental and unorganized and disorderly outbreaks and spontaneous revolts against the autocratic regime of communist authority.[216]

Interviewed in the emigration that summer about the possibility of a popular overthrow of the Bolshevik government, Chernov cautioned that more time and effort would be needed.[217]

The Antonov rebellion—spontaneous, widespread, powerful—would appear the incarnation of the third force predicted by the PSR. It took the government a year, the forces of the entire First Army, and a policy of terror against whole villages to destroy this threat. Yet no other phenomenon so clearly displayed the Socialist Revolutionaries' ambivalence toward mass rebellion. As in the fall of 1917, the tension between hope and fear was resolved by postponing the ultimate confrontation. Even in 1921, the SRs were still waiting for the perfect people's revolution.

Along with peasant war came "tsar hunger." By 1921 the cumulative disasters of seven years of war, compounded by recent droughts, had reduced Russian grain production to half its prewar level.[218] Tens of millions of people faced starvation in the worst famine in the history of modern Europe.[219]

In July 1921 the Central Organizational Bureau of the PSR—a delegation in Russia that acted in the name of the Central Committee, since most of its members were in prison—called on "all citizens" to aid the starving in whatever way they could and appealed through *Revoliutsionnaia Rossiia* to the workers of America and Europe for help.[220] For Chernov, this was an occasion to recall the famine of 1891 and to draw a parallel between the tsarist government's attempts to disguise the poverty of the countryside and the

glowing reports on Russian village life in the Bolshevik press.[221] Even after the
government had been forced to acknowledge the famine, the dimensions of the
impending disaster were minimized in official accounts. Chernov regarded
Russian efforts to negotiate aid from the Western powers in the same light as
the New Economic Policy; this was yet another aspect of the Bolsheviks'
collaboration with bourgeois reaction. He was suspicious as well of the
formation within Russia of an All-Russian Famine Relief Committee, including
a number of prominent non-Bolshevik intellectuals. The only purpose of this
unprecedented appearance of "independent society" was to impress the
Europeans.[222]

This analysis proved to be correct. As Vishniak reported the following
month in *Sovremennye zapiski*, on the day the Soviet government signed an
agreement for aid with the Norwegian philanthropist Fridhof Nansen, the
All-Russian Famine Relief Committee was disbanded and its members arrested
by the Cheka.[223] To Vishniak, the famine provided final, devastating evidence
for the Socialist Revolutionaries' predictions that Bolshevik policies would ruin
the peasantry. Their requisitions had only exacerbated the supply crisis of the
war and revolution, and the recent tax in kind could not remedy the earlier
cutbacks in sown area. The tax, Vishniak noted, had been set at what had
actually been collected during the requisitions and thus represented no loss for
the government and no gain for the peasants. The Bolsheviks had looked
everywhere for someone or something else to blame for the famine—"parties,
peoples, countries, the whole historical past—capitalism, the war, the blockade, tsarism, the Allies, Poland, bandits, Petliura, Wrangel', Antonov,
Noulens, Miliukov, Chernov, Martov"—all to no avail, in his opinion. One
did not have to be an agronomist to see a connection between their economic
system and production on the land.[224] Like Chernov, Vishniak regarded the
Bolsheviks' negotiations with Western individuals and organizations as an
attempt to shore up their authority by dealing with Western capital, an
enterprise in which Russia was bound to lose.[225] But, for Vishniak, there was
no gratification to be had from the government's hypocrisy or from the
economic collapse. It had been a "black year," he wrote from Paris late in
1921.[226]

In Russia, the SR intellectuals were also under seige. NEP, Kronstadt, and
the peasant rebellions of 1920 and 1921 had intensified the government's fear
of opposition. As Lenin emphasized in April 1921, the place for the SRs, as for
the Mensheviks, was jail.[227] By the summer of 1921, most of the SR leadership
had been arrested,[228] and on December 28, 1921, the Bolshevik Central
Committee decided to put the Central Committee of the PSR on trial for
treason.[229]

The SR process of 1922 has been accurately described by its historian Marc
Jansen as a "show trial under Lenin." The SR defendants were charged with
the attempted assassination of Lenin, contacts with the Union for the Regeneration of Russia and with the Allies, the Antonov uprising, and a host of other

crimes. Most of these accusations were either false or covered by the amnesty of 1919; moreover, the indictment was based on a penal code issued in June 1922, after the defendants had been in jail for one to three years.[230] But the trial was not intended as an exercise in bourgeois legality, and its procedures displayed many of the characteristics of the purge trials of the 1930s. The defendants were divided into two groups—a "first" group of twenty-two SR party leaders and a "second" group of collaborators whose testimony served to incriminate their alleged comrades. The first group was not allowed to choose its lawyers, call its own witnesses, or give testimony inconvenient to the case against them. The prosecution was carried out by not only the official prosecutors—Lunacharskii, Pokrovskii, and Krylenko—but also the "defending" lawyers for the second group, among them Bukharin, Tomskii, and Zorin, as well as the three judges and the audience in the courtroom. This was packed with representatives of the Communist party and the police; the defendants' families and friends received few permissions to attend. Western communists also participated in this spectacle: Clara Zetkin was a prosecutor; Jacques Sadoul a defender of the second group. Gramsci was assigned the latter task, but did not fulfill it.[231]

The most innovative aspect of the SR trial was not courtroom procedure, but the state's orchestration of a mass propaganda campaign against the defendants. In February 1922, Lenin had called on the Commissar of Justice to organize "model, noisy, educative trials" to break the socialist opposition.[232] Both through the courts and in the press the Commissariat of Justice was to educate the masses in the "meaning" of these trials and thus "increase the repression against the political enemies of Soviet power and agents of the bourgeoisie (*especially* the Mensheviks and SRs)."[233] These instructions were fulfilled. Before the beginning of the judicial procedures, the government vilified the SRs in the press, the factories, and the streets. The PSR, with the Mensheviks, was held at fault for all the disasters of the past five years—the civil war, the peasant rebellions, and the famine. In street theater performances, Chernov and Martov were killed in effigy. Resolutions demanding the death penalty for the defendants were introduced in factory and Communist party meetings, and lockouts, fines, and arrests were used to enforce attendance at anti-SR demonstrations. During the trial, a select mob was allowed periodically into the courtroom to jeer at the defendants and demand their execution.[234] After one of these turbulent scenes, the lawyers for the "first," authentic, defendants called for a new trial. This plea, although based on the legal code's exclusion of extrajudicial testimony, was ridiculed and rejected. When these lawyers subsequently resigned from the proceedings, three of them were arrested and sent into internal exile.[235]

One other group spoke out in the SRs' behalf. These were European socialists sent to the trial by the non-communist internationals—Emile Vandervelde and Joseph Wauters of the Second International and Theodore Liebknecht and Kurt Rosenfeld of the Vienna Union. Their presence at the trial and a pledge that the defendants would not be executed were the result of negotiations among the three internationals at the Berlin "unity" conference of April 1922.[236] These concessions, granted by Bukharin as the head of the Russian delegation, to the conference, were deplored by Lenin. "We have paid too dear," he wrote in *Pravda* on April 11.[237] Shortly, the bargain was undone. Bukharin compensated for his compliance at Berlin by playing a prominent role in the campaign of character assassination directed at the socialist representatives throughout their stay in Russia.[238] Their participation in the trial was obstructed by garbled translations, denial of access to the stenographic record, and slanderous attacks. After several days in court, Vandervelde and his companions decided to withdraw from the case, believing that their presence served only to give the trial a semblance of legitimacy. This analysis was confirmed when the Western socialists submitted their resignations. They found their departure obstructed by the authorities and had to go on a hunger strike before they were allowed to return to Europe.[239]

Despite the promise made in Berlin and the lack of incriminating evidence, fifteen of the SR defendants were condemned to death, and most of the rest to prison. Although the capital sentences were later commuted to imprisonment, with the goal of holding the prisoners hostage against the activities of their party,[240] the SR leadership in Russia was doomed. The prison terms were followed by exile and new arrests. Only one of the twenty-two defendants survived the Gulag.[241]

Five years after the revolution, populism as a political force in Russia was extinct. The "laboring people" of Russia, decimated by war and famine, were struggling to survive; their defenders in the PSR were abroad, in prison, or dead. In exile, the Socialist Revolutionaries had even less influence on European socialism than had the Mensheviks, whose connections with Western Marxism were stronger.[242] After 1922 the SRs made their most significant contributions to Russian culture, not to politics, as *Sovremennye zapiski* continued to provide Russian literature with an uncensored press.[243]

Nonetheless, Russian populism survived in the minds of its intellectual advocates, a testimony to its ideological essence. Speaking at a convocation of SR leaders in Berlin in December 1922, Chernov persevered in his hopes for the eventual appearance of a popular movement against Bolshevism. Somewhat shaken by the devastation of the party, he recommended that the PSR carry on a limited legal struggle through the Soviets and even enter these institutions, provided there was a "favorable factual relationship of forces." He repudiated "any kind of insurrectionism [*vspyshkopuskatel'stvo*]," yet insisted that the party would never give up its "sacred 'right to revolution.'" This hypothetical path between the evils of Bolshevism and the "Bonapartist danger," this reliance on the "sobering up of the masses," was in its irreality and its substance a repetition of the resolutions of the Fourth Party Congress of 1917. The only lesson Chernov had learned from five years of revolution was the one he had wanted to teach the Central Committee before October—no compromises with the bourgeoisie.[244]

Chernov's inability to break with old ideas was in part a matter of personality. He had built his identity—his contribution to the "capital of history"—on the formulation of the SR program. Apart from its treatment of the peasantry as a revolutionary class and its emphasis on the need for partnership between the city and the country, Chernov's platform offered little that was new—"a little Kant, a little Marx, a little Mach, a little Mikhailovskii and Lavrov, a little syndicalism, and a little of himself," in the words of a hostile contemporary[245]—but it was "synthetic" and it did project the image of a just, harmonic nation to which the SR intellectuals, Vishniak among them, were addicted. One might expect the revolution and civil war to have shattered this idealism. The people had repeatedly failed to carry out the SRs' plans; they had not defended the Constituent Assembly; nor had they produced an alternative to Bolshevism. Instead, their actions—both the support for the Bolshevik seizure of power and the later violent peasant insurrections against Bolshevik control—had been motivated by their "private interests," as the SRs complained in December 1917.

Several aspects of the SRs' history and experience helped them to maintain their faith throughout the revolutionary years. One was the lack of institutions through which the attitudes of others could be known. Before the revolution the intellectuals could maintain their version of the people's will unchecked by the open elections, public referenda, and surveys of opinion that might, had they existed, have provided other points of view. Then, in 1917 the PSR won a victory in Russia's freest election, a sanction to which they laid claim in the coming years. The Bolsheviks' restrictions on elections and on the press only helped to perpetuate the SRs' notion that they spoke for the people as a whole.

In addition, the Socialist Revolutionaries, like many other Russian intellectuals, inherited a Manichean morality from the past. In the traditions of the non-Marxist Russian revolutionary movement, all evil derived from the state. Just as Martov blamed the perversions of the revolution on capitalism, Chernov and Vishniak attributed support for the Bolsheviks to the corruption of the masses by the government. This fixation on the moral dichotomy of state and nation resonated with the Socialist Revolutionaries' reluctance to assume power. The political experience of the PSR had been solely critical, and destructive, of authority; state leadership was a prospect for which the party intelligentsia was psychologically unprepared. The SRs' most concrete program had been terrorism, but after this tactic had been defeated in the first decade of the century, they had counted on the people to make the revolution. The party's commitment to *narodovlastie* served to legitimate certain kinds of action—education, "unmasking," organization—and to preclude the dilemmas of power. There was a moral correspondence between the hatred of state power and the refusal to assume it. "I am an anarchist! Wherefore I will / not on communism and anarchy,[246] asserted the ethical rejection of the state implicit in the SRs' revolutionary slogan: "In struggle you will obtain your rights." In struggle, not in power.

These attitudes lent a peculiar coloration to the SRs' setbacks after 1917. The intellectuals had been accustomed to making their politics through the denunciation of injustice; the new regime gave them ample opportunity to revert to this old role. What the people actually wanted was of secondary importance in the thoughts of intellectuals whose attention was focused once more upon the state. Bolshevik injustice, exploitation, and terror confirmed the populists' view of the new government and obscured their own defeats. Their situation was familiar and, it seemed, predictable. Under the old regime, faith in the people ultimately had been fulfilled; would not the same belief suffice again?

This distance from reality offered the freedom to believe the best. The Constituent Assemby, *narodovlastie*, the third force—all these formulas expressed the Socialist Revolutionaries' extensions of their trust and aspirations to others. Their confidence gave them courage. Vandervelde, meeting with the SR defendants in prison, was startled to find them in lively good humor:

> This is one of the few places here where people chat; perhaps it is the only place where I have seen people talking freely, gaily, not lowering their voices, not always asking themselves whether Moscow is watching or the Cheka listening. They are being threatened with death or, at any rate, with the prospect of remaining in prison for years, and yet they make jokes; they are cheerful with the high spirits of those who are going into battle for a cause they hold dear.[247]

The old regime had taught them how to wait.

3

Two Russian Liberals: Socialism on Trial

Principles and Goals

The Russian liberals' response to the October seizure of power was unambiguous opposition. Their condemnation of Bolshevism was not complicated by the theoretical considerations and self-criticism of the Mensheviks and Socialist Revolutionaries. To the liberals, the Bolshevik takeover lent the Provisional Government a legitimacy it had never established while nominally in control of the state. The only principled course of action from their point of view was to repudiate and defeat the new, unlawful regime.

This absolute hostility was returned in kind by the Bolsheviks. Having based their claim to rule upon the failures and dangers of "bourgeois democracy," the Bolshevik authorities set out to destroy the liberal opposition. On the day after the coup, the Petrograd Military Revolutionary Committee closed seven "bourgeois" newspapers.[1] This suppression of the liberal press—repeated as necessary when newspapers reappeared under different mastheads—was followed by a series of direct actions against the Constitutional Democratic (Kadet) party. In mid-November, the homes of several prominent Kadets were ransacked, and on November 28, the party was outlawed and its leaders in Petrograd arrested and imprisoned.[2] In December the government staged its first political trial: Sofiia Panina, a popular liberal reformer, member of the Kadet Central Committee, and Assistant Minister of Education in the Provisional Government, was arrested for sequestering the Ministry's funds and brought before a Revolutionary Tribunal.[3]

113

These persecutions—censorship, arrests, the banning of the party—recalled abuses endured under the old regime; like the socialists, the liberals met them with fortitude and the optimistic hope that the Bolshevik government would not last. But it soon became clear that the Kadets now faced a different and more dangerous enemy. On January 7, 1918, A. I. Shingarev and F. F. Kokoshkin, two Kadet leaders imprisoned by the government in November, were murdered by Red Guards in the Mariinskii Hospital, where they had been transferred after six weeks in the Petro-Pavlovsk fortress.[4]

The murder of Shingarev and Kokoshkin—both professional men, active in the liberation movement of 1905, prominent members of the Kadet party and delegates to the Constituent Assembly[5]—by sailors, safeguarding the revolution, symbolized the weakness of the liberals' cause in Russia. Liberal goals—the rule of law, political democracy, and civil liberties—were of little significance to the mass of people; yet, from the liberals' perspective, it was only by the achievement of these principles that Russia could begin to advance along the path of Western civilization. The liberals had led the political opposition to the autocracy because they felt that civic freedom and legality were essential to progress. Their program of universal suffrage, representative and constitutional government, and land reform was more radical than the strategies of contemporary European liberalism and evinced their confidence in the values of the population. They assumed that the people of Russia, given an opportunity to exercise their rights, would choose a course of education, work, and individual accomplishment just as they, the elite of society, had done.[6]

The liberals shared both this confidence in the Russian people and their belief in universal progress with the socialist intellectuals. The main difference between these two Eurocentric visions concerned the organization and means of historical advance. The socialists relied upon the proletariat and the class struggle to bring about improvement, and, in theory, their movement was international in scale. The liberals, on the other hand, explicitly embraced the principle of state, not class. Only national government could provide the legal framework essential to individual freedom and achievement. Unlike the socialists' veiled devotion to state power, the liberals' nationalism was consistent with their political philosophy. As Russian patriots, they supported the war effort without hesitation, and, after the revolution, the preservation of the Russian state—with all its territories and peoples—was their foremost goal.

Yet, apart from their commitments to the state, civil liberties, and the rule of law, the Russian liberals agreed on little. True to its principles, the Kadet party was made up of individuals who were not obliged to follow a monolithic party program.[7] The party in this sense reflected its Western prototypes; it attempted to include and resolve tactically the interests of many groups and individuals rather than to represent any one of them. The problem with this strategy in Russia was that the liberals did not command the broad national constituency for which they claimed to speak, nor could they turn their integrating resolutions into state policy.

The divisions within Russian liberalism were reflected in the Kadets' various tactics after 1917. Forced undergound by Bolshevik repression, the party disintegrated into several regional and strategic organizations. The centers of the liberal opposition were the rump Central Committee in Moscow, which formed the nucleus of the National Center, a major alliance of civilian resistance to Bolshevik authority; the Kadet committees in the Ukraine; the Siberian Kadets associated with Kolchak; the short-lived Kadet government in the Crimea; and the political groups connected with the Volunteer Army.[8] Although the Kadets managed to hold several regional party conferences during the civil war, they never adopted a unified national strategy. For all practical purposes, each person acted individually. As with the Mensheviks and Socialist Revolutionaries, those who remained in the capitals were least likely to survive. Kadets in the National Center were captured in 1919 and executed,[9] while many other liberal leaders escaped into the emigration.

After the war against the Bolsheviks was lost, the fragmentation of the party played a role in the liberals' perceptions of the revolutionary years. Some found moral and political lessons in each other's strategic "mistakes"; others were still fighting ideological battles from the prerevolutionary period. The most comprehensive, and idiosyncratic, liberal interpretations of the revolution were those of Pavel Nikolaevich Miliukov and Petr Berngardovich Struve.

Although temperamentally and philosophically unlike, these two outstanding figures in Russian political life shared several intellectual attributes. Both had superb memories, wide-ranging cultural and academic interests, and, despite their active lives in politics, both produced significant scholarly work, Struve in political economy and Miliukov in Russian history.[10] Struve, one of the foremost Marxist intellectuals of the 1890s and the author in 1898 of the founding program of the RSDRP, had turned gradually toward liberal ideas at the end of the decade. He and Miliukov had led Russian liberalism in its best days, helping to build the constitutional movement that culminated in the revolution of 1905–1906. Even at this time, the two had disagreed on the strategies and goals of the liberation campaign, and their differences became more pronounced after the establishment of a parliamentary structure.[11] Miliukov insisted that the Kadet party should have "no enemies on the left," while Struve advocated cooperation between society and the government. In his opinion, the intelligentsia erred in continuing to treat the state administration as its enemy, a view expressed in his 1909 article in *Vekhi* (Landmarks).[12] Rejecting this criticism, Miliukov steered the liberal party on a course of left-wing opposition in the Duma and in *Rech'* (Speech), the party's unofficial newspaper. Struve devoted himself instead to a number of cultural endeavors, in an attempt to build a broader nationalist consensus. He eventually withdrew from the Kadet Central Committee on June 8, 1915.[13]

These disagreements did not prevent Miliukov, the Minister of Foreign Affairs in the first Provisional Government, from asking Struve to join his staff in 1917. In the aftermath of the February revolution, neither man was optimistic about Russia's future. Miliukov, overtaken by the revolutionary crisis he had helped to bring about, worked to form a government based on the authority of the Duma, and then, almost alone among the new ministers, tried to convince the Grand Duke Michael not to abdicate the throne left him by Nicholas II. When Miliukov's efforts to support the autocracy's objectives and commitments in the World War made him a target of anti-government agitation and forced his resignation, Struve left the ministry as well.[14] After two months in government service, Miliukov and Struve returned to their former task of shaping public opinion.

P. N. Miliukov and Bolshevik Power

A few weeks after the Bolshevik seizure of power, Miliukov began writing its history. Completed in the summer of 1918,[15] Miliukov's *History of the Second Russian Revolution* (*Istoriia vtoroi russkoi revoliutsii*)[16] remains today a major source for the events of 1917, unsurpassed in the quality of its narrative and compelling in interpretation. According to Miliukov, his goal in writing this 850-page study was to present "an analysis of events based on a precise understanding of them."[17] This understanding, he insisted in the introduction to the *History*, was not the subjective perspective of the memoirist, but an explanation based upon the facts:

> Facts are subject to objective verification, and to the extent that they are true, the conclusions drawn from them are indisputable. A historian by profession, the author did not want to, and could not, adjust the facts to the conclusions; on the contrary, he drew the conclusions from the facts.[18]

This confidence in the objective nature of the material world and in a direct link between events and meaning was characteristic of Miliukov. A positivist by conviction and in temperament, he brought an unflappable rationalism to his analysis of the revolution and to his promotion of the liberal cause.

Although Miliukov shared a materialist and determinist world view with the Russian socialists, his conception of politics differed significantly from theirs. This is apparent in his writings on Bolshevism, in which the moral outrage and accusatory tone of the socialists are conspicuously missing. Miliukov's equanimity was in part a reflection of his political philosophy. He did not have to defend socialism against its Bolshevik "perversion"; as a liberal, he *expected* that a radical government would be unable to fulfill its promises. In addition, he measured the revolution according to criteria that the moderate socialists and populists were loath, or unable, to apply—his "facts" concerned institutional authority. For Miliukov, the fundamental questions of the revolution concerned power, not justice. The success of the Bolsheviks, he argued in his *History*, was due to the inability of their opponents to see the struggle in these terms.

As presented in the *History*, Miliukov's perspective on the revolution differed from that of most socialists in another respect. The socialists preferred a periodization that started with the October coup and thus ignored their parties' failures earlier in the year. But Miliukov considered the Bolshevik regime a logical result of Russian politics after the collapse of the autocracy. Instead of judging the Bolshevik government as a separate, new phenomenon, distinct from the "conquests of the February revolution," Miliukov viewed the revolution as a single political dynamic, begun in February and culminating in October.

The essence of this process was the inexorable disintegration of state authority. Miliukov's *History* presented the revolution as a tragedy in three acts, from the collapse of the Old Regime to the triumph of the Bolsheviks. The first volume described events from February through the July Days; the second—"Kornilov or Lenin?"—concluded with the defeat of the military alternative to a "revolutionary" state; and the third—"The Agony of Power"—followed Kerensky's last government to its easy defeat by Lenin's party. In each of these studies, Miliukov focused upon the policies of the government. The volumes are filled with quotations from speeches and conversations of the principal politicians, a technique that effectively suggests the grandiloquent incompetence of all the rapidly changing administrations. In Miliukov's view, the successive Provisional Governments increasingly destroyed their own authority, and thereby cleared the way for Bolshevik rule.

Miliukov's description of the revolution consistently distinguished between what the author regarded as the "real" problems of state and the new leaders' perceptions of their task. The real problems, in his account, were the reestablishment of the government's command over the country and the winning of the war. The war, according to the *History*, had precipitated the revolution by "encouraging qualities and habits wholly at odds with those approved of in normal life" and by turning "customary ways of thinking . . . upside down."[19] By failing to provide firm and competent leadership in this crisis, the Russian monarchy lost the allegiance of the population and ultimately its three-hundred-year hold on the state. To Miliukov, consolidating the Provisional Government's power and bringing the war to a successful conclusion were related processes. The members of the young and vulnerable government had to work on both fronts at once if their regime were to survive.

But the new leaders' idea of politics precluded such a course. Instead of coming to grips with the fundamental problems of governance—as Miliukov saw them—the politicians of revolutionary Russia chose to function at an ideological level. Their response to the country's difficulties was not firm action, but "verbal utopianism." The contradictions between the demands of reality and the rhetoric of the authorities explained the turbulent history of the Provisional Government and its ultimate demise.[20]

According to Miliukov, the 1917 revolution was characterized by a "rhythmic pattern" of crises superimposed upon one essential direction—"the constant and progressive disintegration of power." Each revolutionary government lasted for two months before being torn apart. These challenges to state authority increased in severity over time: "Each time the transition between the government that was collapsing and that which was replacing it became more and more protracted and traumatic." In every case, the underlying cause of the breakdown was the inconsistency of the governments themselves.[21]

In Miliukov's account, the Provisional Government that came to power in February 1917 set the stage for these events by abolishing the governing institutions of the old regime without replacing them. This first revolutionary government, which Miliukov labeled a "bourgeois government in the service of socialism," also tolerated and abetted the actions of the Petrograd Soviet, thus further undermining the possibilities for a single state authority. The first "coalition" government, formed in May and made up of socialists and liberals, in turn became the victim of its own "duplicity," of trying, in Miliukov's terms, to be socialist and bourgeois at once. As discipline in the army eroded and the empire disintegrated, the socialists in the government and in the Soviet proclaimed a fictitious "united front" between the "bourgeoisie" and "revolutionary democracy."[22] In Miliukov's view,

> this was a poor and purely formal way not to resolve but to simulate a solution of the profound and insoluble contradiction that existed between the scientific thesis of Marxism, according to which only a "bourgeois" revolution was possible under the prevailing mode of production, and the impatient longing of the majority of Russian socialists to transform the Russian . . . revolution from a political into a social (socialist) one.[23]

It also represented the "first step" down an "inclined plane" for the moderate socialists, a tactic that exposed them to attack from both left and right and resolved none of the problems that beset the country. Forced to make concessions to their opponents on either side, the moderates began a "zigzag" course that was both inconsistent and ineffective. Their halfhearted measures and full-blown utopian rhetoric led to the government's increasing isolation and culminated in the void of Kerensky's last government.[24]

For Miliukov, Kerensky was the symbolic representative of the contradictions and indecisiveness that led to the collapse of state power. Miliukov praised the Prime Minister of the last two Provisional Governments for his efforts to revive the army during the second coalition. But this experience had made Kerensky aware of the need for measures incompatible with the socialists' conception of "revolutionary discipline," and thus had brought him into conflict with the socialists and "with himself."[25] This dilemma was not resolved with the formation of the third coalition:

With all his strength forcing the revolutionary wheel in the direction of firm authority [*tverdaia vlast'*] based on real support, but not venturing at the same time to break with the utopia that pulled that wheel toward the abyss, Kerensky became more and more the sole binding link between flanks that had lost mutual understanding, with a center that was continuing to lose the support of the masses. The political position, understandable and even inescapable in the beginning, turned all the more into an isolated pose, difficult for the actor to maintain and, from the sidelines, unbearable for the spectator to observe. . . . The longer this marching in place continued, the more decidedly the common love for the symbolic personality, embodying the revolution in himself, gave way to the similarly strong feeling of enmity and hatred for the real politician, responsible for his mistakes.[26]

This bitter and astute characterization was based on more than personal animosity. For Miliukov and the liberals, failure to control the revolution meant losing their primary political objective—rebuilding the Russian state according to their principles. Unlike the social democrats, they had no international movement to which they could turn. In addition, Miliukov was repelled by the mythic aspect of Kerensky's leadership. Not only did his "inaction, covered with phrases"[27] encapsulate the naive behavior of the moderates in 1917, but the fact that he could play this role at all was evidence of the power of mystique. In Miliukov's opinion, it was irrationality—the failure of the socialists to follow the logic of their situation—that had destroyed the Provisional Government. Against their self-deceptive symbolic politics, he defended the values of political responsibility and consequent action based on reason.

From this alternative perspective, the Bolsheviks' behavior in 1917 was a model of the rational pursuit of power. Lenin's judgment, wrote Miliukov admiringly, was "highly realistic." He was a "centralist and a statist [*gosudarstvennik*] and relied most of all on measures of direct state violence." While the moderates were muddling about, the Bolsheviks were acting effectively to undermine the authority of their rivals—destroying the army and the navy, increasing their own support in the Soviets and among the soldiers of the capital. The Bolsheviks' tactics during the Kornilov affair, during which they made it seem that Kornilov was attacking the Provisional Government and not their party, was, in Miliukov's words, "very clever and points to their very competent direction."[28]

According to Miliukov's *History*, the Bolsheviks' success in 1917 derived from precisely the qualities that moderate socialists lacked—realism and consistency. Lenin's party had concentrated upon the true locus of power—the army—and had worked effectively to subvert military discipline and to attract the soldiers to their organizations. Far from worrying about the ideological purity of their support, they accepted the money of the nations' enemy for their purposes. In contrast to the confused speeches of the moderate left, Bolshevik propaganda "won the allegiance of the masses by the extreme simplicity and attractiveness of its slogans as well as by a persistent consistency, if not in their execution, then certainly in the repetition and reiteration of these slogans."[29]

Consistency (*posledovatel'nost'*)—this criterion was used repeatedly in the *History* to evaluate the performance of Russia's would-be leaders. As Miliukov's comment on Bolshevik propaganda indicates, what he had in mind was not strict correspondence between promises and acts, but a single, basic political direction, a "steady course" toward a well-defined goal.[30] The moderate socialists had failed not solely because of their inability to fulfill their pledges, but because they did not know what they wanted, or because they wanted two things at once. The title of Miliukov's chapter on the first coalition summed up this dualism: "The socialists defend the bourgeois revolution against a socialist one."[31] In his opinion, such a party could not win.

Although Miliukov acknowledged the skill of the Bolshevik insurgents, he assigned the blame for the October seizure of power to the incompetence of the government. This assessment conformed to the traditional attitude of the Russian left: the rulers, not the opposition, were held responsible for the country's problems. From Miliukov's perspective, the state—after his departure from government on May 2, 1917—had been in the hands of the moderate socialists in the Provisional Government and the Soviet, and they, unwittingly, had led the nation to disaster.

This was the principal analysis that emerged from Miliukov's "precise understanding" of events in the *History of the Second Russian Revolution*. But Miliukov himself had not been entirely consistent in his explanation of the revolution's causes and its "sad outcome."[32] He was too much a historian to ignore the revolution's "roots" in Russia's past. First among the historical factors noted in his study was "the weakness of the principle of the state [*gosudarstvennost'*] in Russian and the predominance in the country of elements who were alien to the state or, as anarchists, hostile to it." This, according to Miliukov, was the consequence of Russia's non-Western political development. He pointed to several other related conditions—the absence of a bourgeoisie, the "utopianism" of the Russian intelligentsia, the formless anarchism of the masses, and the "instinct of self-preservation of the Old Regime and its supporters,"expressed in the autocracy's refusal to reform. He laid particular stress upon the imperial government's "insincere concessions" to society since 1905. The "*Scheinkonstitutionalismus* [pseudo-constitutionalism]" of the Duma period "explains why, after the initial concessions made by the government, the conflict, far from ceasing, assumed a permanent character which led finally to the present catastrophe," he wrote in the historical introduction to the *History*.[33] Here, applied to the old regime, was the same argument that he had used against the false promises of the moderates in 1917. The autocracy, like the revolutionary governments, had fallen victim to its own hypocrisy.

In the narrative of the *History* Miliukov drew attention to another decisive factor in the struggle for power. This was the army. The mutiny of the

Petrograd troops had allowed the February crisis to become a mass revolt; the disintegration of military discipline had undermined the Provisional Government. Ultimately,

> the same thing happened to the Provisional Government in October as happened to the tsarist government in the February days. A fortuitous revolutionary outbreak in the capital was supported passively by the army, because the mood of both the commanders and the soldiers had gone against both governments. In this sense, it would be true to say that the fate of both revolutions in the final analysis was decided by the army.[34]

This attention to the role of the army, and especially to its "mood," brought forward the hidden actors of the *History*—the soldiers, the "dark masses," to whom the Bolsheviks appealed with their "model" propaganda and whose loyalty the moderate socialists had lost. The "people" were present in Miliukov's study, although they were not its principals. Hovering in the wings, or massed in "the street,"[35] they chose the "consistent" promises of the Bolsheviks over the vacillation of the Provisional Government. Miliukov did not hold the people responsible for the consequences of this choice; he regarded them literally as a mass—"a plasma on which history leaves only weak and broken imprints"[36]—incapable of giving form and structure to the state, and thus an object, not a subject, of politics. From his perspective, the masses were part of an elemental process that in an "irrepressible stream" was drawing power away from the central authorities.[37]

This metaphor, and many others, gave the *History* a fatalistic tone. Miliukov's well-chosen facts and his evocative prose spoke past his reasoned case against the moderate socialists. The narration of individual, apparently willful, actions was set against recurrent images of inevitability, of "the tide . . . bearing the ship of state fatally toward the abyss."[38] The tension between these two perspectives—which produces the intellectual dynamism of the work—corresponded to Miliukov's attempt to see the revolution two ways at once. He was trying to explain it as a historical "process," a word he used repeatedly, and also to retain the essentially moral notion of personal responsibility, the concept of the "real politician, responsible for his mistakes."[39]

Although Miliukov's ethical standpoint in the *History* was plain—the good toward which responsibility was to be exercised was the state—it was never made explicit. As a strict Comtian positivist,[40] he could not acknowledge the subjectivity of his goals and judgments. These, like his selection of the "facts," were assumed to be objective and self-evident. Nor did he try to integrate the long and short causalities of the *History*. He commented that the "logic of events was without a doubt on the side of Lenin,"[41] yet he blamed the moderates for the outcome of the revolution. One principle did seem to be operating in both the historical "process" and the immediate political scene: this was Miliukov's favorite notion of consistency. The "logic of events" propelled the revolutionary process; at the same time, the moderates failed to remain in power because they had been inconsistent in their policies. But Miliukov failed to show that the moderates could have controlled events by being more rational. Instead he sustained two separate lines of explanation in the *History*, suggesting only implicitly that reason bound them both.

Despite these evasions and complexities, Miliukov had throughout the *History* made his conception of effective political action clear. Above all, one had to be rational and realistic. This meant behaving consistently: refraining from the reiteration of impossible promises, following a steady political direction, and relying upon real sources of support—the army, the police, and not ideals. In addition, the responsible politican had to act decisively. Few would object to these standards, but in revolutionary Russia they were difficult to apply. For Miliukov in the next few years, reason and realism led to failure.

Sought by the authorities as an "enemy of the people," Miliukov had left Petrograd in November 1917 to join the anti-Bolshevik forces in the south.[42] Although it was obvious to him, and to all the liberal leaders, that the appropriate response to the Bolshevik government was armed opposition, the problem was how to fight. The liberals had no troops of their own, no tradition of underground subversion, and, most important, no mass following. If they wanted an army, they had to turn to others. This strategic question preoccupied Miliukov for the next three years. He tried several solutions.

His first choice was the Volunteer Army, the military force of officers and students formed under General Alekseev in the Don area. Miliukov reached Alekseev's headquarters in the winter of 1917 and immediately became involved in the formation of a civilian "Political Council" to work with the army command, an arrangement that satisfied neither the politicians nor the military leaders.[43] But Miliukov did not stay long with the Volunteers. When the Army was defeated and left Rostov at the end of February 1918 on its "Ice March" to the Kuban,[44] Miliukov stayed behind. He lived in hiding on the outskirts of Rostov until the German Army occupied the city in May. In the spring he decided that the Bolsheviks could best be overthrown by an alliance between the Volunteer Army and the Germans.[45]

At the end of May 1918, Miliukov moved to Kiev, where he tried to convince the German authorities to support the Russian anti-Bolshevik military campaign.[46] This plan outraged many Kadets at the time and sullied Miliukov's reputation in his party for years to come.[47] How could the former Minister of Foreign Affairs, an ardent supporter of the Allied cause, go over to the enemy? This was not how Miliukov saw it. To him, this strategy was not a rejection of the Russian forces, nor a betrayal of his country; his talks with the Germans were entirely in accord with his notion of realistic, pragmatic politics. He conceived of himself as the Volunteer Army's representative, whose task was to negotiate between German and Russian leaders. The potential alliance was thus an expression of national sovereignty as well as a means to defeat the Bolsheviks.[48]

This strategy, however, was based upon an elementary miscalculation. Miliukov's objective was the reunification of Russia; among his conditions for talks with the German authorities were a review of the Brest-Litovsk accords, the reestablishment of Russia's former boundaries, an "All-Russian government," and "the sovereignty of the central administration."[49] Yet it ought to have been plain to any observer, especially to one who understood the motives behind Germany's support for Lenin, that a united, sovereign Russia ran counter to German interests. German support for the Ukrainian separatists in Kiev made this obvious. Yet here Miliukov's desires—his belief that Bolshevism could be defeated through "pragmatic" tactics—overcame his reason. Even in September 1918, two months after he had been informed that his proposals were completely unacceptable in Berlin, he was still hoping that in the long run his wager on the Germans would succeed.[50]

After this fiasco, Miliukov returned to the business of giving advice to the commanders of the Volunteer Army and discussing liberal politics with his fellow Kadets in the south. He was active in the "State Council for the National Unification of Russia," a group of former Duma representatives residing in the Ukraine.[51] At the same time, he prepared his *History* for publication. It was being printed by the Letopis' firm in Kiev, when a gang of "Petliurovtsy," followers of the Ukrainian nationalist Petliura, raided the publishing house and smashed its presses.[52] As a consequence of his unpopular pro-German policy, Miliukov resigned as chairman of the Kadet Central Committee,[53] but he continued to play a leading role in the interminable planning sessions held by groups of liberals in the fall of 1918.[54] At these meetings he insisted on two principles: complete freedom of action for himself and extreme caution for the party. In September at the plenary session of the Kadets' Ukrainian committee, he declared: "For myself, I only ask 'free hands' for reconnoitering [*razvedka*]. I did not misuse my freedom, but I still need it." He then proposed the following resolution, adopted by the meeting: "Not to hurry, but also not to close off possibilities."[55] Miliukov gave his personal sanction to the monarchist slogans popular with the leadership of the Volunteer Army,[56] but he recommended that his party avoid too close an association with the Whites. The Kadets should maintain their political independence, so that after the war was won, they would be free from binding obligations.[57]

It was only in November 1918, when Miliukov left Russia to attend the Jassy peace conference, that he found his proper calling once again. The Kadets' mission to the conference was a failure—they were divided into three separate delegations and unable to present a unified program[58]—but Miliukov was out of Russia and embarked upon a diplomatic task. His strategy now was to persuade the Allied governments to support the anti-Bolshevik armies. After an unsuccessful trip to Paris,[59] he established himself in England, the country where he felt most at home and whose "immortal" values he revered.[60]

In London Miliukov began a campaign of publicity and lobbying directed at the public and the government. He was up against the same obstacles—exhaustion after the war, disillusion with democratic government, and enthusiasm for the Russian "experiment"—that had hindered the Russian socialists in their appeals to European conscience. But this did not daunt Miliukov, whose energy and optimism were irrepressible. His days in London were filled with luncheons, meetings with Members of Parliament, interviews, and speeches; his evenings spent in long discussions with other Russians in what was thought to be the temporary emigration.[61] In addition, during the next two years he edited a weekly news journal and wrote, in English, over seventy articles, two pamphlets, and a book.[62]

The institutional focus of Miliukov's activities in London was the Russian Liberation Committee, an organization of émigrés whose goals were "the overthrow of Bolshevism" and "the restoration of order in and the regeneration of Russia."[63] Throughout 1919, the committee issued a weekly *Bulletin* and a series of pamphlets for distribution in "public libraries . . . workshops and factories,"[64] publications designed to convince British readers of the failures of the Soviet regime and the achievements of the White army. The committee also tried to influence the government through the Foreign Office, with little success.[65]

Miliukov's major contribution to this propaganda effort was a book, provocatively titled *Bolshevism: An International Danger.*[66] The focus of this study, written in 1919 and published early the next year, was the Bolsheviks' involvement, actual and potential, in European politics. Miliukov's discussion reversed the emphasis of the Russian socialists' writings on the revolution. They had concentrated on the destructive consequences of Bolshevism inside Russia and tried to separate the Soviet government from European socialism, the better to criticize the Bolshevik party for its departures from Western orthodoxy. Miliukov, on the other hand, emphasized the international significance of Bolshevism and its connections with the left in Europe. He was, moreover, as critical of the Western socialists as he had been of the Russian Mensheviks and Socialist Revolutionaries.

In *Bolshevism* Miliukov analyzed the revolution, as he had in his *History*, as a political phenomenon. But in this English work he moved beyond the struggle for power in Petrograd. Europe, he insisted, could not stand aside from developments in Russia. The revolution was part of Western politics, in both its origins and its effects.

The roots of Bolshevism, according to Miliukov, could be found in the European theory of "revolutionary syndicalism," a branch of Marxism that chose immediate revolution as its goal. Western social democracy had for the most part renounced this course at the end of the nineteenth century, in favor of a reformist and evolutionary route. But in Russia, where the political situation after 1905 offered no possibility for gradual change, the strategy of violent revolution was especially attractive. The fact that Russia did not have the economic or social development essential for the transition to socialism had not deterred the Bolsheviks from trying to seize power. Lenin's party relied upon a subsequent world revolution to overcome their country's backwardness.[67]

The extremism of the Russian revolutionary movement after 1905 had a corollary in the resurgence of European syndicalism in the same period, Miliukov thought. Georges Sorel, in particular, had revived the militant Marxism of the *Communist Manifesto* and fused it with the irrationalism flourishing in early twentieth-century European thought. This revitalized syndicalism was repugnant to Miliukov in two respects: it both denied a scientific, rational principle of human development and rejected the political foundations of liberalism—democracy, law, the state. Its strategy he described as the "tactics of 'impatience.'" The inspired minority was to overcome the inertia of the majority by appealing to the instincts of the masses, not their reason. In its elitism, Miliukov commented, revolutionary syndicalism "stretches forth its hand to Royalism." "Its political romanticism, its excursions in the sphere of the subconsciousness, its repudiation of democratic principles, its hero-worship—in short, all its psychology it shares in common with . . . the reactionary pole. . . ."[68]

Lenin's contribution to the theory of international revolutionary syndicalism was to bring the state back into this utopianism. His revolution in Russia had filled up "the obscure transitional stage from the general strike to the Social Revolution" with state institutions, manned by his own party members. In theory, these were eventually to disappear, but Lenin's writings showed that he thought it expedient to use the state mechanism against the revolution's enemies. The "last word" of syndicalism in both Russia and Europe was, according to Miliukov, "government by minority." He continued, "This explains why there exists such a strong undercurrent of sympathy with the Bolshevist experiment amongst all partisans of a direct social revolution the world over."[69]

In his presentation, Miliukov was careful not to identify Bolshevism with socialism. "It is a moot question," he noted at the beginning of his book, "whether Bolshevism and its European counterpart, 'Revolutionary Syndicalism' can be called Socialism at all." The significant point, he thought, was that the Bolsheviks and syndicalists, by choosing a revolutionary interpretation of socialism and discarding its scientific theory, had rid their version of Marxism of its inner contradictions while the mainstream European socialists, who tried to be reformists and revolutionaries at once, had not. Moreover, the moderate socialists, with their dedication to party unity, were continually sacrificing their own unsteady principles to the more consistent ones of the syndicalist radicals in order to keep the socialist organizations intact. As in his *History*, Miliukov treated the moderates' compromises and inconsistencies with contempt.[70]

By emphasizing the connection between Bolshevism and European revolutionary doctrine, Miliukov did not intend to lend Lenin's ideas any intellectual prestige. "The Russian practice of Bolshevism did not enrich European theory with any positive data," he wrote in the preface to *Bolshevism*, "and the purely *political* triumph of Bolshevism in Russia is no proof that its social teaching can be applied at all."[71] Miliukov's purpose, however, was not a theoretical critique, but to show that Bolshevism, whatever its weaknesses and strengths, was dangerous to the West. Unlike the Russian socialists, who appealed only for sympathetic understanding, his goal was concrete—to make Europeans aware of a Bolshevik threat and to inspire them to act effectively against it.

The first step in this direction was understanding the enemy, his methods, and his goals. Miliukov cautioned his readers that

> the best way to win the game is not to represent one's adversary as being too stupid, or too dishonest and selfish, or too weak and careless. I prefer to see my enemy at his best in order the better to understand and the better to defeat him.[72]

And to see Bolshevism at its best, to understand it as a menace to the European order, one had only to look at the success of revolutionary socialism in the recent past. Miliukov devoted much of his study to the "progress" of Bolshevism in the last six years. First, there had been the destructive influence of socialist internationalism on the military efforts of the belligerents in the World War. The efforts of the Zimmerwald-Kienthal left to turn the "imperialist" war into a "revolutionary struggle against capitalism" had "strengthened extreme tendencies" in Germany, France, and England, and had been victorious in Russia. There, "internationalist propaganda, introduced into Russia from the outside, . . . led by the group of Russian refugees we know and . . . strongly supported by the International Socialists" had brought about the October insurrection and Russia's withdrawal from the war, to the detriment of the Allied cause. With the triumph of the Bolsheviks, the direction of influence had been reversed; the "internationalized Russian Revolution" began to act back on Europe. But the goal remained that of the Zimmerwald and Kienthal socialists—ending the international war by means of national revolutions. At Brest-Litovsk the Bolsheviks had negotiated with the Germans as if from strength because they had believed in the power of the revolutionary minority and in the imminence of a worldwide crisis.[73]

These revolutionary objectives had not been fulfilled, Miliukov noted, but this was no reason for complacency. It was not European efforts but the campaigns of the anti-Bolshevik armies within Russia that had prevented the Bolsheviks from linking their forces with those of the German Spartacists: "It is fair to say," he asserted, "that if the Bolshevist military contribution to the World Revolution had completely failed in 1919, it was chiefly due to . . . non-Bolshevist Russia's relentless fight against the Bolsheviks."[74]

Even so, the Bolsheviks' military failure had been accompanied by victories in the European socialist movement. Although the Second International had reaffirmed its commitment to democracy at the Berne Conference in 1919, it had nonetheless refused to take a decisive stand against violent revolution. To Miliukov, the contorted resolutions of Western social democrats, like those of Russian socialists, were signs of frailty. The ascendancy of the Third International and of extremism within international socialism was due, he claimed, to the moderates' confusion. Once again, "the Bolsheviks were winning not so much by their own strength as by the weakness and inconsistency of their antagonists within the sphere of doctrine shared by both."[75]

In addition to their consistent radicalism, the Bolsheviks had other weapons in the international struggle. Miliukov warned against the Bolsheviks' diplomacy of "unswerving bluff, almost grandiose in its unattainable cynicism." They would always accept the opportunity to negotiate, he predicted, because to them "discussion meant propaganda." Similarly, they realized that diplomatic recognition offered them the chance to exploit the possibilities of their ambassadors' connections and privileges. In an interview, Lenin had openly declared the policy of using allies whenever they could be found, of "manoeuvring, resting, and biding our time," in order, eventually, to exterminate capitalism.[76] Above all, the Bolsheviks could be effective because they were honest about their ends and not particular about their means. The Russian revolution had demonstrated that "amongst the uncertain and the wavering the Bolsheviks were the only people who knew what they wished to do, and who were ready to use force in order to achieve their aims."[77]

The goal now was world revolution. Although the Bolsheviks had not succeeded in Germany and Austria, the direction of their efforts was clear: first, a revolutionary outbreak in Central Europe followed by the overthrow of capitalism at its centers—London, Paris, and Rome.[78] But victory was not inevitable. Miliukov pointed to the Bolsheviks' internal problems as an indication of their vulnerability: "The probable failure of the Russian Revolution is now being proved true by everything we learn from within Bolshevist Russia." This weakness had forced the Bolsheviks to prepare a "defensive" stage of world revolution in the East, in India, Afghanistan, Turkey, Persia, and China, where "primitiveness" offered the conditions necessary for a successful Communist takeover. According to Miliukov, this retreat served to illustrate that the Bolsheviks were still ready to take advantage of their enemies' inattention and that the British "Hands Off Russia" policy would lead to advances on the other side. By not putting their full support behind the anti-Bolshevik forces in Russia, the British were both prolonging the Communist regime there and encouraging anti-democratic extremism in their own society and in the world.[79]

As he concluded *Bolshevism* in November 1919, Miliukov was optimistic about the ultimate defeat of the Bolshevik government. He contented himself with the suggestion that the British work to control the ideological legacy of the revolution:

> If even Bolshevism is really passing away—as it may be—one has got to take stock of the rather rich inheritance of the Bolshevist ideas and catchwords spread all over the world by the pro-Bolshevist propaganda, and to oppose to it new educational activities or legal action.[80]

A few months later, he was not so sanguine. In the epilogue to the book, added as it went to press in March 1920, Miliukov conveyed his distress at the altered prospects for "revolutionary internationalism." This change was due to two circumstances: the decisive defeat of General Denikin's major offensive against the Red Army and the acceptance of the "Hands Off Russia" policy by European governments generally. Miliukov warned that a "new wave" of Bolshevik propaganda was sweeping Europe and that the Third International was prevailing in the socialist movement.[81] Although European workers remained predominantly reformist,[82] the influence of Bolshevik propaganda could not be ignored. Miliukov's closing words were pessimistic:

> One has had to confess that Lenin's disciples are the only politicians who know what they want and who act in accordance. They meet with half-hearted and disunited opposition, voluntarily ignorant of their far-reaching aims, unmindful of the future, and concerned exclusively with small gains in the everyday struggle, with the preservation of their own momentary power or popularity, or even with realizing the doubtful and illusory benefits which the Soviet power is clever enough to dangle before the "greedy capitalists."[83]

Miliukov's harsher tone presaged a profound change of heart and tactics. His denunciation was uncharacteristically emotional, an expression of his anger at having been betrayed. He had expected the Russian socialists to fail him, but the British government? Here, at the end of his study, Miliukov's reason, so bold in criticizing others' mistakes and so confident that stupidity revealed would not be repeated, led him to a disappointing conclusion. His Bolshevik adversaries seemed to have triumphed once again.

Petr Struve: "The Experimental Refutation of Socialism"

On November 11, 1919, when Denikin's troops were already in retreat, Struve wrote to the Russian general:

> Dear Anton Ivanovich,
>
> I was in Taganrog on the day when you arrived in Rostov and then decided to go to Moscow. Therefore I was not able to report to you. Yet I want not only to present my personal feelings to you but consider it my duty to inform you of some of my observations. For the whole time that I was away from the Volunteer Army I at heart *considered myself in its service and acted in that*

spirit. Now I see here not that band of heroic fighters from whom I parted, but the Great Russian Army that has revived the State. And no matter what kind of difficulties there may be, Russia is arising and in your person is going toward her predestination.

Cordially and faithfully yours,

Petr Struve[84]

It was, doubtless, the news of Denikin's losses that had elicited these words of encouragement and commitment. From Struve's perspective, the spiritual bond between the individual and the nation could not be broken by military setbacks; these defeats only inspired an affirmation of his loyalty to the army, its leader, and its future victory.[85]

Intense patriotism was the foundation of Struve's writings on the revolution. In his pessimistic moments, he regarded the revolutionary crisis as an unmitigated disaster for Russia. At other times, like this one, he thought the challenge to the state could be surmounted. He never accepted the Bolsheviks' claim to represent the nation. In Struve's analyses, Bolshevism served a negative, but illuminating function. The Bolsheviks' victory in 1917 revealed the defects of Russia's past; their government demonstrated that socialism, as a basis for state organization, did not work.

Struve's first published reaction to the October insurrection was a short article in the November-December volume of his journal *Russkaia mysl'* (Russian Thought). In this commentary, entitled "What Is Revolution and What Is Counterrevolution?" he immediately took up the question of the significance of the revolution in Russia's history and for the country's future. The events of 1917 did not deserve the "honorable title of revolution," in Struve's view. They were instead a "soldiers' mutiny [*soldatskii bunt*]" that the intelligentsia had "accepted . . . as a revolution, in the hope of turning the mutiny into a revolution. But this hope had not been realized, and the revolt had turned not into a glorious revolution, but into an immense and disgraceful *all-Russian pogrom.*" (Here Struve used "pogrom" in its general sense of a destructive raid.) To Struve, the developments of the past eight months were but a counterrevolutionary "episode," while the real revolution was an extensive, lengthy movement of social transformation—"the *simultaneous* creation of new *political and social-economic* forms of life"—a process that had begun as early as 1902 and would continue long after the "pogrom" of 1917. Because "the elements who should have actively constructed these new forms of life turned out . . . to be historically incapable of solving this problem," this, real, transformation was and had been "painful" and paradoxical in Russia. The present situation was only a continuation of this ongoing process, and it was illusory to believe that either the calling of the Constituent Assembly or a conclusion of the war would put a quick end to it.[86]

From Struve's perspective, one paradox of 1917 was that despite the need for a strong army and firm authority to bring the external and civil wars to an end, the army itself had turned into an "organized pogrom-making rabble [*pogromnoe bezchinstvo*] of armed people, led by criminals and madmen." Another, more fundamental, paradox lay in the revolution's socialist inspiration and its actual "bourgeois" consequences. Struve felt that the long-term revolution was ultimately a struggle for property—"an immense popular convulsion, out of which must be born in Russia a regime based on private property (first of all in land) of the broad popular masses and on the introduction of propertied conceptions and tastes into their psychology." In this sense, the present upheaval represented a continuation of one of the great accomplishments of the earlier revolution—Stolypin's land reform. To Struve, the peasants' land seizures in 1917 amounted to a demonstration that Russia would take the "path of the creation of universal culture in bourgeois forms" and that "all of Russian agrarian socialism is nothing but intelligentsia ravings, a costume in which the striving for bourgeois possessions of the economically stronger and tenacious peasant element is attired." From this point of view, it was Russian socialism, fighting against the bourgeoisie, the bourgeois structure, and bourgeois values, that was "counterrevolutionary." And as such, it would be "swept away" in the course of historical development.[87]

Condemned to perish in the long run, Russian socialism had nonetheless put the state in jeopardy. By infecting the people's struggle for liberation with "pogrom poison," the intelligentsia had prepared the disasters of 1917.[88] The blame for these was often cast on the old regime or the Bolsheviks, Struve noted, but in his view the entire intelligentsia, by actively or passively promoting socialism despite conclusive evidence that Russia was historically unprepared for it, had to bear a large share of responsibility:

> If one chooses to call the all-Russian pogrom of 1917 the Russian revolution, then I will say directly: the main crime of the old regime is that it prepared this revolution and made it inescapable. Justice, however, demands that one add: the whole progressive Russian intelligentsia participated in this crime by means of the unscrupulous and foolhardy character which it gave to its struggle against the old order, especially after the events of 1905.[89]

Struve's attack on the intelligentsia was a continuation of one of his own long-term struggles. In the aftermath of the 1905 revolution, he had rejected the oppositional politics of both socialists and liberals as destructive and suicidal. Recent events only proved the justice of the accusations he had leveled against the intelligentsia in *Vekhi* in 1909. From his point of view, the intellectuals by virtue of their education and especially their training in Marxist sociology should have realized that Russia needed bourgeois development. They were thus guilty of the "enormous sin" of setting the masses against the bourgeoisie with their inflammatory and illusory propaganda.[90]

Other aspects of Struve's complex intellectual history appeared in his first response to the October events. His analysis was based, at one level, on Marxist concepts of historical development, reflecting his early years as a theorist of

Russian social democracy and his studies in Marxist political economy. But his article expressed as well his gradual repudiation of socialism. While Struve still shared universalistic and deterministic views of history with the left, he had rejected the theory of socialist revolution. His political and philosophical conversion had been founded in part on his reflections on the inconsistencies of Marxist theory, and in particular, on his conclusion, developed in 1899, that violent revolution was incompatible with thoroughgoing social change.[91] This view was reiterated in his assertion in "What Is Revolution and What Is Counterrevolution?" that a real revolution would be a gradual and lengthy process. But, in addition, for Struve the "bourgeois" revolution had become a final goal. It, and not socialism, expressed the values he held to be "universal." This was the underlying point behind his insistence on the episodic qualities of the events of 1917. Eventually, the revolution would have to take on bourgeois forms.

The other side of Struve's support for bourgeois revolution had been his criticism of Russia's socialists as "counterrevolutionary" opponents of progress. In this respect as well 1917 gave Struve more material for his old fights; for him the revolution, or the "pogrom," was another proof of the inadequacy of socialist theory. These themes—the guilt of the intelligentsia, the necessity of "bourgeois" progress, and the failure of socialism—appeared repeatedly in his writings of the next five years.

Since Struve's turn away from the intelligentsia after the 1905 revolution, the major focus of his activities had been Russian culture, not politics.[92] The February revolution had only intensified his efforts to build a broad nationalist consensus based on shared values and traditions. (For Struve, as for Miliukov, the threat to the state began in February, not October.) In addition to editing *Russkaia mysl'*, which he had done for over a decade, he inaugurated a new weekly periodical in the spring of 1917. *Russkaia svoboda* (Russian Freedom) was to carry on the work of *Osvobozhdenie*, the organ he had edited in the liberation movement of 1902–1905. The new journal's goals were the "strengthening of freedom and the growth of culture"; it called on its readers to sacrifice for the common good and for a new life to be based on "complete freedom, love of man, and faith in the good forces of his nature."[93] Connected with *Russkaia svoboda* was the League of Russian Culture, founded by Struve in April 1917 to honor the positive achievements of the past.[94]

Struve's activities in the cause of national rebirth were not confined to education. During the tenure of the Provisional Government, he had taken part, as best he could, in the turbulent politics of the capitals; after October, he devoted himself to the service of the Volunteer Army. He left Moscow in December 1917, joined the civilian council attached to the army, and spent the next two months in the south. When the Bolshevik forces advanced in the Don region, he was not permitted to join the Volunteers on their Ice March. He returned instead to Moscow, where he participated in several liberal and conservative groups opposed to the Bolshevik government, including the Right

Center—until it assumed a pro-German orientation—and, subsequently, the National Center. Through June 1918 he continued to publish truncated issues of *Russkaia mysl'*.[95]

During the spring and summer of 1918 Struve was also involved in the production of a volume of essays on the Russian revolution. He solicited articles from eleven prominent intellectuals who shared his view that the revolution had been a "moral and political catastrophe." Five of the contributors had written for *Vekhi* nine years earlier; a majority were members of the League of Russian Culture. As with *Vekhi*, the book was intended as a compendium of separate articles. Each author was to write "what his conscience and reason dictated." This time the chaos and repression ensured that there was little contact between the contributors. S. L. Frank, living in Saratov, suggested the volume's title—*Iz glubiny* (From the Depths).[96] The verse from Psalm 129—"Out of the depths I cry unto Thee, O Lord"—in both Latin and Old Church Slavonic, was the book's epigraph.

Iz glubiny[97] was printed early in the fall of 1918, just after Fania Kaplan's attempt to assassinate Lenin. In the full-scale terror that followed, it was decided that issuing the book would be "impossible."[98] The printed copies remained in the publisher's warehouse until 1921 when the company's printers sold it privately in Moscow. Suppressed by the authorities, *Iz glubiny* is still banned in Russia. The book survived only because two copies reached the West.[99]

That both its authors and the government considered *Iz glubiny* "impossible" in revolutionary Russia is not surprising.[100] The collection presented an overtly spiritual conception of the nation. In Struve's article, the determinism of his first response to the October coup was absent. In "What Is Revolution and What Is Counterrevolution?" he had looked forward to the future—time would prove that the revolution had to be bourgeois. Now, eight months later, what seemed more conclusive was the past. Forces set in motion almost two centuries earlier appeared to be responsible for the national catastrophe of 1917.

This emphasis on history was suggested in the title of Struve's article: "The Historical Meaning of the Russian Revolution and National Tasks." Struve began by rejecting two "common" explanations of the revolution. The first blamed the Russian people's lack of culture and civilization. This analysis could not stand close scrutiny, Struve countered, for the Russian masses had been less cultured in the days of Stenka Razin and Pugachev, yet then they were not able to bring down the state. Moreover, he added, the Russian masses today were hardly less cultured than the French and English at the time of "their genuine and genuinely great revolutions." The idea of the uncultured masses had to be dismissed as a "superficial and, frankly speaking, simply stupid" notion.[101]

A second widespread opinion placed all the blame on the "old regime," "the old order, and so forth." However, in Struve's view, the institutions of the old regime had been "*technically* satisfactory"; its major failings derived not from the "regime" as such, but from the individuals who had been to some extent "restrained . . . by these institutions." By toppling the established system, the revolution had revealed this more fundamental insufficiency. From the experience of Soviet power, which had brought the worst petty tyrants of Gogol's Russia to the helm of state, one could appreciate the "cultural role" of the old regime's bureaucracy and police.[102]

Struve's explanation was much more extensive in scope and in time than either of these single-cause interpretations. As a "phenomenon," he wrote,

the Russian revolution is explained by the coincidence of the distorted ideological education of the Russian intelligentsia, which it received in the course of almost the whole nineteenth century, with the action of the world war upon the popular masses: the war put the people in conditions that made them especially receptive to the demoralizing propagation of intelligentsia ideas.[103]

The intelligentsia's mistaken and dangerous ideas, condemned earlier by Struve and his fellow dissident intellectuals in *Vekhi*, were hatred of the state and willful ignorance of the "anti-cultural and savage forces, that slumber in the masses." This intelligentsia mentality had grown up in response to the actions of the autocracy, which had systematically excluded first the landed gentry and then the intelligentsia from participation in the construction and administration of the state, thereby turning its natural supporters into "renegades" against their country. The intelligentsia's "renegade spirit [*otshchepenstvo*]" was, in Struve's opinion, "the destructive force that, having spilled out through the whole people and conjoined with their material lusts and longings, smashed a great and composite [*mnogosostavnoe*] state."[104]

This explanation of the revolution shifted the burden of causality away from the people and the present. To the extent that the critical factor was the intelligentsia's ideas, and not the people's character, the revolution's sources lay in the distant past. With his customary intellectual audacity, Struve pointed to a single event as decisive for the rest of Russia's history. This was the constitutional crisis of 1730.

In 1730 Anna Ivanovna, a niece of Peter the Great, accepted an invitation to ascend the Russian throne and then repudiated a set of written limitations upon her authority. According to Struve's account, Anna had achieved this victory for the principle of unlimited authority by relying on the companies of soldiers in the capital and by exploiting divisions within the upper classes. With time, the political crisis was resolved through a division of political and economic spoils: the autocracy retained complete political authority for itself by granting the gentry control over the major economic resource of the country—the peasants. "*The Russian monarchy bought off political reform with serfdom*" was Struve's conclusion.[105]

It was this bargain, struck in the eighteenth century, that ultimately produced the revolution. In Struve's view, the 1730 settlement had delayed the emancipation of the serfs for a century and thereby postponed and finally prevented the establishment of private property for the peasants. At the same time, the upper class either assented to the government's total authority and "*accommodated* and *lowered* its own psychology to this idea of the state" or became "alienated" and joined the struggle against the autocracy. In the latter half of the nineteenth century, this revolt acquired an ideology in the form of "Western-European radicalism and socialism." Subsequent developments made it plain, Struve argued, "that the Russian monarchy was destroyed in 1917 because it for too long relied upon the lack of political rights [*politicheskoe bespravie*] of the gentry and the lack of civil rights [*grazhdanskoe bespravie*] of the peasantry."[106]

In six breathtaking pages in *Iz glubiny*, Struve had sketched an explanation for the intelligentsia worldview he had identified and criticized in *Vekhi* nine years earlier. Then he had pointed to the ideological heritage of the intelligentsia—to its insular "renegade" culture—as the source of its destructive political ideas.[107] Now, he placed the blame for this tradition back upon the state. The time-scale of his argument, its quality of inexorable process, and its appeal to a sense of historical retribution made the revolution appear inescapable and tragic.

But despite the apparent inevitability of the old regime's collapse, Struve felt that lessons for the future could be learned from the revolutionary experience. He devoted a large part of his article to a discussion of what had happened in Russia since February 1917 and in particular to an examination of popular ideas of socialism. The revolution, according to Struve, had shown that socialist conceptions, far from leading to cooperative and constructive actions, had resulted in the destruction of the nation and its economy. This outcome was comprehensible if one paid attention to the real, as opposed to the postulated, values of the masses. Their attitudes toward property, their "class consciousness," and their notions of "socialist" goals were radically at odds with the socialism of the intelligentsia.

Struve's discussion of popular values in *Iz glubiny* indicated that he had begun to revise his earlier prediction that the revolution would establish "bourgeois property" for the peasants. He now took a much more pessimistic view, one based on his analysis of mass behavior. From his perspective, the revolution had not been a struggle for the means of production, but a fight over already existing goods. The people had indeed been influenced by socialist slogans, but these they had interpreted "either as the division of available property or as the receipt of a sufficient and equal ration with the least expenditure of labor and a minimum of obligations."[108] These goals had little in common with the theory of a planned socialist economy, but it was the desires of the people and not the predictions of the intellectuals that were decisive for Russia's future. To Struve, this now looked bleak:

> Socialism, then, as the idea of a division [*razdel*] or redivision [*peredel*] of property, meaning in concrete terms the destruction of a great number of capital assets, rests on the passive consumption, or dissipation, the 'eating up' of goods, following which nothing can be seen except famine and the struggle of hungry people over the meager and ever more meager supply of goods.[109]

This emphasis on the perceptions of the masses and their significance for the "concrete" meaning of socialism led Struve to a discussion of class struggle. In his account, class, as a force in history, could not be explained by objective social-economic criteria such as occupation or salary, but had to be seen as the "psychological fact of class consciousness."[110] This had been clear in the revolution, when, despite the absence or near absence of capitalist classes, the masses had been united by their shared hatred of the privileged, whether capitalist or not. To Struve, this behavior showed that

> it is not the presence of class as an objective category that gives birth to class consciousness, but on the contrary, the presence of class consciousness objectively constitutes a class, as a social-psychological phenomenon, as a sociological quantity.[111]

Lenin, for example, belonged to the proletariat because he had psychologically attached himself to it.[112]

This definition of class was at odds with the deterministic notions of Russian Marxism during the revolutionary period and anticipated the importance ascribed to consciousness by Western Marxists such as Lukács and Gramsci later in the twentieth century. Struve's sensitivity to psychological factors had led him in the 1890s to propose that on their way from "utopian" to "scientific" socialism, Marx and Engels had been followers of Feuerbach, a discovery of the "early Marx" that was also out of phase with contemporary views but a well-founded and modern idea.[113] Now, on the basis of mass behavior in the revolution, Struve once again challenged the left's claim to objectivity and scientific proof. The disparity between the motivations of the crowd and the ideas of the socialist leaders showed, he thought, that the intelligentsia's theories of socialism and class struggle contained the "deepest inner contradictions."[114]

The socialist theory of the intellectuals, according to Struve's article, depended on cooperative economic construction and upon individual self-restraint for the sake of the collective. The masses, on the other hand, were attracted to socialism by the prospect of their own individual gains. For them, the "pathos" of socialism was "purely materialistic and at the same time individualistic, or atomistic." Class struggle amounted to no more than the collective satisfaction of individual desires; in actuality, "class struggle" meant a raid on property. Thus, Struve contended, the "ideas of socialism and class struggle have strength and power as revolutionary ideas for the Russian masses only to the extent that they are individualistic and destructive and not collective and constructive." The experience of the past year had shown that "revolutionary socialism," far from being collectivist in essence, was when enacted socially divisive.[115]

No matter how paradoxical it might seem, Struve argued, " 'bourgeois' society and 'bourgeois' social forms (the state, the army, the church, etc.) [were] much more imbued with the spirit of collectivism (socialism, if you will)

[and] express to a much greater extent the principle of collectivization and social action than militant revolutionary socialism." The difference between the two systems could be seen in two types of war: external war that united society in a shared spirit of self-sacrifice for the sake of the whole and civil war that contradicted the "idea of the whole and the solidarity of its parts." Socialism, with its dependence upon class divisions, led to civil war and destroyed the collectivity expressed by the nation.[116]

But had the Russian nation expressed a collectivity? Why had the idea of class struggle been embraced by the Russian masses? Here Struve pointed to traditional habits, "ancient moral vices, . . . distrust and ill will between classes and individuals, which frequently flared up into hatred." He added, lamely, that the revolution had destroyed the old "national, state, and religious ties" uniting Russian people without replacing them with anything new and positive.[117] The inner contradictions of these—his own—wishful statements he chose to ignore.

The moral of the revolutionary experience, according to Struve in *Iz glubiny*, was that Russians had to turn from the false collective of socialism to the true unity of the nation. And in his definition of the nation, as in his discussion of class, Struve gave primacy to ideas, not material facts. "National consciousness forms the nation just as class consciousness [forms] class," he asserted. But, in addition, the nation had a cultural value superior to the "meager social-economic content" of the class idea; it offered a spiritual idea to all Russians, of all classes, at all times. The task of Russians now was to "educate individuals and the masses in the national spirit." This demanded that Russians free themselves both from the "false ideal" of "class international socialism" and from the worship of specific "political and social forms (such as a republic, the commune, [or] socialism)." These forms, Struve insisted, could not in themselves be national ideals. They were instead different types of social organizations that served only as "the best receptacle [*vmestilishche*] for the national culture" at a given historical moment. A true national ideal could be found instead in Russia's whole historical existence, both in the past and in the years to come. In a material sense, the nation was the "natural [*stikhiinyi*] product of our entire harsh and cruel history." It had to become the "natural force [*stikhiia*] of our existence, lovingly and consciously created," a "higher value" that united all past, present, and future "generations of Russian people." Struve called on Russians to cherish the efforts of the past—"the piety of Sergii of Radonezh, the daring of Metropolitan Fil' \, the patriotism of Peter the Great, the heroism of Suvorov, the poetry of Pusnkin, Gogol, and Tolstoy, the selflessness of Nakhimov, Kornilov, and all the millions of Russians, landlords and peasants, rich and poor, who died intrepidly, without complaint and unselfishly, for Russia." The nation "as a living, assembled personality [*sobornaia lichnost'*] and as a spiritual force" had been created by these people and their self-sacrificing acts.[118]

As this emotional passage indicates, Struve's conception of the nation was inherently religious. It was *belief* in the nation that was to become a motive force for action. The union between the moral idea of the nation and its historical embodiment in the Russian people was based upon an act of faith. Struve's defense of his spiritual commitment was self-conscious, in the tradition of the neo-idealistic revival in Russian philosophy. He accepted the irrational foundation of belief, but he did not presume that a common faith was spontaneously available to all. On the contrary, spiritual values had to be chosen, affirmed, and taught. He argued for belief in the Russian nation as a better faith than socialism, which had proved to be a destructive, self-defeating ideal. The intelligentsia, if it felt a "debt before the people," was obliged to bring not socialism, but the national idea to the masses, because otherwise "neither the rebirth of the people, nor the reconstitution of the government is possible." Reason—the recognition of Russia's national collapse, its causes, and the need to overcome them—could in this way lead to the creation of what Struve called a national "idea-passion." This alone could give Russians the spiritual strength to save their country.[119]

Struve's article in *Iz glubiny* was thus a characteristic combination of passionate idealism, critical theory, and historical determinism. Russian history was called upon to provide the basis for a spiritual revival, while, at the same time, it accounted for the revolutionary debacle. The irresponsibility of the Russian intelligentsia that had seemed so significant to Struve in the immediate aftermath of the October coup now appeared as but one of the consequences of the eighteenth-century political settlement. Struve did not ask himself why that settlement—serfs for power—had lasted for so long or whether it could have been undone. In his analysis, the decisions of 1730 led inexorably to the deformed society of the late nineteenth century. The events of the past year and a half were no longer seen as an aberrant episode in a historical process that would, as in the West, eventually produce a bourgeois order, but rather as the logical outcome of an earlier eccentricity that had thrown Russia radically off course.

After his article for *Iz glubiny*, Struve wrote little on the revolution for over a year. He left Moscow in August 1918, spent four precarious months in northern Russia trying to establish contact with British forces there, and in December escaped to Finland. For the next two years, he devoted himself totally to the military fight against the Bolsheviks.[120] He first campaigned abroad, in London and Paris, to win Western support for the White armies.[121] In September 1919 he returned to the Ukraine where he edited *Velikaia Rossiia* (Great Russia), a highly patriotic and pro-White newspaper. Struve's articles in this publication defended the policies of the Volunteer Army and its Political Council and stressed the ideas he had developed in *Iz glubiny*: the essence of the Russian revolution was the destruction of the state; recovery demanded both belief and sacrifice.[122]

In November 1919 Struve gave a public lecture in Rostov on the revolution and its future. His prognosis was far from optimistic; he only once mentioned the Volunteer Army, which was retreating after the failure of its Moscow offensive. Published later as "Reflections on the Russian Revolution,"[123] Struve's lecture was devoted both to the internal development of the revolution in the last two years and to its international dimension. As his hopes for an early defeat of Bolshevism diminished, he began to see the revolution as a tragedy with moral lessons not just for Russia, but for the world at large.

Struve's "Reflections" were directed in part toward the problem of Western attitudes toward Russia. Like Miliukov, he was concerned about the European governments' unwillingness to give full support to the anti-Bolshevik armies. Since Russia's collapse had been triggered by the war and since Bolshevism was a threat to the Western powers, why had Russia's allies not been more committed to the Whites? According to Struve, the West's recalcitrance was based not on knowledge and real interests, but on impressions and beliefs.

Struve reminded his audience that Russians themselves were partly at fault for the poor image of their country abroad. "We too indiscriminately criticized and defamed our country in front of foreigners," he complained. In addition, Russia as a great power had been the enemy of France and England in the past; these wars and confrontations lived in European memories. On the Polish question in particular Western opinion had always been against Russia. One other traditional attitude influenced the West against the Volunteers; this was the "sincere hostility of Western democratic elements to 'tsarism.'" The collapse of the Russian state was equated with the fall of the autocracy and therefore seen in a positive light. Moreover, Russia appeared to many in the West to have lost the war—although this was in fact the fault of the Germans and the revolution—and thus deserved to bear the costs of the defeat.[124]

In addition to these "historical and psychological" factors, the Allies' attitudes toward Russia were directly affected by their own "internal crisis," a product of the war and revolution. The war, Struve noted, had had in general a "democratic ideology." The masses, in Europe as in Russia, had been called into the national military effort on an unprecedented scale and through their participation "felt their strength." The Russian revolution, the fall of the German monarchy, and the end of war discipline had created a situation in which the popular movements identified with Bolshevism. These factors meant that Western people were for the most "incapable" of understanding that Bolshevism was a product of the immaturity of the Russian people. Instead they imagined that the Russian revolution embodied "that socialism and that rule of the working class about which they had heard so many clever speeches, prophetic soothsayings, and seductive promises." Furthermore, it suited the purposes of the socialist parties in the West to accept this image of Bolshevism. Struve concluded that the "extreme idealization of Russian Bolshevism" among the Western workers was "if you will, childish, but at the same time, precisely for this reason invincible to the arguments of reason or the lessons of history, provided somewhere far away, in that unknown and misunderstood Russia."[125]

The major purpose of Struve's "Reflections on the Russian Revolution" was to elucidate these lessons even if the Europeans were not listening. In his analysis, the "world-historical significance" of the Russian experience was that the "first attempt to establish socialism on a large scale" had failed. The revolution had showed that socialism, as it had been constructed in the minds of intellectuals, was unworkable as a principle of social organization.[126]

In order to develop the lessons of the Bolshevik experiment, Struve turned first, as he had in *Iz glubiny*, to mass values. As before, it seemed to him that the "basis of Bolshevism in daily life" was

the combination of two powerful mass tendencies: (1) the striving of each separate individual from the laboring masses to work as little as possible and to receive as much as possible and (2) the striving by means of mass collective action, not hesitating to use any means whatsoever, to bring about this result and at the same time to spare the individual from the ruinous consequences of such behavior.[127]

It was the *combination* of these aspirations that was new, Struve emphasized. The drive to work less and receive more had always existed, but it had been restrained by the negative results of such behavior for the individual. Bolshevism, however, was a "social-political movement" based on both impulses. It was an attempt to establish the "right to laziness," he concluded, quoting Lafargue.[128]

In Struve's view, an economy based on these conceptions was bound to fail. The intrinsic problem, as he saw it, was in socialist theory. As a political system, socialism was an attempt to realize two incompatible principles— egalitarianism and the national organization of the economy. Although both ideas were fundamental to socialist ideology, when implemented they ran counter to human nature and to each other. The simple fact, according to Struve, was that "on the basis of the equality of individuals, you cannot organize production."[129] The Russian revolution with its disastrous consequences for the Russian economy was a living proof of this fatal contradiction:

Socialism—Marxism teaches—demands the growth of productive forces. Socialism—the experiment of the Russian revolution teaches—is incompatible with the growth of productive forces, and what is more, it means their decline.[130]

Thus the revolution was a refutation of "egalitarian society" and of socialism "in its authentic meaning of the organization of production on the basis of the equality of people."[131]

This judgment was entirely consistent with what Struve had concluded theoretically about socialism long before the revolution. The collapse of the economy in Russia only confirmed his earlier analyses and his own convictions. Like the Russian socialists, Struve was a believer in the virtues of economic growth, but in opposition to the left, he was an advocate of "the idea of the individual's responsiblity for his behavior in general and his economic behavior in particular and the idea of the evaluation of people according to their individual worth, in particular according to their economic suitability." These two principles, given an "economic sanction" in the "institution of private property," were essential to social progress. To Struve, the revolution had demonstrated by omission the necessary role of private property in economic and social advancement. He recalled the words of Chaadaev, one of nineteenth-century Russia's perceptive and despondent figures: "We seem to live in order to give some great lesson to humanity." Now, in 1919, the lesson was clear—"our socialist revolution" had served as the "experimental refutation of socialism."[132]

Russian and European socialists, had they paid attention to Struve,[133] might have objected that a case against socialist theory could not be based on the revolutionary experience in Russia. No Russian social democrat accepted the notion that the Bolsheviks had put socialism into practice, and in this respect, Struve's earlier arguments undercut his conclusion. He had, after all, been insisting that the socialist and collectivist theories of the revolution's leaders had not corresponded to the selfish and individualist ideas of the masses. Was this then a "socialist experiment"? Would not the real experiment take place only when the leaders and the population were both collectivist?

This was exactly the problem, in Struve's presentation. The people of Russia were not collectivist, at least not in a productive sense. They were "collectivist" only toward outsiders, in wanting to divide up preexisting property and in wanting to avoid individual responsibility for their actions. If, as Struve believed, a productive economic system had to be based on private property and individualism, then socialism, by denying these and encouraging a collectivist mentality, would not be able to motivate people to produce and was thus condemned to poverty.

After two years of Bolshevik government, Struve had dispensed with the intricacies of his earlier writings on the revolution—with the distinction between a long-term revolutionary process and its episodes, or with the differences between mass consciousness and theory. His main point was that the revolution represented socialism in action and that it would not work. As before he explained the revolution's origins as a consequence of the chronic exclusion of the population from an active part in goverment, although with time he had become less fatalistic about the old regime. At several points, he now suggested, gradual reforms could have been initiated by the government—in 1881, the early 1890s, and during the Russo-Japanese War. But after 1905, Struve saw both state and society as hopelessly intransigent. The tsarist administration was unwilling to uphold the constitutional principles it had proclaimed, while the leaders of society were unable to see that the real danger to "political freedom and social peace" came from the revolutionary left.[134]

At this point in his analysis, Struve shifted the burden of guilt back onto the intelligentsia. They were "more blind" than the government in not recognizing the danger of revolution. Because of their misunderstanding of the psychology of the masses, the intelligentsia had failed to see that a popular revolution, made by soldiers, would destroy the state, the army, and the war effort. Only the Bolsheviks were "logical" during the revolution and "true to its essence," and, therefore, they won. Even after the fact, "a significant part of the Russian intelligentsia did not have the courage to confess their revolutionary delusions," and to see that they had destroyed their country.[135] In this respect, the Russian revolution was unique: "Russia was killed by the intelligentsia's lack of nationality [*beznatsional'nost'*], the only instance in world history of the brain of the nation being oblivious to the national idea."[136]

As an example of "national suicide," the Russian revolution presented a historical "enigma," commented Struve in his "Reflections". The comparison frequently made with the French revolution was, in the main, wrong. In Struve's view, the French revolution had been true, over time, to its original ideas; they had been put into effect even by the reaction to the revolution.[137] But the Russian revolution had contradicted its own principles:

> It had proclaimed socialism, but in reality it is the living refutation of socialism. In the agrarian sphere it had declared the abolition of private property in land, but the most important psychological result was the growth of proprietary feelings and the proprietary attraction of the masses to the land. . . .

> It declared the abolition of the army, but meanwhile it logically led to the fact that the army acquired a primary significance in the life of the state. It overthrew the monarch and pronounced popular sovereignty, but at the same time dictatorial power, relying on military force, is now the only possible form of state authority for Russia. On the other hand, monarchical ideas are now very strong both among the masses and in the intelligentsia, and there are many convinced monarchists who were made monarchists precisely by the revolution. In a word, nothing from the ideas of this revolution has been realized, and everything that is genuinely being realized contradicts its ideas.[138]

Struve chose instead to compare the revolution with the *smuta*, the "Time of Troubles," Russia's catastrophic national crisis of the early seventeenth century. There were many similarities between the revolution and this period—intrigue and invasion by foreign powers, Russia's weak cultural and national position relative to other states, the absence of courage and patriotism in the upper classes, and the anarchism of the people. During the Time of Troubles, the leaders of the various factions incited popular rebellions of a "pure-Bolshevik" type, setting all groups of the population against each other and calling on their followers to murder, steal, and rape. For Struve's purposes, however, the Time of Troubles had a positive legacy as well. He pointed to the heroism of the Russians who then had come to their country's rescue and drew parallels between the Volunteer Army and the Nizhnii Novgorod militia. The "national movement" of the middle classes in 1611 through 1613, "inspired by the clergy, the only intelligentsia at that time," was his model for Russia in the present. In Struve's presentation, the Time of Troubles had given birth to something that had nothing in common with itself, and this gave him hope that the revolution, too, could bring forth a national revival entirely at odds with its ideas and experience.[139]

But would the modern Pozharskiis and Minins succeed?[140] Denikin's "Great Russian Army" was already falling back after the failure of the Moscow offensive. Struve, characteristically, refused to see this defeat as final and tried once more to turn material losses into lessons for future victories. Two months after his speech at Rostov, he produced a memorandum on the causes of the army's setbacks. From his perspective, it was the demoralization of the army that accounted for its failures.

In his paper, entitled "The Meaning of Events in Southern Russia," Struve argued that the "basic reason for the ruin of the military organization was its mechanical expansion, which led inescapably to its dissolution." Both the Red Army and the Volunteers had resorted to compulsory conscription, using the example of the old regime. Their original, inspired cadres had been replaced by unreliable recruits, causing Denikin to remark to Struve in October 1919 that the "outcome of the struggle depends on which of the two armies . . . disintegrates faster and more thoroughly." This loss of spirit was critical, Struve felt, since the civil war amounted to a "war between minorities" and would be won by the force with the best military organization. He cited several other factors that had contributed to the army's losses—errors of strategy, reliance on the independently minded Cossacks, and, especially, the "military-bureaucratic spirit" of the army staff.[141]

But, in Struve's account, the most flagrant and serious example of the moral failures of the army was the system of "self-supply." Struve was appalled that the army staff had, in effect, sanctioned theft as the means to maintain its soldiers. To him, this was a self-defeating policy:

> The system of self-supply of the army led to pillage, which infected both the higher commanding staff and the officers and the soldier masses. This pillage was dangerous not only and not so much because of the attitude toward the army that it created in the population, but even more because it demoralized and corrupted the army itself.[142]

It was possible, he acknowledged, for a "chronically stealing" army to maintain discipline, but not in the circumstances of the civil war. For the Volunteer Army, and especially for its Cossack allies, the prospect of pillage "kindled the fighting spirit of the army, . . . [but] the results of pillage put it out."[143]

Struve's analysis of the Whites' failures in "The Meaning of Events in Southern Russia" was based upon the same values and conceptions that informed his views on socialism. The self-supply system was just as repugnant to him as a revolutionary "pogrom" and just as suicidal. From his point of view, a policy that permitted individuals to steal for their own needs under the protection of a collective sanction would, ultimately, fail to ensure the survival of the group. His memorandum exhibited as well the immense importance he attached to moral factors. In his perception of the military situation, there was a direct connection between the army's "spirit" and its fighting capability. Both the brigand mentality of the rank-and-file and the "military-bureaucratic" attitudes of the staff were responsible for the Volunteers' losses. A year later, in the emigration, Struve wrote that the Bolsheviks had been "psychologically" better prepared for civil war than the Volunteers. In order to win, the Whites would have had to become "real active revolutionaries."[144]

Struve concluded his 1920 memorandum with several suggestions for the anti-Bolshevik campaign: no outright break with the Cossacks, improved relations with the Allies, amnesty in the rear, legalization of the peasants' land acquisitions, abstention from politics, better material support for officers and soldiers.[145] His advice did not help Denikin, whose forces were decisively beaten in the winter of 1919–1920.

After Denikin's resignation in April 1920, Struve took an active and prominent role in the Crimean government of Baron Wrangel, the Volunteers' new commander-in-chief. As Wrangel's Minister for Foreign Affairs, he once again campaigned for European aid. Struve infuriated the British, who had decided that the civil war was finished, won official recognition of Wrangel's government from France, and, belatedly, concluded a costly and unconsummated arms agreement with the French government. He was abroad on November 1, 1920, when Wrangel was forced to evacuate the Crimea and the war between the Red and White armies came to an end.[146]

Struve: Searching for the Nation

The civil war was over, but not Struve's intellectual battle with the revolution. After the defeat of Wrangel's army released him from his short, improbable career as a foreign envoy, Struve focused his efforts once again on culture and philosophy. He reexamined the issues raised by the revolution in *Russkaia mysl'*, his former "thick journal," reborn in Sofia in February 1921.[147]

Struve's editorial in the inaugural edition of the revived *Russkaia mysl'* was addressed to both "old and new readers." Unlike the Mensheviks' appeal to the international family of socialists in *Sotsialisticheskii vestnik* or *Sovremennye zapiski*'s "nonparty" statement of a Socialist-Revolutionary position, *Russkaia mysl'* was to be free from "servility before political formulas and slogans, from the capitivity of party programs and platforms." Struve called instead for a thoughtful examination of the past. Russians had to have the "daring to look reality in the face" and to "try to comprehend for ourselves the misfortune and catastrophe that has befallen our country." Patriotic spirit was to provide the "courage" for dispassionate understanding, all the more important in the altered circumstances: "The more acute the crisis experienced by Russia, the deeper the fall that we have experienced, the more important and responsible is the work of Russian thought."[148]

As with Struve's critique of Denikin's army, this intellectual activity was to serve as a basis for renewed struggle. Careful thought, inspired by "great patriotic passion," would lead to "daring and firm action." Struve gave no indication of what he had in mind; he only hinted that the process of recovery would be lengthy.[149] In contrast to other émigrés, he did not appeal to foreigners for help or criticize the erstwhile Allies for their failure to carry on the war against the Bolsheviks. The revolution was a problem that Russians had to solve.

For Struve during his first years in emigration, the key problem was still socialism and its "contradictions." Three and a half years of Bolshevik rule gave him more evidence for his view that the revolution had "refuted" socialism. The theoretical conception of socialism, he noted in a speech to "representatives of Russian industry and trade," assembled in Paris in 1921, consisted of the "abolition of private property in the tools and means of production and the transfer of these to the whole society in the person of the state or other public unions." This was exactly what the Bolsheviks had claimed to do, and therefore it was fair to regard their "experiment" as a test of socialist theory.[150]

In his speech, written shortly after the announcement of NEP, Struve reviewed the results of this experiment. He divided Bolshevik industrial policy into two periods. The first stage was that of "forcible destruction of the bourgeois economy, . . . a Communist assault on that structure of economic and state relationships." At this time the Bolsheviks had consciously played on the anarchic and elemental instincts of the masses. The second stage was that of "forcible creation . . . the establishment of a new structure," and in this period, he felt, only the leaders of the party took an active role in shaping policy.[151] Both stages had been economically disastrous, and taken together, they demonstrated the unworkability of a socialist economy.

In the first stage of "workers' control" in 1917 and the beginning of 1918, the expropriation and direct exploitation of enterprises by their workers had rapidly convinced the authorities that workers' control was "either the anarchization of production to the benefit not of society but of more or less random groups or workers," or that it led "by a roundabout means to the reestablishment of the bourgeois economic structure." Thereafter, the state had tried to manage the economy directly. But despite this step toward centralized, socialist organization and despite the replacement of collective by one-man management, production kept falling.[152]

This outcome forced the Communist government to try two new approaches. One was the use of "bourgeois" methods such as piecework and a system of premiums, both of which went against the workers' demands for equalization of pay. At the same time, the Bolsheviks introduced the "militarization of labor." They increased the length of the working day, subjected workers to military discipline, and established a universal labor obligation. While the abrogation of workers' control had been necessary in order to obtain even "minimal" production, this centralist solution was constantly threatened by the "egalitarian pathos" of socialism, expressed in the workers' "reduction of their useful work to a minimum." Thus, once again, the Communist leaders had been forced to resort to "bourgeois" methods—unions for the workers and free trade for the peasants—in order to combat the "demoralization of labor." But these recent expedients would also be undermined by the basic contradictions of the system, Struve predicted. The unions could not be satisfying to the workers because they had been turned into organizations that were "compulsory and completely dependent on the government," and free trade for the peasants would not work because the city had nothing to sell to the country.[153] The final stage of "bourgeois expedients" was reached when the Soviet government had to call in foreigners to replace the native bourgeoisie it had eradicated. This Struve interpreted as a sign of the "deep cynicism" and "extreme weakness" of the regime:

> It cannot, because of political and police considerations dictated by the instinct of self-preservation, admit a national bourgeoisie to economic work on a healthy basis in the country, but it is forced by its economic bankruptcy to seek help from the foreign bourgeoisie. . . . This is a policy of national betrayal: the cynical betrayal of the national principle and national dignity and the equally cynical betrayal of the socialist ideal.[154]

The results of the Bolsheviks' various attempts to run the economy were clear—"an immense economic reaction." The first and most fundamental indication of the catastrophe was demographic. The "dying out of the population, based primarily on the terrible increase in mortality" was the "basic fact of Soviet economics and demography." In the cities people were dying of starvation; in the country from inadequate sanitation.[155] (This was written before the news of the impending famine reached the West. When Struve heard about the disaster, he wrote that it was all the more tragic in that the masses, not those in charge, would pay for their leaders' mistakes.)[156]

A second consequence of the Bolsheviks' policies was the return to a "natural economy." As production in the city ceased, the urban population fled. With the economic links between the city and the country destroyed, the cities became parasitic centers of consumption. The only productive organizations to survive this collapse were "primitive" enterprises that had not been nationalized. As a result, Russia was returning to handicraft manufacture (*okustarenie*). The replacement of mineral fuels with wood was another sign of this economic regression; the Russian metallurgical industry had been set back to the 1870s. In every area of the economy, except the writing of orders and the printing of money, there had been a "terrible qualitative reduction and technical degradation of production, based on the extreme demoralization of labor and the fall in individual productivity of the worker."[157]

At the same time that handicraft production was reviving, other enterprises were being forced into larger and larger conglomerates in the interests of centralization. The interesting fact here, Struve noted, was that while such combinations arose in capitalist societies because of the pressures of unlimited production, in Russia they were formed in conditions of scarcity, to compensate for the lack of raw materials, labor, fuel, and supply networks. The Communist economy in this respect stemmed from so-called "war socialism," the centralist policies adopted to regulate production and distribution when commodities were in short supply, and not from the "scientific socialism of Marx" that was to arise in conditions of abundance.[158]

But while Struve attributed this development ot the legacy of the war, he blamed the collapse of the economy upon the Soviet authorities. The war, he thought, had increased the "productive energies" of the country, even if for "nonproductive" ends, while Bolshevik rule had produced an "economic void." The Bolsheviks' had replaced capitalism with a "parasitic-predatory economy" that lived on goods accumulated in the past. Now these goods had been consumed, and this accounted for the extreme crisis of 1921.[159]

In Struve's analysis, this economic catastrophe had only one parallel in history—the decline of imperial Rome. Then, as now, the "fundamental characteristic of the . . . economic situation was a natural-economic reaction," and, in both cases, the "citizens had been enserfed to the state." The policies of the Roman leaders, like those of the Bolsheviks, bore witness to the " 'madness of power'," Struve noted, only "the Communist madness of the Moscow authorities differed from the madness of the Roman empire in that in the former, as in Hamlet's madness, there was a system."[160] The system of course, was Struve's bugbear—socialism with its insurmountable contradictions.

Struve's 1921 speech summed up his case against socialism as an economic system. The transfer of property to the state was the legal expression of socialism's egalitarian and distributive ideal—the only ideal that appealed to the masses—but the state, once in control of the economic mechanism, found itself unable to produce goods to distribute. It then resorted to "bourgeois" methods, which negated its egalitarian goals. Thus a socialist economy was doomed either to regression, on the basis of its egalitarian principle, or to bourgeoisification, in which case it ceased to be socialist. This was Russia's lesson, demonstrated in practice: "The Russian experience has shown with full clarity, at the cost of terrible suffering, . . . the living tragedy of socialism."[161]

After this sweeping refutation of socialist economics, no one, Struve felt, could believe in Marxism as a feasible, scientific system. Marxism as a "structure," he wrote later in the year, had been relegated to history, where it belonged to the "conservatively historical soil from which it had arisen like a strange revolutionary offshoot, sometime in the epoch of reaction against the French revolution." What remained in the present was a "revolutionary phrase that had lost its ideas and its wings, a phrase that could be believed only by those who had forgotten what they had learned or who had never learned to think scientifically."[162] The most interesting aspect of Marxism in the future, Struve predicted, would be its role as a "psychological and moral postulate" within bourgeois, not socialist, societies. The class struggle depended on the existence and psychology of classes, and, therefore, Marxism was most viable in the West, as an ideology for the social democratic parties.[163]

In Russia all that remained of socialism was the political authority of the Soviet government. There, according to Struve, the rulers had reversed the relationship of economics to politics. The Bolsheviks had seized power in order to restructure the economy. This they then destroyed, while simultaneously creating a powerful political organization. Now, in order to maintain its control, the government could not change its economic policies. The destruction of economic freedom and of personal and property rights of the city population was both a cause of Russia's economic decline and a "necessary condition of the *political* control of the Communist Party." There was no question in Struve's mind about the priorities of the Soviet regime—control came first. "For the Soviet authorities, the Communist policy of welfare had been turned into a policy of security." Any real "evolution" in this system would have to affect both economics and politics; it would be the "condition and signal for a revolt against Bolshevism."[164]

The outcome of the Russian "experiment," with its "unprecedented degree of general political oppression," recalled the lessons of another era to Struve. The eighteenth century had taught and the French revolution had established, he insisted, "that the right of property and the economic freedom of the individual [was] an essential component and at the same time the main guarantee of personal freedom." It was "not in vain" that the Declaration of Rights of Man and the Citizen had included the right of property and that the essential idea of the "truly great revolution" had been "economic liberty." The importance of these values had been demonstrated by the Russian tragedy.[165]

Struve's discussion of the French revolution points to one change in his analysis of the Russian experience since 1917. Earlier he had predicted that the revolution would lead ultimately to the establishment of private ownership and that the peasants' confiscations expressed their striving for property in land. His recommendations to Wrangel had been based on this assumption, calling for the "resolution of the land question on the bases of the consolidation of peasant property and the greatest possible legalization of the *de facto* state of affairs where land is concerned.''[166] But by 1921, Struve had changed his mind. The history of the countryside since 1917 had convinced him that the peasants lacked the "spirit of property" and did not seem likely to develop an interest in it soon. To Struve, this was one more consequence of Russia's deformed—non-Western—past. Over centuries, Russian agriculture had developed the "peasant allotment," not "peasant property," as its fundamental principle. The reforms of the prerevolutionary period had come too late; those peasants who had acquired landed property had been "swept away" by the revolution. In this sense, the revolution had not been, as the left would have it, an attack on "feudalism." For one thing, the serfs had been emancipated earlier, but more significantly, the revolution had replaced one kind of common property with another, before private property attitudes had developed.[167]

This observation, and not his prediction of "bourgeois revolution" in 1917, was consistent with Struve's general perspective on social change. Ever since 1899, when he began his critical reexamination of Marxism, he had been convinced that revolutions—political revolutions—could not accomplish fundamental social transformations.[168] His argument then and later was that if social change were to be full and thoroughgoing, it would have to take place slowly. A seizure of power, a dictatorship of the proletariat, would never in itself accomplish the transition from capitalism to socialism. This perspective was one that some Russian socialists articulated after 1917, a shift that Struve welcomed. Commenting favorably on one of Stepan Ivanovich's articles, Struve reiterated what he had written twenty-three years earlier: The dictatorship of the proletariat was "either completely superfluous or more than insufficient" for the transformation of society, and "the greater the distance that separates society from socialism, the less one can imagine that the forceful means of 'dictatorship' would be capable of eliminating the immaturity for socialism." The results of the revolution only confirmed what he had postulated so long ago.[169]

Struve's developing perspective on the Russian experience recapitulated not only his turn away from revolutionary politics but also his gradual transformation from a socialist to a religious person. Again, this fundamental change had been completed well before 1917, but the revolution had sparked old determinist hopes—as in his initial notion that it would lead to private property—and then forced him to defend and reconfirm his more fully developed values. While even Struve's earliest writings on the revolution were infused with his spiritual commitments, with time, this aspect of his interpretation became more pronounced.

For Struve, the catastrophic results of the revolution were material proof that the idea of progress did not explain human history. Russians "had to have the courage to confess that progress was not at all obligatory for mankind, that evil is the same type of independent real principle in the life of the cosmos and of mankind as is good, that God and the devil were fighting over man in humanity and in history."[170] These forces were at work in the revolution, and toward the revolution one had to take a moral position.[171] Had it been for good or evil?

To Struve, the revolution was an integral phenomenon that combined both "moral-cultural" and "political" dimensions. He demanded that it be judged in its totality, as a "single process," which one had to "accept or reject *spiritually*."[172] His articles in *Russkaia mysl'* were aimed at countering the tendencies of other Russians to "accept" the revolution in one way or another, while criticizing aspects of it. Most left-leaning intellectuals, for example, defended the "conquests of February," and many social democrats, like Martov, regarded the October revolution as progressive, but for its Bolshevik distortions. From Struve's perspective, these attitudes were repugnant: "For me," he wrote in 1922, "the idealization of the revolution accomplished in 1917 is, religiously, a moral lie and, at the same time, historically, a factual untruth, self-deception, and deception."[173] Such "dangerous political romanticism" obscured the real human costs of the past five years and prevented a recovery in the future.[174]

No matter what its ideals had been, the revolution "had been in essence the destruction and degradation of all the forces, material and spiritual, of the people," a "decline in culture" unprecedented in human history.[175] What had it achieved?

> Had the confiscation of the landlords' lands and the ruin of the landlords' economy been worth the death by starvation of many millions of peasants and the return in the end to the greatest, but culturally completely futile, inequality? Had it been worth taking the factories and chasing out their owners in order once again to implant capitalism in a economic void, where some workers had died and from which others had fled, and to breed a new bourgeoisie from the "not-finished-off bourgeois" and the new "Sovbourg [Soviet bourgeois]" . . . ?[176]

There were no conquests of the revolution except death and destruction.

Moreover, Struve felt that the revolution had been evil in its essence, and that this was in large part due to Lenin's leadership. Having known Lenin for twenty-five years and worked closely with him in the early years of Russian social democracy, Struve considered him the " 'representative man' of Bolshevism." The spirit of "malice" that nourished the doctrine of class struggle was "in harmony with . . . [Lenin's] whole being," Struve commented. It was this personal malice that made Lenin totally indifferent to moral criteria and allowed him "consciously" and " 'with pleasure' " to awaken the "ferocity of the savage masses." Lenin's realization that primitive conditions provided the ideal conditions for class war was the "secret of his success" and the "proof of his genuis, if one can speak of a genius of malevolence." The tortures and cruelty of the recent past were not "excesses of Bolshevism but its living historical essence," direct consequences of Lenin's calculated exploitation of barbarism. Lenin was a "theoretician and an idealist of the purest type," but his triumph required more than dogmatism. In it one could see the "cynicism and the genius of the executioner." It was Lenin's ascetic executioner's spirit that had repulsed other socialist leaders in the past, and it was the amoral "genius of the executioner" that allowed him to become the "vivisector of his own people."[177]

To Struve, repudiation of the revolution conducted in Lenin's spirit was the first step toward a Russian "renaissance," a moral and cultural revival that alone could reshape the nation's future. What was needed was not "institutions and forms," but a "rebirth of the national spirit." As before in *Iz glubiny*, Struve called in *Russkaia mysl'* for the "cult and idealization" of Russia's past as the basis for this recovery. "Purely political problems" could be discussed after the "Russian people return once more in spirit to the country of their fathers." They would thus be "purified, liberated by suffering from that spite and malice, godlessness and unbelief, baseness and banality that the Soviet authorities had instilled by violent bureaucratic means in the Russian people and aroused in them."[178]

This assessment of the people's values shows that Struve shared, to some extent, the populist conceptions so common among the Russian intellectuals. Although much of his critique of socialism had been based upon the negative egalitarianism and destructive actions of the "savage masses," he often made statements, like the one above, that blamed Bolshevism for these developments. In his analyses, the people were at some times the makers of the revolution and at others its victims. Philosophically, Struve reconciled these two attitudes by separating them. A rigorous Kantian,[179] he insisted that empirical and metaphysical conceptions should not be confused. Empirically, the "people" meant simply the majority; in this sense, he considered it "blindness to deny that Bolshevism had a certain popular character [*narodnost'*]." In its reflection of mass attitudes, Bolshevism was as "popular [*narodnyi*]" as swearing, he commented. But at the same time, Struve saw the people as a metaphysical ideal, a possibility, and this allowed him to believe in their capacity to overcome Bolshevism and their own imperfections.[180]

Struve's first loyalty was not to the wishes of the majority. "To bow at any given moment before all that triumphs or even simply happens today and to draw from that fact a norm of behavior" was a positivist perversion of ethics. While objective observations provided the foundation for understanding and analysis, they could never become the source of goals and values. What Struve called *faktopoklonstvo*—bowing before the facts—led straight to an acceptance of the revolution because it had taken place and to an acceptance of the Russian people as they were. From his perspective, these attitudes were morally repugnant. The revolution had to be seen not as a fact, but as a crime against the Russian people, against their existence and their spirit. Thus positivists, whose values were confined and determined by what had happened, were guilty of a "lack of confidence" in the Russian people, while he and others who believed in the "metaphysical people, . . . the national spirit expressing itself in genuine and stable thoughts and creations" had an ideal for which they could strive and which affirmed the people's strength and virtue.[181]

The views of Mark Vishniak could serve to illustrate Struve's argument. Vishniak's pessimism about the Russian people—about their commitment to the democratic institutions he valued—was the result of his unusually persistent attempt to confront reality. But from Struve's point of view, Vishniak's commentaries would demonstrate not only his "courage" to see the objective truth, but also the historical dead end to which an atheistic perception led. Vishniak, by following facts alone, had nothing to hope for.

To Struve, it was the spiritual dimension of the revolution that was most meaningful in the long run. He saw the "historical enigma" posed by the revolution as a contest between two attitudes toward life: the religious consciousness, which expressed the idea of the nation as a "collective individuality [*sobornaia individual'nost'*]" that united individuals "organically and lovingly" in a "holy calling [*Bozh'e prizvanie*]", and the anti-religious consciousness, which rested on the "pathos" of "freethinking" along the line of Owen, Bentham, Marx, and Engels. The revolution, he wrote in March 1922, was the "historical confrontation of these two bodies of spiritual thought [*dukhovnye soderzhaniia*] and the struggle of political ideals and social strivings in it is, in a certain cultural-philosophical sense, only the superficial expression and reflection of this deep spiritual confrontation." This struggle, whose depth now was only "vaguely felt," was not over. It was "approaching" its second stage, when spiritual forces would revive. In this new era, Struve felt, the Russian emigration could make its contribution to the nation. The "significance" of the emigration was "almost exclusively spiritual and as such it will count in Russia in the future, when the political struggle in its contemporary forms will move into the background, and social relations will solidify."[182]

Struve's call for spiritual renewal, for the "idealization" of Russia's past, and for a metaphysical faith in the Russian people can be seen as another variant of the ideological escapism so common among the intellectuals in the emigration. But his religious nationalism differed fundamentally from Chernov's "third force," Martov's trust in the working class, and Kropotkin's faith in the cooperative movement. Struve acknowledged the transcendental nature of his hopes. He did not imagine that the Russian people or the proletariat or history sanctioned his ideals; these were the product of his own moral and religious understanding. From his perspective, it was the materialists who were the escapists. Their insistence on founding their essentially moral judgments on experience alone led to self-deception. In order to retain their optimism about the future, they had frequently to violate their empirical principles. Bad but accomplished facts could be ignored or idealized, but not confronted honestly.

Struve kept trying in the emigration to cure the intelligentsia of what he regarded as its philosophical shallowness. Despite his bad repute with the Russian left, he argued seriously and eloquently in *Russkaia mysl'* against the many varieties of intelligentsia positivism.[183] He demanded, as he had in *Vekhi* in 1909, that intellectuals realize that transcendental dualism—the distinction between the material world and the realm of values—was not only philosophically sound, but also that it was the only perspective from which one could hope to overcome the debacle of the revolution. How else could Russians break into the cycle of destruction and disintegration he had described but with the spirit? Struve's Kantian point of view was not that the material and spiritual realms were inaccessible to each other, but that reason informed them both. Reason required an objective evaluation of the revolution's results and an examination of the basis of one's ideals. Both would lead to affirmation of the religious principle.

Was Struve still a liberal? As Richard Pipes has argued, Struve continued throughout his life to blame the revolution upon the Russian state.[184] In Struve's interpretation, the autocracy had set in motion, or, more precisely, had attempted to confine, the forces of Russian history in such a way that a catastrophic explosion became inevitable. This focus on the state, like his commitment to private property, remained unchanged after 1917. Nevertheless, Struve's explicit subordination of institutional reform and "politics" to spiritual rebirth was hardly in the spirit of Russian liberalism. When he wrote that "purely political programs" could wait or that "the establishment of institutions and forms" was not an essential task,[185] he was taking long steps away from notions that had guided liberals in the past. To be sure, much of Struve's criticism of "politics" was directed against the endless and useless party squabbles of the emigration, but the primacy he accorded to ideals could lead to the disregard for other people's values that characterized so many of the intellectuals. Struve's views on popular elections betrayed his willful subjectivity: "Elections signify the opinion and will of the people only at a given moment and one can give them significance for the determination of the real and stable thoughts of the people only with the greatest caution."[186] Vishniak's straightforward commitment to the rule of the majority was a much more democratic sentiment.

One might conclude that Vishniak, the moderate Socialist Revolutionary, was a more consistent liberal than Struve, and that Struve's conservative liberalism was infused with the moralistic populism typical of the Russian left. Struve, however, would not have accepted the latter judgment. His commitment, he claimed, was fundamentally different from that of the socialists, because their empiricism deprived them of a true ethics. Struve was not referring to the evils of pragmatic—"the ends justifies the means"—thinking. He ruled out socialism as a moral philosophy because of the anti-religious ideas on which it was based. These, according to Struve, were the assumptions, first, that "each person is the product of society, its condition, and its structure, which totally determines his behavior," and, second, that "all evil, individual and societal, springs not from the sinful will of man, but from the mistakes and insufficiencies of the social structure." It followed from these ideas that "man was not responsible for his acts and that all the attention of humanity had to be directed to the changing of the social structure, which would then automatically eliminate sinfulness and vice." These ideas, Struve asserted, were antithetical to the religious consciousness. It demanded instead that individuals be personally responsible for themselves and for the world; it considered life to be founded upon the "internal perfection of the human individual." Socialism, with its deterministic ideology, denied the value of personal self-improvement and thus "undercut the deepest root of true religious life."[187]

The only socialist systems that could accurately be described as religious were those, such as early Christian communism or Tolstoyanism, that regarded religion as "their highest sanction," wrote Struve in 1922. Modern socialism, in his view, tried to be both an all-encompassing philosophical system and an economic theory subject to scientific proof. In practice, he observed, socialism functioned as a "secular social and political mythology," interpreted at will "according to the temperament and milieu of its representatives." It could be thought of as "religion or science or technology, but was not any one of these." Struve insisted that socialists could not have it both ways. If socialism was a religious system of belief, it had to give up its claim to scientific verification; on the other hand, to retain its basis in science, socialism would have to be confined to the "modest realm of the scientific technical problem of the economic and social structuring of society." Since he had already eliminated the religious interpretation—a judgment with which most socialists would have concurred—Struve demanded that socialism be considered as a theory of social organization and that, as such, it be subjected to scientific criticism. This brought him back to his chosen battle: "If socialism cannot stand up to such criticism, then that will be proof that we have before us a product of social mythology, a unique phenomenon in individual and collective psychology, born from the most recent conditions of economic and social life and by them, perhaps, likewise condemned to extinction."[188]

Perhaps. Struve, with his sensitivity to psychological needs and his belief in spiritual values, was well aware that the power of ideas did not depend upon their scientific strengths. His own writings displayed major inconsistencies. Had the people been corrupted by the Bolsheviks, were they "poisoned" earlier by the intelligentsia, or were they driven by "anarchic and elemental" instincts? Could the Russian past become a spiritual inspiration when it had led inexorably to national self-destruction? If the evil was in people, why should they change now?

The larger moral problems could be "solved," or at least addressed, by Struve's transcendental metaphysics—he believed that through their efforts and ideals individuals could change themselves and their surroundings for the better. On "scientific" grounds, however, his findings—vivid expressions of a complex individual and of the possibilities and limits of his situation—were inconclusive. Struve had no ideological plan for Russia's future; but he knew, he thought, what had gone wrong before 1917 and since. His writings, for all their lack of system, showed a steady development of two lines of thought. The revolution, in his analysis, was a tragic product of Russia's non-Western history. Its roots lay in the eighteenth century, in a regressive division of powers between the autocracy and the landed classes. In the shorter term, the revolution resulted from the intelligentsia's rebellion against the state, expressed in socialist ideology and fused with the negative egalitarianism of the masses. Struve's second inquiry concerned the results of the Bolshevik "experiment." To him, the contradictions of the new government's policies as well as the death and destruction they had caused demonstrated what he had discovered theoretically many years before—socialism as an economic system did not work.

Miliukov: "The Birth of Russian Democracy"

Struve's critique of the revolution developed over time on the basis of fixed assumptions and in one direction. The years only added evidence to his case against socialism and reinforced his call for patriotic idealism. To Miliukov, on the other hand, time brought change. Eventually, he bowed before some facts.

This transformation began in 1920, a dismal time for Miliukov and the liberal émigrés in London. The year witnessed the end of British support for military efforts against the Bolshevik government and the subsequent defeat of the White armies. The connection between these developments was especially depressing for Miliukov. In his opinion, the British had been instrumental in terminating the civil war.[189]

Miliukov responded to these disappointments with his usual resilience, intellectual flexibility and, finally, renewed optimism. The year of Denikin's defeat closed with another of Miliukov's startling reversals of position. This one was more thoroughgoing than his shift to the Germans and back in 1918, when his concerns had been strategic. Now, in 1920, he changed his estimation of the Allies, the armed struggle, the Russian people, the role of the emigration, and the meaning of the Russian revolution. The single constant that remained was his hostility to the Bolsheviks.

The most decisive setback to Miliukov's earlier calculations was the collapse of Denikin's army after the failure of the 1919 drive against Moscow. In London, the severity of this defeat became apparent in the winter of 1919–1920. Miliukov's first reaction was to intensify his efforts to sway British opinion to the anti-Bolshevik side. On February 5, 1920, the Russian Liberation Committee replaced its *Bulletin* with *The New Russia*, a journal devoted to Russian politics along the lines of its mottos—"No Compromise with Bolshevism" and "Russia United and Free." Miliukov, the editor, wrote a regular "Review of the Week" in this publication. The first question he raised was, should these slogans be changed?[190]

The answer was no. No compromise with Bolshevism was possible because the "final failure of Bolshevism is inevitable." Russian unity, too, could be regained: "We know of no real national interests of the peoples inhabiting Russia which could not be reasonably satisfied without destroying the unity of Russia." Anti-Bolshevism and Russian nationalism were compatible goals, and the first step toward serving both causes was to discover why the Volunteer Army had failed.[191]

The idea of investigating the "mistakes" of the military authorities had a familiar ring. This was Miliukov the pragmatic critic holding the "real politician[s] responsible for [their] mistakes." His analysis, formulated in the first half of 1920, blamed the army's losses on two groups of politicians—the Volunteer Army's civilian administrators and the British government. In addition, as in his *History of the Second Russian Revolution*, Miliukov stressed the attitudes of the masses as a decisive force. This time, however, Miliukov put himself on the people's side.

The "facts" of Miliukov's investigation in *The New Russia* were drawn from sources inside Russia. The most important of these were a "Secret Report to General Denikin," written by an unidentified observer who had lived in Northern Russia before joining the Volunteers,[192] and Struve's memorandum "The Meaning of Events in Southern Russia," although Miliukov did not acknowledge this connection at the time.[193] Miliukov repeated most of Struve's observations: the poor quality of the troops, their lack of discipline, the looting—"almost a profession with a self-supporting army," the unreliability of the Cossacks. In addition, however, he stressed the demoralizing conduct of the administrators who followed in the army's wake. Although the population on the territories formerly under Bolshevik control welcomed the Whites as liberators, the enthusiasm for these saviors was short lived. This was because the Volunteer Army put former officials and landlords back in power. These people, associated in the minds of the local population with the corruption and inequity of the old regime, generally justified their reputations. The Volunteer Army spurned the services of the local intelligentsia—teachers, zemstvo officials, organizers of the cooperatives—and this policy contributed to the population's refusal to support the military.[194]

Miliukov's description of the "passive" attitude of the population, although it repeated Struve's observation, took on a radically different significance. By characterizing the war as one "between two minorities," Struve had pointed to the fact that the outcome depended on the qualitative superiority of one army or the other. Miliukov's discussion debased the contest altogether, on the grounds that it did not involve the population. "Such passive resistance to both sides," he wrote in April 1920, "completely eliminates the population as a factor of the active struggle, and makes it a silent and patient witness of the conflict of minorities.''[195] ''Patient'' is the key word here; it indicates that Miliukov's evolution toward populism was already under way.

In Miliukov's view, the people at fault for this passivity were not the masses, not the ''demoralized'' combatants, and not Denikin—''circumstances . . . were stronger than the individual will of one man''—but the army's Political Council and, especially, the *Velikaia Rossiia* group.[196] Miliukov here singled out those political figures, among them Struve, who had supported the Volunteer Army since the beginning, consistently following the course of force and authority that Miliukov had recommended in his *History*. He, too, had been one of the original members of the Political Council, but he had left it, as he had the Provisional Government, for the role of independent advisor, with ''free hands.'' He was not about to take the blame now, and regretted only that he had been too easy on those who had remained to serve. ''All this,'' he explained in *The New Russia*,

> was tolerated by those who saw more clearly out of a feeling of responsibility for the stability of the only existing power, and in the hope that this power would be sufficiently strong to win a purely military victory, after which a more normal political course would become possible. Now that all hopes of military success have proved illusory, many politicians must be bitterly regretful of having irretrievably lost their opportunity and of having shown too much pliability and reserve.[197]

He had missed an opportunity, but others, who acted, were to blame. This censure of the surrogate state—the politicians of the Volunteer Army—combined with Miliukov's exoneration of himself and of the people, indicated the extent to which Miliukov, for all his political aspirations, had retreated to the role of moral critic.

Miliukov felt betrayed by more than one government. Both after Denikin's resignation and after Wrangel's defeat, he put a large share of blame upon the Allies, especially the British. They had worked to end the civil war, first by pushing Denikin to negotiate with the Bolsheviks[198]—he resigned instead—and later by mediating in the Polish war. As Miliukov pointed out in *The New Russia*, an armistice between the Polish forces and the Bolsheviks could only free the Red Army to attack Wrangel.[199] He found both British enthusiasm for trade with the Bolshevik government and the ease with which Soviet negotiators took advantage of their Western hosts offensive. Throughout 1920 he fulminated against the ignorance and perfidy of the British, who seemed to have chosen the ''doubtful and illusory'' benefits proffered by the Bolsheviks to helping their friends who had fought for a common cause in the World War.

Although Miliukov supported Wrangel loyally in *The New Russia* and even defended Struve's credentials as a representative of the Russian government,[200] he began as early as April 1920 to formulate an alternative to the authority of the Volunteer Army. Until this time, he had described the army as the bearer of legitimate power in Russia; after its failure he began to reconsider:

There is no need to dwell upon the importance we attribute to the rightful succession of power in Russia and to the preservation of this rightful succession in the future. But it is now more than difficult to follow the old lines of merely approving everything this rightful power undertakes. A necessity had now arisen, greater than ever, to analyse the situation collectively and anew, to *revise* the programme of resistance.[201]

The revision was to be made by representatives of Russian society, in particular, by the Russian emigration. The raison d'être of the émigrés, Miliukov asserted, was politics; their position was analogous to that of the "émigrés who sought safety abroad from the persecution of the old regime." Like them, Russians in Europe were to cooperate with their "friends in Russia," against the "new autocracy of Lenin." The new regime, "like the old one, admits of no open political constitutional opposition," and therefore, Miliukov reasoned, "the war of ideas, necessarily in the nature of a conspiracy, must . . . be waged abroad." The émigrés' "obligation to their country" required "their taking part in the common work of Russian political thought."[202]

This analogy made explicit Miliukov's return to old regime traditions. The Duma period, with its complexities, had vanished altogether, as Miliukov recalled the simplicities of the struggle against tsarism before 1905. He collapsed Russian history into a series of synchronic oppositions: society against the state, the emigration against the domestic regime, thought against oppression.

In the light of Miliukov's revised opinion of the British, it is not surprising that he chose France as the base for his new political efforts.[203] Although he continued to write weekly for *The New Russia*, in the spring of 1920 he began to participate in meetings of Russian liberals in Paris.[204] The lengthy sessions of the "Paris Group of the Constitutional Democratic Party" recall the party congresses of the Mensheviks and the Socialist Revolutionaries at the close of 1917. The Kadets were preoccupied by the same two goals that the socialists had pursued before them—condemnation of the Bolsheviks and criticism of their own party's failed policies—with the important difference that the Kadets did not face defeat until 1920. In the liberals' eyes, Russian socialism was responsible for the Bolsheviks' seizure of power, while their own party was inculpated by the losses of the military opposition. Under Miliukov's guidance, the Paris Kadets attributed the defeats of the anti-Bolshevik armies "to a series of grave mistakes, not only of a military, but essentially of a political character" and proposed a program of reforms to Wrangel.[205]

The Kadets' correctives, adopted by the group on May 20, 1920, called for granting the peasants property rights over land they occupied, inviting the local population to take part in government, reestablishing free market relations, negotiating a "new and decentralized form of government" with the border states, and strict observation of civil liberties.[206] A program similar to this one had in fact already been adopted by Wrangel's government, a step that Miliukov praised in *The New Russia* and cited as evidence that "the lessons of the past have been useful.'' He mentioned that the Paris Group had identified the Whites' mistakes and ''the means of avoiding them in the future,'' but made no attempt to associate his group with Wrangel or his advisers.[207]

The discussions of the Paris Kadets laid the basis for Miliukov's activities after the civil war was over. Four weeks after the evacuation of Wrangel's forces from the Crimea, he closed *The New Russia* and gave his full attention to émigré politics in the French capital.[208] His first advice to the liberals there was that the struggle against Bolshevism would have to be entirely transformed. Miliukov's plan, adopted by the Paris Group on December 21, 1920, became known as his ''New Tactic.''[209]

The program Miliukov proposed to the Paris Kadets had four elements: no revival of the armed opposition to Bolshevism by remnants of the evacuated army; the transfer of the leadership of the anti-Bolshevik opposition to the ''foreign centers of the party [and] those elements within the country whom the worker and peasant masses, dispossessed by the Bolsheviks, will follow''; the adoption by the Kadet party of specific positions on the land, national, and constitutional questions without waiting for a revived Constituent Assembly; and a focus on the ''new social structure'' that had emerged in Russia during the course of the revolution.[210]

The ideas behind these proposals were ones that Miliukov had put forward over the past year. The negative program—the rejection of the Volunteer Army and its political leaders—had been articulated in *The New Russia* by April; ''four fatal political mistakes'' attributed to Denikin's staff were identical to the May 20 resolution of the Paris Kadets.[211] The idea of moving the anti-Bolshevik struggle abroad had also been proposed in the spring of 1920.[212] Miliukov supplemented these reappraisals with more criticism of Wrangel's administration—''left tactics by right hands''[213]—an indictment that differed from the earlier ones only in its harsher tone.

The more startling points of Miliukov's New Tactic were the positive ones, in particular his emphasis on the ''worker and peasant masses'' and the ''new social structure.'' The ''patient'' masses who had refused to support the Whites now became the core of Miliukov's program for the future. ''New strata and attitudes have come forward, to which careful attention must be paid, for in them is the pledge of our rebirth,'' he wrote in his proposal.[214] The people, hovering in the wings of *The History of the Second Russian Revolution*, had now moved to center stage.

Miliukov elaborated upon his new conception of the masses in an introduction to the *History*, which he was preparing for publication once again, this time successfully. Dated December 27, 1920, the introduction testified to the profound shift in his analysis:

> If the role of the leaders in the events appears less active, then at the same time the common notion concerning the passive role of the inert masses must also be firmly corrected. The mass of the Russian population, it seems, in fact only

had been *patient*. In the first chapter of the *History* we pointed to the reasons for this passivity, rooted in our past. But now surveying the whole process in its different phases, we begin to arrive at the conclusion that the patience of the masses, all the same, was not completely passive. The masses took from the revolution those things that corresponded to their desires, but immediately set up an iron wall of passive resistance as soon as they began to suspect that events were not leading in the direction of their interests.[215]

Ultimately, the "collective popular wisdom . . . expressed in this behavior of the inert, ignorant and downtrodden masses" solved the problem that was most essential for the people—the "land question." This achievement indicated to Miliukov that the people had learned from the revolution. Even though Russia had been "thrown back from the twentieth century to the seventeenth," "its economy and civilization ruined," "whole classes" destroyed, and its cultural tradition "interrupted," the "people have passed into a new life, enriched by the fund of new experience." Their choices would be decisive in the future, and it was for their sake that the Russian émigrés had to take a "new path."[216]

Miliukov counted on the people to do more than hold on to their property. In a speech given in London on November 30, 1920, he predicted that the Russian people, having achieved their first aim, would go on to appreciate science, enjoy the arts, and reconstruct the government:

> There are signs—and they will increase in number—that the great shock given by history is now operating a great change in the people's mind. Tolstoy's people [the peasants] seem to have learnt from dire experience what ignorance and destruction of state really mean. This people now wants to learn and to know. They already begin to value the art and culture of the cities. We can be sure that the time is not far when the people will become active in rebuilding the state.[217]

With the extravagant, but familiar, assumption that the people would accomplish his own goals, Miliukov completed his populist permutation. His new approach was very similar to that of the Socialist Revolutionaries—in tactics, psychology, and, partially, in content. Like the SRs, he now considered the land the central question of the revolution. In this respect, he was moving in the opposite direction from Struve, who became less sure that the land question had been settled in favor of peasant property as time went on. Just as the SRs in 1918 had continued to act as if the Constituent Assembly were extant, Miliukov now asked the Kadets to behave as if a liberal constitution were in the making. The party would set forth its platform on the land and the form of state; then the people would decide. The Kadets' program was to be a demonstration of their good faith: "It is necessary to take up a definite position so that the country will know where they want to lead her."[218]

The resemblance to the Socialist Revolutionary position was not coincidental. As early as April 1920 Miliukov had taken an interest in the activities of the

SRs in Paris. At his urging, the Paris Group of Kadets decided to cooperate with the Socialist Revolutionaries in the emigration.[219] Their major joint endeavor was the Conference of Members of the Constituent Assembly, held in Paris in January 1921.[220]

Undeterred by the failure of this meeting to produce a working coalition, Miliukov turned to journalism once again. On March 1, 1921, he took over the editorship of *Poslednie novosti* (The Latest News), the foremost Russian newspaper abroad.[221] As he had done with *Rech'* before the revolution, Miliukov used *Poslednie novosti* to promote his own positions.[222] His first editorial pronounced the major lesson of the recent past:

> It is necessary, finally to recognize—and this is the main conclusion of the whole sad experience—that the Russian people is not an inert mass, on which it is possible to perform one or another experiment of liberation and that it wants to be liberated in its own way.[223]

This perspective seemed to leave the emigration little choice but to step aside from politics altogether. But Miliukov thought his newspaper could be of help. In an article concerning the Germans' financial aid to the Bolsheviks in 1917, he suggested that the exposé of Lenin's treachery would be useful to the Russian people: "But Lenin has not yet fallen, and an acquaintance with these documents can create among the popular masses deceived by him the same impression that information much weaker in substance made upon the Petrograd garrison during the July Days of 1917."[224]

How these facts were to reach the Russian people Miliukov did not explain. But apart from the implicit suggestion that his Parisian newspaper would enlighten the popular consciousness, Miliukov's old emphasis on authority and leadership was gone. Justifying his turn toward the Socialist Revolutionaries, he admonished the Kadets to pay attention to the "following historical paradox":

> The SRs in fact began to lose their influence on the masses exactly at the point when they became more reasonable and, having been taught by experience in government and proximity to power, they tried to make truly statesmanslike [*istinno-gosudarstvennye*] "Kadet-type" speeches. Who is to blame for this coincidence?[225]

Although Miliukov had pledged in December 1920 that the "battle against Bolshevism" had to be "continued until the liberation from the Bolshevik yoke,"[226] his program lacked any practical steps toward this goal. With his New Tactic, he left the terrain of pragmatic strategy he had covered so extensively in the past three years and entered the realm of wishful, and often spiteful, thinking. His proposals were not so much plans as dreams and criticisms. To the extent that it reflected the real distribution of force in Russia, the New Tactic was sound, but its timing—just after Wrangel's defeat—and the political censure upon which it was based struck other Russian liberals as callous and vindictive. Within six months after Miliukov's proposal, the Kadet party broke up along ideological lines. Miliukov, defeated at a party congress, seceded with his left-wing Parisian followers; the party majority found a center in V. D. Nabokov's Berlin newspaper *Rul'* (The Rudder); Prince Pavel Dolgorukov left the Central Committee to devote his time to the Volunteer Army.[227] In June 1921 Struve joined Nabokov, Dolgorukov, and other moderates in Paris at a Russian "National Congress," an attempt to unite the liberal emigration around a centrist program of constitutional monarchy and social reform. This gathering included a broader spectrum of Russian political figures than had the Conference of Members of the Constituent Assembly, but its impact on Russia was equally insignificant.[228] The raison d'être of the Kadet party—its integrative function—whatever its inadequacies in Russia, was meaningless abroad.

After the party schism, Miliukov was invited to present a series of lectures on Russia at the Lowell Institute in Boston. He accepted with enthusiasm because, in his words, "by this time I had come to a definite conclusion as to the meaning and the place of the Russian events of the past four years in the history of our revolution." The Lowell lectures, delivered in October and November 1921, and several other speeches given in the United States were the basis for Miliukov's third book on the revolution.[229] In *Russia To-day and To-morrow* Miliukov tried to resolve the duality of perspective that was inherent in his *History of the Second Russian Revolution* and to lay the historical foundations for his new political views. The new history was detailed, lively, and informative, but it utterly failed to substantiate Miliukov's prospectus for the future.

Miliukov's "definite conclusion" as to the significance of the revolution was founded on his conviction that at the end of 1921, a "cycle of events in Russia [had] come to a close." Both the White and Red movements had run their course; the defeat of Wrangel and the famine of 1921 had demonstrated the exhaustion of these forces and would "mark the turning point in the Russian Revolution." Now "its meaning could become patent and a criterion could be found by which these events could be judged in their unity and completion."[230]

For his criterion, Miliukov chose "the historical process" and rejected individual responsibility. The reader was "to discriminate between the passing form and the lasting substance" of the revolution and at the same time to see it in both its "destructive" and "constructive" aspects. While the destructive process was "of necessity presented in detail" in Miliukov's study, he insisted that construction was certain in the future: "We are witnessing the birth of Russian democracy, in the midst of the ruins of the past, which will never return." In the United States, Miliukov felt he had found a people who would be receptive to this message; he dedicated *Russia To-day and To-morrow* to "My American Audiences." The similarities between the structure of the

United States and his federalist plans for Russia, as well as a "truly democratic spirit," bound him to his public.[231]

The historical narrative of *Russia To-day and To-morrow*, presented in Miliukov's straightforward, dynamic style and packed with "facts," covered the period from the February revolution through the famine of 1921. The first sections repeated much of the *History*, but placed a new emphasis on "popular" factors. Gone were the comments about the "universal adaptability and plasticity" of the Russian people.[232] Instead the masses, while still described as "natural anarchists," were transformed into the ultimate arbiter of Russia's destiny and the major force behind the revolt against the old regime:

> A revolution always becomes unavoidable when important and vital reforms are impeded by an authority which has lost its moral prestige and has become powerless to suppress a growing and universal disaffection among the masses.[233]

Similarly, the people's passive "sanction"[234] allowed the Bolsheviks to remain in power after the coup in October 1917. The land question, which Miliukov had ignored in his earlier work, now became an outstanding cause of the revolution. "The transfer of the land from the decaying privileged class to the rural democracy" was one of two vital reforms that the autocracy had refused to enact. The other was the "substitution of a popular constitutional regime for the patriarchal one."[235] In *Russia To-day and To-morrow* the civil war was interpreted according to the most orthodox Socialist Revolutionary tradition: the "turning point" of the military effort was the "coup d'état" against the socialists and liberals in the Directory at Omsk.[236] After this anti-Bolshevik opposition took a course opposed to the "democratic tendencies of the population" that were decisive in the end.[237]

This analysis did not reflect Miliukov's ideas or actions during the civil war—then he had been dead set against the Directory.[238] The judgments in *Russia To-day and To-morrow* were the consequence of Miliukov's shift toward the vocabulary and the conceptions of the Socialist Revolutionaries, although his tone of confidence in the good sense and universal validity of his pronouncements remained unchanged. Both his newfound populism and an inbred historical determinism were apparent in his effort to draw parallels between the Russian and the French revolutions and to present them as analogous and progressive developments. In the *History* he had described the revolution as a regressive phenomenon that its leaders had failed to control:

> Like a mighty geological upheaval that playfully throws off the thin crust of the most recent cultural deposits and brings to the surface layers that were long ago covered up . . . reminding us of the drab old times, of long-past epochs of the history of the earth, so the Russian revolution displays before us our entire historical structure, only thinly covered by the surface layer of recent cultural acquisitions.[239]

Now, four years later, Miliukov came to the conclusion that the Russian revolution was essentially similar to the English and especially the French, as a "violent overthrow of obsolete political and social institutions . . . very likely to come in every civilized community capable of evolving from medievalism to modern democracy."[240]

This complete inversion of his earlier assessment did not affect Miliukov's characterization of the Bolsheviks. They remained the same wily representatives of "international socialism," and they won in 1917, as he had written earlier, by masterfully exploiting the inconsistencies of the moderates. After the October coup, they had had to turn from demagogy to other tactics in order to remain in power. Their first measure was "crushing their opponents."[241] Positive action proved more difficult. The new rulers were not only faced with the task of reconstructing what they had helped to tear apart, they had, in addition, to achieve this with their few party cadres. The Bolsheviks' answers to these problems were centralization and force. The three "pillars" that had kept them in power for four years were "their highly centralized system of administration," the Red Army, and the "secret police and espionage system,"[242] all controlled by the Communist party: "They came to power by promises; they have kept in power by fear."[243]

In foreign affairs as well the Bolsheviks had been quick to adapt their policies to the exigencies of their situation. This meant concentrating their efforts on the "oppressed" nations of Asia and Africa and attacking capitalism as its "weakest point"—"the Eastern frontier of (Western) Europe." Despite their difficulties both inside Russia and abroad, the Bolsheviks were still intent upon achieving world revolution, Miliukov insisted. They were "ready to sacrifice everything, to 'make every concession and promise,' in order to see their vision materialize and to stay in power until they enter their promised land."[244]

But this resolution would not suffice to ward off what Miliukov regarded as the inevitable "degeneration and disintegration" of Bolshevik rule.[245] The "decline of Bolshevism" would come about, he predicted, as a result of its destruction of the Russian economy:

> No human society that consumes without producing can exist. Bolshevism has only succeeded in building a huge machine of bureaucracy and warfare while at the same time it has destroyed all incentive for industry and trade and has had to live on the natural produce of an equally ruined agriculture.[246]

In his discussion of the Russian economy, Miliukov repeated many of Struve's arguments—the analogy with the breakdown of the Roman Empire, the regression to more primitive forms of social organization, the demographic collapse, the decline of the cities, and the catastrophic fall in production—and buttressed these observations with statistical evidence. Like Struve, he pointed to the series of "capitalistic" measures and the militarization of labor as evidence that the Bolsheviks' economic plans had failed.[247] The recent drastic reduction in the number of people entitled to receive state rations was a sign to Miliukov that the Bolsheviks themselves knew that they had reached an economic impasse.[248] The ruling minority was now simply trying to survive, living on the goods of the past and its hopes for the future:

> If left to itself the Red Star will last as long as there will be something to sacrifice and to sell in exchange for its further existence. Its excuse will always remain the same: waiting for the great World Revolution.[249]

In Miliukov's view, only two phenomena could "cut short" this long, degenerative process. One was death; the famine of 1921 represented the "ghastly summary of four years of Soviet domination." For Miliukov, the connection between Bolshevism and the famine was unambiguous. Soviet statistics showed that the major reduction in area under cultivation began only after Bolshevik control. In addition, the new government had proved that it was incapable of saving the country from starvation; foreign philanthropy had provided the crucial aid to the population.[250]

The second way to end the Bolshevik stalemate depended on "the changing state of mind of the popular masses" and their initiation of the "constructive" phase of revolution. Miliukov began his discussion of what he saw as Russia's real future with a quotation from Schiller: "The old crumbles down, time brings changes, and from the ruins blossoms forth a new life." "I used that quotation . . . twenty-five years ago," he wrote, "I am tempted to use it again to sum up what some people are inclined to call Russia's return to barbarism." The present devastation of Russia would not last; it contained the "germs of new life." This, he averred, "makes us hopeful in spite of all and proud of our Russia of tomorrow."[251]

Like his New Tactic, Miliukov's predictions for Russia's future were based on his confidence in the Russian people. The people had given the Bolsheviks their "moral consent" in 1917 on the basis of the party's promises. Later it was Bolshevik terror, the greater danger of a White victory, and the hope, implanted by propaganda, for a world revolution that had kept them passively loyal to the regime. Now that the Whites had vanished, "the people have to rely on themselves for their salvation"; their "isolated uprisings" were expressions of that "change of mind." It would soon be as obvious to them as it was to Miliukov that Bolshevism was not even "minimally acceptable" as a government and that world revolution was a pipe dream. They would then proceed to build a "peasant democracy" in Russia.[252]

Miliukov did not reveal the means by which this transformation from Bolshevik dictatorship to democracy based on universal suffrage would be accomplished. He was confident that peasant parties would arise and that the "free play of democratic institutions . . . [would] forestall new plots and coups d'état." Moreover, the nationalities problem would be settled "peacefully" on the basis of the "free consent of popular assemblies."[253] Those who doubted this were, like the Bolsheviks, guilty of "complete lack of faith in the Russian people."[254] Americans should trust Miliukov's knowledge instead:

> I know the psychology of our people. And I say to all who want to hear: Russia is ripe for democratic change. The change will come. It will come soon. What will emerge from it will be—not the ancient regime, not anarchy, but a great democratic Russia of tomorrow.[255]

The year that had passed since the end of the civil war had transformed the New Tactic into grand optimism about the future. Miliukov had adopted the populist perspective almost completely, adding his own visions of political parties, free enterprise, and development along the Western path. His prediction that the Russian people would proceed to build democracy sounded very much like Chernov's confidence in the third force or Martov's belief in the revival of the working class movement. Of the two principles of explanation at work in his *History of the Second Russian Revolution*—the revolutionary "tide" and the acts of "responsible politicians"—Miliukov had chosen the tide and insisted that it flow west. But despite this resolution, *Russia To-day and To-morrow* was not free from contradictions. Its tensions were not between long and short term causalities, but between the evidence of the past and conclusions for the future. Miliukov's analysis of the Bolsheviks' methods and his assertion that the party's leaders were determined to hold on to power at any cost undercut the prospects of democratic government in Russia. And, while the notion that the people of Russia had acted as an arbiter of the country's fate did explain the outcome of the revolution and civil war, the idea that these people cared about the Western-style democracy and state structures dear to the liberals was unsupported by the facts.

The Liberals and the People

Miliukov's radiant confidence in Russia's democratic future was, of course, anathema to Struve. It was just this kind of wishful thinking that he attacked as *faktopoklonstvo*: the revolution was idolized and reinterpreted because it happened. To Struve, Miliukov's optimistic determinism was a demonstration of his "old regime psychology"; he and his followers at *Poslednie novosti* had taken up their "old positions" as if nothing had changed in the past five years. Their attacks on groups such as the National Congress represented the "purest intelligentsia restoration" and for this reason Miliukov's "ideology" was the "least interesting" émigré interpretation of the revolution.[256] It had all been heard before, before 1917.

But Struve's attack on his old adversary was itself a replay of *Vekhi*'s assault on the left after 1905, and his reconstruction of the deep divide within the intelligentsia failed to take account of changes since the "second" revolution. In several respects, Struve and Miliukov had taken similar positions in the years after 1917. They both remained intransigent opponents of Bolshevism, and refused to recognize Lenin's party as the legitimate government of the Russian state. Their interpretations of the revolution's origins were alike—both saw the revolution as a product of Russia's deficient political heritage, its lack of a state idea—*gosudarstvennost'*, in Miliukov's analysis. Both were critical of the intellectuals' utopianism, yet each put the final blame for the revolution upon the autocracy's refusal to reform. Nationalists to the core, both Miliukov and Struve had turned at times to the monarchy as a means to preserve the state, and each refused to reexamine his deep commitment to a unified "Russian" nation. Unlike the socialists, they both interpreted Bolshevism as a fulfillment of its ideology—"revolutionary syndicalism" in Miliukov's terms, "socialism" in Struve's broader critique. They attacked the Bolshevik government on precisely the same ground—the destruction of the economic system and thus of Russia's viability as a nation.

The differences between Miliukov and Struve concerned not so much the facts, but how they were expressed and what meaning they had for the future. The crucial question was, had the revolution moved Russia "forward" toward the Western values they both admired? Here they parted company, here they despised each other's conclusions, and here the facts were all on Struve's side. Nothing in the Soviet system signaled progress toward private property, individual liberty, and institutional democracy.

Despite the manifest setbacks to the liberal cause, neither Struve nor Miliukov was willing to give up his hopes. Both were able to recover their optimism and to reaffirm their commitments in the face of disaster. The difference once again was in the expression of this trust. Miliukov, hemmed in by positivism, had to find his ideals in historical development. As Struve had indicated, this led Miliukov *ex post facto* to "accept" the failure of the White movement and the victory of the revolution and to give this outcome a moral, progressive significance. From his vantage in the West, he claimed that events had proved the wisdom of the Russian people and their dedication to democratic government. For Struve, on the other hand, morality was not determined by success, and history was not obliged to be progressive. He judged the revolution on the basis of what he saw as its results—millions of starving people and a cynical, exploitative, minority government concerned only with its survival—and concluded that Russia had moved back, not forward. These facts, however, did not deny him the right to believe in a better future. In effect, they made it all the more essential that Russians find a positive ideal, a new national confidence, in order to lift themselves up from chaos and destruction.

The contrast between Miliukov's and Struve's interpretations of the revolution derived, as Struve had suggested, from their different philosophical assumptions. Miliukov, the quintessential "man of the sixties,"[257] had never left the mainstream intelligentsia tradition—radicalism, atheism, and materialism. In several ways his nineteenth-century positivism served him well, informing his energetic campaign for reform before the revolution and providing him with both the theoretical framework and the self-assurance to produce, rapidly, a series of estimable historical studies. It sustained his hopes in the emigration, but at the price of an immense discrepancy between the "facts" and his conclusions. The spectacle of this brilliant scholar predicting the rise of Russian democracy—political parties, the "free play of democratic institutions"—on the basis of what he described as total devastation was, like Kerensky's revolutionary posture, embarrassing to behold.

For Struve, the Kantian idealist, such theorizing amounted to a "moral lie." As a representative of twentieth-century idealism, the major countercurrent in the intelligentsia culture, he was acutely aware of the inadequacy of positivism as a source of moral principles. To him it was imperative to judge not on the basis of what existed but of what was right. A transcendental faith, in that it set eternal standards, meant that failures could be acknowledged without threatening future goals. Indeed, from this perspective, an idealistic standpoint was necessary for progress, because it was the only one that admitted human reason into history. One had to learn from past mistakes, not deny them.

Despite their differences in temperament and philosophy, Struve and Miliukov shared a commitment to liberalism and analyzed the revolution from a similar political perspective. In their writings they took up questions that socialists were disinclined to ask and produced answers that challenged the basic assumptions of the left. Struve in particular developed a historical explanation for the revolution that was much more thoroughgoing than any of the socialists' efforts in this direction. Although Martov had compared the Bolshevik government to the prerevolutionary autocracy, his intent was to criticize, not to provide a causal link. Other socialists, such as Potresov and Zasulich, had pointed to Russian backwardness as evidence of the Bolsheviks' inability to fulfill their promises, but these, too, were attempts to explain why the revolution would fail, not whence it came. Struve's account, on the contrary, represented the revolution as a product of two centuries of social and political history; it surpassed the socialists in determinism and at the same time called their goals into question. Based on the historical consequences of the eighteenth-century division of political and economic power, Struve's analysis suggested that Russia had yet to take the essential first steps toward establishing a bourgeois society. In addition, his interpretation accused the entire intelligentsia, and not just the Bolsheviks, of encouraging the people to tear the country apart.

The actual process of national collapse in 1917 was described by Miliukov in his *History of the Second Russian Revolution.* By focusing on the question of power, he was able to show why the moderates could not lead the nation after the fall of the autocracy. With their bourgeois policies and their revolutionary rhetoric, they had first destroyed the old institutions of authority and then refused, for ideological reasons, to replace them. The Bolsheviks, on the other hand, had put the pursuit of power and later its defense above considerations of principle. By examining revolutionary politics solely at the level of tactics, Miliukov's study avoided moral issues; in this respect, his analysis provided a corrective to the socialists' essentially ethical, and nonexplanatory, critique. He raised an important question for Western democracies as well—how were they going to respond to a new adversary that, in his view, was eager to exploit their tolerance and their greed?

Another "liberal" question involved socialism itself. While the Russian social democrats tried valiantly to dissociate Bolshevism from socialism—and succeeded only in confusing the issue further—Struve took a clear-cut position. The Russian revolution had been initiated by socialist propaganda; the new government was led by intellectuals who tried to pursue socialist goals; and the economic disaster that ensued was a result of the attempt to put socialism into practice. Although he was sensitive to the psychological appeal of socialist ideas, Struve felt that the Bolshevik "experiment" had demonstrated the contradictions between socialism's two basic principles—equality and the central organization of production—and had proved that, as an economic system, socialism was doomed to fail.

In addition to his provocative critique of socialist economics, Struve raised a fundamental philosophical objection to socialist ideology. Could the evil in the world be blamed on social institutions alone? The people of Russia had been quick to grasp what he saw as the human essence of the collectivist idea— socialism did not hold individuals responsible for their acts. To Struve, the consequences of this ethic of individual irresponsibility were clear. He did not deny that institutions had the capacity to shape people's lives for better or for worse; he had, on the contrary, devoted his life to the improvement of the social institutions of his country. But in his eyes, the force for both individual and collective advance derived from each person's desire to improve his or her life and from an individual sense of moral responsibility for oneself and others. From this perspective, the socialists' focus upon external circumstances was bound to be regressive, since it ignored or even sanctioned the evil within each person and provided no inspiration for people to change themselves.

For Struve, progress—or in Russia's case, recovery—depended upon allegiance to a constructive ideal, one created with an awareness of human weakness and a faith in people's ability to strive against their sinfulness and for the good. This faith had no foundation in contemporary events; unlike Miliukov, Struve saw no dialectical imperative in Russia's "ruins." Recovery had to come from love, from the will to believe in a better Russia. Although many Russian socialists were sentimentally attached to their country, their positivist ideologies prevented them from making this emotional commitment explicit. For Struve, however, ideals came first. Only a "lovingly and consciously created" national spirit could give the people of Russia the will to start anew.

Struve's belief in this possibility testified to his religious form of Russian populism. From their divergent points of view, both he and Miliukov had turned in the aftermath of revolution to the Russian people. Miliukov, reversing his earlier focus on government and politics, insisted that the people would now begin to liberate themselves. He was confident in the "healthy foundations of [their] desires and wishes."[258] Struve, while acknowledging that the masses had accepted the socialist "poison" and destroyed the state, trusted in the people as an ideal and a possibility. These expectations evoke the contradictions of Russian liberalism. The liberals' hopes for freedom, for democracy, for the rule of law rested on the assumption of an energetic, participatory, consensual society. But this harmonic individualism could be not imposed. The liberals did not have a large constituency before 1917; it was only in the emigration and in a mythical or idealistic form that they found their Russian people.

4

The Monarchy
in Fact and Fancy

The Autocratic Legacy

The fall of the autocracy failed to provoke a conservative response of any theoretical substance from the Russian intelligentsia. Despite the burgeoning of monarchist sentiment in the emigration, no Russian Burke materialized to make a philosophical case for the old regime. As before the revolution, the best minds were engaged elsewhere.

The poverty of postrevolutionary conservative ideology was due in part to the intelligentsia's culture and experience before 1917. There was little to recover from the past. On a purely intellectual level, monarchism long ago had seemed an old, worn-out idea. Although the dynasty had a few gifted defenders in the nineteenth century—notably, Karamzin and Pobedonostsev[1]—most intellectuals turned to newer notions of social organization. Moreover, in intelligentsia politics, the monarchy for years had been the enemy—of Marxists, populists, and liberals alike. Not only had the autocracy obstructed the intelligentsia's demands for liberty, social justice, and a role in government, it had been unable to defend the nation against its external foes in the Russo-Japanese War and again in 1914. By the reign of Nicholas II, it was impossible for critically thinking individuals to support the monarchy on moral or political grounds, and, for this reason, the intellectual life of Russia at this time tended to divide into oppositional left-wing politics or cultural perspectives on the nation. The autocracy left no room for a constructive, political conservatism.[2]

However, once the monarchy had been destroyed, its adherents multi-plied. Outside Russia, many émigrés turned to an idea for which they had shown no previous enthusiasm.[3] Some liberals, like Struve, saw monarchy as a means to reconstruct the empire. The monarchist abstraction, which merged the individual with the nation and endowed them both—especially after the murder of the imperial family—with an aura of heroic sacrifice, was a seductive image. During the chaos of the revolution and the civil war, many patriots accepted what Miliukov had argued during the succession crisis in February 1917: the country needed a "symbol of authority."[4]

But this new-found appreciation of the Russian monarchy did not stimulate any serious ideological efforts, nor did it override the intellectuals' hostility to the old regime. None but the feeble-minded could wholeheartedly support a return to the past. Unfortunately, these existed and their ideas about the revolution were simple and pernicious.

F. V. Vinberg: "The Forces of Darkness"

Monarchist reactionaries were not prominent in the civil war. After the fall of the autocracy, right-wing extremists gravitated first toward Kiev and the Skoropadsky regime, and then into association with the German occupying forces. Although some reactionaries wrote propaganda for the White armies,[5] most regarded the politicians associated with the Volunteers as too liberal. In general, rightists preferred the Germans to the Whites, and many arrived in Europe with the retreating German armies, well before the major campaigns of the civil war.[6]

Like other émigrés, the monarchists chose to settle in European cities where they felt at home. For enthusiasts of authority, this meant Germany. Berlin and Munich were the centers of Russian monarchism in the West until 1922.[7] In Germany, the new émigrés could join an exile culture that predated the revolution, a milieu that nourished the schemes and fantasies of Alfred Rosenberg and Max Erwin von Scheubner-Richter, both active in Hitler's nascent National Socialist party.[8] Here the Russian rightists found an atmosphere congenial to their operations—the possibility for conspiracy, a free press, and a perception that the citizenry, and many of the authorities as well, were on their side.

Among the reactionaries who arrived in Germany during the civil war was Fedor Viktorovich Vinberg, a fanatic whose activities in the emigration had grim effects. Born in Kiev into a military family, Vinberg made his career in the Imperial Guard and became a colonel and the Stablemaster of the court. Since 1905 he had been an admirer of V. M. Purishkevich, the leader of the extreme right in the Duma period; under his influence, Vinberg had joined the reactionary Union of the Russian People, the Union of the Archangel Michael, and the Philaret Society.[9]

In 1917 Vinberg's association with Purishkevich landed him in jail. After the abortive Kornilov affair, in which he had participated without consequence, he joined Purishkevich and his followers in further discussions about how to overthrow the Provisional Government and replace it with a monarchist dictatorship, again without results. But in December, the Bolsheviks caught up with Purishkevich's group and arrested them for an alleged counterrevolutionary conspiracy.[10] After a trial during which the defendants took great pains to disassociate themselves from the moderate opposition to Bolshevism— Purishkevich declared himself a monarchist, but unable to start a conspiracy because he had no suitable royal candidate to propose—Vinberg was sentenced to three years of hard labor.[11]

Apparently the new government had more dangerous foes, for in the end this sentence was not fulfilled. Vinberg spent only three months in prison, where he had the opportunity to meet some of his liberal and leftist opponents in the flesh. More important for his future, he carried on his discussions of Russia's future with other right-wingers. Among them was Petr Nikolaevich Shabel'skii-Bork, a young cornet who attracted Vinberg with his "obliging, soft character" and the "steadfastness of his monarchist convictions."[12] When the monarchist conspirators were released in the spring of 1918, Vinberg traveled with Shabel'skii-Bork and Sergei Taboritskii, another young officer, to Kiev. Here he published an account of his tribulations with the memorable title, *Imprisoned by the Apes (Notes of a "Counterrevolutionary") (V plenu u obez'ian [Zametki "kontr-revoliutsionera"])*; the book encompassed a rambling record of Vinberg's trial, his encounters in prison, and his monarchist sentiments, embellished with reactionary verses by Shabel'skii-Bork and other prisoners.[13] Vinberg left the Ukraine after the armistice in November 1918 on a train provided by the Germans. Until the Kapp putsch, he lived with Shabel'skii-Bork and Taboritskii in Berlin.[14]

Here Vinberg and his friends began again to publish. The first number of their journal *Luch sveta* (Ray of Light) appeared in the spring of 1919. A hodgepodge of Vinberg's articles and poems, this "literary-political publication" set forth in execrable style the reactionary interpretation of the revolution. Despite his penchant for ornamental bathos and his incapacity for logical argument, Vinberg's main point was clear enough—the revolution was the work of the devil.[15] Russia was but the "first victim" of the "forces of darkness" that were assaulting all mankind.[16]

Although Vinberg had an overarching explanation for how the devil had managed his most recent victory, he refrained "from going into . . . details" in "Before Daybreak," his opening statement in *Luch sveta*.[17] His remarks were devoted instead to a grim description of the contemporary situation and to declarations of faith. From his perspective, *Luch sveta* was the only "ray of light" in a singularly gloomy world. The essence of the present crisis was the struggle between the principles of good and evil, and evil had, it seemed, the upper hand: "The hopeless, dull despair of the forces of light has set in on earth with the triumphant wielding of power and the malicious mockery of the dark forces of malice and evil." As a result of the war and revolution, the "lowest passions, man-hating inducements [*chelovekonenavistnicheskie pobuzhdeniia*], acts of offense and violence, secret dreams of reckoning and revenge have become the motive forces of humanity." After "our disgraceful . . . revolution," only the Russian monarchy remained uncorrupted, the source of everything "creative" and "constructive" in Russian history, and a "clear light" to its followers. The work of Russian monarchists had been obstructed, Vinberg claimed, by conditions in Russia before the revolution. While all other parties had enjoyed the "right" to declare their principles, the monarchists had been obliged to hide their true feelings. Now, finally, the time had come to speak out: "openly and boldly and for all to hear we will declare that we are convinced monarchists, were always such and ever will be."[18]

Such ravings would have left no mark in history, were it not for the vicious anti-Semitism of the Russian reactionaries. The other side of Vinberg's idealization of the autocracy was his consuming hatred of the Jews, and all those whom he considered to be Jews or to be their "agents." The real power behind the "forces of darkness" and the revolution was an international Jewish conspiracy. It was this idea that Vinberg and other Russian extremists managed to communicate to those who were all too willing to listen.

The notion of a Jewish conspiracy to conquer the Christian world was not, of course, a creation of the Russian reaction. The post-revolutionary rightists served their cause by transmitting old ideas. The main "document" of their campaign was the so-called *Protocols of the Elders of Zion*, the anti-Semitic forgery concocted at the time of the Dreyfus affair by Russian police agents living in Paris.[19] Purported to be the instructions of Jewish conspirators, the twenty-four "protocols" comprised both a plan to achieve world domination and a description of the future Jewish state. The basic method of the "conspiracy," according to the *Protocols*, is to use every opportunity offered by liberalism and democracy to undermine the institutions of the Christian nations; once in power, the "elders" will establish a centralized, paternalistic government with strict controls over education, information, and the economy. Civil liberties will be eliminated. It did not disturb the reactionaries who propagated the *Protocols* that the "elders" shared their own contempt for liberalism. The "wisdom" of the *Protocols* appealed to authoritarians by affirming their suspicions.

In Russia the *Protocols* had been published in several versions and editions since 1903, and exploited by extremists on the right to depict the revolution of 1905 as a Jewish plot.[20] But despite the success of pogrom agitators during and after 1905, the influence of the *Protocols* and the extreme right declined with the restabilization of the country in the period of the Third Duma. Even Nicholas II rejected the *Protocols* as spurious, although anti-Semitism and occult reaction were common at the court. But after the revolution, the efforts of rightists like Vinberg gave the *Protocols* a new start in postwar Europe.[21]

The *Protocols* were first revived within Russia as anti-Bolshevik propaganda during the civil war, when reactionaries distributed copies to troops serving in the Volunteer Army.[22] But this dissemination of the *Protocols* in Russia was of little consequence. As Norman Cohn has pointed out, the soldiers could not have understood much from the convoluted document, and, in any case, they needed little encouragement to devastate Jewish communities.[23] The *Protocols* found a mass audience only in Europe, after Vinberg and other officers had established themselves in Germany. Vinberg began to cite the *Protocols* in the first issue of *Luch sveta*; in the third number, published in May 1920, he published the complete text. By the end of 1920, the *Protocols* had been translated and published in Germany, England, the United States, Poland, and France.[24] Through the mediation of Alfred Rosenberg, they entered the mainstream of the Nazi movement.[25]

In addition to serving as a scripture for anti-Semites in the West, the *Protocols* provided Vinberg with the "evidence" for his interpretation—presented as the truth—of the Russian revolution. This he set forth in *The Way of the Cross (Krestnyi put')* a testament of 375 pages, published in Munich in 1921 and translated into German the following year.[26] Replete with falsifications and Vinberg's nonsensical arguments, *The Way of the Cross* embodied the conspiratorial paranoia and fantasies of the monarchist reactionaries.

The *via dolorosa* of the title was that of Nicholas II. Vinberg's book opens with an ode that explicitly compared the emperor to Christ:

> The blind people, duped by liars,
> Insulted you with disgraceful words,
> For the goodness of Your sacred soul,
> They demanded punishment of whom—of You, Yourself!
>
> Was it not like this that the Tsar of crafty Judah fell,
> Truth's Messiah, and the people's dream . . .
> The contemptible Jews crucified their God as well
> On the planks of a shameful cross![27]

These verses, with their profane distortions—note that Christ in this imagery is a Tsar, or Caesar—suggested several of Vinberg's major themes. The revolution, in his mind, had been accomplished by the "blind people," incited by the "liars"—the intelligentsia; behind them both lurked "crafty Judah." The only pure man in Russia was the tsar, his virtue affirmed by suffering and death.

As this construct suggests, Vinberg's view of the Russian population was the antithesis of the populists' confidence and trust. "The Russian people," he asserted, "are in essence a dishonorable, dishonest, lazy, inert people, inclined in their personal interests to isolate themselves from the interests of society and the state."[28] Russians, he was fond of repeating, were weak and inclined to submit to a strong authority. Because of their "soft, flaccid, female Slavic nature," they had given themselves up to the Tatar yoke and later to the Russian autocrats. The harsher the conduct of the ruler, the greater were the people's love and obedience. According to Vinberg, the greatest Russian tsars had been Ivan the Terrible and Peter the Great, whom the people had loved, and Nicholas I, whom they "adored."[29] The secret of the Jews—that is, the Bolsheviks—was that they understood the "character and psychology of the Russian people" and therefore used terror to support their rule:

> Of all the rulers who have ever disposed of the fates of Russia, no one has known and understood the Russian people and been able to lead them as well as Ivan the Terrible, Peter the Great, and . . . Leib Trotskii-Bronshtein.[30]

The liberals, on the other hand, were incapable of understanding the popular mentality. Their attempts at reform and education, according to Vinberg, had only deprived the people of their confidence in God, tsar, and country, and produced the "'revolutionary apes'" of his acquaintance.[31]

While the people were the dupes of others' ignorance and malevolence, both liberals and Bolsheviks were agents of the Jewish conspiracy. In accord with the *Protocols*, and with the Black Hundreds' idea of "*zhidomasonstvo*" ("Yid-Masonry"), Vinberg described the revolution as a two-stage process. From this perspective, the liberals were all, consciously or unconsciously, "*shabbos-goyim*"—the Jews' servants.[32] It was they who had destroyed the monarchy, first by pressing for a constitutional regime, and later by maneuvering Russia into war with Germany. The war, not the February revolution, was the beginning of the end, in Vinberg's eyes. An ardent Germanophile, he advocated cooperation between the two "united and friendly nations." Together, singing "Russland, Deutschland über alles," Russia and Germany were to strive for world dominion. Since Japan was destined to join this chorus, Vinberg regarded the Russo-Japanese War as an earlier Jewish effort to thwart Russia's fulfillment of her "historical calling." In 1914 these imperial prospects had been more decisively obstructed by the success of the Masons in Russia and in England—Vinberg's national *bête noire*—who had set the would-be partners against each other.[33]

The second, Bolshevik, stage of the revolution was that of direct Jewish rule. The "*shabbos-goy*" had only done the "dirty work essential for the Jewish triumph." Now the "false toga-mask" could be thrown away and the true Satan, who was straightforward in his methods, could appear.[34] In case his readers did not recognize the Bolsheviks, Vinberg appended long lists of "Jewish" members of Bolshevik and socialist organizations to *The Way of the Cross*. Lenin was identified as "Jewish on his mother's side."[35] To substantiate his claims, Vinberg pointed to "subsidies" given to "Trotskii-Bronshtein" by the New York firm of Kuhn, Loeb and Co., as well as to the testimony of the *Protocols* and other spurious "documents."[36]

Such was the general "argument" of Vinberg's Russian revolution. But one great attraction of the Jewish-Masonic conspiracy theory was that it could explain not just the general direction of recent Russian history, but every one of Vinberg's deep convictions. For one thing, it accounted for the apparent paradox of the tsar's support of a war against his natural—in Vinberg's eyes— ally. Obviously, Nicholas had been tricked by his advisers into declaring war on Germany, and subsequently, as befitted a virtuous monarch, he had been "true" to his given word. This, for Vinberg, constituted the underlying tragedy of Nicholas's sufferings; he had died because of his own righteousness.[37] The leaders of the Volunteer Army were too moderate for Vinberg—it turned out that they, too, were "Masonic" agents. The entire civil war was both an internal "conflict" between the "Masons" and the "Jews" *and* a part of the greater conspiracy to destroy Russia.[38]

Some people, Vinberg noted, thought the parallels between the civil war and the seventeenth-century Time of Troubles suggested that both were indigenous developments, rooted in the Russian character. Was Lenin not a modern Stenka Razin, and Trotsky a new Pugachev? These arguments had their merits, in Vinberg's account, but they did not refute his causality: such comparisons merely demonstrated that the Jews had used the Russian people and "its History" as a weapon in their battle against Christian culture. The Jewish conspiracy was much older than commonly believed.[39]

Vinberg did not hesitate to apply this reasoning to European developments as well. The common factors in the French and Russian revolutions were suggestive. Discounting the "details" of revolutionary history taught by his "Kadet-professor," Vinberg demonstrated to himself that the Jews were behind the Masons who were behind Voltaire and Diderot. After all, had not the Jews received their freedom from the revolution in France?[40] With this flexible methodology and a large cast of enemies—"We ourselves, Russians," Masonry, Jews connected with Masonry, and the English[41]—Vinberg rewrote history to his satisfaction.

But what of the future? Vinberg's prognosis was not bright. "Israel" had good cause to celebrate, he wrote. Wittingly or unwittingly, a full three-quarters of those who called themselves Christians had been caught up in the Masonic plot.[42] He had only two proposals with which to counter the conspiracy. One was a return to the strong authority of the tsars. A tsarist slogan could unite honorable Russian people and release the forces of good.[43] Vinberg's second plan involved the Church. Orthodoxy, he insisted, should unite with Catholicism in a battle with the enemies of Christ. Unlike Protestants, Catholics understood how to exercise authority, and Russians ought to learn their methods. The first step would be to anathematize the Masons and all of Satan's servants "at Easter week, in all the cathedrals and churches of our homeland."[44] In other words, a nation-wide pogrom.

Was Vinberg mad, but honest? Although there is reason to think that someone who could write *The Way of the Cross* could believe it, the evidence indicates that Vinberg was trying to manipulate his readers and that he was not sincere. He consistently attempted to draw in his audience with respectable arguments before letting loose with the "real" explanation. For the first hundred and fifty pages of *The Way of the Cross*, Jews are called "evrei"; only later do they become "zhidy."[45] This same consideration was apparent in Vinberg's decision not to go into "details" in his opening article in *Luch sveta*. He also provided some camouflage for his tactics: "Not all people understand," he admonished his readers, "that slander is an unpermissible means of struggle, in private, as in public and political life."[46] These little sermons, scattered among the lies, suggest that Vinberg knew what he was about. It made no difference whatsoever to him when the fraudulence of the *Protocols* was exposed by the London *Times* in August 1921.[47] He continued to proclaim their authenticity[48] and quoted from the "1897" version in the 1922 edition of *The Way of the Cross*. Why do otherwise, when he knew from personal experience that people were moved by feelings, not by reason? The "truth" was something to be "felt."[49]

One "truth" Vinberg was eager to establish in *The Way of the Cross* was his own history; he wanted to show that he had been on the tsar's side in the past and to emphasize his intimacy with the right people. A number of his anecdotes—these figured with the *Protocols* and historical parallels as "evidence"—concerned his alleged meetings with the emperor and the empress, the empress's kindness to him, her advice to his wife, and other domestic matters.[50] These devices and Vinberg's clumsy deceptions would seem merely pathetic, if his and others' efforts to propagate the *Protocols* and its message had not been so successful.

Both the deceit and the self-indulgence of *The Way of the Cross* were symptomatic of Vinberg's low opinion of humanity. The ideology of reactionary monarchism placed few demands on its proponents—all evil in the world was explained by the conspiracy and goodness came only from the tsar. The best that one could do was to denounce others and associate oneself with the monarch's cause. While this defensive attitude had an analogue in the ideological politics of the Russian leftists, who also defined virtue through associations and beliefs, the views of the monarchist extremists were radically at odds with the convictions of the intelligentsia. Vinberg's anti-Semitism, his insistence that the Russian people were incapable of self-rule, his devotion to strong authority, and his assertion that monarchy was beneficial to Russia stood populism on its head. And while the left and liberal intellectuals criticized Bolshevik rule on the basis of their moral principles and political aspirations, Vinberg despaired only because the wrong autocrats had won. He had no ethical arguments against the Bolsheviks, apart from accusing them of being Satan's agents. The goal of the "Jewish conspiracy" was exactly what he hoped the Russian-German-Japanese alliance could achieve—the conquest of the world.

S. S. Ol'denburg: The Best Case for the Sovereign

Although the defense of the Russian monarch was, for the most part, a cause
for bigots like Vinberg, one intelligent and thoughtful individual attempted to
speak up for the old regime. This was Sergei Sergeevich Ol'denburg, who in
Berlin in 1922 published a perceptive biographical essay on Nicholas II.[51] This
study was unique among the writings of Russian intellectuals in the five years
after 1917, for it was sympathetic to Nicholas and stressed the positive
achievements of the monarchy.

The singularity of Ol'denburg's perspective was related to his age. He was
younger than the outstanding figures in the intelligentsia and had not seen the
ambitions of a lifetime thwarted by the autocracy. Sergei Sergeevich was the
son of S. F. Ol'denburg—a prominent Orientalist, a member of the Kadet
Central Committee, and, for a time, Minister of Education in the Provisional
Government.[52] Although his father remained in Russia after the revolution,
Sergei Sergeevich emigrated. He became a regular contributor to Struve's
Russkaia mysl'.[53]

While many moderates in the emigration were committed to monarchy as a
political form, only Ol'denburg was willing to turn to the past to support his
views. Any positive representation of the Romanovs was regarded as eccentric,
if not depraved, by the intelligentsia in the 1920s; even those who considered
monarchy a constructive element of Russia's future polity were loath to
reconsider their prerevolutionary judgments of the dynasty.[54] Ol'denburg's
intention in his short study of Nicholas II was to break through the intellectuals'
prejudices and to explain the tsar's actions on the basis of his character and
situation. The goal was not exoneration, but understanding.

The lack of mutual comprehension between society and sovereign had been
at the base of the revolution, according to this account, and, in contrast to
other intellectuals, Ol'denburg did not place the blame for this estrangement
on the autocracy alone. The educated people of the old regime had kept
themselves willfully uninformed of matters concerning the emperor, he wrote
in *The Sovereign Emperor Nicholas II Alexandrovich (Gosudar' Imperator
Nikolai II Aleksandrovich)*. An interest in the lives and activities of the royal
family had been considered perverse by prerevolutionary society; it had been
"almost a sign of bad taste to know the names of the Grand Princes and their
degree of relationship." (Here Ol'denburg used "society" (*obshchestvo*) to
mean the intelligentsia in its broad sense of educated people.)[55] The
intelligentsia had exercised its own unofficial censorship against the
monarchy—verse dedicated by the great Russian poets to members of the
imperial family had been "subjected to a silent boycott." This "intentional
ignorance", Ol'denburg thought, was responsible for the inability of many
intellectuals to comprehend Russia's history and especially the events
connected with the two revolutions.[56]

Nicholas in his turn had been far from well informed about the country that he ruled and especially about society and its opinions, Ol'denburg admitted. This was again partly the intelligentsia's own fault: the emperor's isolation behind the high walls of the imperial palaces and the protection of his Cossack guards was a rational response to a long series of assassinations that "had not met with a sufficient moral rebuff on the part of society." But far more important than the physical separation of the emperor from his subjects was the misleading ideology that this condition protected. Like the intelligentsia, Nicholas lived in a world of political "fictions and conventions."[57]

According to Ol'denburg, the most insidious of these notions was the illusion that the tsar could rule without the upper classes. Ever since the reign of Nicholas I, the "distinctive policy" of the autocracy had been the attempt to govern "relying on the lower strata [*nizy*] over the heads of the intermediate classes." This "populism from the right" was one of the most significant causes of the alienation of society; it represented a denial of the enlightened principles of Catherine the Great and a return to Ivan the Terribles' sixteenth-century campaign against the boyars.[58] The most dangerous aspect of the autocracy's policy was that its guiding premise—"the opposition of the good people to the evil intelligentsia"—led to the "loss of a sense of political realities" and especially to ignorance of the role the intelligentsia would play in forming the people's perceptions:

> The living tie between the ruling authority [*vlast'*] and the population is replaced with a theoretical one. A belief in some kind of real, kind people [*narod*] devoted to their monarch lived in the Sovereign until his last days. He was, perhaps, right, but the Tsar's voice could not fly to that people through the barriers of hostility.[59]

Thus the revolution had been made from both sides under the influence of false ideas—the tsar's "distorted image of society and the people" and the people's and society's "twisted image of the Tsar."[60]

In his sketch of Nicholas, Ol'denburg tried to amend the intelligentsia's perception of the monarch. He insisted that his readers pay attention to facts that they earlier had chosen to ignore. These contradicted the common opinion that Nicholas was uneducated, untalented, stupid, weak of will, and treacherous. In reality, Ol'denburg observed, Nicholas had received an extensive education; he knew three languages well; he had travelled widely in Europe and Asia. His personal qualities were almost entirely admirable: the last tsar had been unpretentious, gracious, devoted to his family. Only the perverse could consider him reprehensible as an individual.[61]

But an evaluation of Nicholas "as a monarch" was, Ol'denburg admitted, "more complicated."[62] Even moderate nationalists like Struve felt that Nicholas had sabotaged Russia's prospects for the future. By thwarting society's attempts at political and social reform, he had driven the country toward revolution. Misleading images alone did not seem a sufficient explanation for this course, and they certainly did not constitute a justification. Nonetheless, Ol'denburg felt that Nicholas' motivation had to be understood in order to judge his conduct. From the tsar's own perspective—if one could comprehend his standpoint—he had acted in the best interests of the country.

The clue to Nicholas's behavior, according to Ol'denburg, was his sense of duty. He had been brought up to regard imperial power as a personal obligation: "power, bringing with it great responsibility—this was the basic characteristic of his political world view." In the emperor's mind, power and responsibility for Russia had been given to him by God, and no earthly authority could take this duty from him. Both by education and conviction, he was "without doubt an absolutist," and his performance as a ruler was consistent with this philosophy. Nicholas declined to delegate authority not because he loved control, but because this would be a violation of his calling. Thus, after the Russo-Japanese War, he refused to take Kaiser Wilhelm's advice to have the Treaty of Portsmouth ratified by the Duma, a course the Kaiser urged in the interest of the emperor's reputation. If the treaty turned out to be unpopular, Wilhelm had argued, others, in the parliament, would have to take the blame. Nicholas would not accept this strategy. In his view, he alone was responsible for Russia "before God and history" and therefore he alone could decide how to conclude the war.[63]

In theory, Nicholas's absolutism did not prevent him from allowing society to participate in government, as long as he continued to retain ultimate control and responsibility. But, as Ol'denburg described it, each time Nicholas took a step in the direction of sharing power, he was persuaded by the country's response that he had made a mistake. The October Manifesto had not been welcomed by the nation. On the contrary, this major concession to society had provoked malicious criticism in the press and a full-scale insurrection in Moscow. The convocation of the First Duma provided a setting for demands and threats, not constructive governance. "Was the sovereign wrong," asked Ol'denburg, "when after vacillating he did not consider it possible to entrust the direction of the turbulent country to *those forces*?" The irresponsible behavior of those "who had been demanding rights so loudly" forced the tsar back upon the resources of his own government.[64]

Yet here, too, the tsar had been reluctant to grant authority to others. Even Ol'denburg was willing to admit that Nicholas's idea of his own accountability had frequently "ruined" his relations with his ministers. The tsar's need to retain personal control meant that he was uncomfortable with advisers "whose goals and means he could not fully grasp." He did not like ministers who were "stronger and smarter" than he, and he readily dismissed them when there was a difference of opinion.[65]

Nicholas's conflicts with his ministers had occasioned much spiteful commentary in prerevolutionary society, where the tsar had been accused of being "weak-willed" and "treacherous." Although Ol'denburg did not fully approve the emperor's conduct, he insisted that these characterizations were unfair. The emperor did not lack will, but he expressed his authority in an unfamiliar way. His "type of will" was not like a "hammer or a sword, [which] crushes obstacles or is broken on them," but analogous to a mountain stream that "when meeting with an obstacle . . . bends around it, goes to one side, but steadfastly, inescapably flows down from the peak and nears its goal." Nicholas had grown up with people—his father, his mother, and Pobedonostsev—whose will was direct and harsh, "like a sword," and he had learned to get what he wanted by quiet persistence. He dealt with advisers who opposed him in this fashion, listening politely, appearing to accept their opinions, and then discharging them from their posts. "This external passivity . . . in conjunction with the mildness of His manners" had earned Nicholas many enemies, wrote Ol'denburg. But such behavior was neither a sign of weak will—the tsar after all did have his way—nor evidence of "craftiness." The idea that such dismissals stemmed from "intrigue" and "dark forces" rather than from a straightforward disagreement on policy reflected more the insecurity of the advisers than the character of the tsar. "Who knows," Ol'denburg demurred, "the future might prove the Sovereign to have been right on a critical question."[66]

Although Ol'denburg's interpretation of Nicholas's personality was more attractive and faithful than the hostile suspicions of the intelligentsia, it was not in itself a defense of Nicholas "as a monarch." A political judgment, Ol'denburg insisted, had to be based upon the achievements of the nation under Nicholas's rule, and these, he thought, were many and important. For the twenty years before the war, the country had made spectacular economic and social progress. The average size of the grain harvest had increased by 78 percent since the preceding reign; the number of cattle by 63.5 percent; annual production of coal, sugar, cotton, copper, iron, steel, and manganese had at least tripled; the railroad network had been doubled. The increase in the population during this period—40 percent—had been exceeded by the growth in production, and this, according to Ol'denburg, was a decisive indication of a significant advance in material well-being.[67]

Progress had been made in other areas as well. New legislation had emancipated the peasants form communal restrictions; limits on the working day, a factory inspection system, Sunday holidays, and sickness insurance for industrial workers had been introduced. The achievements in education had been far-reaching—a huge increase in literacy, and a rapid expansion of the school system, especially in the number of women's institutions and of female students. From the perspective of civic freedoms, life had changed immeasurably in the second decade of Nicholas's reign. The Duma included representatives who called publicly for the violent overthrow of the government; Lenin's articles were published legally in the capital. Against these developments one had to weigh that which had not been done and the "many . . . mistakes made in internal and external affairs," Ol'denburg cautioned. But on balance, he insisted, the last tsar had presided over an era of tremendous national advance.[68]

The problems began with the war. It was during this prolonged crisis that the mutual misunderstanding of government and society became fatal. Ol'denburg reminded his readers that Nicholas had been an advocate of peace; up until the last he had tried to prevent hostilities. But once the war began, Nicholas had dedicated himself to its successful conclusion. His much-criticized assumption of the army command in the fall of 1915 was consistent with his idea of personal responsibility. The inability of the politicians in the capital to appreciate the extent of Nicholas's patriotism and his sense of obligation had contributed to the steady degeneration of relations between the Duma and the emperor. Only people ignorant of Nicholas's character could have accused his government of incompetence and the imperial family of treason in the expectation that these attacks would bring concessions to parliamentary government. Instead the slanderous attacks upon the empress, like the murder of Rasputin, convinced the emperor once again of the complete irresponsibility of the intelligentsia and destroyed any chance of accommodation between the Duma politicians and the monarchy.[69]

Nicholas's intransigence when faced with wartime opposition appeared wholly in accord with his ideology of duty, as Ol'denburg understood it. But why had the tsar suddenly and completely capitulated on March 1, 1917? Nicholas's abdication seemed at odds with Ol'denburg's portrait. Could a man who felt himself "responsible before God and history" give up his post? For Ol'denburg, Nicholas's dedication to winning the war and his conviction that this was essential to the nation's welfare helped to explain the abdication. It was the disaffection of the military leaders that had persuaded him to resign. The generals' support for the Duma government and the prospect of an internecine conflict within the army should he remain in power were the decisive factors for the monarch.[70]

The primacy of the war in Nicholas's considerations was made clear in his farewell address to the army, a document "hidden" by the Provisional Government and published in full by Ol'denburg. In it Nicholas called on his "beloved forces" to be loyal to the Provisional Government and their commanders and to consider anyone who called for peace a traitor to the country, urgings that reflected his concern over the grave threat to the Russian state. The tsar's last manifesto concluded with an ambiguous declaration: "I firmly believe that boundless love for our Great Country has not died out in Your hearts."[71] This pathetic assertion of his faith suggested that Nicholas, too, had begun to doubt. Did the "good people" perhaps still live only in the tsar's imagination? In the captivity that followed his abdication, Nicholas was freed, finally, from his responsiblity for these people and for Russia. He seemed "almost happy," Ol'denburg observed, and he faced his executioners with the "simple and serene majesty" that had made him a "real, . . . very Russian tsar."[72]

By entering into the psychology of the monarch, Ol'denburg had created a "loving" and forgiving image, one that would seem to answer Struve's call for an empathetic understanding of the past. In addition, the biography was a healthy corrective to the intelligentsia's fixation on its own martyrdom; from Ol'denburg's point of view, society was not the only victim of the revolution, nor was it free from blame. But *The Sovereign Emperor Nicholas II Alexandrovich* was not successful as a political defense of the Russian monarchy. In spite of itself, Ol'denburg's truthful essay revealed both Nicholas's failings and deep faults in the autocratic system.

That Ol'denburg chose to make his case by writing a biography illustrated the fusion of personal and political spheres in the monarchical tradition. In the right circumstances, this was not a weakness; the expression of national strength in the fiction of an all-powerful monarch could function as a unifying, inspirational mythology. But Nicholas failed to understand the essential symbolism of his role. As Ol'denburg's sketch indicated, the last tsar took his absolutism seriously. Although the monarchist ideology was in itself, as Kaiser Wilhelm had recognized, a recipe for political difficulties, Nicholas's personality made his problems worse. "Simplicity" and "serenity" were virtues for tsars who lived in calmer times. In modern Russia, a tsar willing to let his ministers' divergent views find a parliamentary resolution might have survived, and a tsar who outlawed divergent voices altogether had probably an even better chance—this was closer to the Bolshevik solution—but a tsar who listened politely and then quietly went his way was doomed. Society's aversion to Nicholas's mild manner was an educated echo of Vinberg's demand for authoritarian control. By concentrating on the ethical qualities of Nicholas's behavior, Ol'denburg avoided coming to terms with the fact his analysis suggested—Nicholas was despised more for his weakness than his strength.

Ol'denburg's study pointed, again indirectly, to another obstacle in the way of Russian monarchy. Nicholas's personality was an accident of genetics, but his ideology was not. By stressing Nicholas's upbringing, Ol'denburg had shown the force of the autocratic idea within the tsar's own culture. Nicholas, like the Russian intellectuals, was a prisoner of his beliefs, and these, as Ol'denburg demonstrated, were not conducive to sharing power. The monarch's image of the intelligentsia made it especially unlikely that responsibility would ever be granted to the representatives of Russian society, let alone the people. One of the strengths of Ol'denburg's work was its emphasis on the influence of "fictions and conventions" upon the political impasse of the old regime.

In general, however, *The Sovereign Nicholas II Alexandrovich* did not specifically address political problems and this was one of the work's major flaws. Ol'denburg's case for the monarchy did have a basis in the economic statistics and social achievements he enumerated, but these were not the concerns of the intelligentsia and the people at the time of greatest pressure on the state. The war had to be considered part of Nicholas's reign as well. While Ol'denburg had not hesitated to attribute the favorable "balance" of the prewar reign to Nicholas, he discarded even this crude measure after 1914. In his sympathetic identification with the tsar, he accepted the notion of autocratic responsibility and then applied it selectively. Especially after the fall of 1916, when the political mood of the capital had gone decisively against the emperor, Ol'denburg, like his subject, just gave up.

Ol'denburg's view of the revolution attributed a decisive role to ideas. It was the hostile imagery of the intelligentsia and the tsar that had set them so totally at odds. "The true tragedy," wrote Ol'denburg of the break between the Duma leaders and the monarch in the fall of 1916, was that "both sides, at heart, were fully convinced that they were right."[73] At the same time, this study called attention to the role of absolutist ideology and absolutist symbolism in the old regime. Nicholas had absorbed the ideology, but not the symbolism. He was not a "a sword," not personally fit for the familiar, forceful dictatorship that might have forestalled the revolution. Yet his conviction of his own responsibility did not permit him to supervise a transition to participatory government. Nicholas retained absolute authority without embodying it. This was a complete reversal of the course taken by the monarchy in the West and it proved fatal in Russia in 1917.

Monarchist Politics, 1921–1922

Like socialists and liberals in the emigration, Russian monarchists attempted to organize themselves abroad. In their efforts they were not guided or restricted by earlier alignments; the conservative parties of the old regime—both Octobrists and Nationalists—had vanished with the autocracy.[74] While the émigré associations of Mensheviks, Socialist Revolutionaries, and Kadets were based on prerevolutionary ties and, for the most part, prerevolutionary principles, the monarchists started fresh. In addition, they enjoyed the opportunity offered by a growing number of enthusiasts. In the other world of emigration politics, the monarchists now faced the challenge of uniting many individuals in a single cause.

But unity—that enticing standard of so many Russian political movements—eluded post-revolutionary monarchism from the start. In 1921 two distinct organizations adopted monarchist programs and refused to have anything to do with one another. The National Congress that met in Paris in June 1921 served as a forum for moderates whose monarchist sentiments were integrated into a liberal program of social and economic reconstruction in Russia. The leaders of this short-lived group deliberately refrained from inviting right-wing monarchists to their meeting.[75] This exclusion provided an excuse for vitriolic comments, but it could hardly have hurt feelings. The right-wing monarchists held their own conference at Bad Reichenhall in Bavaria from May 29 to June 6, 1921. Although the Reichenhall congress was nominally an attempt to form a "general monarchist" movement, its leaders were for the most part extremists connected with the anti-Semitic *Aufbau* society, a German-Russian group organized by Max von Scheubner-Richter in the winter of 1920–1921. German rightists were responsible for local arrangements at Bad Reichenhall and participated in some of the festivities. The Russian leadership of the conference was dominated by General Biskupskii, a notorious intriguer, and E. N. Markov II, a founding member of the Union of the Russian People and an editor of *Dvuglavyi orel* (The Double-headed Eagle), a scurrilous monarchist publication based in Berlin.[76]

At Reichenhall, the monarchists held the perfectly orchestrated party congress. Their goal was symbolic unity and affirmation, and it was achieved by strict organizational control and a well-designed appeal to conformist and authoritarian temperaments. The organizers of the conference took care to construct a "facade" of national monarchist committees—Great Russian, Ukrainian, and Belorussian—and to invite an impressive array of church dignitaries, officers, non-Russians, and sympathetic intellectuals to the meeting.[77] The orderly and pastoral setting held great allure for the 150 participants, as did the smart ceremony of the proceedings.[78] According to E. Efimovskii, an erstwhile liberal whom the Berlin group had included in the planning stages, a "secret congress" before the actual meeting had agreed to propose two principles: "unity in diversity" and "the worst monarchy is better than the best republic."[79]

The leaders of the congress had planned its elections and resolutions well. All reports made at the conference were accepted unanimously, as were the prearranged nominations to the Supreme Monarchist Council (*Vyshii monarkhicheskii sovet*).[80] This triumvirate was composed of Markov II; Prince A. A. Shirinskii-Shikhmatov, a prominent rightist active in the administration of the Orthodox Church, and A. M. Maslennikov, a former Kadet.[81] The regulations for the monarchist association, also adopted unanimously, were a paradigm of hierarchical organization and informal politics. The highest organ of the "general-monarchist movement" was to be the yearly congress of delegates, their provenance and method of selection unspecified. The "executive organ," which would act in the stead of the congress between the yearly sessions, was the Supreme Monarchist Council, chosen at the yearly meeting. The Council had the right to coopt its own members, both permanent and temporary. The highest authorities of the Orthodox Church in exile were declared honorary members of the Council, which was to have its own newspaper.[82]

Thus the right wing of Russian monarchism began its political life in the emigration with the sanction of a representative assembly and an organization controlled from the top. Its ideology was noncontroversial. For formal purposes anti-Semitism was dropped; the positive program called for the primacy of the Russian Orthodox Church, the denationalization of property, free trade, and, of course, monarchy.[83]

But who was to be king? For all their learning from the past, the Russian monarchists could not resurrect the dead. Nicholas's legal successors had perished with him, and none of the Romanovs abroad had claimed the right to rule. The Reichenhallers were obliged to send a delegation to the Dowager Empress Maria Feodorovna to request that a family council choose one of the surviving grand dukes as a guardian of the throne.[84] The dynasty was not quick to answer. In September 1921, four months after Reichenhall, Efimovskii began to despair. "Perhaps the Russian monarchists themselves have not merited a monarchy," he wrote in his new weekly *Griadushchaia Rossiia* (The Future Russia). "Some of them contributed to the fall of the monarchy, while others were not able to avert this fatal event."[85]

Efimovskii represented a minority at Reichenhall who were willing to blame themselves and not the liberals or the Jews for the collapse of the old regime. His *Griadushchaia Rossiia* attracted more respectable contributors than either *Luch sveta* or *Dvuglavyi orel*.[86] But by the end of 1922 all these publications had collapsed.[87] Even as it began, the monarchist movement in the emigration disintegrated into quarrelling factions. In late 1921, a Council of the Russian Orthodox Church in Serbia endorsed the monarchy, an act that alientated liberals who wanted to keep the church out of politics.[88] While the moderate monarchists, sympathetic to Russia's former allies, retained their Paris connections, in Germany the monarchist organizations disintegrated as the government drew closer to a pro-Soviet policy and support from native reactionaries dwindled.[89] To complicate matters further, the Romanov family had by 1922 produced not one but two contenders for the throne. Both the Grand Duke Kirill Vladimirovich, Nicholas II's cousin, and the popular Grand Duke Nikolai Nikolaevich, a nephew of Nicholas's grandfather, had separate followings in the emigration.[90] In addition to these live rivals, ghosts of Nicholas's immediate family began to assert their claims.[91] Adding to these difficulties, by the time a second monarchist congress convened in Berlin in March 1922, only thirty-five delegates were present.[92]

At the Berlin conference, held at the Rotes Haus restaurant, "unity in diversity" was based on a cautious pledge of loyalty to the Romanov dynasty—candidate unnamed—and to the Supreme Monarchist Council.[93] Once again a vague formula enabled moderates like Efimovskii and Ol'denburg to cooperate with reactionaries of Markov II's ilk. This symbolic unity was terminated by the actions of the extreme right wing. Vinberg and his collaborators, Shabel'skii-Bork and Taboritskii, had been forced to move to Munich after the Kapp putsch, but they were still intent upon exposing the Jewish-Masonic conspiracy behind the revolution.[94] Now their plans included murder. On the night of March 28, 1922, while the monarchist conference was still in session, Shabel'skii-Bork and Taboritskii tried to assassinate Miliukov.

Miliukov was in Berlin to address an émigré gathering at the Philharmonic Hall. As he left the stage after his speech, one of the assassins stepped forward, drew a gun, and fired. Thrown to the ground by a member of the audience, Miliukov was untouched, but V. D. Nabokov, the editor of the liberal newspaper *Rul'*, was killed while trying to prevent the gunman from attacking again. After the shooting, Shabel'skii-Bork and Taboritskii announced their act as vengeance for the "murder of the Russian tsar" and shouted anti-Semitic insults. Both were caught by the audience and one almost lynched before they were handed over to the German police.[95]

This tragedy not only deprived the liberal emigration of one of its most sensible and humane leaders,[96] it damaged the monarchist movement as well. When Shabel'skii-Bork and Taboritskii were arrested, the German authorities were quick to make the wrong connection. The monarchist conference at the Rotes Haus was broken up by the police and the delegates carted off for questioning. This abrupt ending of the Reichenhall collaboration was, it seems, superfluous. Not many monarchists were still in attendance at the conference when the police arrived. According to a participant, "the fruitlessness of the business and the boredom" had already driven them away.[97]

The Kingdom of Ideals

Russian monarchism, like Russian populism, could not be eradicated by arrests. Despite the setbacks suffered by the monarchist groups in Germany, the monarchist idea continued to attract adherents throughout the emigration. Unlike the parties of the left, monarchism had no capital city abroad. Its sympathizers were everywhere. In 1925, they accounted for 85 percent of the emigration, in Struve's rough estimation.[98] As in 1921, many flowers bloomed, but none bore any fruit, except for Vinberg's poisonous variety. Shabel'skii-Bork and Taboritskii, convicted of the murder of Nabokov, did not serve out their prison terms. Later they offered their services to the Nazis.[99]

The popularity of various monarchist ideas in the emigration was related to new circumstances. Russian monarchism after the revolution was no longer tied to the Romanovs and their government. Outside the national territory and in the absence of a ruler, monarchism became what the reformist opposition had always been—a primarily ideological phenomenon. Rid of the reality of dynastic power, the monarchist ideal attracted a broad spectrum of supporters. Liberals like Struve felt the need for a compelling national symbolism and supported constitutional monarchy as a safeguard of civil liberties.[100] Reactionaries, on the other hand, believed that a strong monarchy could control the Russian people, who were by nature vulnerable to evil forces. Both moderates and extremists regarded the monarchy as able to enforce and legitimate their own ideas, exactly as the populists had envisioned the Russian people.

Elevated to a pure abstraction, monarchism had some advantages over rival constructs. Unlike Russian socialism, populism, or liberalism, it had at least existed in the past. And, in contrast to the notion of proletarian power, the monarch's authority was not, in theory, particularistic. In its reductive imagery, Russian monarchism placed the tsar outside and above the disparate groups and individuals in the nation. His power obviated confrontation with the will of others, and it freed the individual from the perils of autonomy. To some survivors of the collapse of liberal initiatives in Russia, the abdication of individualism, one's own and that of others, came easily. A "firm authority" (*sil'naia vlast'*) had to exist, many felt, and it was best and strongest coming from above.

In addition to its authoritarian appeal, the monarchy had a communal mythology to offer. The Reichenhall "principle" of "unity in diversity" was easily accomplished in the monarchist imagination. Through his physical and spiritual embodiment of the entire empire, the monarch provided a symbolic resolution of differences. A shared belief in the monarch did not do away with conflicts of interest, but for many the monarchical symbol was more compelling than the socialist vision. Socialist harmony was only a promise for the future—in the present socialism demanded class struggle—while the monarchist synthesis, because it existed in the mind, was available immediately.

The monarchist cause was easy to believe in but difficult to serve. Acts of personal symbolism, like the assassination of Nabokov, were well suited to the emblematic quality of monarchist belief, but incapable of bringing a ruler into power.[101] At the least, the post-revolutionary monarchists needed a candidate for the throne, but in this matter the émigrés and the Romanovs were equally ineffectual. As for the intellectual defense of monarchism, this had been sabotaged by the dynasty itself. Those intelligent and patriotic Russians who might have been expected to advocate a restoration on conservative principles could not bring themselves to argue for the old regime. They kept silent, or, like the intellectuals on the left, wrote memoirs that ended before the war.[102] Ol'denburg alone took the monarch's part, yet even his compassionate biography did not absolve the tsar.

Thus after 1917 the idea of monarchy flourished in the absence of the institution. This, in part, explained the vacuousness of the orchestrated conferences at Reichenhall and Berlin and the extremists' penchant for fantasy and mysticism. Invention was carried to a perverse extreme in Vinberg's anti-Semitic propaganda, in which authoritarian fanatics could find an enemy worthy of their own failed dreams. I. F. Nazhivin, a tough-minded observer interested in the revival of monarchist sentiment among the Russian peasants, was repulsed by what he discovered in the monarchist emigration. It was the same "romantic nonsense" he had heard on the left, the same "dreary vaudeville."[103] Russian monarchists in Germany, he wrote,

> understood their role to be pushing us back into the old, rotten swamp, assuring everyone that it was not a swamp, but the heavenly kingdom; but if it had been the heavenly kingdom, then we would have nothing to do on the banks of the Spree, we would still be in the heavenly kingdom, and since we

were on foreign soil, then, obviously, there were some weighty reasons for this. The main one was a secret to no one: the old regime had rotted to the root, crashed down, and crushed millions of people in its fall.[104]

But, with the exception of Ol'denburg, the monarchists paid little attention to the problems of the old regime. For the extremists, the tsar was perfect and the revolution was easy to explain: the people, the intelligentsia, Russia's foreign rivals, and the Jews had caused it all.

5

A Different Culture

From the Depths

While the leaders of various Russian parties and factions measured the revolution against their political goals, other, more speculative, observers felt that contemporary events called all these aspirations into question. For those intellectuals whose primary concern was culture, not politics, the country's collapse into anarchy, war, and famine proved that the course chosen by the intelligentsia before 1917 had been based on ignorance of the Russian nation, its people, and its possibilities. Recovery from the devastation of the revolution had, they thought, to be based on a reexamination of Russian values and Russian culture. Not until the intelligentsia had come to understand the country for which it claimed to speak could the nation begin to heal itself.

This countercurrent of Russian thought was not new in 1917. Like the political opposition to Bolshevik government, cultural nationalism derived from prerevolutionary ideas. Since the beginning of the century, many of Russia's outstanding intellectuals had been attracted to philosophical perspectives that rejected the conventions of the nineteenth-century revolutionary tradition. The creators of the "renaissance"[1] in Russian culture repudiated materialism, positivism, and atheism in favor of idealism, aesthetics, and faith. Struve was a leader of this intellectual about-face, along with the philosophers Nikolai Berdiaev and S. L. Frank, and the theologian Sergei Bulgakov.[2] Their turn away from Marxist politics and their support for individual endeavor outside the political arena coincided with the explosion of artistic and scholarly creativity in the prerevolutionary period.[3] Although the new movement was eclectic and individualistic, a spirit rather than a doctrine, it produced two collective works that represented its general direction. The first of these, *Problems of Idealism* (*Problemy idealizma*), a philosophical critique of positivism, was published in 1903. It was followed in the aftermath of the 1905 revolution by *Vekhi* (Landmarks), the idealists' all-out assault on the assumptions and actions of the radical intelligentsia.[4]

Although this new attention to the irrational foundations of consciousness and culture reflected a general trend in European social thought, in Russia the idealist movement met with great hostility and only partial success. The profuse and venomous counterattack against *Vekhi* indicated that the intelligentsia was unwilling to abandon its old commitments. To positivists such as Miliukov or Martov, the idealists' insistence on the primacy of cultural and religious values was triply pernicious; these ideas abetted the formation of an elite culture, drew off the energies of society from politics, and undermined the theoretical foundations of progressive politics.[5] But the essence of the quarrel between the *vekhovtsy* and the representatives of the materialist tradition did not concern the exclusivity of politics and culture, but the question of how best to serve the nation. The idealists were explicitly patriotic, and some, like Struve, were active in political life. They differed from the radical intelligentsia in the importance they attached to the cultural transformation of Russian society and Russian people. Moral reform, they felt, rather than the single-minded attack upon the state, was essential to the nation's well-being. In this respect, the conflict between Russian interpreters of two Western philosophies—nineteenth-century positivism and twentieth-century subjectivism—was also the ancient debate between materialists and moralists. The *vekhovtsy* did not think that political revolution by itself could change Russia for the better.

The revolution only reinforced the convictions of both sides in this dispute. As the political intelligentsia resumed its criticism of the state, idealists took up their pens against the radical tradition. Their first and most coherent onslaught was voiced in *Iz glubiny* (From the Depths), the literary symposium on the revolution organized by Struve in 1918. In addition to Struve's essay, "The Historical Meaning of the Russian Revolution and National Tasks," the volume contained articles by Berdiaev, Frank, and Bulgakov; two liberal journalists A. S. Izgoev and V. N. Muraviev; the poet Viacheslav Ivanov; S. A. Askol'dov and P. I. Novgorodstev, philosophers; and two specialists on law—S. A. Kotliarevskii and I. A. Pokrovskii.[6]

The participants in *Iz glubiny* viewed the revolution as an immense national and spiritual tragedy. Unlike the left-wing intellectuals, they did not focus their attention on the Bolsheviks. From the idealists' perspective, the sufferings endured since 1917 could not be blamed on political oppression alone; they had more profound causes in the history and culture of prerevolutionary Russia. Of the articles in the collection, Struve's was eccentric in its historical specificity; he alone argued for the responsibility of the state. The rest of the contributors, with the exception of Viacheslav Ivanov who offered a lyrical tribute to the Russian language, suggested that the entire nation was suffering from a great moral flaw, not easily defined but pervasive and corrupting. The masses were, to some degree and to some of the *Iz glubiny* writers, infected with this moral illness. In Askol'dov's apocalyptic interpretation, the revolution had released the "beast" within the Russian people,[7] and other writers concurred with their representations of the masses as a passive, crude, materialistic force.[8] But all the contributors agreed that the intelligentsia was the true culprit and malefactor of the revolution. It was educated individuals who had promoted the "lies" of socialism and revolution, who refused to understand the values of the law and of the state, who looked at the world through the "rose and black glasses" of their abstract principles.[9] These were not the faults of the Bolsheviks alone, but of the whole of political society. The liberals, like the socialists, wrote Frank,

> considered all the ruled good and only the rulers evil. Like the socialists, they did not acknowledge or insufficiently acknowledged the dependence of every government [*vlast'*] on the spiritual and cultural level of society, and consequently, the responsibility of society for its government.[10]

This indictment reflected *Iz glubiny*'s direct descent from *Vekhi*. Once more the idealists rejected the conventions of the left. They repudiated the moral polarity of society and state, and suggested that the people and especially their educated leaders could be held accountable for the deficiencies of life in Russia.

Although the contributors to *Iz glubiny* stressed the responsibility of the intelligentsia for the revolution's destructive course, they did not therefore whitewash the old regime. Theirs was not a world of moral opposites—society versus the state, or, in the monarchist reversal, the good tsar and the evil people—but rather a vision of the nation as a single community. Their ideal was an organic connection between state and nation, and this, they felt, had been missing long before the revolution. The old regime, wrote Novgorodtsev, had failed to unite the nation with its "dogmatic and isolating" ideology of "Autocracy, Orthodoxy, and Nationality," whose inadequacy the intelligentsia had attacked without providing anything positive in its place.[11] In this respect, the *Iz glubiny* writers were not conservatives—they had no kind words for the recent past and many harsh ones for the prerevolutionary right[12]—but instead the advocates of a national community that had yet to appear.

For all their criticism of intelligentsia "utopianism," the idealists' response to their situation was distinctly otherworldly. As before the revolution, criticism of the intelligentsia provided no answers for the future.[13] The majority of the articles in *Iz glubiny* concluded with hopes for a spiritual revival, auguries almost as formulaic and certainly more pompous than the democratic slogans of the party politicians.[14] The nation, Russian culture, the state—these absolute values would be appreciated as a consequence of the revolutionary scourge, and in their service, the intelligentsia could begin the process of national renewal.

These vague prophecies were based on the most dubious reasoning and raised more questions in their turn. The contributors to *Iz glubiny* provided little foundation for their hopes other than the strength of their own faith and a kind of dialectical reasoning worthy of Bakunin. The very enormity of the revolutionary destruction would chasten Russia into self-transcendence, they appeared to say. They did not indicate how moral rebirth could bring about political change, and none of their high goals had specific social content.[15] Moreover, the idealists, who were constantly berating other intellectuals for their ignorance of life, failed to provide an image of the Russian nation to which one could in good conscience be true. Their criticism in *Iz glubiny* cast doubt upon the moral qualities of both the people and their leaders. What were the possibilites of Russian culture, and if the intelligentsia could be converted to this ideal, how was it to serve the nation? In the years following the revolution, nationalist intellectuals proposed several radical solutions to these problems.

Nikolai Berdiaev: "The Peculiarity of Bitter Russian Fate"

Of the contributors to *Iz glubiny*, Nikolai Aleksandrovich Berdiaev offered the most provocative psychological interpretation of the revolution. Berdiaev's view of Russian culture was profoundly critical. He found the Russian people—both the masses and the intelligentsia—to be suffering from a "sickness of the moral consciousness," unable to sustain a disciplined, responsible, and honorable way of life, and incapable of creating or appreciating cultural values. The severity of this indictment followed from Berdiaev's willingness to take the idealist standpoint to its logical extreme and to defend individualistic and explicitly aristocratic notions of creativity and ethics. If the mass of the Russian people did not share the moral or aesthetic sensibilities of the elite, this did not surprise him, nor did it necessarily place limits on the future of the nation. From Berdiaev's lofty perspective, the "Christian spirit of Russia" could act through a "minority" who were the bearers of national ideals.[16]

Berdiaev's early writings on the revolution exhibited the eccentric flamboyance that caused him later to appear in Western eyes as the apotheosis of the Russian soul.[17] But, unlike Berdiaev's subsequent works, these studies from the first years after 1917 expressed a malevolent and disparaging account of Russian life, the most hostile analysis to appear in the revolutionary period. At this time, Berdiaev was a fervent admirer of Joseph de Maistre and seemed to regard himself as the creative "reactionary" of the Russian revolution, a philosopher whose spiritual quest would, like his hero's, lay the groundwork for a century of thought.[18] Although Berdiaev's voluminous, contradictory, and unsystematic opus was not equal to this task, his open elitism allowed him to discuss the disparity between elite and mass values, a difference in culture that the populist intelligentsia was unable to confront directly.

Unlike must Russian intellectuals, Berdiaev did not believe in progress. Thus, while he considered the revolution a catastrophe, he did not therefore dismiss it as a temporary aberration from the forward course of history. On the contrary, for Berdiaev, the revolution was a repugnant, but logical consequence of the Russian past. Not only was the Bolshevik regime a direct successor to the anarchy released by the February revolution, it was also a return to older habits. Nothing has changed, Berdiaev wrote in November 1917 in an article entitled "Has There Been a Revolution in Russia?"[19] What we call a revolution is only the force of inertia:

> All of the past is repeating itself and acts only behind new masks. The turbulent processes occur only on the surface. These processes are only the rotting of the ragged clothes of unregenerated Russia. We are living out the consequences of our old sins; we suffer from our moral illnesses. *In Russia there has been no revolution.*[20]

The moral illnesses to which Berdiaev referred afflicted the people, not the state. It was true, he commented, that the old regime had "ingloriously fallen like an apple from a tree," but this was no sign of real change. The "rot" was in Russians themselves; the ugly anarchy released in 1917 was part of the people's character. They spent their energies not on political reform, but in malicious vengeance. Under the direction of the intelligentsia, the masses had vented their anger on the "bourgeoisie," which to them meant all of educated society. But there was nothing new here, Berdiaev insisted. In the old days, too, the tsarist regime had relied upon the "illiterate, dark masses of soldiers"; now the Bolsheviks would do the same. The habits of force and terror would return, the same "violation of freedom and rights, the same scoffing at the dignity of man." Nothing resembled democracy or socialism; the Bolshevik revolution was only a "moment" in the ongoing decay of Russia. The people had not changed: their present "hatred of the bourgeoisie" was the "dark East's age-old hatred of culture."[21]

Culture, Christianity, and individual freedom were Berdiaev's central concerns, and he was sure that Russian people cared nothing for them. From his perspective, the masses were rebelling not against a corrupt government, or against the "bourgeoisie," as the left would have it, but against the "higher" culture, the way of life, of educated society. Both in the city and the provinces, all educated individuals, not just political enemies, were subject to the mob's caprice. "The people have revolted against the work of Peter [the Great] and Pushkin," Berdiaev wrote in January 1918. To him, the significance of the revolution was that it made plain the conflict between "barbarianism" and culture.[22]

In his essay for *Iz glubiny*, Berdiaev tried to describe the "old national diseases and sins" that, he thought, had produced the revolution and shaped its distinctive features.[23] For his study of national character, entitled "Spirits of the Russian Revolution," he turned to nineteenth-century Russian literature—to Gogol and Dostoevsky, the two writers who, he felt, had most perceptively revealed the moral flaws in Russian life, and to Tolstoy, who, in Berdiaev's view, had displayed these flaws himself. This resort to literary evidence expressed Berdiaev's confidence in the superior insight of the artist; the creative writer was able to uncover truths no social theorist or politician could discuss. That these literary images derived from the last century did not perplex Berdiaev. In his opinion, most Russian people had not entered the modern age; it was the confusion of new and traditional values, "of the fourteenth with the twentieth centuries" that hindered the development of a unified national life.[24]

Gogol, the master satirist, had come closest to identifying the elemental defects in the Russian character, Berdiaev wrote in "Spirits of the Russian Revolution." With his "exceptional . . . sense for evil," Gogol had captured Russian people in their preposterously normal state of immorality. He had understood that Russian vices—greed, pomposity, deceit, malice, despotism—were too petty to merit tragic, human, forms. For this reason, the characters in Gogol's novel, plays, and stories frequently appeared as pieces of human beings—a nose, as in the famous story—or as bits of speech, never as whole people. This technique, Berdiaev commented, was an anticipation of cubism, and it expressed the same perception of reality. By dissecting and distorting his characters' physical forms, Gogol deprived them of humanity. "Gogol saw the same monsters . . . as Picasso," thought Berdiaev. His creativity was "homicidal," and in this way, true to the "inhuman caddishness" of Russian nature.[25]

This Russian spirit had not vanished with the revolution, according to Berdiaev. The autocracy had fallen, but Gogol's characters had not only survived, but come to the surface of politics. Bribery remained the "constitution" of the country, and Khlestiakov, the impostor of Gogol's play *The Inspector General*, had now elevated himself to the summit of authority. The speeches of the "revolutionary Khlestiakovs" could be heard daily: " 'I'm not joking; I'll show them all. . . . I am so! I don't give a damn about anyone. . . . I'm everywhere, everywhere.' " Chichikov, the swindler of *Dead Souls*, was likewise omnipresent—always on a special train, scattering telegrams far and wide, dealing hastily in the "dead souls" of the fictitious revolutionary economy. The whole agrarian reform was, in Berdiaev's eyes, a "Chichikovian" enterprise—grand in scope and a vast fraud in reality.[26]

It was the great self-deceit of the revolution that reminded Berdiaev of Gogol's grotesque world. Gogol had understood that schemes like Chichikov's and Khlestiakov's were founded on a propensity to wishful thinking, a lack of reasoning in one's approach to life—in Berdiaev's terminology, a "lack of ontology [*neontologichnost'*]." A second characteristic, connected with this willingness to fall for profitable illusions, was a deep-seated fear of getting caught in one's own lies by a higher, but not necessarily better, authority. The possibility always remained that one day, as in Gogol's play, the real inspector-general would arrive to uncover and exploit the duplicities of others. This attitude—"the perpetual fear of the gendarme"—could be seen in the masses' dread of counterrevolution; according to Berdiaev, their apprehension betrayed the underlying "irreality and falsity of the revolution's achievements." Even the Gogolian supporters of the revolution saw it as something that could be swept away at any time. People whose experience was saturated with hypocrisy were incapable of believing in their own ascendancy.[27]

If the Russian people had a low opinion of themselves and others, the intelligentsia was all too ready to embrace ideas of human perfectibility. This, according to Berdiaev, was one of the lessons of Dostoevsky's great psychological novels. To Berdiaev, Dostoevsky was the "prophet of the Russian revolution," the genius who had uncovered the "dialectic of . . . revolutionary thought."[28] Long before 1917, Dostoevsky had perceived that the Russian intelligentsia would be attracted by the idea of socialism, that the essence of this idea was the denial of God, and that its consequences in Russia would be catastrophic.

In Dostoevsky's view, as Berdiaev recreated it in "Spirits of the Russian Revolution," socialism appealed to the Russian intelligentsia not by virtue of its class-based ideology, but as a secular religion, a new faith that promised the kingdom of God on earth. This promise was accepted by the intelligentsia out of moral weakness. Instead of coming to grips with the complexities of historical existence, the revolutionaries were drawn to the notion that evil itself could be abolished.[29] This apocalyptic Russian socialism shielded the intelligentsia both from the realities of life and from their own inadequacies. As Petr Verkhovenskii, the nihilist conspirator in *The Possessed*, remarked, "the cement that binds all together is the shame of one's own opinion." The fear of thinking independently, the suspicion that one's own thoughts were worthless, was what led the intelligentsia to abdicate its mind to the collective and its soul to those who, in Verkhovenskii's words, "worked on this 'sweet little fact' so that not a single private idea remained in anyone's head."[30] It was easier to believe in the collective than to strive for understanding on one's own, and if the kingdom of God could come on earth, then collective opinion would be good.

The search for some kind of "apocalyptic or nihilistic" truth was a "deep national trait," Berdiaev commented. The favorite questions of "Russian boys," drinking in their "stinking taverns," concerned the existence of God and the possibilities for humankind. Dostoevsky had captured the essence of these endless discussions in the "Legend of the Grand Inquisitor," when Ivan Karamazov asked Alesha if he, in order to achieve happiness and peace for all mankind, would be willing to torture a single baby. The very expression of this thought demonstrated the fundamentally irreligious quality of Russian moralism, Berdiaev observed. Any Christian knew the answer to this question, but only an atheist could pose it. The question was itself a revolt against God, the blasphemy of "the Russian nihilist-moralist [who] thinks that he loves man and suffers with man more than God," who believes that he can "correct God's plan" and eliminate suffering and sacrifice from life. At the base of this question was not Christian love, but "some kind of false Russian sensitivity and sentimentality, a false compassion for man, developed into a hatred for God and for the divine meaning of earthly life." In his irreligious pathos, Ivan Karamazov was typical of "untold numbers of Russian boys, Russian nihilists and atheists, socialists and anarchists." He had "mistaken Western negating hypotheses for axioms and begun to believe in atheism."[31]

Dostoevsky had tried to warn his readers of the dangers of these blasphemous ideas. *The Possessed*, his famous novel about a radical conspiracy, portrayed the consequences of succumbing to apocalyptic fantasies, of believing that revolution could establish God's kingdom on earth: the "right to dishonor [*pravo na beschest'e*]" led the conspirators in the novel to murder and suicide, not salvation.[32] To Dostoevsky, Christianity was not only the true faith, but also an essential one for Russia. Atheism, he suggested in his novels, would release the devils in the weak Russian spirit—if God did not exist, then all would be permitted—and under the regime of "Russian boys," life would be turned into hell.[33] In *The Brothers Karamazov* Father Zosima had expressed this fear in his description of the revolutionaries:

> In truth they have more visionary fantasy than we! They conceive of arranging things justly, but having repudiated Christ, they will end by flooding the world with blood, for blood calls forth blood, and he who lives by the sword shall perish by the sword. And if it were not for Christ's promise, they would annihilate each other, even to the last two men on earth.[34]

The revolution, thought Berdiaev, had borne out Dostoevsky's intuition. It had confirmed that the "humanism" of the revolutionaries was false, that it led to the destruction of humanity, not to a better life on earth.[35] Russians were eager to make "a story about God from a child's tear," but they were not willing to suffer themselves in order to reduce the amount of pain in the world. Instead, they tried to destroy existing society, and their actions, released from the moral constraints, only "increased the quantity of . . . tears." Moreover, Dostoevsky's positive vision—his faith that the Russian people and their church would prevail against the temptations of the Antichrist—had been disproved. This was one more "populist illusion" destroyed in the past year.[36] The Russian people—Gogol's people—and the Russian intelligentsia— Dostoevsky's "boys"—had both given themselves up to the revolutionary temptation.

It remained for Berdiaev to unmask Tolstoy as the incarnation of the Russian spirit. To him, Tolstoy's collectivism provided a key to understanding Russian attitudes and helped to explain how atheistic humanism could lead to disregard for human life. His extreme egalitarianism, which abolished differences among people and even among humans, animals, and plants, was an "eastern, Buddhist sentiment." This submersion of the personal into the collective appealed to Russian values by releasing the individual from a moral obligation to himself and disguising this license as ethics. Thus it encompassed both "Russian moralism" and "Russian amoralism"—"two sides of the same sickness of the moral consciousness."[37]

To Berdiaev, this refusal to take an individualistic perspective on one's life was the fundamental problem with the Russian character. "I see the sickness of the Russian moral consciousness," he emphasized,

> above all in the denial of personal moral responsibility and personal moral discipline, in the weak development of a sense of duty and a sense of honor, in the absence of consciousness of the moral value of a range of personal qualities. The Russian person does not feel morally accountable to a sufficient degree, and he inadequately respects the qualities of an individual.[38]

This attitude meant that a Russian person did not consider himself "the master of his own fate." Lacking faith in his own positive qualities, he despised them in others. He regarded every effort at improvement with suspicion; every higher culture seemed a "series of moral pretensions."[39]

In Berdiaev's account, Tolstoy's theory of art expressed this hatred for culture, a hatred born from lack of self-respect. In his later works, Tolstoy had denied the value of every human institution—the church, the state, the nation—in favor of a leveling equality. No other genius, wrote Berdiaev, had been so sunk in animal life and so hostile to the spirit, yet almost the whole intelligentsia considered Tolstoyan ethics "as the highest that could be achieved by man." The intellectuals accepted and admired Tolstoy's desire for absolute equality, for the abolition of the hierarchical historical world, for nonresistance, for anarchy. Like Tolstoy, they ignored original sin and imagined that natural man was good. The results of this ignorance were now plain, Berdiaev felt. Tolstoyan morality "killed the instinct of strength and glory in Russian nature and left behind the instinct of egoism, envy, and malice." It had "morally prepared the historical suicide of the Russian people." Dostoevsky was the revolution's prophet; Tolstoy was its philosopher.[40]

From Berdiaev's essay in *Iz glubiny* it seemed that the "spirits" of the revolution were commonplace specters, reflections of a national personality. To be Russian, according to this bleak and haughty view, meant to be susceptible to the ideal of human perfectibility and, at the same time, incapable of taking responsibility for one's life. Russians combined Tolstoyan ideals with Gogolian behavior. Their belief in impossible goals and their lack of confidence in their own abilities left them unprotected against the temptation of utopian promises. In Berdiaev's eyes, Western people, especially Catholics with their heightened awareness of evil, were spiritually fortified against the enticements of the Antichrist, while Russians suffered from the inability to distinguish between good and evil, to acknowledge the fullness and variety of life, to experience it "immanently." They preferred to live with their deceptions, addicted to the false hope that God's kingdom would come to them on earth. The only positive result of the revolution was to expose this fatal weakness and thus to offer the nation a chance to begin anew.[41]

Berdiaev developed this pessimistic perspective further in *The Philosophy of Inequality* (*Filosofiia neravenstva*), a book he composed in Moscow in 1918, but whose publication was not allowed in Russia.[42] First published in Berlin in 1923, this volume contains fourteen long "letters" on political topics— socialism, anarchism, liberalism, the state, and war among them. By describing the essays in *The Philosophy of Inequality* as letters, Berdiaev aspired to an exalted place in the tradition of Russian political thought. His book would be another epistolary consideration of Russia's destiny, a successor to Chaadaev's *Philosophical Letters* written ninety years before and a rebuttal to Lavrov's populist *Historical Letters* from the 1860s. But the foremost inspiration for *The Philosophy of Inequality* was Joseph de Maistre, whose "appearance" Berdiaev described as the "most significant result of the French revolution."[43] Berdiaev, in turn, considered himself the contemporary spokesman for creative, spiritual reaction; his objective in *The Philosophy of Inequality* was to attack not just the errors of Russian society, but the entire rationalist tradition. He now saw the revolution not only as divine retribution for Russia's sins, but also as a lesson for all humanity. It was a "great experiment" that "intensifies all the basic problems of social philosophy."[44]

Speaking for the values of culture and Christianity, Berdiaev attacked the Russian people, as he had in *Iz glubiny*, for their spiritual deficits. The Russians' "Eastern" frame of mind was to blame both for their losses in the World War and for the development of the revolution. Their inability to act courageously and forcefully for their nation he attributed to a "false relationship between the male and female principles" in the Russian psyche. Unlike the Europeans, whose national character had been formed in a "masculine" spirit, the Russians had remained "female," thought Berdiaev.[45] Alluding to the role of foreigners in forming and ruling the Russian state, he claimed that the Russian land was like a young bride,

> always waiting for a bridegroom from afar. . . . The Russian people could never produce a male authority from their own womb, they looked for it abroad, called in the Varangians or the German bureaucrats.[46]

When church and state were organized on borrowed principles, the people had remained pagan, Berdiaev continued. No true marriage of the people and the government had taken place. When at last a truly "masculine" autocrat appeared, the people did not accept him: Peter the Great was "more ravisher than husband," and through him the people became more embittered rather than reconciled with their national leadership. "The schism in the Russian soul" lasted to this day; it had led to the revolution and the destruction of the Russian state.[47]

This same passivity and irreconcilability were characteristic of the intelligentsia. According to Berdiaev, the intellectuals, like the people, waited for a bridegroom from abroad. Unable to discover a "masculine spirit" within, they borrowed it from the West, in particular from the writings of Karl Marx. Like the people, the intelligentsia was both apocalyptic and nihilistic in its attitudes. Fearful of the "Russian Eastern chaos" in its depths, it absorbed the latest Western teaching all the more voraciously. But these ideas, too, were not compatible with national life. Russian intellectuals did not regard their country as German intellectuals regarded Germany; instead they looked at Russia from outside, as German intellectuals looked at Russia.[48]

Vilification of the Russian national character was not Berdiaev's main objective in *The Philosophy of Inequality*. He castigated the intelligentsia not so much for borrowing from the West, as for borrowing the wrong ideas. In his opinion, socialism, anarchism, and democracy were pernicious doctrines. The products of Western rationalism, these political philosophies were mistaken in their assumptions about the human condition.

Underlying the misconceptions of these world views, according to Berdiaev, was a refusal to accept the irrational, historical realities of life. The "sociological" perspective of the nineteenth century denied any value to "real, ontological communities," such as the church, the state, the nation, and culture. Instead it reduced the world to abstract combinations of atoms, of human beings treated as atoms, as if there were no history and no religion to give their lives specific and unique significance.[49] This abstract attitude toward life was expressed most clearly in the idea of the equality of man, an idea that Berdiaev rejected as false and destructive. Not only was it obvious that people were natively unequal, the evidence of the past proved that inequality was the source of human achievement.

Berdiaev's arguments against equality were founded on a Nietzschean conception of value. All culture, he insisted, had been the product of exceptional individuals, not equals, of an elite, not whole societies. The highest achievements of each nation were not those of the "people," but of its geniuses. Pushkin, a member of the gentry, and Dostoevsky, an *intelligent*, were "a thousand times more national" than the Soviets of workers' and peasants' deputies. The true bearers of the national spirit were these "chosen individuals."[50] In economic life as well, inequality was the source of national prosperity. The fact that a small number of materially privileged people existed in society was not in itself an evil; taking away their riches would not alter the lives of the masses significantly. Indeed, to improve the fortunes of the masses, inequalities of wealth, which provided the means to increase human control over nature, were essential. Berdiaev was not arguing against amelioration, but against socialist economics. Like Struve, he felt that economic progress depended not on improving distribution, but on increasing productivity.[51]

There was, moreover, a direct connection between inequality and the possibility of cultural advance, from this point of view. Berdiaev, bucking the intelligentsia tradition, was an unabashed advocate of social hierarchy—of "aristocracy," in his terms. An aristocratic society was superior to a democratic one, he thought, because only aristocrats free of envy could act nobly and generously for the good of others. This argument was both elitist and self-serving—Berdiaev came from an aristocratic background—but it was not a defense of the old regime or of the prerevolutionary aristocracy. The absence of chivalry in Russia meant, Berdiaev commented, that no truly heroic tradition had ever developed in the country. In addition, he acknowledged that Russia's most talented class, the gentry, had declined in quality since the early nineteenth century. Nonetheless, the potential for aristocracy remained in Russian blood and it was to be these natural leaders, whose genius gave them precedence, that Berdiaev turned. Like Nietzsche, he hoped for an aristocracy of the spirit, based on birth, to be sure, but on the gifts of individuals, not the claims of groups.[52]

Berdiaev's attack on equality was based not only on the merits of aristocratic culture, but also upon his advocacy of total freedom. Freedom, he wrote later in his biography, was the foundation of his philosophy; it was the absolute for which he had struggled all his life.[53] Although Berdiaev was never able to define what this ideal meant for society, it was clear what it meant for him. He refused to be constrained by the desires, opinions, rules, and arguments of others. To him, democracy—that egalitarian "fiction"—represented a limitation on his self-assumed rights. "There is no more bitter and degrading dependence than dependence upon human will, on the arbitrariness of those who are equal to oneself," he carped. Submission to the power of priest or tsar was possible in the name of service to the higher principles of church and state, "but why should I have to surrender to the interests, instincts, and lusts of the human mass?"[54]

These protests against the "tyranny" of democracy[55] were symptomatic of Berdiaev's fears. His inability to trust the reason of other citizens and to accept them as political equals led him to mystical authorities instead. To him, church and state were bulwarks against humanity's evil nature, and as such history's highest creations. Their value was not related to institutional principles or established procedures—he was horrified by anything that smacked of "forms" or "mechanisms"—but to a simple victory of order over chaos. These sentiments provide an insight into Berdiaev's spiritual universe: he conceived of life as a battle between the "cosmic" principles of hierarchy, creativity, and culture against the anarchy of undifferentiated, "atomized" barbarism.[56]

In Berdiaev's mind, this cosmology merged with Christian ethics, and it was from a Christian perspective that he rejected socialism. Within bourgeois society, he acknowledged, socialism could be understood as a "noble and unselfish movement of the human spirit," an aristocratic impulse of generosity toward others.[57] Moreover, by unmasking the democratic "illusion," socialism had performed a useful function in the past. But as a system of social organization and as an ideology, socialism, in Berdiaev's view, was false. Like democracy, it violated his notion of freedom. The proletariat was just "a new fiction, a new fetish" with which the social democrats replaced the "people."[58] In a more profound and Christian sense, Berdiaev objected to what he called the "compulsory brotherhood" of socialist theory. Brotherhood—the love of people for each other—was not a secular phenomenon; in his eyes, it existed only through Christ. "In the natural order men are not brothers to each other but wolves," he wrote, and socialism itself derived from this worldly struggle. Society could require respect for the dignity and rights of each individual as a citizen, but the decision to love was a religious choice, made in freedom, through Christ's grace, by each person for himself. To Berdiaev, the socialist notion of "comradeship" was nonsense. Built on the theory that people were divided into hostile classes, and yet postulating a mutuality determined by material interest, "comradeship" was a sham and an impossibility, a "monstrous confusion" of the religious with the civil spheres.[59]

In addition to the fallacy of "compulsory collectivism," socialism violated Christian ethics. Its class-based morality, its legitimation of hatred, contradicted the message of the Gospel. "Christ taught people to give their wealth away; socialists say to take the wealth of others," Berdiaev gibed.[60] But beyond the obvious contrasts in their ethical systems, Christianity and socialism were based upon radically different attitudes toward life. True Christians knew that Christ's kingdom was of the spirit, while socialists thought that paradise could be built on earth. In *The Philosophy of Inequality*, Berdiaev expanded on this point, which he had made repeatedly before. He now considered socialism's amalgam of Christian eschatology with historical experience a product of "Jewish chiliasm." It was "no accident that Marx was Jewish," he noted, for his theory was a secular form of Jewish messianism.[61]

This notion that socialism was a Jewish world view had nothing in common with the anti-Semitic deliria of reactionaries such as Vinberg. For Berdiaev, socialism was not a Jewish conspiracy, but a theory that held a particular attraction for Jews. His basic idea had been expressed in *Iz glubiny*: socialism relied upon a millenarian deception that no true Christian could accept. But now he made a more historical argument; the messianic and socialist inclinations of Jews and Russians were products of their similar, though not identical, circumstances. Both peoples were cut off from an "organic" nationalism—the Jews had lost their country; the Russians had failed to develop an authentic national consciousness. These lacks led not to a lowering of expectations, but to a heightened sense of destiny. Both Russians and Jews felt that they had universal missions, and it was this mentality to which socialist ideas appealed.[62] But the results of such attitudes were catastrophic, Berdiaev warned. Messianism inspired people to extremes of sacrifice, to a kind of "madness in Christ" that destroyed nations and their cultures. The Russian revolution and the historical experience of the Jews both testified to the tragic results of messianism. From a Christian perspective, Christ's revelation meant that there could be no chosen people and no kingdom of God on earth. There were only nations and individuals within them who, in order to carry on a Christian life, had to accept the limitations of the historical world.[63]

Could Berdiaev himself do this? The answer was hardly clear from the misanthropic *Philosophy of Inequality*. The book, addressed to his "enemies in social philosophy,"[64] was a bitter denunciation of others' theories, rather than a plan for national reconstruction. Berdiaev's "creative" idea amounted to the negation of the Enlightenment tradition and no more. The "letters" were riddled with contradictions and gave every evidence of Berdiaev's lack of discipline—his poor and unrefurbished memory,[65] his habit of writing down and if possible publishing everything that came into his head,[66] and his complete disregard for order in his presentation.[67] What was most interesting in this work was its quality of psychological suggestion, the way it captured the mentality Berdiaev was attempting to describe. The disordered thoughts of the advocate of discipline, the mean-spirited diatribes about Christian love—were these the bold truths of a free spirit? As always, it was difficult to argue with a defender of the irrational.

Berdiaev's observations were consistent with Struve's idea that socialism appealed to Russians by promising the opportunity to work less, or to steal, without having to suffer the consequences. But Berdiaev suggested that this was not the way that Russian people would have described their choices to themselves; their preferences were not based on rational, calculated choices, or, as Struve explained it, an insufficient understanding of private property. In Berdiaev's explanation, Russians accepted the idea that theft could lead to paradise on earth out of lethargy—an unwillingness to take a responsible, constructive role in their own lives. The absence of chivalry and the influence of Russian orthodoxy were two historical factors contributing to this passivity, he felt. Russian models were martyrs, not heroes; Russians learned forbearance, not enterprise. These influences had a bearing upon the inadequate development of an individualistic ethic and the lack of self-discipline that inclined Russians to accept the authority of others. "Either the tsar or full anarchy—popular thought oscillated between these two poles," he commented.[68] In the spiritual realm, Russian attitudes were similarly extreme, swinging wildly from apocalyptic to nihilistic expectations. For this reason, Berdiaev argued, it was difficult for a Russian to contribute to the creation of a historical culture: "He just hoped that as soon as possible everything would finish in all or nothing."[69] These weaknesses were those of the intelligentsia as well. Instead of working to build a strong national tradition, they had seized upon ideas ready-made in the West. Of these, socialism had taken hold because its messianic and apocalyptic message appealed to the nationless, self-suspecting Russian psyche.

This analysis offered little hope for change. Unlike Struve, Berdiaev did not fall back upon a transcendent faith in the Russian people. According to his theory, Russian culture would have in any case to be created by an elite.

Clearly, Berdiaev considered himself one of those aristocrats capable of culture-building. Throughout the civil war, he remained in Moscow to carry on this task.

Although Berdiaev's criticism of the revolution was more radically hostile than the opposition of the moderate socialists, the authorities considered it less dangerous. For the first four years after 1917, he, like many members of the artistic elite, was permitted to pursue his cultural interests in relative security. While an old revolutionary like Kropotkin was forced out of the capitals, Berdiaev was allowed to keep his family's apartment and his books. He was even allotted a double ration as one of twelve well-known writers protected by the Bolsheviks—and nicknamed the "immortals."[70] This ration, income from a bookshop, and the earnings of his sister-in-law in a government post supported Berdiaev after the closing of the periodical press.[71] As "bourgeois," he and his family were forced at times to do compulsory heavy labor; he was arrested twice and imprisoned for a time in connection with a political trial;[72] the family had to sell or burn for fuel many of their personal possessions. But such hardships were commonplace, and Berdiaev's life in Moscow was one of privilege. Although he, for the most part, could not publish, he could write. Four books completed in these years appeared later in the West.[73]

In this period, Berdiaev led an active professional and social life. Unable to fit into party politics before the revolution, he found himself at home in the cultural controversies that occupied the nonparty intellectuals after 1917. Political organizations had been forced out, but the spirit was definitely in. Although the Orthodox Church had, with state help, torn itself apart in the revolution and civil war, religious sentiments flourished again in the intelligentsia.[74] Berdiaev held a regular open house on Tuesdays in his apartment, gatherings at which lectures on "spiritual" topics were delivered and discussed. For a time, he was a leading figure in the All-Russian Union of Writers and a frequent petitioner in the cause of members of the union who were imprisoned or harassed. In 1920, despite his lack of academic credentials, he was appointed Professor of Philosophy at Moscow University.[75] More important in the intellectual life of these years was Berdiaev's Free Academy of Spiritual Culture (*Vol'naia akademiia dukhovnoi kul'tury*), an association formed in the fall of 1919 to preserve and continue the Russian idealist movement.[76]

The academy, a free-form institution, held its courses and meetings in the halls of Soviet institutions where its sympathizers worked.[77] In 1919–1920, Berdiaev gave lectures on the philosophy of history and religion; the next year he led a seminar on Dostoevsky. These classes were the basis of his later books, *The Meaning of History* and *The World View of Dostoevsky*.[78] The writers Andrei Belyi and Viacheslav Ivanov and the philosopher S. L. Frank were among the other instructors. "The crisis of culture, the crisis of philosophy, on Christian freedom, on the essence of Christianity, . . . on the magic nature of the word, on Polish messianism, . . . Russia and Europe''—these and other topics dear to the minds of the idealists proved attractive to Soviet society.[79]

Encouraged by their overflow audiences, Berdiaev and Frank began in the spring of 1922 to organize a Philosophical-Humanistic Faculty (*Filosofsko-gumanitarnyi fakul'tet*) under the auspices of the academy.[80] But this project never had a chance. A year after the systematic suppression of the political opposition, the Soviet government turned its attention to the more ethereal intellectuals. Those who spoke for ''spiritual culture''—the idealists, the *vekhovtsy*, and other survivors of the Russian ''renaissance''—were now silenced. Berdiaev and Frank were among twenty-five intellectuals, most scholars or philosophers, expelled with their families from Russia in September 1922.[81] Before the expulsion, Berdiaev was told in prison that if he ever crossed the border back into Russia, he would be shot.[82] The Free Academy of Spiritual Culture was closed with his departure.[83]

That the problem from the government's point of view was not anti-Bolshevik, but un-Bolshevik ideas was clear in Berdiaev's case. By 1919 he had begun to modify his opinion of the revolution. While he did not approve of the new rulers, Berdiaev began to see the revolution as part of a worldwide turn away from individualism and the culture of the West. He now put less emphasis on the insufficiencies of Russian civilization and more upon the general cultural crisis. Humanity, he wrote in 1919, was experiencing the ''end of the Renaissance.''[84]

Berdiaev's essay on this topic was an extension of his attack on rationalism in *The Philosophy of Inequality*. He now turned history against his old enemy, and claimed to know that a cycle of social and cultural development—most of which was repugnant to him—was complete. Human civilization had been unable to sustain the high level of creativity released by the Renaissance, when humanistic thought had been informed and inspired by Christian principles. Since that time, he asserted, humanistic thought had declined according to a self-annihilating dialectic: the idea of God within humanity had led to a revolt against God and would lead ultimately to the eradication of humanity itself. The reformation, the Enlightenment, the French revolution, positivism, socialism, and anarchism had all served to tear apart the Renaissance idea of man. Abstract art, modern machinery, the collectivism of Marx, the godless individualism of Nietzsche—these were signs that the great optimistic culture of the Renaissance was dead. Russia, he wrote, had had the great misfortune of having missed the Renaissance and absorbing only the products of its decay. The revolution had taken humanism to its limit, destroying culture, freedom, and law in its name.[85] There was something terrible and unfair in this belated borrowing:

> we experience futurism, which is hostile to the Renaissance, without having experienced the creation of the Renaissance; we experience socialism and anarchism, hostile to the Renaissance, without having experienced the free

flowering of the national state; we experience philosophical and theosophical movements hostile to the Renaissance, without having experienced the Renaissance rapture in epistemology. It was not our lot to experience the joys of free humanity. In this is the peculiarity of bitter Russian fate.[86]

By adopting this perspective, Berdiaev had shifted the blame for Russia's ills away from indigenous culture and onto the Europeans—these were *their* bad ideas—or even into the cosmos. His lamentations suggested that some kind of universal injustice had been done. This was no longer cynicism, but fatalism, with a big dose of unaristocratic rancor. The confident elitism of *The Philosophy of Inequality* had disappeared; Russia was not rejected, but pitied. However, Berdiaev now felt that Russian intellectuals had a special mission to fulfill. The country's destiny was to live out the humanist destruction to the finish, to take humanity through the end of history and into a new epoch of the spirit. According to Berdiaev's four-stage cosmology, after barbarism, culture, and civilization would come religious transcendence.[87] Humanity would return to a new Middle Age, when the spirit once again would reign. It was the task of Russian philosophy to explain this future to a desperate world. "Russian religious philosophy," with its particular sensitivity to historical destiny, had a "unique mission in the recognition of the end of the Renaissance and the end of humanism."[88]

Berdiaev arrived in Germany in the fall of 1922 with this personal destiny in mind. With the help of the American Y.M.C.A., the Free Academy of Spiritual Culture was reformed in Berlin as the Religious-Philosophical Academy.[89] The academy's program declared:

> Only religious rebirth can save Russia and heal Europe and the whole world. All political forms and all social organizations are impotent and fruitless, unless they are filled with content and subordinated to the spiritual aims of life.[90]

This association took shape in the manner of the reformations of the political émigrés: its declared purpose was spiritual unity, but those who thought differently were turned away. Berdiaev would not unite, and share the Y.M.C.A. largesse, with another Russian cultural organization—V. V. Zenkovskii's Union of Russian Philosophers in Berlin.[91] Not only did he dominate the academy, Berdiaev managed to alienate many other émigrés. From the beginning he had been determined to despise them as reactionaries.[92] In the West as in Russia, his primary loyalty was to his freedom.[93]

One of the last of Berdiaev's works published in Russia was an essay on Spengler's *Decline of the West*, entitled *"The Last Thoughts of Faust."* Predictably, Berdiaev insisted that Spengler's ideas came as no surprise to him. "It's our kind of book," he wrote;[94] he had "sensed" the crisis of European culture even before the war. Furthermore, a series of Russian thinkers, from

Danilevskii to Leontiev, had anticipated Spengler's criticism of Western civilization. These observations did not prevent Berdiaev from welcoming Spengler's book as a confirmation of his own idea about the end of European culture. The degeneration of the modern age could be seen, he thought, in modern physics; entropy, radioactivity, relativity—these discoveries all indicated that the material world was falling apart. But at the same time, Berdiaev described a syncretic tendency in contemporary thought. As in the period of Hellenic decline, there was a movement toward consolidation of various mystic cults, a will to world unification expressed in both imperialism and socialism, a shift from individual to universal culture, and a rapprochement between East and West. The "over-civilized people" of Europe were "searching for light from the East." In contrast to Spengler, Berdiaev believed that this reorientation meant that spiritual culture would, after all, survive. Even if it perished "in quantities," it would survive "in qualities" through the barbaric times to come.[95]

The prediction and the idea of East-West synthesis gave Berdiaev and other representatives of the Russian spiritual elite a new importance. No longer simply prophets of Russia's doom, they could now speak for the East. They were "in a more fortunate position than Spengler and the people of the West," Berdiaev thought, for they could understand both Europe and Russia. "For this reason," he wrote in "The Last Thoughts of Faust," "the horizon of Russian thought must be wider; for in it, the far off is more visible." Russian philosophers of history had to emerge from their isolated existence and reveal Russia's "secret" to the West. Although the essence of this "secret" was not yet clear, Berdiaev was confident of two things: it was connected with the crisis of European culture and with the "solution of some great theme of universal history."[96]

This return to Slavophile jingoism constituted Berdiaev's last word upon the revolution in the five years after 1917. He had more, much more, to say in his later life as a Russian guru among the Europeans,[97] but at this time the concept of a universal historical crisis prevailed. In favor of Berdiaev's prediction was his welcome in the West. Europe *was* looking to the East, and reason was out of fashion. But for Russia and Russian culture, Berdiaev's revolutionary odyssey had a more ambiguous and complex significance. On the one hand, his writing in 1918 had painted the most dismal picture of Russian life. Unlike the majority of the intellectuals, he had looked behind the populist screen and found the people passive, gullible, and corrupt. The vaunted Russian soul was, he thought, prone to apocalyptic fantasies and nihilistic acts. The intelligentsia shared these characteristics with the people, and the revolution was a natural development of this psychological predisposition. True culture—historical, national, and Christian—was confined to the elite, to people like himself, who were the bearers of the national spirit.

During Berdiaev's tenure as a Soviet "immortal," these specific, Europhilic judgments sublimed into a mystic haze. Berdiaev came to see the revolution as part of a larger crisis in European, not Russian, values. His rhetoric disguised the fact that he had shifted the focus of his criticism. Before, Russians had failed to live up to European standards; by 1922 European culture was at fault for Russia's misfortunes. Moreover, Berdiaev's writings in this later period hinted at Russia's superiority to the West: its Eastern "secret" held the key to the meaning of history. With this elevation of perspective, the Russian people and their weaknesses dropped out of sight. The task of the elite, however, was magnified in proportion to Berdiaev's world-scale goals. Russian thinkers could now mediate between East and West, not at the sordid level of politics, but in the cause of the spiritual transfiguration of earthly life. In this new Russian messianism and his revolt against history, Berdiaev fell victim to the apocalyptic and nihilistic attitudes he had earlier decried.

N. S. Trubetskoi: The Rebellion of the Despised

There were others in the emigration who shared Berdiaev's enthusiasm for the values of the East, but felt that Russian intellectuals should turn their backs on Europe. Their task was not the salvation of the world, but the building of an authentic Russian culture. According to the "Eurasian" school of thought, Russia's involvement with Europe—with the West's economy, politics, and culture—had been a huge historical mistake, forced upon a population whose natural ties were to the Asian continent and the cultures of the steppe. The revolution, thought the Eurasians, represented one last ruinous attempt to impose a European system upon the Russian people. Now it was time to reexamine Russia's roots and to understand the nation at its true and ancient core.[98]

Eurasianism seemed to be one of the most novel intellectual developments of the Russian emigration. Its leaders asked that the intellectuals retrain their minds, reject European culture, and recognize their kinship with the Russian folk heritage. But the movement was not as new as it was radical. Its rebellion against the West was in accord with the Slavophile tradition, and its demand that the intellectuals adjust their values to those of the people was yet another variety of Russian populism. The movement was a direct descendant of the prerevolutionary fascination with Asia expressed in Russian philosophy, literature, and scholarship. The visions of Vladimir Soloviev and D. S. Merezhkovskii, the Mongol themes in the novels of Andrei Belyi and the poems of Aleksandr Blok, as well as the flourishing Orientalist studies at the University of St. Petersburg were central to the Eurasians' cultural heritage.[99] In addition to these ties to the Russian intellectual tradition, Eurasianism was linked to contemporary currents in European thought, especially relativism and formalism. Its foremost theorist was Prince Nikolai Sergeevich Trubetskoi, in

1917 a brilliant young scholar, later a founder of the Prague school of linguistics.[100]

The Trubetskoi family could have provided a model for Berdiaev's notion of aristocratic virtue. In late imperial Russia, the Trubetskois were, as in the past, outstanding participants in political and cultural life. Both Nikolai Sergeevich's father, S. N. Trubetskoi, and his uncle, E. N. Trubetskoi, were philosophers; they and another uncle, G. N. Trubetskoi, were active in liberal politics. S. N. Trubetskoi, the rector of the University of Moscow, was one of the contributors to *Problems of Idealism*, the seminal collection of idealist writings to which Struve and Berdiaev had contributed.[101]

A precocious scholar, Nikolai Sergeevich published his first article on Finno-Ugric folklore in 1905 at the age of fourteen. In 1916 he was made a professor at the University of Moscow, where he specialized in comparative linguistics and Sanskrit and immediately became the leader of a rebellion against the reigning school of linguistic reconstruction. The civil war caught Trubetskoi in the Caucasus, where he had traveled for research and rest. He made his way with difficulty to Rostov; there for a year he taught linguistics and worked on a history of phonology. Evacuated from Rostov in December 1919 and later from the Crimea, Trubetskoi was given a post in Slavic philology and comparative linguistics at the University of Sofia.[102] There, in addition to pursuing his teaching and research, he wrote a small book that precipitated the Eurasian movement. Its suggestive title was *Europe and Humanity (Evropa i chelovechestvo.)*[103]

Trubetskoi's book, published in 1920, was a direct attack on European values, a defense of cultural relativism, and an assertion of the need for indigenous national development. This study was connected with his long interest in problems of ethnology and nationalism. Since 1909–1910, he had intended to write a trilogy called "The Justification of Nationalism"; *Europe and Humanity* was the first volume of this project.[104] According to his introduction to the book, Trubetskoi had not published his thoughts on this topic before the war because he had found them rejected and misunderstood, "almost organically unacceptable" to educated people. Now, after the great loss of faith in "'civilized humanity,'" he discovered that these same ideas met with "understanding and even agreement."[105] It was time, therefore, to publish them, so that they could be subjected to wider scrutiny. "Each [reader] *must* decide for himself personally," he admonished:

> It's either one or the other. Either the thoughts I defend are *false*—but then it is necessary to refute them logically—or these thoughts are *true*—but then it is necessary to draw some practical conclusions from them.[106]

Trubetskoi professed himself ready to abide by his readers' verdict, and, no matter what the answer, he enjoined his compatriots to reply to his analysis. (To facilitate this response, he included his address in the introduction.) If he was right, then an entirely new "system" would have to be developed, a task that demanded "collective" work. On the other hand, if his thoughts were false, then they were "dangerous" and had to be refuted "in order to save those who had come to believe in them . . . from errors."[107] Confident that his demonstrations could stand this test, Trubetskoi set out to prove that European ideas had no place in Russia or in any part of the non-"Romano-Germanic" world.[108]

His first step was to dispose of the idea of universal values.[109] That which passed for "civilized humanity" in the eyes of Europeans or Europeanized individuals was only the part of humanity that had accepted European culture. This culture was a product not of all humankind, but of a "specific ethno-graphic-anthropological unit." Its "cosmopolitan" assumptions did not derive from an extant human community, but from the Europeans' past—their civilization formed by the historical merger of Romanic and Germanic populations and by the "supernational" ideals of classical antiquity. To Europeans, the idea of a universal culture came naturally, but this did not make it true. Their cosmopolitanism was actually "Romano-Germanic chauvinism," Trubetskoi warned. The psychological basis of European culture, in both explicitly chauvinistic and falsely cosmopolitan forms, was simple "egocentrism."[110]

To Trubetskoi, this exposé deprived the concept of universal values of any scientific validity. If cosmopolitanism was only an egocentric delusion, then any "honest Romano-German" would have to give it up.[111] His major concern, however, was not Europe, but Russia and its cosmopolitans. How could they be liberated from their Western conceptions, from the "hypothesis of words" with which the Romano-Germans masked their chauvinist ambitions? Trubetskoi proposed that those intellectuals who had been "stupefied" by the Europeans consider five questions: (1) Could it be objectively shown that Romano-Germanic culture was more perfect than all other cultures existing today or in the past? (2) Was it possible for a people to assimilate a foreign culture fully without anthropologically merging with that foreign people? (3) Was the acquisition of European culture a good or an evil? (4) Was general Europeanization inescapable? and (5) How could one struggle against its negative consequences?[112]

Characteristically, Trubetskoi proposed to take up these studied questions according to the strictest logic. In answer to the first, he argued that since there was no rational basis upon which to judge historical progress, no culture could be considered "higher" than another.[113] All that we knew "objectively" was that different cultures were more or less like each other, and all that we understood about other cultures was their likeness to our own. The European and the "barbarian" knew only that each other's ways were different, and both were inclined to consider the other "childish," for his possession of the most elemental human attributes without the advanced knowledge particular to the subject's culture.[114] Although Europeans considered their culture greater than all others and judged different peoples according to the degree of their divergence from European norms, this measurement was only another egocentric fallacy. It was not objectively possible to prove that Romano-Germanic culture was superior.[115]

Trubetskoi approached the question of cultural acquisition according to several sociological assumptions—the ethnocentrism of which he did not acknowledge or discuss.[116] He defined a cultural value as "any purposeful creation of man that becomes a common possession of his compatriots." Such creation was always an additive process: it combined old cultural values—the means of understanding—with something new. Only if its components were comprehensible to the larger society could a "creative" discovery spread into the wider culture. Thus, the development of culture required a "common stock of cultural values" and a shared perception of the worth of new discoveries. "In order for a given discovery to be accepted by all or the majority," Trubetskoi asserted, "it is necessary that the tastes, predispositions, and temperament of its creator not contradict the psychological structure of a given society—and for this a unified heredity is necessary."[117]

From these definitions—a far cry from Berdiaev's elitist notions—it followed that no foreign culture could be totally acquired without an anthropological mixing of peoples. No culture could ever become the same as another because values would always be absorbed in a distinct fashion by people of different cultural heredities.[118]

On the basis of this schematic perspective, Trubetskoi could now answer his third question. Although it might appear that Romano-Germanic discoveries could add to other cultures, in fact they would have evil consequences for the borrowing society. From the beginning the borrowers would not be able to assimilate the European discoveries as quickly as the Europeans could. Thus the borrowing culture was doomed to always be behind. It would waste its energies on the effort to absorb Western ideas, while the Europeans were busy coming up with new ones. Borrowing from Europe meant borrowing that country's psychology and with it the criteria of "cosmopolitan" European standards. To the extent that the borrowing country accepted these standards, it would acquire a poor image of itself:

> Comparing themselves with the native Romano-Germans, the Europeanized people [*narod*] will come to the recognition of their [the Europeans'] superiority to themselves, and this consciousness combined with the constant complaint of their stagnation and backwardness gradually leads to the result that people stop respecting themselves.[119]

The result would be a decline in patriotism. National pride would be the "concern of only a few separate individuals, while national self-affirmation is reduced for the most part to the ambitions of the rulers and the ruling political circles."[120]

At the same time, Europeanization led inevitably to the fragmentation of a nation, to divisions between generations and between higher and lower layers of society, as European values were differentially diffused. These divisions led in turn to an intensification of class struggle, which further aggravated social stresses by obstructing movement between classes.[121] The effect of this differentiation and of the aggregate "backwardness" of the Europeanizing culture was that the non-European societies were forced to make "sporadic historical leaps." A lack would be perceived; the borrowing culture would muster its forces to catch up with the West; then, exhausted by its immense efforts to cover the same ground more quickly and without the historical resources of the Europeans, it would fall back into a period of "apparent (from the European point of view) stagnation":

> Exactly like a man who, trying to match stride for stride a fellow traveler who walks faster and having with this intent resorted to the strategy of periodic leaps, in the end inevitably wears himself out and falls down in total exhaustion, the Europeanizing people, having started on the path of evolution, inevitably perishes, having pointlessly wasted its national forces. And all this—without belief in itself, without even the strengthening of the feeling of national unity, long ago destroyed by the very fact of Europeanization.[122]

What could be done to counter this degenerative process? Trubetskoi's logic suggested that the struggle was hopeless. Europeanization seemed to be an "inescapable world law."[123] Throughout most of *Europe and Humanity* Trubetskoi tried to keep his argument abstract and "objective," avoiding criticism of any specific sins—such as militarism or capitalism—of which the European nations stood accused. His point had been that no matter what the content of Europeanization, it would damage native culture. However, he did not disguise his opinion of European culture. In his view, the root of the European evil was not capitalism or socialism, but "unsatisfied greed, lodged in the very nature of the international plunderers—the Romano-Germans, and . . . egocentrism, which has permeated their whole notorious 'civilization.'"[124] Trubetskoi predicted that socialism would soon replace capitalism, but that this transformation would only hasten the imposition of Western egocentrism upon other nations. As the ultimate expression of Romano-Germanic cosmopolitanism, socialism could be established only as a European system, he felt, and then the Europeans would follow out their internationalist mission to the end:

> If a socialist system were established in Europe, the European socialist states would be obliged first of all to install the same system by fire and sword throughout the world, and after that vigilantly to see to it that not one people would betray this system. Otherwise—that is, in the case that somewhere a corner of the globe remained untouched by socialism—that corner would immediately become the hotbed of capitalism. And then in order to guard the socialist system, the Europeans would have to keep their military technology at the former level and remain armed to the teeth.[125]

Since armament always threatened the independence of other nations, the "state of armed peace" would then spread throughout the world. The "socialist" Europeans would resume their "colonial" trade and all the old imperatives of military technology and factory production would reappear with one difference—the demand for a "single socialist way of life" would be imposed upon all the trading partners of the socialist state.[126]

But this dismal prospect did not settle the question of inevitablity, a problem that Trubetskoi left unresolved. In self-defense, a threatened country would have to arm itself and keep its weaponry up to European standards, he suggested, and to do this it would be forced to borrow and to imitate. But in this area, the effects of backwardness were less disruptive and easier to surmount that in more abstract fields. They made a visible impact only in the "lesser intensity of industrial life."[127]

As for how to fight against the "negative consequences" of Europeanization, here Trubetskoi's answers were more direct. A rising of all humanity—"not that humanity of which the Romano-Germans love to talk, but the real humanity, its majority composed of the Slavs, the Chinese, the Indians, the Arabs, the Negroes, and other tribes, all those who without regard to the color of their skin languish under the heavy yoke of the Romano-Germans and waste their national forces on the procuring of raw materials needed in European factories"—would perhaps succeed but seemed impossible to organize. What appeared more promising and more vital was the struggle for consciousness. All the non-European nations had to free themselves from Romano-Germanic ideas, escape from the hypnosis of European egocentrism, recognize that they had been deceived, and begin to respect themselves. This was above all the task of the intelligentsia, whose "psychology" needed to be "fundamentally transformed." Up to the present, the intellectuals had been the "agents" of Europeanization, but once they came to understand Romano-Germanic cosmopolitanism as a "naked deception" and Europeanization as an "unconditional evil," they would no longer aid the enemy. And without the help of the Europeanized intelligentsia, the Romano-Germans would not be able to accomplish the "spiritual enslavement of all the peoples of the world." This was to be a generous and united battle, Trubetskoi instructed his readers. The unmasking of the European evil did not provide an excuse for native nationalism or for "partial solutions" like Pan-Slavism. There was only one "true" opposition in the coming struggle—"the Romano-Germans and all the other peoples of the world, *Europe and Humanity*."[128]

In this dramatic fashion, Trubetskoi concluded his investigation of contemporary nationalism. The incongruity of the passionate ending was apparent even to the author. The next year in a letter to his friend Roman Jakobson, he confessed that the last part of the book had been written hastily and much later than the rest:

I had wanted the book to put an empty space in front of the reader and to make him give some thought to what could fill this void. But the impression was given that I myself was trying to fill up this void with a hazy surrogate.[129]

The subjective conclusion was not the only flaw in *Europe and Humanity*. Trubetskoi had, after all, employed a "cosmopolitan" method to attack the Europeans, attempting to demonstrate with logic that their values were not universal. And what of logic? It was, in his description, the principle at the very foundation of European culture: "Its whole spiritual culture, its entire world view, is based on the belief that unconscious emotional life and all prejudices based on that emotional life must give way before the instructions of reason, of logic, that it is only on logical, scientific grounds that any theory whatsoever can be built."[130] Was logic then to go as well? And if it did, what happened to Trubetskoi's conclusions? Or, if it was a universal value, were there others? Trubetskoi used logic, to be sure, against what he saw as the West's arrogant violations of its own standards, but his own commitment to the "instructions of reason"[131] passed unexamined. His unquestioning confidence in the power of scientific thought to "decide" ethical questions on a universal scale was a symptom of the problem of understanding he had so poignantly described.

Other assumptions about thought and human nature deprived Trubetskoi's arguments of the "objectivity" he sought. His theories of cultural development were profoundly conservative and monolithic. A nation, from his perspective, was by definition united in its values, an assumption that dismissed both pluralism and class conflict as deformations of a natural community. Furthermore, he wrote as if a nation's creative energy were a fixed and scarce resource. The argument that Europeanizing countries would always be behind the West ignored the possibility of increases in "cultural" productivity, or qualitative shifts in demands and expectations. In Trubetskoi's view, culture was a strictly linear, step-by-step process, and the non-Western countries were slow walkers.

The language of *Europe and Humanity* revealed the anger behind this purportedly objective work. Trubetskoi consistently weighted his words against the Europeans. By any objective criterion, they were, despite the title, *part* of humanity. But in this presentation, European civilization was a product of an "ethnic-anthropological unit [*edinstvo*]," while non-European societies were real "peoples [*narody*]";[132] a stylistic attack along this line was carried on throughout the work. Although it followed from Trubetskoi's argument that European civilization represented only one of many human cultures, none of which could be judged better than another, this was not the message that the book conveyed. By the end of the study it appeared that the special attribute of European society was not its egocentrism, but its greed and drive for conquest.[133]

Like the Europeans he criticized, Trubetskoi could easily be faulted on the grounds of logic. The fact remained that *Europe and Humanity*, with its emotion and its reason, was a provocative, perceptive analysis of Russia's interaction with European culture and, more generally, of the relationship between Europe and the non-Western world. Trubetskoi's description of Europeanization and its effects helped to explain the immense social stresses experienced by Russia in the recent past. The divisions between old and young, between "high" and "low" culture, the lack of cohesion and of patriotism, the inferiority complex vis-à-vis the West—these phenomena had plagued the country before 1917. Trubetskoi's explanation of the onset of this process—the need to remain abreast of European military technolgoy—fit the Russian case. And the mélange of "cosmopolitan" scholarship with Russian xenophobia in the book only illustrated his idea that foreign concepts were always subject to a native transformation.

Trubetskoi's goal, however, was not description, but destruction. He had tried to unmask the logical fallacies of "cosmopolitanism" and the pernicious effects of Europeanization in order to set Russia on a different path. Although he was dissatisfied with the anti-colonial rhetoric of his conclusion, he still hoped that *Europe and Humanity* would achieve what his conception of cultural conservatism made unlikely—a fresh start. Once "certain idols" had been knocked down from their pedestals, the "revolution in consciousness" could begin.[134]

In 1921, the year after the appearance of *Europe and Humanity*, Trubetskoi with three other émigrés issued the first manifesto of the Eurasian movement. Published in Sofiia, *Exodus to the East* (*Iskhod k vostoku*) was a collection of articles exploring the great cultural transformation that its authors believed to be in progress. As the title of the volume indicated, the self-proclaimed "Eurasians" had found something to fill Trubetskoi's "empty space." Culture, they felt, was moving eastward; it was time for Russia to proclaim this "universal truth."[135]

The boldness of the Eurasians' feelings was matched by the vagueness of their thoughts. Here there were few attempts at rational persuasion, and little uniformity of opinion. The contributors to *Exodus to the East*, like the authors of *Iz glubiny*, took care to point out that they disagreed on several issues. Trubetskoi; the theologian G. V. Florinskii; P. N. Savitskii, an economist; and P. P. Suvchinskii[136] were united, however, in their "presentiments and dethronements"[137]—in their sense that the world was undergoing a "historical spasm" analogous to the conquests of Alexander the Great or the great migrations. While the duration of this cultural shift was unknown, some of its structures and consequences could already be perceived. The Eurasians agreed that the "'epoch of science' was once again giving way to the 'epoch of faith,'" and they based this prediction upon the lessons of the Russian revolution. It had at last revealed Russia's great "truth"—"the repudiation of socialism and the affirmation of the Church."[138]

This interpretation of the revolution, while superficially akin to Struve's, made no distinction between the realms of fact and faith. The Eurasians wrote as if socialism had already been defeated and the Church had triumphed:

"Together with the huge majority of the Russian people, we see how the Church is reviving with the new strength of Grace, and once again is acquiring the prophetic language of wisdom and revelation." Confident that destruction was giving birth to "charity and illumination," and that they were the voices of this change, the Eurasians called for "submitting" to the revolution, as if before "an elemental catastrophe." They expressed their outrage at the "lack of humanity and the abomination" of Bolshevism, but felt that the truth of religion had been revealed so clearly only thanks to the Bolsheviks' unprecedented "daring." Since in time Bolshevism would "negate itself," the Eurasians dismissed political opposition as superfluous.[139]

Despite their hostility to politics, the Eurasians had a "worldly" message to announce. Russia had a grand place in the new epoch. An "elemental and creative Russian nationalism" was emerging, a spirit that went beyond the "confining . . . limits of 'nationalisms' on a Western European scale" and extended further than the ethnic orientation of the Slavophiles.[140] The Russian people could now begin to see themselves as the leaders of two continents:

> The introduction of the whole circle of Eastern European and Asiatic peoples into the conceptual sphere of world Russian culture stems . . . in equal measure from the innermost "affinity of souls"—which makes Russian culture understandable and close to these peoples and, conversely, determines the fruitfulness of their participation in Russian affairs—and from the community of economic interest, from the economic interconnectedness of these people.[141]

From this functional perspective, the Russian people were "neither Europeans, nor Asians." Instead, the contributors to *Exodus to the East* concluded, "merging with our kinfolk and with the elemental force of culture and of life surrounding us, we are not afraid to pronounce ourselves—Eurasians."[142]

With this declaration, the Eurasians opened wide the compass of Russia's "natural" empire. The Russians were not only to be mediators between Europe and Asia, they were the leaders of a new "world" culture. The imagery of their future—a circle with Russia in the middle—duplicated Trubetskoi's diagram of European cultural chauvinism in *Europe and Humanity*, except that Russia now took Europe's central place.[143]

The articles in *Exodus to the East* were personal elaborations upon this inchoate blend of Orthodoxy, anti-Bolshevism, sentiment, and sublimated chauvinism. The Eurasians put forward several justifications for the "turn toward the East,"[144] among them the dynamism of the "youthful" cultures of America and Russia,[145] the benefits of a "continental" economy,[146] and Russia's unique role as an "Orthodox-Moslem, Orthodox-Buddhist country."[147] The most imaginative of these explanations was Savitskii's theory of cultural migration. According to his calculations, the center of world culture had moved along a declining temperature gradient at a rate of five degrees centigrade approximately every thousand years: from ancient Mesopotamia and

Egypt with an average yearly temperature of 20° C; to Greece and Rome at 15° C; to Gaul (10° C); to northern Europe (5° C). No historical evidence could be decisive, he admitted, but this trend boded well for Canada and Russia in the third millennium A.D.[148]

Amid these fantasies, Trubetskoi's contributions to *Exodus to the East* shone with the light of reason. His two articles were condensed versions of the second and third parts of his projected trilogy on nationalism.[149] Both were more tentative and reflective than *Europe and Humanity*; the emphasis was no longer on anti-colonialism but on the search for an authentic Russian culture.

In the first of these studies, "On True and False Nationalism," Trubetskoi repeated his arguments against European egocentrism, while cautioning non-European peoples not to develop similar prejudices. No civilization was "the center of the universe, the hub of the world [*pup zemli*]." The duty of each non-European people was to conquer its own egocentrism and, at the same time, to guard against the "deception of 'universal culture.'" This duty, wrote Trubetskoi, was expressed in two aphorisms: "know yourself" and "be yourself." Self-knowledge and self-respect were the keys both to moral life and to collective, national well-being. The intelligentsia's refusal to "be itself," its striving to become "truly European," accounted for the absence of "true nationalism" in Russia at the present.[150]

Without specifying its content, Trubetskoi suggested the premises upon which a new, productive nationalism could be founded. Its basis could not be the state, militant chauvinism, or exclusive loyalty to the past, but instead the living culture of the people. Trubetskoi insisted that each people formed a "psychological whole" analogous to the complex personality of the individual. The duty of the nation, as of each person, was self-knowledge; indeed, these two endeavors reinforced each other. Individuals in discovering themselves grew to know their national characteristics and thus affirmed their membership in the nation, or, if they were creative, even added to the national culture. Just as personal happiness depended upon the "harmony of all elements of spiritual life," so a true national culture answered the "ethical, aesthetic, and utilitarian demands" of the whole nation. "Under such conditions," Trubetskoi commented, "the individual can take part in the cultural life of his people completely sincerely, without hypocrisy [*ne krivia dushoi*, literally "not bending his soul"], not pretending to others or himself that he is something that he never was and never will be."[151]

Where was such a culture, for Russia, to be found? This was the concern of Trubetskoi's second article in *Exodus to the East*, "The Heights and Depths of Russian Culture." Not surprisingly, he chose to look for Russian culture in the "depths." The basis for a distinctive Russian nationalism could be found, he thought, through ethnographic study of the Eastern Slavs.

Trubetskoi's linguistic investigations had convinced him that the Slavs' earliest ancestors had been in contact with both Western Indo-European and Proto-Iranian people. From this he concluded that, even in ancient times, the

Slavs had served an intermediaries between East and West. But in addition, according to Trubetskoi's reconstructions of the Proto-Slavic language, the Slavs' ties to East and West had been qualitatively different. The sound patterns of the Proto-Slavic dialects were closer to the Iranian than the European system, and certain basic elements of Slavic vocabulary were shared with Proto-Iranian. Most important, according to Trubetskoi, words concerning religion and spiritual ideas suggested the Slavs' ties to the cultures of the East. The Slavs' Western connections were of a more material type; here the linguistic traces showed a common technical and geographic vocabulary. Thus, already at the end of the Indo-European epoch, the Slavic "soul" was attracted to the East, and its "body" to the West.[152]

This pattern endured in the Slavs' later history, Trubetskoi averred. The material connections with the West had continued to develop, but the Slavs' cultural choice had been Byzantium:

> Everything received from Byzantium was assimilated organically and served as a model for creative work, adjusting all these elements to the demands of the national psyche. This was especially the case for the areas of spiritual culture, of art, and religious life. On the other hand, everything received from the "West" was not organically assimilated, did not inspire national creative work. Western wares were imported and purchased, but not reproduced. Master craftsmen were engaged, not to teach Russian people, but to fulfill orders.[153]

These "general outlines," Trubetskoi believed, revealed the authentic Russian disposition, an "instinctive feeling of repulsion from the Romano-Germanic spirit, a consciousness of its inability to create in that spirit." This orientation was "true" to the Slavs' prehistoric past; it was natural and distinctive; and it had been destroyed by Peter the Great.[154]

Peter's reforms, according to Trubetskoi, had obliged Russians to act in a "Romano-Germanic" spirit. The result had been to shatter the national community into high and low cultures. The elite, educated in Western style, lost touch with ancient ways; even its attempts to represent folk culture were undertaken in the spitit of Western exoticism. As far as Russia's future was concerned, the way of the intelligentsia was a dead end. In the "lower layers," however, the old traditions were preserved, and there, Trubetskoi maintained, the early connection with the steppe could still be seen. Russian folk music, dances, and tales provided living evidence of Eastern origins and of a spiritual connection with the Asian races. "The inclination to contemplation and the devotion to ritual characteristic of Russian piety" tied Russia not only to Byzantium, but also to the "non-Orthodox East," he wrote. Even the Russian idea of heroism—"*udal'*" (daring)—was a "pure steppe virtue," appreciated by the Turks, but not the Europeans or the Slavs. It was to these time-honored traditions that contemporary Russian culture had to turn.[155]

While Trubetskoi's Eurasianism was decidedly more earthbound than that of the other writers in *Exodus to the East*, there were some inconsistencies in his argument. Even apart from the problems of linguistic evidence, his discussion finessed one of the most important national questions. Who were these Russians? Trubetskoi had begun by describing the cultural heritage of the Slavs and had based his analysis on their distinctive combination of Eastern and Western traits. But he had ended with the Russians, whose ethnicity appeared to be a blend of Slavic, Finno-Ugric, Iranian, Turkic, and even Chinese elements. In his search for Eastern roots, the distinction between ethnic origins and ethnic representations had been lost, and the scope of "Russian" culture had been extended far.

As in *Europe and Humanity*, Trubetskoi's theorizing in *Exodus to the East* reflected his ideals. True national culture could be only integrating and harmonious, an affirmation of the psychic identity of the individual with the nation. It had to be conservative as well: the force of the ethnographic argument depended upon the notion that ancient roots were best. From the folk heritage, Trubetskoi presented only evidence that linked the masses with the past; upon their apparently undifferentiated wisdom, a new collective could be built.

Although Trubetskoi admitted that the "concrete forms" of this new Russian culture were difficult to predict,[156] he later suggested two of its essential components. In the second Eurasian miscellany, *On Our Way (Na putiakh)*,[157] he wrote about the religious and political elements of the Russian culture of the future. One article, "The Religions of India and Christianity," praised the Orthodox church. Despite the attractions of a higher synthesis of Orthodoxy with the religions of the East, Trubetskoi maintained that Orthodoxy—"the purest form of Christianity"—was the only religious basis for Russian culture, the "treasure" for which the "whole Russian land" should be forever grateful. It offered protection against the decaying churches of the West—against the "Satanic temptation of earthy dominion that had conquered Catholicism and . . . the temptation of pride in human reason and revolt against authority that afflicted Protestantism."[158] As for politics, Trubetskoi concentrated on foreign relations in his article "The Russian Problem." In September 1921, he found immediate prospects dismal: in order to reestablish the national economy, Russia would have to turn again to Europe, to the "rapacious beast," greedily waiting to turn the country into a colony. Even world revolution, he reasoned as he had before in *Europe and Humanity*, would only lead to European exploitation. The one consolation for Russia was that it thus would enter the "family of colonial countries . . . under quite favorable auspices." The country's "new historical role" was to become the "leader of the liberation of the colonial world from the Romano-Germanic yoke."[159]

The aggressive nationalism of Trubetskoi's article in *On Our Way* was a return to the blustery conclusion of *Europe and Humanity*. Since 1920, he had given the problem of organizing "humanity" against "Europe" much thought and had decided that the colonial nations were ready to revolt. The Europeans had taught the "natives" military skills and set them against rival "Romano-

Germans'' during the World War. They had educated the indigenous intelligentsia in European culture, a step that would result eventually in disillusionment. (Other intellectuals, he implied, would follow his own path.) On the other side, the Bolsheviks, even as they ruined Russia economically, had prepared the country for its new role.[160] Everywhere in the Asiatic world, they had discovered the same thing—while "pure Communist" ideas held little appeal, anti-European propaganda was enormously successful:

> Communist propaganda was understood as a nationalist sermon against the Europeans and their stooges. They take "bourgeois" to mean any European merchant, engineer, bureaucrat, exploiting native, any Europeanized native intellectual who accepts European culture, wears a European suit, and has lost his ties with the native people.[161]

Even though the Bolsheviks were not entirely pleased with this "incorrect" interpretation, the damage had been done. Bolsheviks, "and with them Russia," were associated in many Asian countries with the "idea of national liberation, with the protest against Romano-Germans and European civilization." Turkey, Persia, Afghanistan, India, parts of China, and other countries of East Asia were now bound to Russia by ties of mutual interest; Russia was "no longer a great European power, but a huge colonial country, standing at the head of her Asiatic sisters in their common struggle." This was the way for Russia to escape from the present devastation, Trubetskoi asserted: "'The Asiatic orientation' is becoming the only one for a real Russian nationalist."[162]

Despite this prospect, the intelligentsia was still tied to its European past. In "The Russian Problem," Trubetskoi repeated his earlier calls for a revolution in ideas: "We must become accustomed to the thought that the Romano-Germanic world with its culture is our worst enemy," he insisted. The special task of the Russian emigration was to prepare the spiritual opposition to European civilization, to destroy its own "social ideals and prejudices," and to educate the younger generation in an authentic national spirit.[163] The restrictions on intellectual life in Soviet Russia made it all the more important that the émigrés make use of their opportunities in the West:

> We émigrés are not oppressed by the Soviet censorship; it is not required that we be, obligatorily, Marxists. We can think, talk, and write what we want, and if in some country where we are living temporarily some thought or other of ours provokes repression . . . , we can change our place of residence. And therefore our duty consists of carrying out that great cultural work which in Russia is attended with frequently insuperable obstacles.[164]

Thus, with the *udal'* of the steppe bandit, Trubetskoi instructed the intellectuals to prepare the anti-colonial revolution on the enemy's terrain. In European conditions, there was no need to choose between high and low culture and no need to confront the contradictions between his sheltered life of scholarship and the vast revolt against European culture that he preached.

Protected by the Romano-Germans, Eurasianism flourished, spreading from its first home in Sofiia to several capitals of the Western world. A half dozen serial publications appeared under the Eurasian banner between 1921 and 1936, and many books and articles developed aspects of Eurasian thought.[165] Although the Eurasians' predictions were not fulfilled in their original form—the Orthodox revival came later than expected and many Asiatic, anti-colonial movements were led by the Bolsheviks after all—the "revolution in consciousness" was significant outside Russia. This was particularly evident in émigré scholarship, with its attention to Asian, Iranian, and Mongol influences on Russia's culture. Both Roman Jakobson's early linguistic studies and George Vernadsky's histories had Eurasian roots.[166]

The success of Eurasian ideas in the Western academy testified to the movement's creative impulse. Eurasianism had always been a spirit rather than a creed; it had more room for new ideas—and fantasies—than did the émigrés' political organizations. Its repudiation of Western notions of historical development permitted the unthinkable to be said—perhaps the Russian people were "slow walkers" and perhaps they were repulsed by the "civilization" that had so profoundly shaped their lives. "In essence, popular 'Bolshevism' at home in Russia and in Asia is not a rising of the poor against the rich, but of the despised against the despisers," Trubetskoi insisted in 1921. The Communists tried to put the "red mask of Marxism" on Russia's "Asiatic or half-Asiatic face," but in fact the "sharp edge" of the revolt was directed "above all against those self-satisfied Europeans, who regard all non-European humanity as mere ethnographic material, as slaves, needed only to provide Europe with raw materials and to buy European goods.[167] Whatever Russian people felt, Eurasianism gave its youthful advocates in the emigration[168] a chance to vent their anger. Their attacks on Western culture struck not only at the West, but at the Eurocentric visions of their parents. Moreover, Eurasianism supplied the answer to their own divided consciousness: the European intrusion into Russia explained their alienation from the "true" national community.

Still, Trubetskoi's princely notion of true nationalism was no more real than the populist visions of the older generation. There was little reason to believe that steppe virtues or an Eastern sensibility or Orthodoxy or the three combined could of themselves produce a harmonious collective. Nor was there any evidence that this was what the Russian people or, especially, their "Asiatic sisters" wanted. Despite his claim to stand for objectivity, cultural diversity, and tolerance, Trubetskoi's relativism lapsed into imperialism where Russian interests were at stake. "Small" peoples could not have a "true" nationalism, he thought. Their " 'national self-determination,' as it is understood by former President Wilson and various little proponents of 'independence' [*samostiiniki*] like the Georgians, Estonians, Letts, and so on is a typical form of false nationalism."[169]

Yet for all his flagrant breaks with reason, Trubetskoi had fine political intuition. He recognized the emotional power of the anti-colonial idea and the

fear that would keep an established socialist power "armed to the teeth" until
the last capitalist country was destroyed. In addition, the Eurasians had the
good sense to see that they, the intellectuals, were not wanted. "Men of pure
science" would feel "superfluous" in Russia, wrote Trubetskoi in 1920.[170]
Instead, they stayed on in the West, "bending their souls," and defending an
ideology that repudiated both "Romano-Germanic" civilization and their own
high culture.

N. V. Ustrialov: Changing Landmarks

Of all the intellectual currents in the Russian emigration, the most unorthodox
was *smenovekhovstvo*—the Change of Landmarks movement. Its proponents
advised the intellectuals to return home to serve the state. Like the Eurasians,
the *smenovekhovtsy* felt that their first duty was to defend the nation as it was,
not to attack it for what, according to Western standards, it had not become.
But the decisive factor for the *smenovekhovtsy* was not cultural integrity, but
national power. For its sake they endorsed the revolution.[171]

Nikolai Vasil'evich Ustrialov, the major figure in this new intelligentsia
heresy, was born in 1890.[172] An aspiring academic and an active member of the
Kadet party at the time of the revolution,[173] he pursued a pragmatic course of
opposition to the Bolsheviks for two years. In the spring of 1918 Ustrialov
published a short-lived weekly called *Nakanune* (On the Eve) with his friends
Iu. V. Kliuchnikov and Iu. N. Potekhin. The *Nakanune* group opposed using
the slogan of the Constituent Assembly as part of the anti-Bolshevik campaign,
a sentiment shared by many Kadets at the time. But few in the Kadet leadership
were sympathetic to what Ustrialov called an "orientation of free hands," his
proposal that the liberals accept Russia's withdrawal from the war as final and
reconsider their relationship to the Allies. Like Miliukov, who was out of
contact in the south, Ustrialov felt that the Kadets should break their wartime
ties and put national interests first. His resolution to this effect was soundly
defeated at the party's underground conference in Moscow in May 1918.[174]
Ustrialov and Kliuchnikov eventually found a place for their ideas in the service
of Kolchak's Siberian army, where Kliuchnikov became Minister of Foreign
Affairs and Ustrialov was a director of the Russian Press Bureau and a leader
of the Eastern Committee of the Kadet party. Ustrialov was an enthusiastic
supporter of the military dictatorship: only a strong authority, he felt, could
muster the unwilling forces of the people and impose discipline upon their
leaders in order to win the civil war.[175]

In January 1920, after the fall of Kolchak's authorities in Irkutsk, Ustrialov
escaped to Manchuria. The collapse of the anti-Bolshevik forces in Siberia
forced him to reconsider the entire military effort. Like Miliukov, he came to
the conclusion that the Whites would inevitably lose, but unlike the Kadet

leader, Ustrialov did not wait until the civil war was over to make his opinion known. The armed struggle against the Bolsheviks had failed, he wrote in a Harbin newspaper on February 1, 1920, and it should be renounced immediately.[176]

With the courage to "look truth in the eyes," one could see that Kolchak's defeat was not accidental, Ustrialov insisted in his article "The Turning Point." There was "something fatal, like the will of history in the victories of Soviet power." The outcome of the war on the eastern front could not be blamed, as in the Socialist Revolutionary interpretation, upon the "reactionary" policies of the Whites. "In methods of administration, the Bolsheviks were far more reactionary than the defeated government," he commented, but this was not significant.[177] What seemed decisive was the international dimension of the struggle in Siberia, where the Whites had been assisted by the Allies.[178] This collaboration, Ustrialov felt, had undermined the war against the Bolsheviks. Kolchak's forces had "tied themselves too closely to foreign elements," thereby providing Bolshevism with a "certain national halo, essentially alien to its nature."[179] The experience of the Siberian war showed that

> the odd dialectic of history has unexpectedly advanced the Soviet government [*vlast'*] with its ideology of the International into the role of the national factor of contemporary Russian life, at the same time that our [the Whites'] nationalism, while remaining steadfast in principle, has waned and faded in practice, as a consequence of its chronic alliances and compromises with the so-called "Allies."[180]

Thus for Ustrialov, the Bolshevik victory became the triumph of the Russian nation, and on these grounds he called for an end to military operations. The intelligentsia did not have to accept Bolshevism, for the system, he felt, would change peacefully with time. But Russian patriots should put aside their ideological differences with the Soviet rulers in the interest of their most important and common goal—"the unification and resurrection of our homeland, her power in the international arena."[181] These pronouncements contained the xenophobic and fatalistic germs of the *Smena vekh* movement and the theory later known as "National Bolshevism."[182]

Throughout 1920, Ustrialov carried on a lonely literary battle in this spirit in Harbin.[183] His articles in the Harbin paper *Novosti zhizni* (News of Life), collected and published as *In the Struggle for Russia* (*V bor' be za Rossiiu*) at the end of the year, elaborated upon the ideas he had suggested in "The Turning Point." First among the reasons for Ustrialov's ongoing support for Bolshevik power was Russia's altered image in the West. Anyone could see, he wrote in February 1920, that "Russia's prestige abroad was increasing daily." It was true that "hatred for the external form of national Russian rebirth" was growing among Western leaders, but "this hatred was far better than the condescending scorn" with which Clemenceau and Lloyd George had treated the Whites' representatives at the Paris Peace Conference.[184] The clue to the Bolsheviks' ability to frighten Russia's former partners was their bold and flexible foreign policy, Ustrialov thought. They had from the beginning freed themselves from the albatross of "loyalty to our loyal allies" and played on the European leaders' fears of internal disorder. Thus the Bolsheviks' ideology had become an "excellent weapon of Russian international politics," and any patriot who wished to deprive Russia of this weapon was "blind" to its effects.[185]

Even more attractive to Ustrialov was the prospect that the Bolsheviks would carry out their threats. He had no illusions about the "peaceful" character of the new government. It was clear, he wrote in March, that the Soviet leaders considered their achievement as only the first "stage of the world socialist revolution," and this was all to the good. Russia had not yet earned a "real peace," he thought; her task, after the civil war was over, was to establish herself "with her rights as a great power." The first step was to reconquer the former empire.[186]

Unlike so many of the intellectuals, Ustrialov was a conscious and explicit Russian chauvinist. He counted on the Bolsheviks to bring the "pygmy states" on Russia's borders back into the fold. The Soviet government's commitment to "self-determination of peoples" was only a tactical measure, he assured his readers, a "typical 'petty bourgeois' principle" totally at odds with "world-wide proletarian revolution" and the "dictatorship of the proletariat." Under these devices, the Russian Bolsheviks would first unite with the forces of "proletarian revolution" in the border countries as a "line of least resistance."[187] The "little people [narodtsy]," he predicted,

> are too infected with Russian culture not to assimilate its latest product, Bolshevism. There is sufficient flammable material. . . . Agitation among them is relatively easy. . . .
>
> Under such conditions, being a neighbor of Red Russia can hardly lead to the well-being and harmless prosperity of our borderlands. . . . There can be authentic "honest" peace between the borderlands and the Bolsheviks until the system of Soviets is extended over the whole territory.[188]

Here was another area in which the interests of the Bolsheviks and of Russian patriots coincided. Despite ideological differences, the "practical course" was the same.[189]

The war with Poland goaded Ustrialov into more vindictive bluster:

> In addition to the endless Latvias, Georgias, Azerbaijans (although today already deceased) and so on and so forth, now a new Poland appears on God's earth, proud of her ancient glory, her miraculous resurrection, and, it seems, her eternal dream.[190]

The Poles, in their spite against their former rulers, had refused to aid Denikin in his offensive against Moscow in 1919. Now Russian patriots could pay them back in kind. A Bolshevik victory over Poland would mean that Russia could once again open a "window on Europe."[191]

Ustrialov's argument that the Bolsheviks should be supported as a government with the force and drive essential to restore Russian national power applied to internal affairs as well. The Bolsheviks alone, he insisted, were able to hold the country together, and for this reason, Russian patriots should stop counting on popular revolts against the state. Opponents of the government ought to ask themselves what would happen if a rebellion should succeed. The answer, according to his article "Green Noise," was "unlimited anarchy, a new paroxysm of 'Russian revolt [*russkii bunt*],' a new *Razinovshchina*, only of unheard of proportions."[192] To remind the advocates of "Green" rebellion of the real consequences of peasant "rule," Ustrialov offered his description of a raid on a Siberian town. After overpowering the guards, the peasants

> chased the commissars, caught some of them and slit their throats then and there. They killed the Jews that fell into their hands. Then they began a pogrom through the entire town. Looted the shops, looted the houses, took everything they came upon. Then they set things on fire and admired the "illuminations." Then they left for home.[193]

Although the peasants' individual interests were obviously a motive for this attack, there was another shared purpose to their actions, "something common, 'principled' [*'printsipial'nyi'*]—smash the whole town, level it to the ground, only then will life be possible [*tol'ko togda i zhit'e budet*]." That was "today's anti-Bolshevism," Ustrialov emphasized, and it threatened more than the Soviet regime. Not just the Jews, or the Communists, but "everything connected with city culture" would be fair game. No hypothetical "strong authority" could step in to control this force; the peasants would revolt against authority itself.[194]

But of course the intelligentsia would try the impossible. If a peasant rebellion were successful, Ustrialov predicted, the intelligentsia would appear like an "eastern magus, able to call up a genii, but powerless to control it." Thus, the beginning of the revolution would be repeated; a reaction of the most destructive type would commence; and "our 'liberals' . . . would be horrified, but as always, when it was too late." Following upon the enormous losses and disruptions of the last three years, this struggle would destroy the state, perhaps forever. And, in any case, the empire would not hold. Plunged into anarchy once again, Russia would dissolve into a "mishmash of 'liberated peoples' with an 'independent Siberia' to the east, an 'independent [*samostiinaia*] Ukraine' and a 'free Caucasus' to the south, and 'Great Poland' and a dozen 'lesser' nationalities to the west."[195] Thus, for the sake of empire, for the sake of the state, and for the sake of their own culture, Russian patriots should forget their dreams of mass rebellion.

Underlying each of Ustrialov's arguments for Bolshevik rule was the same imperative—the Russian state's authority over its subjects and its subject nations. In contrast to the patriotism of the idealist generation, this new nationalism had no spiritual or ideological sanction. Ustrialov did not appeal to Orthodoxy, Russian culture, history, or ethnicity. Although he supported "Russian" control of non-Russian people, he felt that this prerogative belonged to the state, not to its Russian population. The state in turn justified its claims by conquest: in Ustrialov's formulation, the measure and the goal of national power was territory.

In the Struggle for Russia was in part a defense of territorial nationalism as a basis for the state. "A person who considers territory a 'dead' element of the state . . . is profoundly mistaken," Ustrialov argued in an essay called "The Logic of Nationalism." On the contrary, "territory is the most essential and valuable component of the state soul."[196] It was the source of national culture:

> Only a "physically" powerful state can possess a great culture. The souls of "small powers" are not deprived of the possibility of being refined, noble, even "heroic"—but they are organically incapable of being "great." For that a big style is necessary, a big range, a big scale of thought and action—"a picture by Michelangelo." A German, Russian, or English "messianism" is possible. But take, for example, Serbian, Rumanian, or Portuguese messianism—that offends the ear, like a wrong note. . . .[197]

Although it was conventional to regard government and population as essential elements of the state, Ustrialov dismissed them as secondary phenomena. History had demonstrated that the "form" of government has the least impact upon the "extent and 'style' of state culture," although it affected its "concrete, temporary content." "Rome remained Rome," he asserted, "both under the government of the republic and under the emperors' command." Population, too, meant nothing for "state culture" unless the people had been transformed into a "nation," and such a "historical-social formation" depended in turn upon territory. It was the national territory that provided a population with material and cultural resources. Large territories enriched these opportunities, while reductions in space were "losses of life force." Thus, Ustrialov concluded, "all nationalism, if it is serious, must first of all be 'topographical.'"[198]

In accord with this underlying principle, Russian patriots were bound to support "that government, no matter what type it may be, that today is bringing about the unification of Russia within her great-power [*velikoderzhavnye*] borders."[199] The Bolsheviks' aggressive internationalism promised the broad interpretation of these "borders" that followed from Ustrialov's "logic." Moreover, as he noted in August 1920, the new government had already had a positive effect:

> When now Lloyd George speaks in the House of Commons with a perplexed expression of the "great Soviet empire," it's true, you hear these words with

a feeling of joyful spiritual relief and not without a sensation of national pride.[200]

Ustrialov's enthusiasm for the Bolsheviks as leaders of a powerful Russian state did not extend to their explicit ideology nor to their domestic policies. He was fond of pointing out that he, personally, was no friend of Bolshevik ideas. Economic materialism, the "religion of humanism . . . and paradise on earth"—these were "false" conceptions of Russia's current leaders. One had to recognize, nonetheless, that they were part of "Russian culture," of the tradition of historical materialism shared by many supporters and opponents of the revolution, and, in this sense, the revolution had expressed the "national genius." The task of Russian patriots who rejected these ideas was not to oppose the revolution and the all-important political authority it had achieved, but to "sound other strings in the national lyre" and thus to strengthen Russia's power.[201] Ustrialov's particular "string" was the impossibility of a national economy run on socialist principles. A year before NEP he predicted that the Soviet government would have to make the "greatest compromise" with capitalism in order to survive. "An economic Brest [Litovsk] is apparently in store for Bolshevism," he wrote in March 1920 from Harbin. The "logic of things" would lead Bolshevism from a Jacobin to a Napoleonic "style" of government, and Lenin, "with his characteristic tactical flexibility," was just the man to carry this conversion off.[202]

The intelligentsia, too—and this was Ustrialov's major point—would have to make concessions. Their first obligation, he insisted, was to end the civil war and reconcile themselves to Soviet power. Reconciliation would give the country a chance to revive its economy, would protect it from foreign intervention, and would promote the "evolution" of the system. The final article of *In the Struggle for Russia* reminded its readers that a chronic problem for the Russian state was the lack of qualified personnel. "I tell you frankly," Kolchak had confessed to the author,

I am struck by the absence of decent people. It's the same with Denikin . . . and with the Bolsheviks. This is a general Russian phenomenon: no people.[203]

The solution, Ustrialov thought, was for the intelligentsia to lend its skills and sympathies. He called on the émigrés to "go to Canossa," to support the "government, in many ways alien to us, in many ways antagonizing to us, full of defects, but the only [one] capable at this time of ruling the country, taking it in hand, surmounting the anarchism of the tired and agitated revolutionary masses, and especially important, able to be dangerous to our enemies."[204]

By the time *In the Struggle for Russia* was published at the end of 1920, the White Armies had lost the war and Ustrialov's call to give up the military struggle was out of date. But the basic problem of intelligentsia opposition still remained, Ustrialov felt, and he hoped that his book would persuade the

Russian émigrés in Europe to renounce their hostility to the Soviet government and rejoin the nation, as he saw it.[205] He sent a copy of his book to his old companion Kliuchnikov in Paris and thus catalyzed the Change of Landmarks movement.

Kliuchnikov, whose encouraging letters had succored Ustrialov in his Manchurian isolation, now heard a kindred spirit. Thanks to Ustrialov's letters and the book, he responded,

> I feel, despite all my loneliness here, stronger than all those SRs, Kadets, blacks and whites, parliamentary and national committees, right up to the Constituent Assembly, diligently destroying Russia on the peaceful banks of the Seine. The future belongs to *us*, and not to them. From this moment our words have an explosive force that no other words have.[206]

This emotional outpouring—the resentful focus on the émigré organizations, the concern for the "force" of words, the instant transformation of Ustrialov's ideas into a movement with both an opposition—the emigration—and a future—was typical of Kliuchnikov. Like other younger intellectuals in exile, he rankled at the prominence abroad of established political figures in the intelligentsia and its associations, but outside the Russian polity, he had no claims against their leadership. Ustrialov's book gave Kliuchnikov a cause, and within four months he had organized a circle of like-thinkers.[207] Their manifesto, with articles by Ustrialov, Kliuchnikov, and Potekhin—the former colleagues of the *Nakanune* group—and S. S. Lukianov, A. V. Bobrishchev-Pushkin, and S. S. Chakhotin appeared in the fall of 1921.[208] Not accidentally, it was titled *Smena vekh*.[209]

Kliuchnikov's lead essay put the question. In 1909, Struve, Berdiaev, and the other contributors to *Vekhi* had accused the intelligentsia of maximalism, a devotion to abstract principles, and willful ignorance of the Russian people; could not these same charges be leveled now at Struve and the anti-Bolshevik opposition? The true maximalists, Kliuchinov asserted, were those who refused to face up to the reality of the revolution. They were traitors to the authentic "state mystique" apparent "*in everything that originated from Russia, the country of the Soviets, from Moscow, the capital of the International, from the Russian peasant, the ruler of the destiny of world culture.*"[210] It was finally time to heed the lessons of 1909. Now, after the revolution Struve and the idealist had tried to avert, the intelligentsia should cease its opposition to the state.

As this variant of Ustrialov's call for reconciliation indicates, Kliuchnikov had shifted the emphasis of *In the Struggle for Russia*. He and the other European *smenovekhovtsy* agreed that the revolution had to be accepted and that the Bolsheviks could provide the "strong authority" needed to run the country; Ustrialov's book, they acknowledged, was the "first decisive step" along their common path.[211] What was new in *Smena vekh*, in addition to a grand sweep of patriotic passion and a bold enthusiasm for almost everything in Russia including the Bolsheviks, was the attack on the émigré intelligentsia. The young men of the moderate right—former Kadets and Octobrists who had been associated with the anti-Bolshevik armies in the civil war—were now turning the *Vekhi* legacy against their former mentors in the idealist generation. For Kliuchnikov, an erstwhile student of the religious philospher E. N. Trubetskoi, the chance to teach his intellectual fathers had great appeal. Presenting himself as the contemporary spokesman for a great heritage, he called Struve and Miliukov, the leaders of the older generation, to task. They were to accept the revolution, and the first step was to acknowledge their mistakes.[212] The barrage of accusations was kept up by the other European contributors to the manifesto. Potekhin's article blamed the anti-Bolshevik opposition for a "significant share" of responsibility for the famine in Russia,[213] while Bobrishchev-Pushkin, a former Octobrist, scolded the intelligentsia in Europe for its enthusiastc response to the Kronstadt revolt. Kronstadt meant anarchy, not order and reconstruction; the émigrés' endorsement of the rebellion showed that their hostility to the Bolsheviks outweighed their love of country.[214]

Ustrialov's contribution to *Smena vekh* combined two articles he had published in *Novosti zhizni* during the past year.[215] The title of his essay, "Patriotica," echoed one of Struve's prerevolutionary publications,[216] and, compared to the other authors, Ustrialov took a more positive and persuasive approach toward the emigration. Less concerned with the errors of the past than intent upon convincing the intellectuals of his point of view,[217] he offered them two new reasons to support the Bolshevik government. The revolution, he asserted, should be accepted for its authentically Russian character and in the confidence that great destruction could lead only to great achievement.[218]

In Ustrialov's view, the revolution was not a product of Bolshevik excesses, as the socialists would have it, nor a consequence of "Western" ideas, as in Berdiaev's analysis. It was instead a true expression of the Russian nation and therefore to be revered. Had it not begun with a "typical Russian rebellion 'senseless without mercy,'" in Pushkin's famous phrase, and did it not at the same time conceal "some moral depths, some kind of distinctive 'truth'"? In the revolution he saw not only the anarchy of the masses, but also the intelligentsia tradition—the spirit of the Slavophiles, Chaadaev's pessimism, Herzen's "revolutionary romanticism," Pisarev's utilitarianism, the Marxism of the 1890s led by Bulgakov, Berdiaev, and Struve, and the writings of Dostoevsky, Gorkii, Belyi, and Blok. The revolution belonged therefore to both the people and the intelligentsia. "It is ours," he asserted, "it is authentically Russian, it is entirely in our psychology, in our past, and nothing similar can be or will be in the West." Even if the leaders of the revolution were shown "mathematically" to be 90 percent foreigners or Jews, this did not affect the essentially "Russian" character of the movement.[219]

Some might object, Ustrialov continued, that this "Russian" phenomenon had only been destructive. It had, after all, eradicated the old way of life, robbed the museums, sold the nation's art collection to foreigners, shot and starved and driven out the "best people" of the country. But all this, he claimed, was only a promise of a better life to come—"every great historical phenomenon was attended by destruction." Christianity had begun by destroying the culture of antiquity; the barbarian invasions had prepared the way for modern history; now the Russian revolution meant the beginning of a "new epoch." In the future, he predicted, "our grandchildren when asked 'what makes Russia great,' will reply with pride: 'Pushkin and Tolstoy, Dostoevsky and Gogol, Russian music, Russian religious thought, Peter the Great, and the *great Russian revolution.* . . . ' "[220]

In contrast to Kliuchnikov's arrogant rejection, Ustrialov tried to appeal to the cultural conscience of the emigration: the revolution was part of the legacy they all would want to claim. But like the other contributors to *Smena vekh*, he relied upon nationalist sentiment and a Bakuninist dialectic to make his point.[221] The revolution had to be accepted because it was Russian—anarchic and destructive—and because it was anarchic and destructive, it would be great. This reasoning was a perversion of the notions of the original *vekhovtsy*, with their emphasis on the need for cumulative cultural growth, but it nonetheless pointed up the shortcomings of the nationalism that Struve and his collaborators had encouraged. The absolute demand for love of country and a disregard for political content degenerated easily into "our" revolution, Russian and therefore right.

Ustrialov's hopes for the future inclined him to see "evolution" in every report from Russia. He was delighted to see his prediction of an "economic Brest" fulfilled in the New Economic Policy.[222] "*To save the Soviets, Moscow sacrifices communism,*" he had gloated from Harbin in the spring of 1921.[223] Lenin, a "great utopian and at the same time a great opportunist," had recognized the failure of "immediate communism" and was ready to compromise with the bourgeiosie. From Ustrialov's perspective, the Soviet pejorative "radish"—red on the outside, white within—could be applied not just to individuals, but to the country as a whole. The red exterior was "a signboard that caught the eye, useful for the distinctive attraction it held out to foreign eyes, for its ability to 'impress.' " The white core was the reality of the reviving state—"the *new* aristocracy, the *new* bourgeoisie, the *new* bureaucracy." Their reappearance indicated that Russia was on its way to "normal" economic and political development, revitalized by the movement of new people into these social ranks.[224]

After the appearance of the *Smena vekh* collection, Ustrialov continued to defend his notion of a nationalist revolution from Harbin. He now felt sure that there were good reasons both for the Bolsheviks' triumph in 1917 and for their ongoing guidance of the state. Of all the contenders for power, the Bolsheviks were the truest to the character of both the Russian intelligentsia and the people, and they were able to use this affinity in the interest of national power. In the winter of 1921–1922, Ustrialov developed these ideas in a two-part study, "The Intelligentsia and the People in the Russian Revolution." Here he tried to smooth over his differences with the *smenovekhovtsy* in Europe and to present their "common philosophy of the revolution." Kliuchnikov published the first article in his Paris weekly *Smena vekh* and the second in its replacement, *Nakanune*, a newspaper printed in Berlin.[225]

The revolution, Ustrialov asserted in these essays, should be seen "first of all as a struggle of the Russian intelligentsia with itself," a struggle in which the Bolsheviks had appealed to and exploited the intelligentsia's dominant traits. Their "fanatical, *religious* worship of material culture and material progress had actively prepared the way for the materialistic cult of the October revolution"; their hatred for the nation and the state had found an outlet in the Bolsheviks' internationalist ideology; and their traditional utopianism, born of lack of political experience, inclined them to live a "golden dream" and ignore reality. These time-honored values had prevailed against the voice of the *Vekhi* dissidents in 1909 and again in 1917, when the World War placed Russia's fate in the intelligentsia's hands.[226]

By that time nothing was left of "Petersburg absolutism," Ustrialov noted, except its premature offspring, the Provisional Government. Under its aegis, the intelligentsia ran through its entire history of political fantasies within a few months—"from the ideas of the Decembrists, to the liberalism of the Westernizers and Slavophile romanticism to the nihilistic negations of the men of the sixties, to the utopias of Chernyshevskii, to the French and German formulas of Bakunin." Once they had seen these dreams embodied in their most extreme form, the major part of the intelligentsia drew back in revulsion, joined the opposition once again, this time fighting against its own earlier ideas and destroying itself in the process.[227]

The Bolsheviks, however, not only provided the masses with an ideology corresponding to their desires, but also encouraged their revolt against property, the army, and the state. Unlike the rest of the intelligentsia, they accepted the wave of anarchy and its consequences. In this, Ustrialov thought, the Bolsheviks came closer to the masses and abolished the age-old division between the people and the state.[228] Even their liquidation of the turbulent, free rebellion of the first stage of revolution corresponded to the instincts of the people:

> Anarchy, having fulfilled its negative mission, did not realize the popular expectations and inevitably turned into a war of all against all. The people did not find the peace they had wanted in the flare-up of hatred, nor the awaited material prosperity in the fact of absolute licentiousness. There was no genuine peace, no sure bread, no real freedom. . . . Deprived of the historical guardianship [*opeka*] of the State, the people felt acutely the necessity of order and strong authority.[229]

The other side of Russian anarchy, Ustrialov felt, was the longing for a boss—*nachal' stvo*—and for a "healthy state of a grand scale and caliber." In the revolution, the people, like the intelligentsia, had fought a "terrible battle with itself": "it not only learned to rule, but it also had to learn consciously to obey." The government that the Russian people had put forward was one that wore its "national face" and would, at the same time, fight against its "dangerous qualities," its passivity and fatigue. Bolshevik rule expressed the "deeply and elementally statist" spirit of the people. Thus anchored in the national culture, the new government would extend its "world-historical truth" beyond the borders of the state and turn Russia into the "rainbow of the world."[230]

This was Ustrialov's resolution of the national problem with which so many of the intellectuals had grappled. In particular it was an answer to Struve, his erstwhile mentor and present correspondent, and Struve's search for national ideals.[231] According to Ustrialov, the revolution was the unifying force. It had merged state and people; the Bolsheviks' nihilism, authoritarianism, and internationalism all corresponded to aspirations of the masses. And in addition, the Bolsheviks had abolished the intelligentsia's isolation: "In the Bolsheviks and through Bolshevism the Russian intelligentsia surmounts its historical apostasy against the people and its psychological apostasy against the state.[232]

What institutional forms would this new state assume? Although Ustrialov supported free enterprise with ardor, he was not an advocate of "bourgeois" politics. He considered himself a democrat, but, like most of the intellectuals, on his own terms. As a "national democrat," he recognized the need for "national political self-definition by means of special state organs of a representative character," but this did not mean the political systems of the West. The vital consideration was not the "form of the state structure," but its "organic" representation of the national experience, of the nation's "character" and "style." Neither "formal, parliamentary, 'arithmetical' . . . democracy of the Western models" nor "canonized Communist schemes" could fulfill this new criterion for state culture, Ustrialov wrote in October 1922. What was needed was an "evolution of the awakened and agitated popular soul into an authentic spiritual self-consciousness," and a sloughing off of the Europeans' "civilization." For Ustrialov, this was the promise of the revolution. It had "brought Russia to the fore of the world stage," and he was confident that a new "cultural-state type, authoritative for the West" would be its result.[233]

Sustaining this grand vision required careful husbandry of Ustrialov's self-vaunted realism. He did not mention the famine in his articles from Harbin, and he interpreted the abolition of the Cheka in February 1922—a formal measure, which Martov had dismissed as window-dressing—as "one of the most splendid acts of the Russian revolution" and a sign of the "new Russia."[234] He refused to see anything of significance in the Bolsheviks' "attachment" to their ideology. Communist terminology was only the "brake" with which they smoothed their descent from utopia to reality, he thought. It allowed the new governors to gain practical experience at a gradual pace and to cover up their past mistakes with handy labels, such as "*SR* [not

Bolshevik] immediate communism.'' Far from criticizing such slanders, Ustrialov felt that they should be welcomed as a means of facilitating progress. Had not Machiavelli taught that in times of change ''it was necessary to preserve the shadow of the former ways so that the people would not suspect the change in the system?'' The ''dream of world revolution'' served a useful, fortifying purpose. It strengthened Russia's international position and, at home, inspired the reconstruction of the state, the rebirth of the army, and a ''sober'' economic policy.[235]

Although Ustrialov had been able to ignore the persecution of the political opposition—from his perspective, the Mensheviks' and SRs' concerns were irrelevant—the expulsion of Berdiaev and other prominent ''idealist'' intellectuals in 1922 forced him to define the intelligentsia's place in the new Russia. He admitted that the recent ''repression'' was ''sad''; it showed that ''full recovery'' was not imminent. But the intellectuals, he argued, would have to be patient. After all, even the ''means of suppression''—exile—had been ''relatively humanitarian.'' And had not the intellectuals themselves looked forward to a ''fresh nation''; had they not idolized the possiblities of a primitive authentic culture? Why should they be surprised when the ''new Scythians'' had bad manners? Now was not the time for ''bourgeois'' morals.[236]

There was no room for ''pure thought'' either, Ustrialov wrote in December 1922. The course of national healing was slow, and the '' 'brain of the country' . . . ought not in any way to hinder this process.'' Of what use were ''critically thinking individuals'' to a nation that was all ''raw appetite,'' just recovering its most ''elemental'' forces after a lengthy crisis. It was time for the intelligentsia to ''rest'' and to refrain for a while from its ''primary function— thought.'' ''Wise men'' would ''keep their lighted candles in the catacombs of personal consciousness, not carrying them aloft, for above there is now too much flammable material.'' And if the intellectuals did not voluntarily choose such a course, it would be forced upon them.[237]

Ustrialov's caution was at odds with the ideas of the *smenovekhovtsy* in Europe. From the first he had argued that the *émigrés* could serve their country best by defending its interests abroad, persuading the ''civilized world'' to accede to Russia's interests, and preparing to return home later, after the Russian Thermidor, when they could be useful.[238] But Kliuchnikov and his colleagues advocated immediate return to Russia and participation in the national reconstruction. When Chakhotin echoed Ustrialov's call ''To Canossa'' in the *Smena vekh*, manifesto, he meant a journey of the body and the mind. The émigrés, if they returned, could not only fill the depleted ranks of the professionals who had remained in Russia as guardians of the national culture—the museums, laboratories, and libraries—they could also aid the economic recovery. The special task of the intelligentsia should be technology, not politics, thought Chakhotin. They could use their acquaintance with the new princples of industrial organization developed in the West to ''Americanize'' Russian production.[239]

While Ustrialov found the notion of borrowing from the West abhorrent,[240] the Soviet government recognized the utility of these ideas. Lenin in particular found *Smena vekh* intriguing; the enlistment of the intelligentsia in state service fit the conceptions of the New Economic Policy, and, in addition, he liked Ustrialov's blunt defense of bourgeois economics. It was refreshing to hear the "class enemy" speak without pretense, Lenin told the Eleventh Party Congress in March 1922. Ustrialov's idea of "evolution"—that NEP would lead back to capitalism—expressed the "main and real danger" facing communism. The challenge, from Lenin's point of view, was to use NEP tactically, to exploit the skills and knowledge of the bourgeoisie without bringing about the fundamental transformation that Ustrialov had predicted.[241]

In accord with this perspective, the Soviet government subsidized *Nakanune* and other *Smena vekh* publications in Europe, [242] and permitted a number of journals defending the ideas of the *smenovekhovtsy* to appear in Russia in 1922.[243] When Kliuchnikov and Potekhin followed their own advice and returned home that year, they were allowed to conduct a series of lectures on the movement in several major cities.

This outright collaboration with the Bolshevik authorities was not to Ustrialov's taste. His idea had been that the intelligentsia had to wait and return to full participation in national life only later, when communism had been transformed. For a long time he had been suspicious of his colleagues' Bolshevik "illusions,"[244] and Kliuchnikov's experience in Russia—where he cooperated with the authorites at the SR trial[245] and wrote a series of glowing articles on Soviet life for *Nakanune*[246]—only confirmed Ustrialov's fears. Perhaps Kliuchnikov and Potekhin were right, he grumbled in his diary; with their "mimicry" they could "buy" the opportunity to go home. But he was an "ideologue," concerned with the "internal sense of a given position," and thus unwilling to praise the Bolshevik system as a whole.[247] It was still "too early" to return, he wrote to Bobrishchev-Pushkin in October 1922.[248]

Although the *Smena vekh* movement made few converts among the émigrés, it enjoyed some popularity in Russia, especially among engineers and other industrial specialists.[249] But while the *smenovekhovtsy* appealed to the notion of nonpartisan, professional service to the state, their ties to the emigration and to "bourgeois" economics were not forgotten. In the mid-twenties, the movement's Soviet journals were shut down and some of its prominent exponents expelled.[250] Kliuchnikov, however, continued to defend Russian nationalism and imperialism under the auspices of the Commissariat of Foreign Affairs,[251] while Ustrialov's ideas played an important role in the debates over socialism in one country. Ustrialov finally returned to Russia in 1935 and taught at Moscow University.[252]

Despite their heretical plea for reconciliation with the Bolshevik revolution, the *smenovekhovtsy*'s assessment of Russian culture was consistent with the views of other nationalists. Berdiaev, Trubetskoi, and Ustrialov all suggested that the

Russian people were not the frustrated democrats and socialists the parties of the left presumed to serve. They did not have Western political ideas, Western customs, or Western values. Whether this was cause for alarm, as in Berdiaev's early works, or for hope, as in Trubetskoi's, the idea that Russia's culture was non-European assumed a new significance in the years after 1917.

What Russians *were* was more difficult to describe, although several characteristics appeared repeatedly in these postrevolutionary evaluations. One common focus was on a dualistic attitude toward authority. Both Berdiaev and Ustrialov emphasized the masses' capacity for extreme rebellion, for destruction aimed at every evidence of social differentiation. Yet at the same time they noted a willingness, even a desire, to submit to strong authority—the "fear of the gendarme," in Berdiaev's phrase, Ustrialov's *nachal'stvo*. These two contrary sentiments were thought to be reinforcing; they fueled the oscillation between passivity and violence in Russia's history. The people, these analyses suggested, acknowledged the need to be "taken in hand," but this imposed control stirred them later to rebellion. No equilibrium was achieved. Related to such erratic, hopeless discontent was a lack of self-confidence. This Trubetskoi attributed to the imposition of Western culture, which had made Russians feel they were inferior. Berdiaev, speaking for high culture, had a different explanation. Russians lacked self-confidence because they had never developed the sense of individualism and individual responsibility associated with Western civilization. Without the experience of chivalry, without the ideas of the Renaissance, Russians had not learned to believe in their actions and ideas.

The nationalist intellectuals attributed this lack of social virtue and individual dignity—deficiencies from the Western point of view—to Russia's "Eastern" sensibility. To Berdiaev this meant formlessness, chaos, "female" passivity, and an inability to assimilate the individualist ethic of Christianity. Russian Orthodoxy, all observers agreed, expressed a religious spirit different from that of the Western churches. It was more "organic," more collective; in Trubetskoi's analysis, it was a sign of an "Asiatic" attitude, a soulfullness hostile to the "technical" creativity of the West. The more pragmatic *smenovekhovtsy* pointed to the absolute quality of Russian religion. To Potekhin, the convicts' message to Dostoevsky—"It is necessary to kill him . . . he does not believe in God"—represented Russian nature.[253]

If these propensities defied the categories of Western thought, they had nonetheless revealed themselves in revolution. According to these nationalist perspectives, the people had acted on their hatred not only of the government, but of the "city," the "bourgeois," the Jew, everything not their own. It had been a revolution against, not for, in Ustrialov's view. The object had been to "level" the town to the ground, and to enjoy its flames. Every member of the intelligentsia was, potentially, an enemy, and it was to the credit of intellectuals like Berdiaev, Trubetskoi, and Ustrialov that they admitted this fundamental opposition. In their reconstructions, the revolution had been a mass revolt against the alien culture of the educated.

Although this vast attack on "civilized" society might have been attributed to divisions within the Russian nation, the nationalist intellectuals preferred to speak of East and West. This formulation derived from the education and traditions of the intellectuals themselves. Even if in principle they rejected the values of the West, in practice they adopted its standards and vocabulary. As Berdiaev had suggested, they looked at Russia with the eyes of European intellectuals. It was no wonder that what they saw best was differences from Europe and that their definitions of "Eastern" ways were negative and vague. Moreover, by establishing an opposition between East and West as their primary frame of reference, they elicited certain answers to Russian problems and ignored other questions altogether.

One answer that corresponded to this kind of thinking was xenophobia, in a variety of forms. The hypothesis of East-West opposition inclined these Russian patriots to blame the West for their country's crisis. Even Berdiaev, who in 1918 had decried Russia's lack of European culture, turned his attention to the pernicious effect of Western "humanism" by the time he was expelled from Russia. Trubetskoi's ethical relativism changed rapidly into warmongering against European civilization—the "worst enemy" of "humanity." Ustrialov's aggressive nationalism lacked such theoretical embellishments—it just made him happy to see the former "Allies" squirm.

One question that the East-West view ignored was class. To Lenin, all the patriotic fervor of the intellectuals could not disguise the fact that they were, in his view, the witting or unwitting agents of world capitalism. The nationalists could not argue this point, for their view of an "organic" nation, regardless of its economic structure, gave class-based opposition no fundamental meaning. Related to this was the question of the intellectuals' place in Russia. To the extent that Russian nationality was identified with an elemental, Asiatic collective, the intelligentsia was an alien interloper. Such a conclusion could not distress Berdiaev; culture for him had always been the province of a distinguished and free-thinking few. And, in his anticipation of the end of history, Russian intellectuals like himself had an international—even cosmic— mission. Trubetskoi, despite his theoretical rejection of Westernized high culture, also had secured the intellectuals a precarious and temporary role in shaping Russia's future. Outside the Soviet system, they were to exploit the permissiveness of Western civilization in order to promote their Eurasian creed. That a systematic application of his theories would eliminate the Westernized intelligentsia and several centuries of "cosmopolitan" achievement in Russia did not concern Trubetskoi. The vision of social harmony was more enticing. It was easier for him and other Eurasians to maintain the strict division between East and West than to examine and defend their own complex values.

Only the *smenovekhovtsy* were rigorous in applying their theories to themselves. Having reduced the national principle to territorial control, they had good reason to support the state. Although Ustrialov disagreed with communism as an ideology, he recognized and approved the Bolsheviks' government. It provided the guardianship and strong authority that Russian people needed. As for the intellectuals, it was time for them to cease their "opposition for opposition's sake,"[254] to defend Russia against its foreign enemies, and thus, even in exile, to join the peasants and the workers in service to their country. For now, Ustrialov thought, the tradition of critical thought had no place in Russia. What the nation needed was labor, not ideas.

6

The Revolution and
the Intelligentsia

With his call for service to the state, Ustrialov enjoined intellectuals opposed to Bolshevism to renounce their past and take a new role in Russia. This was the objective of the Soviet leadership as well. There was no room for the defense of alternative ideals in a nation that was building socialism. Ustrialov suggested that the "brain of the nation" take a "rest";[1] Lenin wanted to put it in jail, or at least to send it out of the country. The events of 1922—the SR trial, the suppression of the remnants of the Menshevik organizations, the expulsion of both political opponents and unruly eccentrics like Berdiaev—all pointed in the same direction.[2] The prerevolutionary intelligentsia, with its self-chosen functions of free inquiry and speaking for the nation, was to be abolished.

The new Soviet intelligentsia would do "mental" labor, but its members would be "white-collar" workers—the managers, administrators, educators of a unified society.[3] More serviceable and compliant people would replace the obstreperous, demanding individuals whose ideas had helped destroy the old regime. Returning home as the nonconforming intellectuals were expelled, the *smenovekhovtsy* were accepted for their technical and propagandistic skills and for their willingness to abandon the old oppositionist assumptions.

But most of the people whose ideas have figured in this study refused to relinquish the principles that had guided them before the revolution. They considered independent analysis, criticism, and theory to be their service to the nation; these ends were not to be given up in order to go home. Socialists, liberals, and nationalists continued to pursue the life that they had chosen long ago and refused to accept the new terms the Bolsheviks pronounced. In addition, most of these intellectuals continued to develop and defend their specific and various prerevolutionary ideologies; they were loyal to their own revolutions, rather than to the one that had taken place. In some cases, old approaches led to new conclusions, as with Vishniak's admission that Western-style democracy was not popular in Russia, but for the most part, the hopes and goals and attitudes of intellectuals before 1917 shaped their later views. The revolution did not change ideas, it confirmed them.

In the world of intelligentsia theory, the experience of five years of revolutionary Russia had given new life to each of the currents of thought that had coexisted so unhappily in the Duma period. Those who had always regarded the state as the source of Russia's problems now found a new enemy worthy of their wrath. The Bolsheviks, more plausibly than the Romanovs in their final, feeble days, could be accused of "dictatorship" and held responsible for the "corruption" of the masses. Leftists who had called for "revolutionary democracy" before 1917 were the more strident in their criticism of the Bolsheviks' "false socialism." Similarly, intellectuals of the *Vekhi* school, who for years had argued that the radical abstractions of the intelligentsia would result in a national collapse, saw their worst fears fulfilled. And those who sensed that Russia's crisis was in essence cultural—the lack of individualistic, "Western" ethics—found reasons to believe that their analyses had been correct.

But despite the divergence of these interpretations of the revolution and despite the fact that theoretical and political differences remained unresolved in 1922, many of the intellectuals' observations concerning the revolutionary experience were concordant. From these notions a composite image of the revolution emerges—a revolution that caught the intelligentsia by surprise, challenged its expectations, and evoked its critical response. Although individual theorists emphasized the incompatibilities of their positions, in fact the revolution drew forth descriptions and opinions that reflect values shared by these adherents to the intelligentsia tradition. These underlying affinities of perspective are clearest in intellectuals' views of the new government and its methods, of Bolshevism's roots in Russian history, and its immediate consequences for the Russian economy.

About the Bolshevik leadership, its procedures and institutions, there was little disagreement. Russian intellectuals accepted the government for what Lenin said it was—a dictatorship. The effectiveness of the new regime and its significance for Russia were matters of dispute, but intellectuals agreed that the means of rule were repressive and authoritarian; the Bolsheviks maintained their leadership with terror and the suppression of dissent. Unlike many in the West, Russian observers did not believe the rhetoric of government by the laboring people and the "power of the Soviets." To them, Soviet democracy was a sham, the revolutionary tribunals meant organized persecution, and the new constitution was a facade for the real government of the Bolshevik party leaders.

Intelligentsia descriptions of Bolshevism converged in other ways as well.

The party leaders were condemned by most, and praised by some, for reviving the practices of the old regime. "Everything is as under the tsar," grieved the Menshevik press in 1918.[4] The "commissarocracy" had refurbished the former institutions of control—the secret police, the censorship, the centralized bureaucracy—and what the ruling party lacked in skill was made up in violence. Shooting, the Menshevik "right" complained on May Day 1919, was the method of dealing with any "manifestation of independence among the workers."[5] Many of the procedures and regulations of the Soviet state, such as the internal passport system, honorific titles, and the hierarchical electoral plan, had been borrowed directly from the tsarist government. Most important, from the intellectuals' perspectives, was the attempt to base the state on interests of classes not individuals, an endeavor that both critics and supporters in the intelligentsia interpreted in the shadow of Russia's past. To those who advocated the equality of all citizens, class-based legislation was a regression to absolutist principles. Vishniak's *Le régime soviétiste* indicted the Bolshevik government for its division of society into separate "estates" and its reliance upon the differential allocation of duties and rewards.[6] But others welcomed the reorganization of the population according to its work as a sign of national recovery. According to Chakhotin in *Smena vekh*, the peasants, workers, and "laboring intelligentsia" were the "three bases of the state." The government's task was to "harmonize [their] interests and activity . . . and to build upon them the well-being of the country."[7] By Russian Marxists, of course, the theory of class rule was accepted; what was questioned was its practice. If the Bolsheviks turned their supporters into a new "Praetorian guard" and a new corrupt bureaucracy, what good did this do the working class?[8]

These views of Bolshevik government as a revival of absolutist principles and practice were reflected in intellectuals' predictions for the future. To many it appeared that the new regime would end in one-man rule. The dictatorship already existed; the estate system was in place; the missing element was the autocrat. Martov, whose frames of reference were both the Russian past and the French revolution, wrote even in December 1917 that "some kind of Caesarism" was likely.[9] Lenin did not fit this role exactly. Although it was clear to these observers that Lenin led the government, he did not, in their eyes, support or embody the principle of autocratic authority. He was "Lenin-Pugachev," the rebel; "Lenin-Arakcheev," the administrative zealot; or, in Struve's passion, Lenin, "the executioner"; but not a Russian tsar. Other Bolsheviks, especially Trotsky, attracted the attention and imagination of the intelligentsia at this time. The autocratic solution, longed for by reactionary fanatics and feared by reformers, had not yet taken shape, they felt.

In addition to examining the Bolshevik government's connection to prerevolutionary state politics, intellectuals looked for sources of Bolshevik theory in the Russian past. One common explanation of Bolshevism, as an ideology, was its derivation from the nineteenth-century revolutionary movement and in particular from Bakuninist principles. Struve considered Bolshevism the culmination of the intelligentsia tradition and pointed to the intelligentsia's "apostasy," rebellion against the state, as a cause of the revolution. While nationalists like Struve and Berdiaev condemned the entire intelligentsia for its disloyalty, Mensheviks were eager to distinguish between their own convictions and those of their Bolshevik opponents. In their efforts to separate Bolshevik party practice from Marxist tradition, both Martov and Axelrod associated Bolshevism with a primitive stage of Russian socialism, one based on terrorism, conspiracy, and the cynical exploitation of anarchistic sentiment. Their charges of "Bakuninism" accorded with the judgments of the *vekhovtsy*. Kropotkin's testimony, however, was at odds with this prevailing view. As a systematic anarchist, he blamed Bolshevism on the centralist and statist assumptions of Marxist thought.

Although most of the intellectuals considered here agreed that Lenin's party represented at least a part of the intelligentsia's own past, there was one respect in which the Bolsheviks appeared to be anomalous. They alone possessed the skill and the audacity to seize and maintain power. This was acknowledged even by their opponents, at least by those who were willing to confront the problem of political authority. The "maximalist illusions" so criticized by the moderate socialists were to Miliukov a sign of the Bolsheviks' political realism. Their slogans, unlike those of all other parties, were clear, "consistent," and immensely appealing to the masses in 1917. Moreover, as Ustrialov observed, the Bolsheviks had been willing to ride the wave of anarchy and destruction, and to wait until the energies of revolt had been exhausted before asserting their control. Struve, too, recognized the Bolsheviks' ability to speak to popular desires; as he saw it, the deceit that people would be able to work less and receive more had had enormous success. Only the Bolsheviks had been "logical" during the revolution and civil war, Struve felt; they were "psychologically" prepared to win.[10]

This revolutionary spirit had outlived the end of the war in Russia, intellectuals observed; in their views, it animated the militant foreign policy of the Soviet government. Russian socialists criticized the Bolsheviks for their violations of "internationalism": Martov charged them with manipulating the European socialist organizations for their own ends and with making unprincipled alliances with nonsocialist movements in the East. These were the same trouble spots singled out by Miliukov in *Bolshevism: An International Danger*. The Bolsheviks would use every means to advance their cause in Europe, Miliukov advised. Set back temporarily by the failure of the German and Hungarian revolutions, they were now preparing the world revolution in Asia. These warnings would have been soothing to Ustrialov's xenophobia. He supported the Bolshevik government because of its ability to threaten Europe and to absorb the "pygmy" nations on its borders.

Although Bolshevik politics had been effective in Russia and promised results elsewhere, the party's economic program had been a failure. Russian critics almost unanimously pointed to the economy as the weakest link in the

Bolshevik system. The attempt to build socialism in backward, war-torn Russia made sense to no one, least of all to Mensheviks who believed in progress through essential stages of development. The Socialist Revolutionaries realized that the land "redistribution" had meant no gains in agricultural output and that the requisitions policy amounted to starving first the countryside and then the country. As Struve pointed out, harsh controls over labor could not by themselves stimulate production in a system with little to eat and nothing to sell. Both he and Miliukov thought that the Bolshevik economy depended upon products accumulated in the past and that such a system could not last. Ustrialov was just as insistent that the Bolsheviks would have to repudiate "communism" in order to survive. While the New Economic Policy of 1921 confirmed the widespread opinion that the experiment in state socialism had failed, it did not inspire confidence in the future. The *smenovekhovtsy* welcomed the prospect of an economy revitalized by the technical intelligentsia and free enterprise, but most observers remained sceptical.

Thus, though drawn from different perspectives, these views of the Bolshevik government were consistent. The new regime was a dictatorship. Its techniques—the propaganda of revolt and justice, followed by authoritarian controls—fused the traditions of conspiratorial populism with the politics of autocracy. Bolshevik tactics had been successful in Russia, and they posed a threat to other states. On the other hand, the economic policies of the new administration had been a failure and this, in these theorists' eyes, threatened to undermine the political victory.

Russian intellectuals' interpretations of the revolution as a whole, of its causes and significance for the future, were less congruent than their assessments of Bolshevism. It was easy to repudiate the hostile government, but to pronounce the revolution a failure would have meant a defeat of their own hopes for a new Russia. In 1922, most of these critics did not regard the revolution as completed; it still posed "problems," "tasks," or "lessons" to Russia and the world. This sense of still being in the revolutionary period allowed intellectuals to believe in the ultimate success of their own principles, but it was also a perceptive judgment. To their credit, many of these witnesses regarded the revolution as a question, not an answer.

One of the problems that troubled Russian intellectuals was the origin of a revolution that conformed so little to their expectations. Only the most determined positivists, such as Kropotkin, accepted the simplistic explanation that the revolution was an expression of historical progress. Others—socialists, liberals, and nationalists alike—were provoked to search for more specific causes. These they found in Russia's past, in social and political developments, and in the aggravating circumstances of the World War. Of all the explanations based on Russia's political history, Struve's was the most far-reaching and deterministic. He felt that the bargain struck in the eighteenth century between the autocracy and its potential rivals had condemned Russia to a warped, non-European future. The autocracy had purchased its monopoly on power with serfdom—by granting absolute control over the peasants to the gentry on the condition that the economically dominant class would not meddle in affairs of state. According to Struve, this arrangement prevented the growth of private property and participatory government, and it had produced the agent of its own demise—the intelligentsia.

Although Struve blamed the revolution, ultimately, upon the Russian autocracy and its refusal to share power, he accused the intelligentsia of willfully bringing down the state without regard to the consequences for the nation. The idea of the intelligentsia's responsibility for the national collapse was shared by many intellectuals, and not solely those of the *Vekhi* orientation. Berdiaev, of course, despised the intelligentsia for what he saw as a lack of individualism and self-respect. In his view, the inability to trust one's own opinion had inclined Russians to embrace collectivist, leveling ideals antithetical to creative work. But some socialists, too, pointed to the intelligentsia's shortcomings. Vishniak reproached the entire left for not taking democracy seriously; Potresov condemned the Mensheviks for their narrow-minded dogmatism. The charges of impracticality and utopianism appeared to have been vindicated by the incompetence of the Provisional Government and the moderate leaders of the Petrograd Soviet. When given a chance to run the state, the left had failed miserably, as Miliukov's *History* had stressed. Although the intellectuals tended to blame each other or the Bolsheviks for the outcome of the revolution, in aggregate their criticism accorded ''intelligentsia ideas'' an important place in the destruction of the old regime and the disintegration of state authority.

But the old regime had been in no shape to fight. As Berdiaev commented, the autocracy fell ''like an apple from a tree'';[11] Nicholas II, in Ol'denburg's account, gave up without protest. After its demise, the autocracy vanished from the intellectuals' consciousness, reappearing only as a polemical abstraction with which they could compare their enemies. The reactionaries, of course, wanted the monarchy to return, but of the serious theorists few had anything positive to say about the prerevolutionary government. Contrary to the accusations of the socialists, the liberals seemed as intent upon forgetting the Duma period as any of their opponents. The intelligentsia as a whole preferred to contemplate the heroic days before 1905. No one thought that but for the revolution of 1917, Russia would have evolved toward democracy or socialism or national consensus on the basis of the prerevolutionary political system.

Similarly, few spoke with enthusiasm about the prerevolutionary economy. Russia was seen as a ''backward,'' not a thriving, nation. While intellectuals generally condemned the Bolsheviks' policy of immediate socialism as ''utopian,''·this did not mean that they recommended a return to the policies of the past. Social democrats wrote of the necessity for a bourgeois stage of production, but among their major theorists only Potresov was willing to admit the merits of the Russian bourgeoisie. Struve spoke of the vital importance of private property, but was well aware that it had not been established as a principle in Russian life. Supporters of capitalism and free enterprise like Struve and Ustrialov regarded them as goals for the future, not as achievements of the old regime.

That after the revolution with its disappointments Russian intellectuals mustered no support for the prerevolutionary government, or for its political or economic potential, suggests the extent of their alienation from the state before 1917. To them, the revolution did not appear as a sudden, freakish challenge to a strong and well-established system, but as a long-anticipated chance for old and serious problems to be resolved. The question had been when and how, not if, the old regime would fall.

The event that most observers pointed to as the immediate cause of revolution was the war. It seemed to have deepened the divisions between society and government, stretched everyone's nerves, and created the possibility for a radical break in the stalemated system. Most important, the war brought new people to political life. As Struve noted, in wartime, the masses both in Europe and in Russia, had "felt their strength."[12] Martov believed that the war, and the capitalists behind it, had "corrupted" the people and destroyed their confidence in the "moral" values of socialism;[13] Potresov, on the other hand, thought the war had simply revealed a "peasant" mentality that socialists had overlooked before. But no matter what the genesis of the masses' attitudes, the war and revolution had made one thing clear to intellectuals: the people— peasants, soldiers, and proletarians—preferred their own "selfish interests" to the salvation of the Russian state.

The war, the unworkable political arrangement inherited from the past, "intelligentsia" ideas—these figured repeatedly in intellectuals' writings on the origins of the revolution. But what of its future? What did the revolution mean in the forward course of Russia's history? For the intelligentsia, the revolution revived all the "accursed questions" of the past and gave them vital significance. Three issues in particular dominated the post-revolutionary debates and provoked a variety of answers; these were Russian socialism, the place of the people in the new state, and the relationship of Russia to the West.

The controversy over whether the Bolshevik revolution represented socialism began with the October seizure of power. The Russian social democrats considered here insisted that the Bolshevik government had betrayed their cause. There were two aspects to this judgment, one based on the Mensheviks' commitment to Marxist economic theory. Despite Martov's early optimistic prediction that a socialist government could guide a revolution along the necessary "bourgeois tracks," by 1918 the leader of the Menshevik party had returned to a position more consistent with Marxist premises—Russia did not have the economic resources for socialist organization. As he argued to the Congress of Trade Unions in January 1918, without plentiful production, exploitation could not disappear.[14] When Martov sided with the revolution against its enemies, his support was conditioned by his loyalties in the class struggle—the need to fight against the capitalists—rather than by an acceptance of Bolshevik ideology. This notion that the revolution could not be socialist because of Russia's "backwardness" was shared and defended more consistently by Plekhanov, Potresov, and Zasulich.

There was another, related, dimension to the moderate left's claim that the Bolsheviks and their system were not socialist. This was a political argument, one that helped to clarify the left's vague prerevolutionary commitment to "democracy". The experience of the revolution made Mensheviks and Socialist Revolutionaries more conscious, by negative example, of the value of democratic procedures and of their importance to a socialist society. By destroying the independence of the unions and eliminating the right to strike the Bolsheviks had created a "dictatorship *over* the proletariat," in Axelrod's phrase. More fundamentally, one-party rule seemed to undermine the vision of socialism as a liberating and participatory system. Martov, Chernov, and Kropotkin each in different ways thought that socialism would mean that people could shape their own lives and share in the decisions that formed their society. A party dictatorship was therefore, as Kropotkin wrote to Lenin, "positively harmful for the building of a new socialist system,"[15] for it destroyed the initiative and self-reliance essential to a free, consensual nation. To the moderate socialists before the revolution, socialism had meant, among other things, individual freedom.[16] After 1917, they found socialism without liberty and democracy not worthy of the name, and in this cause subjected Bolshevism to a more thoroughgoing libertarian critique than did any of the non-socialist intellectuals.

While leftists refused to accept the revolution as socialist, others wanted to judge the revolution with the Bolsheviks' own terms. Struve, Miliukov, and Ustrialov accepted the Bolsheviks' claim to the socialist banner, the better to discredit Marxism. For each of these critics, the main issue was economics. The postrevolutionary economy represented an attempt to put socialist theory into practice, they insisted, and its disastrous failure demonstrated that socialism would not work. If socialists had taken this argument seriously instead of dismissing all moderate opinion as "reaction," they would have responded that since Russian conditions were too "backward" for socialism and since the government was not socialist in its practice, this general indictment was based on false premises. Struve—as usual compensating for the lack of dialogue by anticipating and countering objections—felt that such excuses were insufficient. One could not ignore the result of the Russian experience: there was a fundamental contradiction in socialist ideology that would never disappear. As the revolution showed, the principle of equality was contrary to the goal of productivity. In order to produce, a socialist state would have to resort to "bourgeois" incentives that undermined its egalitarian objectives. The consequences of a policy that eliminated private property and economic freedom would be, as the years of Bolshevik control had shown, "socialized" poverty and death.

A second problem revived and vitalized by the revolution was the relation of the Russian people to the state. In the past, radical and reformist intellectuals had assumed an opposition, actual or latent, between *narod* and *rezhim*—people and the government. The purpose of the intelligentsia had been to eliminate this polarity, by speaking for the people's interest, destroying the imperial state, and creating a new united nation. Where did the people stand after 1917, and had the revolution resolved or altered this time-honored question? Five years after the October coup, intellectuals had to face the fact that the Bolsheviks' ideas had been popular. And, for all the misery of the population, the Bolsheviks had won support—first, during the seizure of power and later in the civil war. Was this a new beginning?

To moderate socialists and liberal reformers, the idea that the people had voluntarily chosen government by the Bolsheviks was repugnant. This explanation of the Bolsheviks' success contradicted their view that the Russian people were the bearers of their own democratic and nationalist ideas. Thus, for the most part, critics on the left focused their attention on the "deception" of the people by the Bolsheviks. Once the new governors were "unmasked" as despots, assumed Mensheviks and Socialist Revolutionaries, the people would refuse to follow them. Several concepts—the notion that the Bolsheviks had used one "part" of the working class against another or that they had exploited divisions between the city and the country—helped these theorists to account for the Bolsheviks' popularity in the capitals in 1917. In addition, the idea that the Bolsheviks had "corrupted" the masses was frequently adduced, as in Vishniak's account of Kronstadt. These efforts to counter the Bolsheviks' claim to represent the people were, however, undercut by the refusal of the Menshevik Central Committee and the SR leadership to support rebellions against the new government. Only the "right" wing of the left—represented here by Potresov and his followers—encouraged working-class opposition to the regime and thus acted in accord with the view that popular opinion was on the other side.

Difficult as the confrontation with mass support for Bolshevism was, some intellectuals tried to integrate it into their interpretations of the revolution. Struve, the Kantian nationalist, solved the problem transcendentally: yes, the people had supported the Bolsheviks; yes, they had fallen for the chance to divide up accumulated wealth and the promise that more was, easily, to come; but no, they were not thereby united with the Russian state, because under Bolshevik rule a healthy, productive, self-sustained nation was impossible. The true unity would appear only in the future when the people had transformed themselves into the Christian nationalists he believed they could become.

Others looked at this problem from cultural, rather than political perspectives. To Berdiaev, the revolution had revealed a national unity—a negative one. The entire population, he felt, was suffering from a "disease of the moral consciousness."[17] Both intelligentsia and *narod* were not Christian, but apocalyptic in outlook. The masses would rather bring everything down to their own level than strive for self-improvement. The key to the success of the cleverest "Russian boys" was their understanding of this mentality and their cultivation of the individual's wish to give in to the collective will. "The shame of one's own opinion" was the "cement that binds all together."[18]

Of these views of the people and the state after 1917, Ustrialov's was the most radical in its break with earlier interpretations. He felt that the correspondence between Bolshevik slogans and popular desires had a profound and positive significance for Russia as a nation. The Bolsheviks, he wrote, were the "most Russian" members of the intelligentsia; it was natural that the masses had identified with them:

> The worker-peasant revolt needed a suitable "ideology" that corresponded to itself. The new *Pugachevshchina* sought slogans and found them in the group of Bolshevik-*intelligenty*, who not only did not fear anarchy, but "took" [*priiavshie*] it to the end and even tried to intensify it.[19]

After the destructive energies of the masses had been spent, the Bolsheviks provided the strong authority the people then desired. For Ustrialov, the Bolsheviks' political triumph would allow Russia to create a "new cultural-state type." The Westernized ideals of the intellectuals had been rejected; the "St. Petersburg period" of Russian history was finished.[20] The revolution represented a union of the people with the state.

Ustrialov's nationalist interpretation of the revolution was linked to his hopes for the revival of Russian power in world affairs. Russia's emergence as a "great and united state"[21] meant strength in future conflicts with the nation's enemies—the Western countries. The notion that the revolution would have a profound impact upon world history and in particular upon Russia's relationship with Europe was shared by many intellectuals at this time. But here again, their conceptions of the question and their answers were radically at odds.

Liberals and socialists took an abstract, moralistic approach to the issue of the revolution's international significance. Both Vishniak and Struve, for example, conceived of the revolution as a tragic political lesson, an affirmation by negative example of the validity of "Western" principles. Europeans could learn from Russia's experience that democratic institutions, according to Vishniak, and private property, in Struve's analysis, were essential to national well-being. Although Russian socialists identified their interests with the European proletariat and maintained their opposition to capitalism and imperialism, they saw the revolution as a source of wisdom. Most agreed with Kropotkin's judgment that the Bolsheviks were demonstrating how not to build a revolution.

With respect to future international developments, these normative interpretations implied that political initiative and strength belonged to the West: the Europeans—governors, proletarians, intellectuals—would be enlightened and presumably fortified by the Russian experience. But other Russian intellectuals, who addressed political consequences directly, felt that the revolution posed a direct threat to Western society, a challenge deriving from an expansion of militarism, a revival of Russian national power, and Russian alliances with colonial nations. Underlying these views was the idea that the upheaval in Russia was linked to a radical reorientation of international politics. That the revolution had taken Russia out of the European war appeared a sign of things to come. The fundamental antagonism was no longer between different European imperialists, but between Russia and her enemies.

The impression that the revolution would lead to a general increase in hostilities was shared by people of different ideological persuasions. Vera Zasulich's vague prediction of an "outburst of militarism" was connected with her alarm at Russia's withdrawal from the World War. Bolshevik policy would strengthen Germany, she thought, intensify world conflicts, and thus lead to the indefinite postponement of the "possibility of socialism."[22] For Trubetskoi, on the other hand, it was socialism itself, which he associated with "Romano-Germanic civilization" and not with Russia, that would keep the world an armed camp until the last outpost of capitalism was destroyed.[23] These ill-defined and pessimistic thoughts expressed a common mood; no one thought that the revolution would lead to peace.

To Ustrialov, of course, the prospect of conflict with the West was not unwelcome. He was pleased by the effect of Bolshevik militancy upon the Europeans and eager to recognize the Bolsheviks as the heirs of Russian imperialism. It was the Bolsheviks' break with the "so-called 'Allies' " that had induced him to forsake the White armies.[24] To Ustrialov, Bolshevik ideology was strictly a weapon to be used against Russia's enemies. Slogans such as "national self-determination" would mean nothing when Russia had the strength to expand her territory. From his pragmatic, chauvinist perspective, the revolution had provided Russia with a leadership and an ideology suited to her "world mission."[25]

To the Eurasians, this mission meant turning to the East. Russia's natural allies were the other victims of European domination. Like Ustrialov, Trubetskoi noted the utility of Bolshevik propaganda: in the colonies it had been associated with the "idea of national liberation." Through the revolution, Russia had acquired the possibility of "standing at the head of her Asiatic sisters" in a struggle against European culture, their "worst enemy."[26] Thus Trubetskoi welcomed the revolutionary agitation that Martov and Miliukov alike deplored. An alliance with "primitive" countries was not pernicious; it was a logical and a national imperative.

These reflections on the international dimension of the revolution suggested that there was an unanticipated power in Bolshevik slogans, an attraction that had little to do with the Eurocentric visions of socialists like Martov. As Trubetskoi pointed out, what worked for the Bolsheviks in Asia was not "pure-Communist ideas," but propaganda "against the Romano-Germans and Romano-Germanic culture." Russia's "Asiatic sisters" interpreted "bourgeois" to mean the European shopkeepers, engineers, and bureaucrats in their midst as well as native, "Europeanized" intellectuals.[27] Other commentaries indicated that similar "misunderstanding" had taken place at home. In Ustrialov's description of a peasant raid, the peasants had seized property, but they had also burned down the town and enjoyed it. This had been their point, their "principle": the town had to be destroyed for their lives to be possible.[28] From Berdiaev's aristocratic perch, the preaching of the "Russian boys" had only sanctioned the masses' "Eastern" hostility to elite culture. Incited against the bourgeoisie, the people had attacked all forms of alien dominance—the state, the city, the intelligentsia. The revolt had been directed at the whole of educated society.

That the revolution had been against them—or against things they stood for—this was the rudest challenge to the intelligentsia's self-image. It was given substance by the physical extrusion of non-Bolshevik theorists from Russia. Of the intellectuals considered here, by 1922 three had died in Russia; one—Potresov—remained there in broken health; two, who supported the new government, had returned from exile; and the rest lived abroad. In this concrete sense, the non-Bolshevik intelligentsia had lost its battles, but what effect had the preceeding five years had upon its consciousness, upon "intelligentsia ideas"?

The outstanding feature of the intelligentsia in 1922 was how little it had changed. Not only had individual intellectuals remained true to their prerevolutionary ideals, they had, collectively, with their paper politics reconstructed a divided opposition. To be sure, some individuals had budged an inch or two, and new fissures had opened up between people who had thought they stood together, but these were, for the most part, developments consistent with prerevolutionary attitudes. The revolution renewed and intensified old quarrels, as the polemical struggles between radicals and reformers, and among members of the same party, were taken up again in emigration. Among the subjects of this study, the major differences in postrevolutionary ideology were related not to the revolution, but to generation. Those who had fought the autocracy before 1905 remained firmly attached to Europhilic, determinist views of historical development, continued to assume that Russia would, eventually, pursue a course similar to that taken by the West, and, whether liberals or socialists, stressed the importance of liberty. Younger individuals who had grown up in the relative freedom of the Duma period did not defend these traditional intelligentsia values. Their ideas—Ustrialov's xenophobic nationalism, Trubetskoi's Eurasianism, Ol'denburg's sympathetic portrait of Nicholas II—broke with nineteenth-century conventions.

But even the novel constructions of younger intellectuals conformed to the intelligentsia's most fundamental assumption—the idea that it spoke for the Russian people. The populism of the Russian intelligentsia, the unconscious merging of one's own views with a mass wish, not only survived the shock of the revolutionary years, it emerged strengthened by the ordeal. This common confidence took a variety of forms.

The most compelling testimony to the power of populist ideals is the extent to which they figured in the writings of the people's harshest critics. Ustrialov could not have been more explicit about the cruelty and anarchism of the masses or more elitist in his conceptions of political and economic power; nonetheless, he insisted that the Russians were a "deeply . . . statist people"[29] and that they would thrive under the aggressive, nationalist regime he recommended. Miliukov, who in 1918 had dismissed the people as a passive object of politics, discovered their democratic proclivities after the defeat of his several wartime plans. Even Berdiaev, disdainful as he had been of Russian values, suggested in 1922 that Russia's "Eastern" sensibility provided a guide to the "spiritual" stage of life on earth—and that he was its spokesman.

As for the socialists, their conviction that they represented the interests of the masses went, for the most part, unexamined. Some, at times, recognized that "the people," or some of them, were not behaving as their would-be leaders had expected; neither the pursuit of "selfish interests" nor violent rebellion against the Bolshevik state were to Martov's and Chernov's tastes. But both continued to believe that the workers, or the "whole laboring people," would come eventually to support the ideas and projects of social democracy, or the PSR. To explain the gap between their image of the people and reality, socialist intellectuals turned back to an old enemy. It was the new state—the "banditry" of the new elite, their use of the "dregs" of the population to terrorize the rest, their suppression of the press—that accounted for the people's temporary lapses.

The extremes of Russian populism are reflected in the visions of Struve and Trubetskoi, whose philosophies were diametrically opposed. Struve, a Kantian and a Christian, based his confidence in the people explicitly on faith; he *believed* in their capacity for spiritual rebirth and national reconstruction, in their willing service of his values. Trubetskoi, as a positivist and an opponent of the Westernism of his father's generation, advocated that Russians eliminate the intelligentsia's "Romano-Germanic" ideas altogether and base their nation on the people's "low" culture.

The strength of these different confidences in the people seems all the more pronounced when set against intelligentsia denunciations of the Bolsheviks. "The people—it is I"—this was Martov's cut at "Lenin, Trotsky, Stalin and their brotherhood,"[30] but was this not true of the anti-Bolsheviks as well? One of their major charges against the government was that its claim to represent the people was duplicitous, yet the intellectuals outside the state remained impervious to doubts about their own support. What did this protean, insistent populism in the discarded intelligentsia mean?

From a functionalist perspective, these intellectuals' dedication to their visions of the Russian people has a basis in a group psychology. Belief that the people would themselves act for the goals set by the intelligentsia meant that the opposition intellectuals had not lost the revolution and, what was more, they did not have to fight their own battles. Eventually, the people—the working class, the "third force," Miliukov's "peasant democracy"—would do it all.

However, if such calculations played any role in the intelligentsia's postrevolutionary choices, they could not have been articulated. Most of the intellectuals considered here thought of themselves as active in the revolutionary period and were: Mensheviks and Socialist Revolutionaries tried to inform and guide their parties; Kropotkin struggled to protect and promote cooperative ethics; Struve and, until the end, Miliukov served the White Armies with their diplomacy and propaganda; Ustrialov worked for Kolchak and then against the Whites. These were not lazy, pacific, or unambitious people.

How intellectuals acted in this period, rather than the question of activity, provides a glimpse into their frames of mind. Their behavior was conditioned by the ideas and experience of the past, a past in which the people's values had been adduced, but not confronted. Neither the rigid structures of the autocracy, nor the complex and hierarchical compromises of the Duma period had let the people's voices through, and what had been heard from 1905 and 1906 was selectively interpreted. The political context was such that anyone could speak for the people, without fear of decisive contradiction. In the relative freedom of the Duma years, the intelligentsia had cultivated the remembrance of a heroic past of opposition, without examining its place in a changing society or breaking with its own anarchism and authoritarianism. And even in this most cosmopolitan of times, intellectuals took in only what they wanted from European thought. Positivism, socialism, and idealism were embraced by individual enthusiasts, but pluralism remained an alien idea. Each preferred the assumption that his or her ideas were shared by all—or rather by the people— to the tolerance of differing perceptions.

But it was more than the language of Russian politics or a loyalty to the old heroism that kept this mentality alive. How could intellectuals confront the question of popular support for their ideas, without endangering the nationalist constructions they had produced? Each had a vision of Russia, an image of a united society that could exist if only one's own plan—for socialism, *narodovlastie*, private property, national service, spiritual transfiguration— were followed. By extending their ideas to the people, intellectuals gave themselves a nation, a nation in which they, with their education, their theories, their mixed and complex culture, would have a place.

The tension between these integrative projections and the conflicts that devastated Russia from 1917 through 1922 emerges in the arguments intellectuals applied to their opponents in the intelligentsia and to questions affecting the nation as a whole. When dealing with, or dismissing, the ideas of their peers, intellectuals had sharp eyes for contradictions. The socialists repeatedly condemned the Bolsheviks for the divergence between their slogans and their actions; Miliukov attacked the moderate left on these same grounds. Inconsistencies in one's opponents' theories, or between words and deeds, were seen as fatal, as if systems based on contradictions could not survive and would give way before the force of reason. But when looking at the revolution as a whole, many accepted a different kind of dialectic: it was tempting to believe a phenomenon could lead to its opposite, that from the collapse of the old society, something new and better would arise. This was the view of the *Iz glubiny* patriots: both Struve and Berdiaev felt that religious rebirth would result from the material destruction of 1918. Miliukov, too, predicted that Russian democracy would follow Bolshevik tyranny. Even Ustrialov, the most pragmatic patriot, was vulnerable to the seductive "logic" of "light from darkness."[31] "Destruction," he wrote, was a "sign of life," accompanying "every great historical event."[32] The Russian people, having destroyed the "historical Russian state," would not only discover a new national ideal; they, "indigent" and "hungry," would turn Russia into the "rainbow of the new world."[33] These distortions of the tractable Hegelian heritage denied the continuity of history and made room for hope.

Another sign of intellectuals' ability to disguise discordant evidence, as well as of their need for affirmation, was their behavior in the emigration. Leaving Russia distanced them physically from the people they believed they served and perpetuated their populist abstractions. Firm in their convictions, they continued to reject the legitimacy of each others' views. The same intolerant individualism, the same insistence upon a single correct analysis, related to a single correct idea of Russia, reemerged abroad—in the exclusionary politics of the Menshevik Central Committee, in Struve's dogmatic insistence that one had to "accept or reject" the revolution as a whole, in Trubetskoi's "logical" demonstrations in *Europe and Humanity*. At the same time, the geographic dispersion of émigré intellectuals reflected their desire to be with those who thought alike. The Mensheviks established themselves near their German comrades in Berlin, while the obstinate "rightist" labor representatives sought help from trade unionists in London. Miliukov headed for London as well in order to consult with the politicians who, he thought, were most dedicated to the values of liberalism and fair play. Trubetskoi indulged his Slavophile fantasies on the eastern periphery of Europe; while Ustrialov, true to his hatred of the "so-called 'Allies,' " refused to leave Harbin.[34]

Miliukov's dedication of *Russia To-day and To-morrow* to his American audiences and his pleasure in the thought that they shared the democratic and federalist sympathies he attributed to the Russian people illustrates the hopeful and fanciful world of Russian intellectuals in 1922. Like the rest, Miliukov sought legitimacy by assigning his ideals to others, and his career can serve as a paradigm for the intelligentsia's experience. On the surface, from his words, Miliukov sounded like a Western politician, exceptionally clever and eloquent, of course, but dedicated to the pragmatic pursuit of political ends—the integrity and power of his nation, the primacy of his party and of himself within it. But the relationship of these words to what was happening in Russia was tenuous in the beginning and became immaterial with time. Once Miliukov was forced out of the Provisional Government, his schemes and strategies, his heretical negotiations with the Germans, his zealous defense of his right to "free hands," and his equally ardent critique of the British and their "Hands Off

Russia'' policy, his New Tactic and the consequent disintegration of the Kadet party—all this energy, all this ''common sense''—these were connected to the revolutionary struggles in Russia only by strands of wishful thought.

To an imaginative cynic, these intellectuals may appear as in a dollhouse on the stage of Russian history—in a mansion to be sure, each room a different blend of new European imports with the mixed comforts of the past, each window with its separate view—but in miniature and in a set within a set. The domestic quarrels in this building could seem unrelated to the grander drama of the revolution, but only if one forgets some facts and overlooks possibilities of interpretation.

Most obviously, these theorists and critics were Russians, too, and they had been part of the revolution. One of the virtues of their writings was to reveal which part. They did not cast themselves as principals—these roles were reserved for the Bolshevik leaders and the masses—but as observers, analysts, and critics. They acted within the confines of a particular tradition—the notion of the intelligentsia as defenders of ''truth and justice''[35] and of critical thought as a contribution to national well-being.

The result of this confidence in free inquiry was a rich legacy of interpretation and description of the revolutionary years, a spectrum of ideas that can be set against and seen within their historical context. Socialists, mindful of their own ideal, subjected the Bolshevik government to a libertarian critique: to both Mensheviks and Socialist Revolutionaries, the Soviet government meant political dictatorship and repression and corruption of the masses. Struve drew an economic lesson from the upheaval. The attempt to put socialism into practice had demonstrated that its egalitarian principle destroyed incentive to produce. Russian socialism was the division of accumulated goods and the subsequent nationalization of poverty. Several intellectuals stressed the international dimension of the revolution. To nationalists, it presaged the revival of Russian imperialism and a confrontation between colonial and Western nations. Berdiaev and Trubetskoi saw the revolution as the culmination of a profound cultural crisis in Russia and as evidence of the failure of Western values. Unfortunately, none of these provocative conclusions entered Western consciousness as directly as the lies of the Russian anti-Semites; to them the revolution was proof of an international Jewish conspiracy.

Yet even as they hoped for their projects to come alive, the serious social theorists of this period thought of their views as hypotheses to be tested. ''All these 'syntheses' are worked out by life completely independently of our desire and opposition,'' wrote Ustrialov in 1922. ''We are only registrars; that infamous 'future historian' will draw the conclusion.''[36] For those who need to be convinced that these old ideas are worthy of analysis, it is instructive to recall that, from today's perspective, Russia's intellectuals writing in the revolution were right about several of its major consequences.

First, they, and not the government, were correct from the beginning about the problems of socialist construction. When Martov argued on the basis of Marxist theory that the prerequisites for a plentiful and just economy were not present, or when Struve, from his philosophic and informed hostility, predicted that the Bolsheviks would have to turn to bourgeois incentives in order to produce, they anticipated the major crisis of the revolution. Second, the intellectuals' sense of the revolution as a world-historical event cannot be disputed. Through their peculiar position within a hybrid culture, they were sensitized to the attack on Western assumptions that was imbedded in the Russian revolution. Even those who could not address this threat directly "registered" their shock and this was a sound indicator of future realignments. Third, and here the intelligentsia tradition served a critical role, the intellectuals were quick to spot the reappearence of political oppression. If the revolt against authority took unexpected directions, the structures and supports of the Bolsheviks' government were familiar, and, for those who sought after liberty, the change in ideology did not make terror, control over elections and the press, and a centralized, corrupting bureaucracy more palatable. To the dismay of most of these observers, no democracy, no merging of the rulers and the ruled, had taken place. Their old enemy—the state—had won.

The weaknesses of these interpretations are also informative. Historians of Russia, especially Western ones, can learn a useful scepticism about their own approaches from the inadequacies of the intelligentsia's ideas. They looked at Russia with Western eyes, Berdiaev thought, and this meant a narrow focus, partial visions, certain blindspots. Of these attempts to fit the revolution with a theory, the analyses of the Westernized reformers were most at odds with their observations. Both Martov and Struve expected Russia to take the course of Europe—despite their disagreements about the endpoint of the route—but by 1922 both socialist and liberal variants of progressive thought seemed brittle impositions on the revolution they tried to encompass. The cultural nationalists, for all their isolation as individuals, were more able to confront divisions between the intelligentsia and the people, to listen to the voices of rebellion, and to imagine the birth of a new nation on its own terms.

Right and wrong, adherents to the intelligentsia idea, with their criticisms and their speculations, were pushed out of Russia; their failure as a class is as significant as their partial victories as thinkers. After 1917 they had tried to function as before, pursuing the mission of independent inquiry, publicity, articulation of political and cultural alternatives. Perhaps it was only in bourgeois societies that defenders of these values had a place. Or perhaps the exclusion of opposition and potential opposition was a fulfillment of Russian culture, for the intelligentsia both before and after 1917 shared with the governors a wish for organic, uncontested politics. These are not questions with scientific answers, but the sloughing off of the intelligentsia tradition meant that Russia faced the future with different resources.

New people had torn the old society apart; new people came to take old places. Even the opponents of the government recognized that there was something "popular" about Bolshevism, in its appeal to vengeance and its promise of relief. Ustrialov felt that the new government spoke to the authoritarian instincts of the masses and that on this base a powerful Russian nation could be built. But this was a minority opinion, a victory most intellectuals would not concede. If the revolution meant new state oppression supported by the people, their mission of enlightenment had failed.

Notes

Introduction

1. One other perspective on the revolution, based upon Russian Orthodoxy, developed later and is not represented here. The renaissance of Orthodox theology began only in the mid-1920s and belongs, primarily, to the history of the Russian emigration. For the history of the church in Russia in this period, see John Shelton Curtiss, *The Russian Church and the Soviet State, 1917–1950* (Boston: Little, Brown, 1953).
2. See, from the rich historiography, David Shub, *Lenin, A Biography*, rev. ed. (Harmondsworth: Penguin, 1966); Isaac Deutscher, *The Prophet Armed: Trotsky: 1879–1921* (New York: Oxford University Press, 1954); Stephen F. Cohen, *Bukharin and the Bolshevik Revolution: A Political Biography, 1888–1938* (New York: Alfred A. Knopf, 1973); Barbara Evans Clements, *Bolshevik Feminist: The Life of Aleksandra Kollontai* (Bloomington: Indiana University Press, 1979); and Robert Vincent Daniels, *The Conscience of the Revolution: Communist Opposition in Soviet Russia* (Cambridge, Mass.: Harvard University Press, 1960). William G. Rosenberg's *Bolshevik Visions: First Phase of the Cultural Revolution in Soviet Russia* (Ann Arbor: Ardis, 1984) presents a survey of Bolshevik theory and prediction from the revolutionary period. Two of the most profound statements on the nature of the revolution are Lenin's *The Proletarian Revolution and the Renegade Kautsky* and Trotsky's *Terrorism and Communism*.
3. The literature on the intelligentsia is voluminous. A concise and stimulating discussion of the formation of the intelligentsia, the nineteenth-century consensus, and the twentieth-century crisis is Michael Confino, "On Intellectuals and Intellectual Traditions in Eighteenth- and Nineteenth-Century Russia," *Daedalus*, 101, no. 2 (Spring 1972), 117–149.

4. Between 1859 and 1900, sixty thousand people were trained at Russian universities, followed by forty thousand more between 1900 and 1913, figures that do not include students at European institutions, or in Russia's medical, law, and other professional schools: V. R. Leikina-Svirskaia, *Russkaia intelligentsiia v 1900–1917 godakh* (Moscow: Mysl', 1981), p. 23. The role of this class in the revolutions of 1905 and 1917 is, as Leikina-Svirskaia's work suggests, one of the most interesting problems in the history of modern Russia.

5. "Realism dictated not the pursuit of the 'bluebird' of socialism, but the search for a profitable place in a capitalist enterprise," complained one social democrat looking back: G. Aronson, "Samoopredelenie intelligentsii," *Sotsialisticheskii vestnik*, no. 5–6 (51–52) (16 March 1923), p. 3.

6. See, among other sources on the high culture of the period, John E. Bowlt, *The Silver Age: Russian Art of the Early Twentieth Century and the "World of Art" Group* (Newtonville, Mass.: Oriental Research Partners, 1979); Martha Bohachevsky-Chomiak and Bernice Glatzer Rosenthal, eds., *A Revolution of the Spirit: Crisis of Value in Russia, 1890–1918* (Newtonville, Mass.: Oriental Research Partners, 1982); Gleb Struve, "The Cultural Renaissance," in Theofanis George Stavrou, ed., *Russia Under the Last Tsar* (Minneapolis: University of Minnesota Press, 1969), pp. 179–201. Alexander Vucinich's article in the Stavrou collection, "Politics, Universities, and Science," pp. 154–178, examines higher education.

7. Leikina-Svirskaia makes this case very effectively: Leikina-Svirskaia, *Russkaia intelligentsiia*, pp. 86–217.

8. P. Miliukov, *Iz istorii russkoi intelligentsii*, 2nd ed. (St. Petersburg: Znanie, 1903).

9. Iu. Martov, *Obshchestvennye i umstvennye techeniia v Rossii 1870–1905 g.g.* (Leningrad-Moscow, 1924). This work was written in 1910 for *Istoriia russkoi literatury*, a collective work edited by Ovsianiko-Kulikovskii.

10. Ivanov-Razumnik, *Istoriia russkoi obshchestvennoi mysli*, 3rd ed., 2 vols. (St. Petersburg: Tipografiia M. M. Stasiulevicha, 1911; reprint ed., The Hague: Mouton, 1969), p. 12. All translations are my own unless otherwise indicated.

11. See Jacob Walkin, "Government Controls Over the Press, 1905–1914," *Russian Review*, 13, no. 3 (July 1954), 203–209.

12. *Vekhi: Sbornik statei o russkoi intelligentsii* (Moscow, 1909).

13. Christopher Read's outstanding study of the prerevolutionary intelligentsia, *Religion, Revolution and the Russian Intelligentsia 1900–1912: The **Vekhi** Debate and its Intellectual Background* (London: Macmillan Press, 1979), focuses on this controversy. See also Pierre Pascal, "Les grands courants de la pensée russe contemporaine," *Cahiers du monde russe et soviétique*, 3, no. 1 (January–March 1962), 5–89.

14. On the response to *Vekhi* see Read, *Religion, Revolution*, pp. 141–161.

15. On the religious concerns of the intelligentsia, see Jutta Scherrer's studies: *Die Petersbürger Religiös-Philosophischen Vereinigungen*, Forschungen zur Osteuropaischen Geschichte, 19 (Berlin: Otto Harrassowitz, 1973), and "Intelligentsia, religion, révolution: Premières manifestations d'un socialisme chrétien en Russie, 1905–1907," *Cahiers du monde russe et soviétique*, 17, no. 4 (1976), 427–466; and 18, nos. 1–2 (1977), 5–32.

16. On the liberals in this period see William G. Rosenberg, "The Kadets and the

Politics of Ambivalence, 1905–1917,'' in Charles Timberlake, ed., *Essays on Russian Liberalism* (Columbia, Mo.: University of Missouri Press, 1972), pp. 139–163; on the Socialist Revolutionaries, Oliver H. Radkey, *The Agrarian Foes of Bolshevism* (New York: Columbia University Press, 1958), pp. 47–126; and on the social democrats, Abraham Ascher, ''Introduction,'' in Abraham Ascher, ed., *The Mensheviks in the Russian Revolution* (Ithaca: Cornell University Press, 1976), pp. 8–31.

17. Aleksandr Blok, ''Stikhiia i kul'tura,'' in his *Sobranie sochinenii v vos'mi tomakh* (Moscow: Gos. izd. khudozhestvennoi literatury, 1960–1965), 5:351.

Chapter 1

1. *Novyi luch*, no. 3, 3 December 1917, p. 4. The Extraordinary Congress is the subject of Leopold Haimson, ''The Mensheviks After the October Revolution, Part II: The Extraordinary Party Congress,'' *Russian Review*, 39, no. 2 (April 1980), 181–207.

2. *Novyi luch*, no. 3, 3 December 1917, p. 4.

3. For an analysis of Martov's position at the conference and the drafting of the party resolution, see Haimson, ''Mensheviks After the October Revolution, II,'' pp. 186–189, 192–194.

4. See Lenin's argument in *Imperialism, the Highest Stage of Capitalism*, which while directed against the reformist strategies made possible by imperialism, still describes monopoly capitalism as preparing the way for socialism: V. I. Lenin, ''Imperializm, kak noveishii etap kapitalizma,'' *Polnoe sobranie sochinenii*, 5th ed., 55 vols. (Moscow: Gospolizdat, 1958–1965), 27:299–426.

5. This statist interpretation of Marx, which ignored the specificity of his arguments, and assumed that countries were distinct units of history, following each other along the path pioneered by the Western capitalist nations, was characteristic of socialism in this period. Marx himself toward the end of his life was moving in a different direction. See Teodor Shanin, *Late Marx and the Russian Road: Marx and the 'Peripheries of Capitalism'* (New York: Monthly Review, 1983).

6. Cited from Richard Pipes, *Struve: Liberal on the Left, 1870–1905* (Cambridge, Mass.: Harvard University Press, 1970), p. 195. The program was written by Petr Struve.

7. On the Mensheviks before October 1917, see Ziva Galili i Garcia, ''The Origins of Revolutionary Defensism: I. G. Tsereteli and the 'Siberian Zimmerwaldists','' *Slavic Review*, 41, no. 3 (Fall 1982), 454–476, and John D. Basil, *The Mensheviks in the Revolution of 1917* (Columbus: Slavica, 1984).

8. For a comprehensive and sympathetic biography of Martov, see Israel Getzler, *Martov: A Political Biography of a Russian Social Democrat* (Cambridge: At the University Press, 1967).

9. Menshevik memories of Martov are invariably fond, despite political disagreements. For examples, see the outpouring of grief after his death in *Sotsialisticheskii vestnik*, special issue (10 April 1923), and the ongoing cult of Martov in this journal. Even Martov's opponents and enemies agree that his personal qualities were exceptional: see Lunacharskii's sketch in A. Lunarcharskii, *Revoliutsionnye siluety* (Khar'kov: Gosudarstvennoe izdatel'stvo Ukrainy, 1924), pp. 68–75, reprinted in I. M. Getzler, ed., *Stat'i, posviashchen-*

nye Iu. O. Martovu (New York: Inter-University Project on the History of the Menshevik Movement, 1961).

10. An account of this episode is provided by Getzler, *Martov*, pp. 147–149. See also Alfred Erich Senn, *The Russian Revolution in Switzerland 1914–1917* (Madison: University of Wisconsin Press, 1971), pp. 222–232. Martov postponed his departure in the vain hope of returning as part of an exchange between the German and the Russian governments, while Lenin decided earlier to deal directly with the German authorities.

11. See Martov's speech and resolution in the Petrograd Soviet, cited in Abraham Ascher, ed., *The Mensheviks in the Russian Revolution* (Ithaca: Cornell University Press, 1976), pp. 101–103.

12. See his articles in *Novaia zhizn'* and *Iskra* in the fall of 1917.

13. "Kak byt' s burzhuaznoi revoliutsiei," *Vpered*, no. 159, 16(29) October 1917.

14. Ibid.

15. Ibid.

16. Ibid.

17. Martov to Axelrod, 19 November 1917, Nicolaevsky Collection, no. 17, box 1, folio 2, Hoover Institution, Stanford University, Stanford, California.

18. Martov to Axelrod, 19 November 1917. A significant minority of the Bolshevik Central Committee—Zinoviev, Kamenev, Rykov, Miliutin, and Nogin—as well as many Bolshevik commissars and officials broke with Lenin and Trotsky on this and the related issue of freedom of the press in November 1917, but soon returned to the fold. See Martov's "Le parti socialiste démocrate en Russie bolcheviste," Nicolaevsky Collection, no. 6, box 1, folio 16, on the resignations from the Bolshevik Central Committee and the account in Leonard Schapiro, *The Origin of the Communist Autocracy*, 2nd ed. (Cambridge, Mass.: Harvard University Press, 1977), pp. 70–80.

19. These were the preliminary results, but the final returns were just as bad: around 1.25 million for the Mensheviks, less than the Kadets (the liberals) with just under 2 million, the Bolsheviks with between 9 and 10 million, and the Russian Socialist-Revolutionaries who won the election with between 15.8 and 17.5 million votes. These figures are from Oliver Henry Radkey, *The Election to the Russian Constituent Assembly* (Cambridge, Mass.: Harvard University Press, 1950), pp. 16, 17. This source provides a full discussion of the statistics on the election as well as an analysis of the results. See also Lenin's view of the results in I. S. Malchevskii, ed., *Vserossiiskoe uchreditel'noe sobranie* (Moscow: Gosudarstvennoe izdatel'stvo, 1930), pp. iii–xix.

20. Martov to Axelrod, 19 November 1917.

21. Ibid. The Bulygin Duma, the tsarist government's first institutional concession in 1905, was a proposal for a consultative assembly of elected representatives who would participate in the "preliminary elaboration and discussion of legislative bills." Its provisions are cited in Michael T. Florinsky, *Russia: A History and an Interpretation*, 2 vols. (New York: Macmillan, 1960), 2:1172.

22. When the Menshevik Defensists and Socialist Revolutionaries left the Second Congress, Martov stayed on to defend, ineffectually, the necessity of an inclusive, all-socialist government, and then, with his Internationalists, walked out a few hours later: Martov to Axelrod, 19 November 1917. For an account of the

meeting, see Alexander Rabinowitch, *The Bolsheviks Come to Power: The Revolution of 1917 in Petrograd* (New York: Norton, 1976), pp. 291–298, 301–304.

23. Martov to Axelrod, 19 November 1917.

24. Arakcheev, a powerful administrator under Alexander I, established a system of military colonies to supply the state with soldiers. His name stood for reaction and despotism in the intelligentsia tradition. Pugachev was the Cossack leader of the massive peasant rebellions against the state in 1773–1774.

25. Martov to N. S. Kristi, in *Martov i ego blizkie* (New York, 1959), pp. 48–49.

26. Ibid., p. 49.

27. Letter to Axelrod, 19 November 1917.

28. "Ne po puti," *Novyi luch*, no. 14, 17 December 1917.

29. Martov to Axelrod, 1 December 1917, Nicolaevsky Collection, no. 17, box 1, folio 2.

30. Martov to Axelrod, 1 December 1917.

31. Martov to N. S. Kristi, in *Martov i ego blizkie*, p. 48.

32. His "Resolution on the Current Situation," eventually the majority declaration, began: "The Russian revolution cannot bring about the socialist transformation of society in so far as such a transformation has not begun in the advanced capitalist countries and in so far as the productive forces in Russia itself are at an exceedingly low level of development, but also because the huge mass of the laborers, who are striving in this revolution to conquer or to strengthen their economic independence are not interested in the destruction of capitalist society and not capable of the organization of socialist production" (*Novyi luch*, no. 3, 3 December 1917, p. 4).

33. *Novyi luch*, no. 3, 3 December 1917, p. 4.

34. See Martov's comment in 1905: "Our task is not so much to 'organize' a revolution as to unleash one. The revolution existed already potentially in the thoughts and feelings of the broad masses" (cited in Getzler, *Martov*, p. 101).

35. "Skazochka. Dlia detei izriadnogo vozrasta," *Vpered*, no. 216, 24 November (7 December) 1917.

36. Consult Anna Bourgina, *Russian Social Democracy: The Menshevik Movement* (Stanford: The Hoover Institution, 1968), p. 347, for the publication record.

37. *Shchit*, no. 1, 30 November 1917.

38. "Rol' partii proletariata," *Novyi luch*, no. 18, 22 December 1917. For a brief account of the military campaign, see John Bradley, *Civil War in Russia 1917–1920* (London: B. T. Batsford, 1975), p. 40.

39. "Rol' partii proletariata," *Novyi luch*, no. 18, 22 December 1917.

40. For the final programmatic call on the eve of the meeting, see *Novyi luch*, no. 3(27), 5 January 1918.

41. *Pravda* consistently described both the Constituent Assembly and the demonstration as attempts by the bourgeoisie to "seize" power from the Soviets. See, for example, the headlines on January 3, 1918 (O.S.)—"Comrade workers, soldiers, peasants, sailors! Under the mask of the defense of the Constituent Assembly, the bourgeoisie is preparing a treacherous attack on the Soviets of workers', soldiers' and peasants' deputies. . . . Be on your guard. Hold tight to your rifles"—and on January 5, the day of the demonstration and the convening of the assembly, "Today the hyenas of capitalism and their hirelings want to tear power from the

hands of the Soviets" (*Pravda* no. 2, 16[3] January 1918 [evening edition], and no. 3[320], 18[5] January 1918).

42. *Novyi luch*, no. 3(27), 5 January 1918.

43. Ibid.

44. See *Novyi luch*, no. 5(29), 12 January 1918, on the memorial arrangements.

45. Ibid.

46. The paper was reopened in a truncated version six days later: *Novyi luch*, no. 5(29), 12 January 1918.

47. The stenographic record of this congress, *Pervyi Vserossiiskii s"ezd professional'nykh soiuzov* (Moscow: Izdanie Vserossiiskogo tsentral'nogo soveta professional'nykh soiuzov, 1918), is a vivid source on revolutionary politics. Many of the speeches at the Congress continued the debate over the role of the Constituent Assembly and its dissolution. The Congress is discussed in John L. H. Keep, *The Russian Revolution: A Study in Mass Mobilization* (New York: Norton, 1976), pp. 299–304.

48. *Pervyi . . . s"ezd prof. soiuzov*, pp. 69,70.

49. Ibid., pp. 74, 75.

50. Ibid., p. 76. As Martov noted in his speech, the Bolsheviks had begun to call the revolution "communist" three days before: see *Pravda*, no. 3(230), 18(5) January 1918. Both "socialist" and "communist" were used by Bolshevik speakers and writers in this period.

51. The following text condenses Martov's two major speeches at the congress: *Pervyi . . . s"ezd prof. soiuzov*, pp. 76–82 and 112–116.

52. *Pervyi . . . s"ezd prof. soiuzov*, p. 77.

53. Ibid., p. 114.

54. Ibid., p. 79.

55. Ibid., p. 82.

56. Martov also used the labels "state capitalism" and "war socialism": *Pervyi . . . s"ezd prof. soiuzov*, pp. 80, 115.

57. *Pervyi . . . s"ezd prof. soiuzov*, p. 82.

58. Ibid., pp. 115, 116.

59. Ibid., p. 112.

60. Ibid., p. 124. Twenty delegates voted for a Left SR proposal and 42 abstained.

61. *Pervyi . . . s"ezd prof. soiuzov*, p. 82.

62. See the decree of the Council of Peoples' Commissars, 17 December 1917, translated in James Bunyan and H. H. Fisher, *The Bolshevik Revolution, 1917–1918: Documents and Materials* (Stanford: Stanford University Press, 1934), pp. 308–310.

63. *Klich* [*Luch*], no. 5, 6 December 1917.

64. "Konstitutsiia Trutovskogo," *Novyi Luch*, no. 10, 18 January 1918. In the same issue, Ia. Piletskii made a similar argument about the army: Soldiers in the army had voted for the Bolsheviks "because under their leadership, they could without difficulty do what was profitable for themselves alone, not taking into account either the general conditions and needs of the country or the interests of socialism" ("Krest'ianskaia kontr-revoliutsiia," *Novyi Luch*, no. 10, 18 January 1918).

65. Martov, "Konstitutsiia Trutovskogo," *Novyi luch*, no. 10, 18 January 1918, p. 1. The draft constitution is translated in Bunyan and Fisher, *Bolshevik Revolution*, pp. 396–397.

66. *Novyi luch*, no. 10, 18 January 1918, p. 1.

67. Ibid.

68. Martov used the stick of "Bakuninism" liberally. See his "Ot Bakunina k Marksu i obratno" in *Novyi luch*, no. 6, 13 January 1918, p. 1, where he argued that Lenin's theory of socialist revolution in a backward country is a reversion to Bakunin's "special calling of the Slavic peoples."

69. *Novyi luch*, no. 10, 18 January 1918, p. 1.

70. "Kommunizm i desiat' zapovedei," *Vpered*, no. 69(315), 23(10) April 1918.

71. *Novyi luch*, no. 25(49), 19(6) February 1918.

72. "Kommunizm i desiat' zapovedei," *Vpered*, no. 69(315), 23(10) April 1918.

73. See Martov's article in *Vpered*, no. 67(313), 20(7) April 1918, in which he compares the Bolsheviks' treatment of the Mensheviks in the Central Executive Committee of the Soviets to the harassment of the opposition in the Third Duma.

74. "The autocracy taught us that temporary measures are the most lasting ones," he responded to Trotsky's project for the Red Army (*Vpered*, no. 69[315], 23[10] April 1918).

75. G. Aronson, "Stalinskii protsess protiv Martova," *Sotsialisticheskii vestnik*, vol. 19, no. 7–8(435–436) (28 April 1930), pp. 84–89, provides an account of this incident. See also *Vpered* for April 1918 and the file on the Martov affair in Nicolaevsky Collection, no. 6, box 2, folio 27.

76. *Vpered*, no. 63(309), 14(1) April 1918.

77. *Vpered*, no. 72(318), 26(13) April 1918.

78. Aronson, "Stalinskii protsess," p. 89.

79. For an account of this largely unstudied period, see William G. Rosenberg, "Russian Labor and Bolshevik Power After October," *Slavic Review*, 44, no. 2 (Summer 1985), 213–238.

80. See Vladimir Brovkin, "The Mensheviks' Political Comeback: The Elections to the Provincial City Soviets in Spring 1918," *Russian Review*, 42, no. 1 (January 1983), 1–50.

81. For information on the Assemblies of Factory and Plant Representatives, see Leopold H. Haimson, ed. *The Mensheviks: From the Revolution of 1917 to the Second World War* (Chicago: University of Chicago Press, 1974), pp. 150–152; G. Aronson, "Stranitsy proshlogo," in V. Dvinov, ed., *Protiv techeniia: Sbornik* (New York, 1952); the documents in M. S. Bernshtam, ed., *Nezavisimoe rabochee dvizhenie v 1918 godu: Dokumenty i materialy* (Paris: YMCA Press, 1981); and G. Ia. Aronson, *Dvizhenie upolnomochennykh ot rabochikh fabrik i zavodov v 1918 godu* (New York: Inter-University Project on the History of the Menshevik Movement, 1960).

82. *Novaia zaria*, no. 1 (22 April 1918), p. 3. For the Menshevik position on the Brest peace, see the resolution of the party conference in May, "Brestskii mir i raspad Rossii," in *Novaia zaria*, no. 5–6 (10 June 1918), pp. 79–81, and the party's agitational literature for May Day 1918: "Den' 1 Maia," *Novaia zaria*, no. 2 (1 May 1918), pp. 3–6.

83. See the minutes of the fourth convocation: *Chetvertyi Vserossiiskii s''ezd sovetov rabochikh, krest'ianskikh, soldatskikh i kazach'ikh deputatov. Stenograficheskii otchet* (Moscow: Gosudarstvennoe izdatel'stvo, 1919).

84. For Martov's summation of Menshevik tactics in this period and a passionate

defense of "unarmed" organization of the masses, see his final speech at the CEC on June 14, 1918: *Chetvertyi . . . s"ezd sovetov*, pp. 425–426; also available in *Martov i ego blizkie*, pp. 163–165.

85. "Rabochie i gosudarstvennaia vlast'," *Novaia zaria*, no. 1 (22 April 1918), pp. 12, 14.

86. Ibid., pp. 12–15.

87. Ibid., pp. 14–16.

88. For an example, see his outburst on May 14 after Sverdlov dismissed the speech of a Socialist Revolutionary as coming from a party "stained with counter-revolutionary activities": "In no reactionary bourgeois parliament, or in any rotten Russian State Duma, was it the case that a representative of one of the opposition parties would, in response to expressing his opinions, be characterized by the presiding officer as having besmirched his hands in some or another crime." During this stormy debate Martov had to call upon the chair to restrain someone from physically attacking him (*Chetvertyi . . . s"ezd sovetov*, pp. 278, 288).

89. Ibid., p. 279.

90. Ibid., p. 349.

91. Ibid., p. 226.

92. Ibid., p. 355.

93. Ibid., p. 439.

94. On the persecution of the party press, see Martov's letter to A. N. Shtein from June 16, 1918, published in *Sotsialisticheskii vestnik*, vol. 6, no. 7–8(125–126) (25 April 1926), pp. 16–18.

95. See, for example, Zinoviev's vicious denunciation of the Mensheviks and SRs as the agents of capital in his speech delivered to the Petrograd Soviet on June 15 and published by the CEC: G. Zinov'ev, *Kontr-revoliutsiia i zadachi rabochikh. Rech' na zasedanii Petrogradskogo soveta 15 iiuna 1918* (Moscow: Izdatel'stvo Vserossiiskogo tsentral'nogo ispolnitel'nogo komiteta Sovetov R.,S.,K., i K. deputatov, 1918).

96. In the case of Admiral Shchastnyi, who was condemned to death and summarily executed on Trotsky's evidence; see Schapiro, *Origin of the Communist Autocracy*, pp. 115, 119.

97. "Doloi smertnuiu kazn'," excerpted in *Martov i ego blizkie*, pp. 149–153; a reprint of an English edition is in *The Opposition, At Home and Abroad, Seeds of Conflict*. Series 4: *The Russian Revolution*, 3 vols. (Nendeln: Kraus Reprint, 1975), 1.

98. "The Social Democratic Labor party has always rejected political murders. . . . It objected to them even when the revolutionaries murdered the hired guns of tsarism. It taught the working class that it would not improve its lot by such murders, even of the worst enemies of the people, but by a fundamental change of the whole political system, of all the conditions which give rise to oppression and the use of violence" ("Doloi smertnuiu kazn'," in *Martov i ego blizkie*, p. 152).

99. *Martov i ego blizkie*, pp. 152, 153.

100. See the party's explicit condemnations of workers' rebellions in "Rezoliutsiia tsentral'nogo komiteta RSDRP o Iaroslavskikh sobytiakh . . . ," "Rezoliutsiia ot 27-go iiulia," "Rezoliutsiia TsK RSDRP ot 2-go avgusta 1918 goda," all in Nicolaevsky Collection, no. 6, box 1, folio 14, as well as Martov's consistent

accounts of Central Committee policy in "Sobiraiut materialy," *Sotsialisticheskii vestnik*, no. 16(38) (16 August 1922), p. 7 (on the Iaroslavl' uprising); "Vospominaniia renegata," *Sotsialisticheskii vestnik*, no. 23–24(45–46) (9 December 1922), pp. 15, 16 (on the Maiskii affair); and "Martov o partii 1918/1919 gg.," *Sotsialisticheskii vestnik*, vol. 7, no. 7(149) (4 April 1927), pp. 3–10.

101. "Ko vsem partiinym organizatsiiam," 16 October 1918, Nicolaevsky Collection, no. 6, box 1, folio 4. For the Central Committee's explanation of this change, see *Partiinoe soveshchanie RSDRP 27 dek. 1918—1 ian. 1919: Rezoliutsii* (Moscow: Izd. Biuro Ts. kom. RSDRP, 1919), pp. 23–25, in Nicolaevsky Collection, no. 6, box 3, folio 32.

102. Cited in Haimson, *The Mensheviks*, p. 184.

103. "Marks i problema diktatury proletariata," in Martov's *Mirovoi bol'shevizm* (Berlin: Iskra, 1923), pp. 98–100, 107, 108. The essay is available in English in Martov, *The State and the Social Revolution* (New York: International Review, 1938).

104. "Iu. O. Martov," *Sotsialisticheskii vestnik*, no. 7–8(77–78) (4 April 1924), p. 20; Martov, *Zapiski sotsial demokrata* (Berlin: Grzhebin, 1922).

105. See his articles in *Vsegda vpered* in January and February 1919 and his speech to the Congress of Trade Unions in January, *Vsegda vpered*, no. 1 (22 January 1919).

106. Bourgina, *Russian Social Democracy*, p. 345. See also the issues of *Vsegda vpered* (Always Forward) in the Hoover Library at Stanford University. Martov analyzed the brief and limited legalization as window-dressing intended for the German Social Democrats: "Novyi kurs v sovetskoi Rossii," *Mysl'*, no. 1–2 (January 1919), pp. 9–14. During this period, the Menshevik Central Committee lent its services to the Bolshevik effort to influence European opinion. Their appeal to Western socialists to mobilize against Allied intervention in Russia and to support peace negotiations was published in *Izvestiia*. See "K sotsialistam i rabochim vsego mira," Nicolaevsky Collection, no. 6, box 1, folio 7.

107. Martov was put under house arrest for a short time. Later, he spent several weeks at a dacha outside Moscow, a sign of the impossibility of political activism. See D. Dalin's "Dva aresta," *Sotsialisticheskii vestnik*, no. 7–8(77–78) (4 April 1924), pp. 15–16, and his "Obryvki vospominanii," in *Martov i ego blizkie*, pp. 103–104.

108. See, for example, his cautiously optimistic article in *Mysl'* (Khar'kov): "Novyi kurs v sovetskoi Rossii," no. 1–2 (January 1919), pp. 9–14, and his vicious criticism in "'Sotsializm' dikarei," *Vsegda vpered*, no. 13 (22 February 1919), and "Poslednii ukus zmei," *Vsegda vpered*, no. 14 (23 February 1919).

109. The first essay appeared in *Mysl'*, no. 10 (April 1919), pp. 333–343, followed by two more articles in later issues. My citations are to the Berlin reprint of all three parts: Martov, *Mirovoi bol'shevizm* (Berlin: Iskra, 1923). Parts two and three were translated and published in Martov, *The State and the Socialist Revolution* (New York: International Review, 1938), as "The Ideology of Socialism" and "Decomposition or Conquest of the State."

110. This change was reflected as well in the Mensheviks' statements of party policy, which called now for political and economic reforms of *Soviet* government, thus granting the regime a legitimacy they had denied in the first half of 1918. See, for example, "Chto delat'" from July 1919, in *Sotsial-demokratiia i revoliutsiia*

(Odessa: Izd. Gruppa Sots. Dem., 1920), pp. 9–16, in Nicolaevsky Collection, no. 6, box 3, folio 32.

111. *Mirovoi Bol'shevizm*, p. 92.
112. Ibid., p. 93.
113. Ibid., p. 39.
114. Ibid., p. 94.
115. Ibid., p. 13.
116. Ibid.
117. Ibid., p. 17.
118. Ibid., pp. 10–17, 20–22.
119. Ibid., p. 25.
120. Ibid., p. 28.
121. Ibid., p. 20. Emphasis in the original, as in all subsequent citations.
122. This had been a hope expressed in Menshevik position papers in 1918; see Martov's report on the international situation, "Mezhdunarodnoe polozhenie i zadachi russkoi revoliutsii," in the resolutions of the party conference at the end of the year: *Partiinoe soveshchanie RSDRP 27 dek. 1918-1 ian. 1919* (Moscow: Izd. Biuro Ts. Kom. RSDRP, 1919), pp. 8–13, in Nicolaevsky Collection, no. 6, box 3, folio 32.
123. *Mirovoi bol'shevizm*, p. 25.
124. Ibid., p. 26.
125. Ibid., pp. 54–60.
126. See *Oborona revoliutsii i sotsial-demokratiia* (Petrograd: "Kniga," 1920) for the Central Committee's call to arms in support of the Bolshevik government, especially Dan's "Oborona revoliutsii," pp. 8–12.
127. When the regime was strong enough to clamp down, it did; when it needed to mobilize worker or international opinion, it allowed Menshevik voices briefly to be heard. For an account of this period, see Schapiro, *Origin of the Communist Autocracy*, pp. 190–209. On the many arrests in August 1920, see Martov to Axelrod, 29 September 1920, Nicolaevsky Collection, no. 17, box 1, folio 2, and the Menshevik Central Committee's letter to "all comrades," 28 September 1920, Nicolaevsky Collection, no. 6, box 1, folio 4.
128. B. A. Skomorovskii to Axelrod, 3 September 1920, Axelrod Archive, International Institute of Social History, Amsterdam (I.I.S.H.). Lenin, concerned about Martov's health, supported his request for an exit visa: R. Abramovich, *Men'sheviki i sotsialisticheskii internatsional (1918–1940)* (n.p., n.d.), p. 19. See Getzler, *Martov*, p. 208, note 18, for anecdotal evidence of Lenin's attitude toward Martov.
129. Quoted in F. Dan, "Pamiati Iu. O. Martova," *Sotsialisticheskii vestnik*, no. 7–8(77–78) (4 April 1924), p. 8.
130. See Grigorii Aronson, *K istorii pravogo techeniia sredi men'shevikov*, Inter-University Project on the History of the Menshevik Movement Paper no. 4 (New York, 1960), pp. 3, 4. This is the major study of right Menshevism. A "left" wing of the party favored entering the Bolshevik government.
131. Aronson, *K istorii*, pp. 40, 173.
132. There were subsequent "conferences" in the civil war years, but no full-scale congresses. Much later, in the emigration, a "rightist" point of view again became important and finally dominated in the party; see André Liebich, *Les*

Mencheviks en exil face à l'Union soviétique, Cahiers de recherche du CIEE, no. 4 (Montreal: Centre interuniversitaire d'Etudes européennes, 1982), pp. 14, 42–58.

133. Martov's vindictive campaign for strict party unity began at the Extraordinary Congress, and, as Haimson notes, "ill became the leader of a faction that had not hesitated to violate Party discipline when it had been in the minority" (Haimson, "The Mensheviks after the October Revolution, Part II," p. 199). The Central Committee's right to expel individuals and groups from the RSDRP was asserted by a party conference in December 1918 and reaffirmed by another conference in April 1920: "Rezoliutsiia o polozhenii del v RSDRP," in *Sotsial-demokratiia i revoliutsiia*, pp. 44ff.

134. For short biographies of leading right Mensheviks, see Aronson, *K istorii*, pp. 243–262.

135. The two exceptions were Martov and Lenin.

136. For an account of Plekhanov's last year in Russia, see Samuel H. Baron's intellectual biography, *Plekhanov: The Father of Russian Marxism* (Stanford: Stanford University Press, 1963), pp. 343–354, and his article with documents, "Plekhanov in War and Revolution, 1914–1917," *International Review of Social History*, 26, part 3 (1981), 325–376. Another informative source on Plekhanov's role in Russian social democracy is Arthur P. Mendel, *Dilemmas of Progress in Tsarist Russia: Legal Marxism and Legal Populism* (Cambridge, Mass.: Harvard University Press, 1961), pp. 105–118.

137. See the accounts of the raid and the moves in Plekhanov's wife's letters to her daughters: 28 November 1917, in Baron, "Plekhanov in War and Revolution," pp. 372–374, and 28 February 1918, Plekhanov Archive, I.I.S.H. A biographical essay by Iu. Arzaev is included in G. V. Plekhanov, *God na rodine*, 2 vols. (Paris: J. Povolozky, 1921), 1: XLII–XLIV.

138. *Edinstvo* was shut down in November and renamed *Nashe edinstvo* in December. See the publishing record in Bourgina, *Russian Social Democracy*, p. 361.

139. Plekhanov, *God na rodine*, 2:246, from "Otkrytoe pis'mo k petrogradskim rabochim," *Edinstvo*, no. 173, 28 October 1917. *God na rodine* is a collection of the articles Plekhanov wrote in Russia in 1917 and 1918.

140. "Buki az-ba," in *God na rodine*, 2:267, from *Nashe edinstvo*, nos. 14 and 16, 11, and 13 January 1918.

141. *Pravda*, no. 221(152), 4 January 1918(22 December 1917).

142. "Not revolution for the triumph of . . . tactical rules, but . . . rules for the triumph of the revolution," he elaborated. "Buki az-ba," in *God na rodine*, 2:261.

143. Ibid., pp. 259–268.

144. "A vse taki dvizhetsia," *Edinstvo*, no. 3, 18(5) June 1918, pp. 2, 3, reprinted from *Nashe edinstvo*, 19 December 1917.

145. On the funeral and memorial services, see *Novaia zhizn'*, nos. 107 (322), 4 June (22 May) 1918, 108(323), 5 June(23 May) 1918, 112(327), 9 June(27 May) 1918, 113(328), 11 June(29 May) 1918; *Edinstvo*, no. 3, 18(5) June 1918.

146. *Novaia zhizn'*, no. 107(322), 4 June (22 May) 1918.

147. See the moving account of the funeral in K. M. Ermolaev to P. B. Axelrod, 17 June 1918, Nicolaevsky Collection, no. 16, folio 99.

148. *Chetvertyi . . . s''ezd sovetov*, pp. 374, 375.

149. On Plekhanov's death and funeral, see his wife's letter to her children in Paris, R. G. Plekhanova, 29 August 1918, Plekhanov Archive, I.I.S.H.

150. For Potresov's biography, see St. Ivanovich, *A. N. Potresov: Opyt kul'turno-psikhologicheskogo portreta* (Paris, 1938), and B. Nikolaevskii, "A. N. Potresov: Opyt literaturno-politicheskoi biografii" in A. N. Potresov, *Posmertnyi sbornik proizvedenii* (Paris, 1937), pp. 9–90.

151. "Rech' na s''ezde S. D. partii," in Potresov, *Posmertnyi sbornik*, p. 255.

152. See the description of Potresov's mood in Ivanovich, *Potresov*, pp. 121–134.

153. "Rokovye protivorechiia russkoi revoliutsii," in Potresov, *Posmertnyi sbornik*, pp. 230–242.

154. Ibid., p. 237.

155. Ibid.

156. Ibid., pp. 238, 239.

157. "L'stetsam proletariata," in Potresov, *Posmertnyi sbornik*, pp. 259, 260.

158. See, for example, "Zagadka," *Polnoch'*, no. 2, 25 November 1917; "Izmena i kontr-revoliutsiia," *Griadushchii den'*, no. 1, 28 November 1917.

159. "Polumarksistam," in Potresov, *Posmertnyi sbornik*, p. 279; from *Novyi den'*, 17(4) February 1918.

160. See, for example, "Polumarksistam," *Novyi den'*, 17(4) February 1918.

161. On this newspaper and its struggle to survive, see Ivanovich, *Potresov*, pp. 146–158.

162. "Mertvye dushi," in Potresov, *Posmertnyi sbornik*, p. 268; from *Griadushchii den'*, 7 December 1917.

163. "Na perevale," in Potresov, *Posmertnyi sbornik*, p. 271; from *Griadushchii den'*, 10 December 1917.

164. "Mertvye dushi," in Potresov, *Posmertnyi sbornik*, p. 268. For an analysis of Potresov's speech at the Extraordinary Congress, see Haimson, "Mensheviks after the October Revolution, Part II," pp. 184–186.

165. "Na perevale," in Potresov, *Posmertnyi sbornik*, p. 271.

166. "Polumarksistam," in Potresov, *Posmertnyi sbornik*, pp. 278, 279. See also "Pafos stroitel'stva," *Den'*, 21(8) February 1918, a response to *Luch*'s rebuttal.

167. "Obshchenatsional'noe delo," in *Den'*, no. 3(1674),28(15) March 1918.

168. See, for example, "Novye variagi," *Novyi den'*, no. 1, 14(1) February 1918; "Grazhdanskii mir," *Novyi den'*, no. 6, 20(7) February 1918; "Natsional'noe ob''edinenie i kruzhkovshchina," *Novyi den'*, no. 17, 13 April (31 March) 1918.

169. "Polumarksistam," in Potresov, *Posmertnyi sbornik*, pp. 277–278; from *Novyi den'*, 17(4) February 1918.

170. "Na perevale," in *Posmertnyi sbornik*, p. 271.

171. "Natsional'noe ob''edinenie i kruzhkovshchina," *Novyi den'*, no. 17, 13 April (31 March) 1918.

172. See, for example, "Osadi nazad," *Den'*, no. 7(1678), 2 April (18 March) 1918.

173. "Porugannyi den'," *Novyi den'*, no. 32, 1 May (18 April) 1918.

174. The Cossack leader of a widespread and violent peasant rebellion along the Volga in the seventeenth century.

175. "Gore ot uma," *Novyi den'*, no. 34, 4 May (21 April) 1918.

176. "G. V. Plekhanov," in Potresov, *Posmertnyi sbornik*, pp. 289, 290.

177. "Privet 'Russkomu bogatstvu'," in *Posmertnyi sbornik*, p. 281; from *Novyi den'*, 15(2) February 1918.

178. Ibid.

179. Nikolaevskii, "A. N. Potresov," p. 80. For a brief description of the Union, see William Henry Chamberlin, *The Russian Revolution*, 2 vols. (New York: Grosset and Dunlap, 1965), 1:421.

180. Ivanovich, *Potresov*, pp. 133, 152–159; A. N. Potresov, "Vera Zasulich," *Novyi den'*, no. 17, 13 April (31 March) 1918.

181. See, for example, the broadside of the Petrograd Group of SDs in response to the Menshevik party conference in December 1918, reprinted in Ivanovich, *Potresov*, pp. 158, 159.

182. Ivanovich, *Potresov*, pp. 160–165; Nikolaevskii, "A. N. Potresov," pp. 80–83. After a lapse of several years, Potresov took up his battle with the Menshevik leadership again. See his *V plenu u illiuzii (Moi spor s offitsial'nym men'shevizmom)* (Paris, 1927).

183. A. N. Potresov, "V. I. Zasulich," *Novyi den'*, no. 18, 14(1) April 1918. For Zasulich's life, see Jay Bergman's study, *Vera Zasulich: A Biography* (Stanford: Stanford University Press, 1983).

184. "Sotsializm Smol'nogo," *Nachalo*, no. 2, 2(15) February 1918. The Bolshevik party headquarters in Petrograd was the Smol'nyi Institute, formerly a private school for girls.

185. Ibid.

186. Ibid.

187. Ibid.

188. Ibid.

189. Ibid.

190. Bourgina records only two issues in *Russian Social Democracy*, p. 350.

191. Bergman, *Zasulich*, p. 214. See also Martov's letter to P. B. Axelrod, 23 January 1920, Nicolaevsky Collection, no. 17, box 1, folio 2.

192. An account of the rebellions in Iaroslavl' and elsewhere is provided in Haimson, *The Mensheviks*, pp. 163–175. See the documents in M. S. Bernshtam, ed., *Ural i Prikam'e noiabr' 1917—ianvar' 1919: Dokumenty i materialy* (Paris: YMCA Press, 1982).

193. See Aronson, *K istorii*, p. 58, for an incomplete list of newspapers published outside Soviet control.

194. See, among other pamphlets, "1-e maia 1919 goda"; "Gruppa sotsial. demokratov," [untitled broadside], 2 March 1921; "Predstaviteli fabrik i zavodov Petrograda, Petrogradskaia gruppa sotsial-demokratov," 11 March 1921; "Rossiiskaia sotsialdem. rabochaia partiia" [untitled declaration], May 1921; "Protiv edinogo front s bol'shevikami," 1 May 1922, all in Portugeis Collection, I.I.S.H.

195. "1-e maia 1919 goda," Portugeis Collection, I.I.S.H.

196. *Nasha zhizn'*, no. 4 (November 1922). For an account of the rightists' activities in 1921, see B. G. Vasil'ev to P. B. Axelrod, 6 August 1921, Axelrod Archive, I.I.S.H.

197. Martov to Axelrod, 23 January 1920, Nicolaevsky Collection, no. 17, box 1, folio 2.

198. See, for example, "Men'sheviki i sovetskaia vlast'," "Protiv edinogo fronta s bol'shevikami," in the Portugeis Collection, I.I.S.H.

199. I. Upovalov and G. Strumilo to Martov, 18 February 1921, Portugeis Collection, I.I.S.H..

200. See Ivanovich's discussion of this party loyalty, in *Potresov*, pp. 159–163.

201. For Axelrod's life and role in Russian politics, see Abraham Ascher's excellent intellectual biography, *Pavel Axelrod and the Development of Menshevism* (Cambridge, Mass.: Harvard University Press, 1972). As Ascher notes, Axelrod was not sure of his birthdate, but believed he had been born in 1849 or 1850: Ascher, *Axelrod*, p. 7.

202. Ibid., pp. 319–333; Martov to Axelrod, 19 November 1917, Nicolaevsky Collection.

203. "Je crois à mon devoir de contribuer à la destruction de cette légende": "Avis aux lecteurs," *Les Echos de Russie*, no. 15/16, 15 June 1918.

204. On Axelrod's relationship with Kautsky, see Abraham Ascher, "Axelrod and Kautsky," *Slavic Review*, 26 (March 1967), 94–112, and Ascher, *Axelrod*, pp. 83–88.

205. On Axelrod's activities after October 1917, see Ascher, *Axelrod*, pp. 331–379, and Aronson, *K istorii*, pp. 105–114.

206. Pavel Borisovich Aksel'rod, *Perezhitoe i peredumannoe* (Berlin: Grzhebin, 1923), pp. 71–73.

207. Ibid., pp. 130–131; see also Ascher, *Axelrod*, pp. 26, 27.

208. See, in addition to Ascher, Leopold H. Haimson, *The Russian Marxists and the Origins of Bolshevism* (Cambridge, Mass.: Harvard University Press, 1955), pp. 26–48.

209. *Sotsialisticheskii vestnik*, no. 15/16 (1925), p. 15.

210. For a while in Europe Axelrod and his wife made and sold kefir for a living. On Axelrod's various labors, see Ascher, *Axelrod*, especially pp. 28, 82–88.

211. Axelrod's position statements from 1903 and 1906 are cited in Abraham Ascher, ed., *The Mensheviks in the Russian Revolution* (London: Thames and Hudson, 1976), pp. 45, 46, 59–64.

212. Axelrod to Martov, September 1920, in "Tov. P. B. Aksel'rod o bol'shevizme i bor'be s nim," *Sotsialisticheskii vestnik*, no. 6 (20 April 1921), p. 6. This long letter, published in *Sotsialisticheskii vestnik*, no. 6 (20 April 1921), pp. 3–7, and no. 7 (4 May 1921), pp. 3–5., is translated in Ascher, *The Mensheviks*, pp. 130–136. Axelrod used the concept of the dictatorship over the proletariat repeatedly in his writings and speeches. See, for example, P. B. Aksel'rod, *Kto izmenil sotsializmu? (Bol'shevizm i sotsial'naia demokratiia v Rossii)* (New York: Narodopravstvo, 1919), p. 27. Martov, too, used this phrase in 1919 as a subtitle in his *Mirovoi bol'shevizm*, but then appears to have dropped the epithet: *Mirovoi bol'shevizm* (Berlin: Iskra, 1923), p. 42.

213. *Les Echos de Russie*, no. 15/16, 15 June 1918, p. 2.

214. Axelrod to Martov, September 1920, in "Tov. P. B. Aksel'rod," *Sotsialisticheskii vestnik*, no. 6 (20 April 1921), p. 6.

215. The essay was published as a pamphlet by Russian émigrés in New York: *Kto izmenil sotsializmu? (Bol'shevizm i sotsial'naia demokratiia v Rossii)* (New York: Narodopravstvo, 1919).

216. Ibid., p. 6. A discussion of the separate path, its history and role in the revolutionary movement can be found in Richard Pipes, *Struve: Liberal on the Left, 1870–1905* (Cambridge, Mass.: Harvard University Press, 1970), pp. 35–44.

217. *Kto izmenil sotsializmu*, pp. 6–8, 23.

218. Ascher, *Axelrod*, pp. 23–55.

219. Aksel'rod, *Kto izmenil sotsializmu?*, pp. 9–13, 22, 23.

220. Ibid., pp. 10–11.

221. Ibid., pp. 21–23.

222. See Axelrod's foreword to a German biography of Lenin, in which he described Lenin as the "major author" of the return to the "antimarxist tendencies, goals, and programs" of the early revolutionary movement: "Geleitwort," in A. Charach, *Lenin* (Zurich: Art. Institut Orell Fussli, 1920), p. 5.

223. *Kto izmenil sotsializmu*, pp. 24–27.

224. Axelrod to Martov, September 1920, in "Tov. P. B. Aksel'rod," *Sotsialisticheskii vestnik*, no. 7 (4 May 1921), pp. 3–5; see also "Zapis' besedy Anan'ina s Pavlom Borisovichem v Tsurikhe v 20 godu," Nicolaevsky Collection, no. 16, box 6, folio 113.

225. "Le discours du camarade P. Axelrod à la Conférence socialişte internationale de Berne," *Echo de Russie* (July 1919), p. 18. Excerpts from this speech are translated in Ascher, *The Mensheviks*, pp. 127–130.

226. "Le discours du camarade P. Axelrod à . . . Berne, *Echo de Russie* (July 1919), p. 23.

227. See his correspondence in the Axelrod Archive, I.I.S.H., especially B 69 IV, B 78 I, B 78 IV.

228. See Ascher, *Axelrod*, pp. 355–356.

229. J. B. Severac to Aksl'rod, 13 October 1920, Axelrod Archive, I.I.S.H.

230. The Berne speech called vaguely for "active" intervention on the part of the International ("La discours du camarade P. Axelrod," p. 23), but in his letter to Martov in September 1920, Axelrod specifically opposed a military campaign ("Tov. P. B. Aksel'rod," *Sotsialisticheskii vestnik*, no. 6 [20 April 1921], pp. 3–5).

231. Axelrod to Martov, September 1920, in "Tov. P. B. Aksel'rod," *Sotsialisticheskii vestnik*, no. 7 (4 May 1921), p. 5.

232. "P. B. Aksel'rod: Cherti dlia kharakteristiki," *Sotsialisticheskii vestnik*, no. 15/16 (18 August 1925), p. 17. Tsereteli writes with pride of this impracticality.

233. "Zapis' besedy Anan'nina," Nicolaevsky Collection.

234. Russian social democrats were caught in a "vicious circle," Axelrod argued; they could not have a successful struggle against Bolshevism without the opportunity to organize the masses, yet the Bolsheviks prevented that organization. Thus, there was no way out without the help of the international movement: Ibid.

235. P. B. Aksel'rod, "K voprosu o sotsialisticheskoi interventsii, 1920 g.," Nicolaevsky Collection.

236. B. A. Skomorovskii to Axelrod, 6 August 1920 and 3 September 1920, Axelrod Archive, I.I.S.H.; Martov to Axelrod, 29 September 1920, Nicolaevsky Collection, no. 17, box 1, folio 2.

237. See "Mirovaia sotsial'naia revoliutsiia i zadachi sotsial-demokratiia" and "Politicheskaia revoliutsiia i diktatura proletariata" in *Sotsial-demokratiia i revoliutsiia* (Odessa: Izd. Gruppa Sots. Dem., 1920), pp. 24–28, in Nicolaevsky Collection, no. 6, box 3, folio 32.

238. See, for example, Martov's correspondence with Axelrod, renewed in January 1920 after two years of silence: Nicolaevsky Collection, no. 17, folio 2.

239. Letter from the Central Committee of the RSDRP to "all comrades," 28

September 1920, Nicolaevsky Collection, no. 6, box 1, folio 4; Martov to
Axelrod, 29 September 1920, Nicolaevsky Collection, no. 17, box 1, folio 2.
Martov worried that his presence served as a deterrent to the total destruction of
the party. For this reason and on the grounds of a desperate need for "authority"
in the party, there had been much opposition to his trip abroad: Martov to Axelrod,
4 August 1920, Nicolaevsky Collection, no. 17, box 1, folio 2.
240. On the Foreign Delegation and its relationship to the party leadership at home, see
Haimson, *The Mensheviks*, pp. 250–255, 289–309. For the history of the
Mensheviks abroad, see Liebich, *Les Mencheviks en exil*.
241. The journal proved to be the longest-lived Menshevik periodical; it ceased
publication in 1963.
242. *Sotsialisticheskii vestnik*, no. 1 (1 February 1921), p. 1.
243. *Sotsialisticheskii vestnik* was not the only outlet for the Menshevik intellectuals in
Europe. In 1921 and 1922 Mensheviks also wrote in *Freiheit*, the organ of the
USPD; see Robert C. Williams *Culture in Exile: Russian Emigrés in Germany,
1881–1941* (Ithaca: Cornell University Press, 1972), p. 231. Foreign-language
bulletins of the RSDRP were published sporadically later: see Bourgina, *Russian
Social Democracy*, pp. 353, 354.
244. The invitation had been extended in Moscow by Dittmann and Crispien:
Abramovich, *Men'sheviki*, p. 14. On the Mensheviks at the Halle congress, see,
in addition to Abramovich, Getzler, *Martov*, pp. 208–212; Williams, *Culture in
Exile*, pp. 194–196; and Branko Lazitch and Milorad M. Drachkovitch, *Lenin and
the Comintern* (Stanford: Hoover Institution Press, 1972), 1:425–433.
245. "Rech' na zasedanii 15-go oktiabria 1920g.," in Iu. Martov, *Bol'shevizm v
Rossii i v internatsionale* (Berlin: Sotsialisticheskii vestnik, 1923), pp. 14–19.
246. Ibid., p. 15.
247. Martov described the Bolsheviks' response to the assassination of Uritskii and the
attempted assassination of Lenin in the summer of 1918—eight hundred prisoners,
people arrested for their hostility to the revolution *before* these acts took place,
were shot and their names printed in *Izvestiia* as a warning to others: Ibid., pp.
19, 20.
248. Ibid., pp. 19–21.
249. Ibid., p. 17.
250. Ibid., p. 24.
251. See Lazitch and Drachkovitch, *Lenin*, 1:427–429. Martov wrote to Axelrod that
Zinoviev's speech was a "pearl of demagogic art": Martov to Axelrod, 17
October 1920, Nicolaevsky Collection, no. 17, box 1, folio 2.
252. The speech was delivered by Alexander Stein, who had difficulty reading
Martov's handwriting (a problem students of Menshevism can appreciate): Martov
to Axelrod, 17 October 1920, Nicolaevsky Collection. On Stein, see Williams,
Culture in Exile, pp. 190–194.
253. See the account in Abramovich, *Men'sheviki*, p. 22.
254. Martov to Axelrod, 17 October 1920; Abramovich, *Men'sheviki*, p. 23.
255. Lazitch and Drachkovitch, *Lenin*, pp. 431–432. Abramovich, *Men'sheviki*, p. 23,
reports a tally of 236 to 150.
256. Martov to Axelrod, 15 October 1920 and 17 October 1920, Nicolaevsky
Collection, no. 17, box 1, folio 2.
257. Martov, *Bol'shevizm v Rossii*, p. 5.

258. Ascher, *Axelrod*, p. 359.
259. On the Vienna International, see Julius Braunthal, *Geschichte der Internationale*, 3 vols. (Hannover: J. H. W. Dietz, 1963), 2:249–272. For Tsereteli and the Second International, see W. H. Roobel, *Tsereteli, a Democrat in the Russian Revolution: A Political Biography*, trans. by Philip Hyans and Lynn Richards (The Hague: Nijhoff, 1976), pp. 218–249.
260. "Po puti k Internatsionalu," *Sotsialisticheskii vestnik*, no. 1 (1 February 1921); see, among Martov's articles on this subject, "K Venskoi konferentsii," *Sotsialisticheskii vestnik*, no. 4 (18 March 1921), "Sumerki kominterna," *Sotsialisticheskii vestnik*, no. 12 (22 July 1921), "Vosstanovlenie Internatsionala," *Sotsialisticheskii vestnik*, no. 13 (5 August 1921), and "V bor'be za edinstvo," *Sotsialisticheskii vestnik*, no. 11(33) (3 June 1922). Much of Martov's writing in the emigration on the question of the International is collected in Iu. O. Martov, *V bor'be za internatsional* (Berlin: Iskra, 1924).
261. Martov, *Bol'shevizm v Rossii i v Internatsionale*, p. 5.
262. "V bor'be za edinstvo," *Sotsialisticheskii vestnik*, no. 11(33) (3 June 1922).
263. "Problema internatsionala," *Sotsialisticheskii vestnik*, no. 21(43) (2 November 1922).
264. Martov's first letter to Axelrod after two years of silence was dated 23 January 1920. It does not appear that any letters from Axelrod got through to him. See the file in Nicolaevsky Collection, no. 17, box 1, folio 2.
265. Axelrod, on the other hand, was eager for a meeting, even without the prospect of agreement: Axelrod, draft letter on Bolshevik terror, 4 September 1920, Axelrod Archive, B 78 V, I.I.S.H.; Axelrod to S. D. Shchupak, 7 December 1920, Nicolaevsky Collection, no. 16, box 5, folio 91. For Martov's attitudes, see his letters to Axelrod in the fall of 1920, especially, 28 October 1920 and 25 November 1920, Nicolaevsky Collection, no. 17, box 1, folio 2.
266. Martov to Axelrod, 25 November 1920, Nicolaevsky Collection, no. 17, box 1, folio 2.
267. Martov to Axelrod, 14 December 1920, Nicolaevsky Collection, no. 17, box 1, folio 2.
268. Axelrod to S. D. Shchupak, 10 December 1920, Nicolaevsky Collection, no. 16, box 5, folio 91.
269. Axelrod to S. D. Shchupak, 24 December 1920, Nicolaevsky Collection, no. 16, box 5, folio 91.
270. "Tov. P. B. Aksel'rod o bol'shevizme i bor'be s nim," *Sotsialisticheskii vestnik*, no. 6 (20 April 1921), pp. 3–7, and no. 7 (4 May 1921), pp. 3–5; Martov to Axelrod, 5 April 1921, Nicolaevsky Collection, no. 17, box 1, folio 2.
271. See, for example, Martov to Axelrod, 27 April 1921, 13 May 1921, 31 August 1921, Nicolaevsky Collection, no. 17, box 1, folio 2. On Axelrod's care and respect for Martov, see his memorial article, "Pamiati Martova," *Sotsialisticheskii vestnik*, special issue (10 April 1923), pp. 2, 3.
272. London Group of the RSDRP to Central Committee of the RSDRP, 15 September 1920, Portugeis Collection, III, Strumilo Dossier, I.I.S.H. According to the Strumilo dossier, the following people were associated with the London Group of the RSDRP, or London Group of Social Democrats: V. F. Breitveit, A. V. Baikalov, Zundelevich, Upovalov, Strumilo, Krugliakov, Stentsel-Lenskii, Nosov, Laskin, and Khvostenko.

273. Martov to A. V. Baikalov, 6 November 1920, Portugeis Collection, IV.
274. Ibid.
275. Martov to the London "Group of SDs," 5 February 1921, Portugeis Collection, IV.
276. "Chto delat'," in *Sotsial-demokratiia i revoliutsiia* (Odessa: Izd. Gruppy sots. dem., 1920), pp. 9–16.
277. "In reality, Lenin took our supply platform in its entirety" (Martov to Axelrod, 24 March 1921, Nicolaevsky Collection, no. 17, box 1, folio 2). Martov claimed in this letter that the Bolsheviks had physically stolen the economic program in the form of documents confiscated from the Menshevik Central Committee. Subsequently, Lenin had announced it "as his own."
278. Martov, "Nasha platforma," *Sotsialisticheskii vestnik*, no. 19(4 October 1922), p. 4.
279. Ibid., p. 5.
280. "Na puti k likvidatsii," *Sotsialisticheskii vestnik*, no. 18 (15 October 1921).
281. "From the moment the Bolshevik government began to serve the non-Communist 'new economic policy', its own (subjective) relationship to democracy was changed in principle" (Martov, "Dialektika diktatury," *Sotsialisticheskii vestnik*, no. 3(25) (3 February 1922), p. 5.
282. "Russkii rabochii pri gosudarstvennom kapitalizme," *Sotsialisticheskii vestnik*, no. 19 (1 November 1921).
283. "Dialektika diktatury," p. 4–7.
284. Martov, "Nasha platforma," pp. 3–7.
285. Ibid., p. 6.
286. Ibid., p. 7.
287. *O prodovol'stvennom naloge (Znachenie novoi politiki i ee usloviia)* in Lenin, *Polnoe sobranie sochinenii*, 43:241–242. See also the "Political Results and Conclusions" section of this work, pp. 243–245. The last sentence repeats the threats against the political opposition.
288. Dan, Aronson, and Nicolaevsky left Russia at this time. On the Butyrki hunger strike, see Abramovich, *Men'sheviki*, pp. 38–41. Martov wrote to Axelrod that the Central Committee had forbidden this strike, which the participants intended to keep until death: Martov to Axelrod, 7 January 1922, Nicolaevsky Collection, no. 17, box 1, folio 2.
289. "Vybory v sovety i SD partiia," *Sotsialisticheskii vestnik* (21 September 1922), p. 3.
290. See, for example, his article, "Preventivnaia bor'ba," *Sotsialisticheskii vestnik*, no. 18(40) (21 September 1921).
291. *Sotsialisticheskii vestnik*, no. 1 (1 February 1921).
292. "Pobeda [!] na Butyrskom fronte," *Sotsialisticheskii vestnik*, no. 9 (5 June 1921). This statement seems a pathetic echo of Lenin's claim in his brochure on NEP that the Bolsheviks had created an "*avant-garde* of the proletariat" that was "steel-like and tempered" (Lenin, *O prodovol'stvennom naloge*, in *Polnoe sobranie sochinenii*, 43:240).
293. "Perechesivaiutsia," *Sotsialisticheskii vestnik*, no. 4 (23 February 1922), p. 1.
294. "Ili-ili," *Sotsialisticheskii vestnik*, no. 17 (10 October 1921).
295. Martov, "Vosstanovlenie gosudarstvennykh dolgov," *Vsegda vpered*, no. 8, 16 February 1919.

296. "Problema internatsionala," *Sotsialisticheskii vestnik*, no. 21(43) (2 November 1922).
297. "Martov o partii 1918–1919 gg." *Sotsialisticheskii vestnik*," vol. 7, no. 7(149) (4 April 1927); Martov, "Nasha platforma," *Sotsialisticheskii vestnik*, no. 19 (4 October 1922).
298. "Iu. O. Martov," *Sotsialisticheskii vestnik*, no. 7–8(77–78) (4 April 1924), p. 20.
299. "Mnimoe bankrotstvo marksizma," *Sotsialisticheskii vestnik*, no. 10(32) (16 May 1922), p. 7.
300. St. Ivanovich, *Potresov*, p. 170; S. Zagorskii, "Kto my?," and St. Ivanovich, "Vmeste s kommunistami ili protiv nikh," *Zaria*, no. 1 (15 April 1922), pp. 1–10. This first number contained an article dedicated to the memory of Vera Zasulich. Members of the London SDs on the *Zaria* editorial board included A. Baikalov, V. Breitman, A. Zundelevich, and G. Strumillo. For a glimpse of Martov's bitterness toward Stepan Ivanovich's group, see his letter to E. A. Ananin of 8 March 1922, in which he tries to dissuade Ananin from publishing in *Zaria*: Lydia Dan Archive, IX, 32, I.I.S.H.
301. "Liberal'nyi sotsializm," *Sotsialisticheskii vestnik*, no. 1(47) (1 January 1923), pp. 7–11. St. Ivanovich's offending article, "The Democratization of Socialism," had been published in *Sovremennye zapiski*, an SR publication. This sign of Ivanovich's alliance with the SRs was especially irksome to Martov. See also Martov's response to other rightists two weeks later in his "Otvet kritikam," *Sotsialisticheskii vestnik*, no. 2(48) (17 January 1923), pp. 10–13. This is yet another defense of the Central Committee's stance against militant opposition to the Bolshevik government.
302. "Liberal'nyi sotsializm," pp. 7–9.
303. Ibid., p. 9.
304. Ibid.
305. Ibid., pp. 10–11.
306. Ibid., p. 11.
307. From their letter in response to Martov's dismissal of the London Group: I. Upovalov and G. Strumilo to Martov, 18 February 1921, Portugeis Collection, IV.

Chapter 2

1. One sign of the Marxists' ideological victory in the 1890s was that the word "*narodnichestvo* [populism]" was used as a pejorative epithet. On the origins of this term in Russian and its polemical usage, see Richard Pipes, "Narodnichestvo—A Semantic Inquiry," *Slavic Review*, 23, no. 3 (September 1964), 451–458. I am using "populist" in its broad sense to describe those individuals who, according to their theoretical statements, wished to see Russia's future determined by the "*narod*," the people, in contrast to the state or any elite leadership. For a discussion of populist theories in the 1880s and 1890s, see Richard Pipes, *Struve: Liberal on the Left, 1870–1905* (Cambridge, Mass.: Harvard University Press, 1970), pp. 30–51, 79–117; Richard Wortman, *The Crisis of Russian Populism* (Cambridge: Cambridge University Press, 1967); and Andrzej Walicki, *The Controversy over Capitalism* (Oxford: Clarendon Press, 1969).

2. For the history of the Socialist Revolutionary party in the prerevolutionary period, see Maureen Perrie, *The Agrarian Policy of the Russian Socialist-Revolutionary Party: From its Origins Through the Revolution of 1905–1907* (Cambridge: Cambridge University Press, 1976); Manfred Hildermeier, *Die Sozial-revolutionaere Partei Russlands: Agrarsozialismus und Modernisierung im Zarenreich (1900–1914)* (Cologne: Boelau Verlag, 1978); Jacques Baynac, *Les Socialistes-Révolutionnaires de mars 1881 à mars 1917* (Paris: Robert Laffont, 1979); Donald W. Treadgold, *Lenin and His Rivals* (New York: Praeger, 1955), pp. 60–82, 148–153, 207–218; and Oliver H. Radkey, *The Agrarian Foes of Bolshevism* (New York: Columbia University Press, 1958), pp. 3–87.

3. For a brief summary of Chernov's life and work, see B. Nikolaevskii, "V. M. Chernov," in V. M. Chernov, *Pered burei: Vospominaniia* (New York: Izdatel'stvo imeni Chekhova, 1953), pp. 5–16. For his role in the formulation of SR policy through 1907, see Maureen Perrie's informative study, *Agrarian Policy*, especially pp. 14–33, 58–69, 143–152.

4. See his memoirs, Viktor Chernov, *Zapiski sotsialista revoliutsionera* (Berlin: Izdatel'stvo S. I. Grzhebina, 1922), pp. 97–339, and Perrie, *Agrarian Policy*, pp. 14–23.

5. Chernov read Struve's Marxist polemics in jail and commented, later, that although they seemed to have been written by "an inhabitant of another planet," they had helped him to define his own, different, point of view· Chernov, *Zapiski*, p. 233.

6. Ibid., pp. 336, 339.

7. Perrie, *Agrarian Policy*, p. 42.

8. See Perrie, *Agrarian Policy*, pp. 143–152, on the party congress.

9. "Programma Partii sotsialistov-revoliutsionerov," in *Sovremennyi moment v otsenke Partii sots.-revoliutsionerov (Fevral'–mart 1919g.)* (New York: N'iu Iorkskaia gruppa Partii sotsialistov-revoliutsionerov, 1919), pp. 53–59.

10. Ibid., p. 59.

11. Ibid.

12. Ibid., pp. 59–64.

13. Ibid., p. 53.

14. See Perrie, *Agrarian Policy*, pp. 74–83, for an excellent discussion of SR views of class and politics in the countryside.

15. "Programma partii," p. 62.

16. Ibid., p. 64.

17. In Oliver Radkey's phrase, "Populism was less an ideology than a state of mind" (Radkey, *Agrarian Foes*, p. 3.)

18. On Azef, see B. I. Nikolaevskii, *Istoriia odnogo predatelia* (Berlin: Petropolis, 1932.)

19. Radkey makes a critical assessment of Chernov's career in government in *Agrarian Foes*, pp. 322–334.

20. V. M. Chernov, *Pered burei* (New York: Izdatel'stvo imeni Chekhova, 1953), p. 345. For Chernov's disagreements with the other SR leaders, see the protocols of the Central Committee of the PSR for the fall of 1917, especially 4 September, 6 September, 7 September, and 11 September: "Protokoly zasedanii Ts.K.Partii S.–R.," Nicolaevsky Collection, no. 7, box 1, folio 10, Hoover Institution, Stanford University, Stanford, California.

21. On the origin and significance of Chernov's leadership, consult Radkey, *Agrarian Foes*, pp. 457–461. For Chernov's stature before 1917, see Mark Vishniak, *Dan' proshlomu* (New York: Izdatel'stvo imeni Chekhova, 1954), p. 123. Chernov himself recognized his lack of organizational skills: "He [Chernov is speaking of himself] . . . never wanted or never was able to control [*derzhat' v svoikh rukakh*] the party machine" ("Kommentarii V. M. Chernova k protokolam Ts.K.P.S.R.," Nicolaevsky Collection, no. 7, box 3, folio 54, pp. 38–39).

22. "Protokoly zasedanii Ts.K.Partii S.-R.," 8 December 1917, Nicolaevsky Collection, no. 7, box 1, folio 10. On the Congress, see Oliver Henry Radkey, *The Sickle Under the Hammer* (New York: Columbia University Press, 1963), pp. 163–202.

23. See Leonard Schapiro, *The Origin of the Communist Autocracy: Political Opposition in the Soviet State*, 2nd ed. (Cambridge, Mass.: Harvard University Press, 1977), pp. 111–114, and Radkey, *The Sickle Under the Hammer*, pp. 95–162.

24. Even Chernov was involved briefly in an abortive scheme to form an alternative government based on the support of the Allies. The SRs' early efforts to unseat the Bolsheviks are chronicled in Radkey, *The Sickle Under the Hammer*, pp. 13–61, 73–91.

25. "Tekushchii moment i zadachi partii: Rezoliutsiia IV–go s"ezda," Nicolaevsky Collection, no. 7, box 1, folio 11.

26. Ibid.

27. Ibid.

28. Ibid.

29. Ibid.

30. The SR Central Committee supported the Constituent Assembly simultaneously with the notion of an all-socialist government to replace the Bolsheviks. On November 14, during its fruitless attempts to organize an all-socialist government, the Central Committee specified that such a government would act only until the convocation of the Constituent Assembly: "Protokoly zasedanii Ts.K.Partii S.-R.," 14 November 1917, Nicolaevsky Collection, no. 7, box 1, folio 10.

31. "Tekushchii moment i zadachi partii: Rezoliutsiia IV–go s"ezda," Nicolaevsky Collection, no. 7, box 1, folio 11.

32. After the party congress had adjourned, the Central Committee asserted that there was to be "no terror" against the Bolsheviks in defense of the Constituent Assembly: "Protokoly zasedanii Ts.K.Partii S.-R.," 8 December 1917, Nicolaevsky Collection, no. 7, box 1, folio 10. Chernov wrote later in his memoirs that "everything, in our perspective, depended on not giving the Bolsheviks the least shade of moral justification for going over to bloodletting" (Chernov, *Pered burei*, p. 357).

33. The vote was 244 for, 151 against: I. S. Malchevskii, ed., *Vserossiiskoe uchreditel'noe sobranie* (Moscow: Gosudarstvennoe izdatel'stvo, 1930), p. 9.

34. Ibid.

35. See Radkey's account of the session in *The Sickle Under the Hammer*, pp. 386–409. For the Bolsheviks' strategy at the meeting, see the memoirs of I. Z. Steinberg, the People's Commissar of Justice at the time: *Als ich Volkskommissar*

war: Episoden aus der russischen Oktoberrevolution (Munich: R. Piper & Co., 1929), pp. 41–87.

36. Malchevskii, *Vserossiiskoe*, p. 27.
37. For the text of this legislation, see Malchevskii, *Vserossiiskoe*, pp. 112–113.
38. *Tezisy dokladov dlia partiinykh agitatorov i propagandistov*, no. 1: *Direktivnoe pis'mo partiinym organizatsiiam*, Nicolaevsky Collection, no. 7, box 3, folio 52.
39. Ibid.
40. Ibid.
41. Ibid.
42. *Tezisy dokladov dlia partiinykh agitatorov i propagandistov*, no. 9: *Bol'shevizm i "rabochii kontrol'*," Nicolaevsky Collection, no. 7, box 3, folio 52. Both the Mensheviks and the SRs turned away from "workers' control" when they saw its effects. While the Mensheviks complained about the backwardness of the workers's attitudes, Chernov pointed to the need to include the intelligentsia in the production process.
43. *Tezisy dokladov*, no. 1, Nicolaevsky Collection.
44. Chernov, *Pered burei*, pp. 368–374; V. Chernov, *Mes tribulations en Russie soviétique* (Paris: Povolozky, 1921), p. 7.
45. On the Ufa conference and the Directory, see the congress's declaration, "Towards National Unity," in *The Russian Commonwealth*, 1, no. 1 (1 November 1918), p. 17, and M. V. Vishniak, *Vserossiiskoe uchreditel'noe sobranie* (Paris: Sovremennye zapiski, 1932), pp. 170–217; I. Maiskii, *Demokraticheskaia kontr-revoliutsiia* (Moscow: Gosudarstvennoe izdatel'stvo, 1923), pp. 215–343; Vladimir Zenzinov, *Iz zhizni revoliutsionera* (Paris, 1919), pp. 109–112.
46. "Zhirondisty byli, *mutatis mutandis*, kadetami Velikoi Frantsuzskoi Revoliutsii": "'Chernovskaia gramota' i Ufimskaia direktoriia," Nicolaevsky Collection, no. 7, box 3, folio 55.
47. "'Chernovskaia gramota'," Nicolaevsky Collection; Vishniak, *Vserossiiskoe*, pp. 195–196.
48. Zenzinov, *Iz zhizni*, p. 112; V. Chernov, *Mes tribulations*, pp. 7–20.
49. *Mes tribulations*, p. 20.
50. SR policy during the civil war can be followed in the newspapers and bulletins published by party members in Paris; see *Le Bulletin de la Ligue russe pour la défense révolutionnaire, La République russe, La Russie démocratique*, and *Pour la Russie*, from 1918 through 1921.
51. Chernov, *Mes tribulations*, pp. 18–23.
52. Chernov, *Mes tribulations*, pp. 21–33. The attempt to sign an accord with the PSR caused another split—or rather a splinter—in the party, and is known in the SR annals as the Volskii affair; see Marc Jansen, *A Show Trial Under Lenin: The Trial of the Socialist Revolutionaries, Moscow 1922* (The Hague: Martinus Nijhoff, 1982), pp. 5–12.
53. "Pochetnaia kapitulatsiia," *Vsegda vpered*, no. 1, 22 January 1919.
54. "Izveshchenie o IX sovete Partii Sotsialistov-Revoliutsionerov," Nicolaevsky Collection, no. 7, box 1, folio 7. Chernov had used the notion of the third force—a new way avoiding two evils—in an analogous manner during the World War to support his internationalist position: V. M. Chernov, *Voina i "tret'ia sila": Sbornik statei*, 2d ed. (Petrograd, 1917); Radkey, *Agrarian Foes*, pp. 107–109.

55. "Izveshchenie o IX sovete Partii Sotsialistov-Revoliutsionerov," Nicolaevsky Collection.
56. Ibid.
57. Ibid.
58. Olga Chernov Andreyev, *Cold Spring in Russia* (Ann Arbor: Ardis, 1978), p. 11.
59. Chernov, *Mes tribulations*, p. 51.
60. They were finally released from prison and various house arrests in 1922 and allowed to go abroad. See the memoir of these years by one of the children: Olga Chernov Andreyev, *Cold Spring in Russia*, pp. 209–283. In response to his family's arrest, Chernov sent Lenin a letter congratulating him on this "major success on the internal front." Parts of this letter are quoted in M. V. Vishniak, *Chernyi god* (Paris: Franko-russkaia pechat', 1922), p. 13.
61. On the Printers' Union and its opposition to the Bolsheviks and its connection with right Menshevism, see Grigorii Aronson, *K istorii pravogo techeniia sredi men'shevikov*, Inter-University Project on the History of the Menshevik Movement, no. 4 (New York, 1960), pp. 79–81.
62. The British Delegation was one offshoot of Axelrod's proposal for a socialist investigatory commission. The visitors were generally discouraged from making contacts with the socialist opposition; the printers' meeting was an exceptional event. See Aronson, *K istorii*, pp. 79–80; Abramovich, *Men'sheviki i sotsialisticheskii internatsional (1918–1940)* (n.p., n.d.), pp. 13–18; Israel Getzler, *Martov: A Political Biography of a Russian Social Democrat* (Cambridge: At the University Press, 1967), pp. 202, 205; and Leopold H. Haimson, ed., *The Mensheviks: From the Revolution of 1917 to the Second World War* (Chicago: University of Chicago Press, 1974), pp. 227–228.
63. "Rech' V. M. Chernova na obshchem sobranii pechatnikov 23–go maia 1920 goda v chest' delegatsii angliiskogo proletariata," *Narodnoe delo*, no. 85, 13 November 1920, pp. 23, 24.
64. Ibid.
65. Ibid.
66. Ibid.
67. Chernov, *Mes tribulations*, pp. 60–61; Abramovich, *Men'sheviki i sotsialisticheskii internatsional*, pp. 17–18.
68. "Rezoliutsii po tekushchemu momentu, priniatye na konferentsii P.S.–R. 8 sentiabria 1920 g.," Nicolaevsky Collection, no. 7, box 1, folio 12. These resolutions were published in *Narodnoe delo*, no. 106, 8 December 1920.
69. Ibid.
70. Ibid.
71. Ibid.
72. He and Martov met on their separate paths out of Russia in Reval: Martov to Axelrod, 29 September 1920, Nicolaevsky Collection, no. 17, box 1, folio 2.
73. "Revoliutsionnaia Rossiia," *Revoliutsionnaia Rossiia*, no. 1 (25 December 1920), pp. 1–2.
74. Ibid.
75. Ibid.
76. See, for example, Viktor Chernov, "Bol'sheviki v derevne," *Volia Rossii*, 28 November 1920. Here Chernov observed that the Bolshevik policy toward the peasants could be summed up in the words of a Communist deputy at the

government's First All-Russian Conference on Party Work in the Village: "Remember, the peasant is a barrel, around which there must be a strong hoop."

77. See the Central Committee's letter to the British Labour Delegation, published in Reval: "Obrashchenie partii S.–R. k delegatsii angliiskoi rabochei partii," *Narodnoe delo*, no. 96, 26 November 1920, and no. 97, 27 November 1920.

78. Chernov harped incessantly on the "living corpse" motif; for example, see "Revoliutsionnaia Rossiia," *Revoliutsionnaia Rossiia*, no. 1 (25 December 1920), pp. 1–2; "Revoliutsiia ili kontr-revoliutsiia," *Narodnoe delo*, no. 81, 7 November 1920.

79. See, for example, Martov's manuscript for a report to European socialists, "Le parti socialiste démocrate en Russie bolcheviste," Nicolaevsky Collection, no. 6, box 1, folio 16, p. 12.

80. "Revoliutsiia ili kontr-revoliutsiia," *Narodnoe delo*, no. 81, 7 November 1920.

81. Ibid.

82. Ibid.

83. Ibid.

84. Ibid.

85. Ibid.

86. Ibid. In Chernov's words: the removal of the "corpse" of Bolshevik socialism was an "urgent demand of revolutionary hygiene."

87. On the preparations for the meeting, see *Poslednie novosti*, nos. 196–213, 11–31 December, 1920.

88. Chernov to the Central Committee of the PSR, 2 June 1921 (attributed date), Nicolaevsky Collection, no. 7, box 1, folio 20.

89. On the Conference of the Members of the Constituent Assembly, see Mark Vishniak, *Gody emigratsii 1919–1969: Parizh-N'iu-Iork* (Stanford: Hoover Institution Press, 1970), pp. 55–65, and Hans von Rimscha, *Der russische Bürgerkrieg und die russische Emigration: 1917–1921* (Jena: Frommannsche Buchhandlung, 1924), pp. 115–120. Rimscha writes that thirty-two delegates attended the conference.

90. See point 15 on "consolidation of [the party's] forces" in "Tekushchii moment i zadachi partii: Rezoliutsiia IV-go s''ezda," Nicolaevsky Collection, and part X, "O partiinoi distsipline" in "Izveshchenie o IX sovete Partii Sotsialistov-Revoliutsionerov," Nicolaevsky Collection.

91. These included Berlin, Berne, Lausanne, and Reval, as well as the main centers in Paris and Prague.

92. On the divisions in the party and the Prague money, see his letter to the Central Committee in Russia, 2 June 1921 (attributed date), Nicolaevsky Collection.

93. *Mes tribulations*, p. 80.

94. P. N. Miliukov, *Istoriia vtoroi russkoi revoliutsii* (Sofia: Rossiisko-Bolgarskoe knigoizdatel'stvo, 1921–1924), 3 vols., 1, part 1, p. 244.

95. On these diplomatic efforts, see Mark Vishniak, *Gody emigratsii 1919–1969* (Stanford: Hoover Institution Press, 1970), pp. 9–40.

96. Among these publications were the *Bulletin de la Ligue pour la défense Révolutionnaire*, *La République russe*, *La Russie démocratique*, and *Pour la Russie*.

97. In his memoirs, Vishniak describes the choice of Paris as "instinctive" for these people (*Gody emigratsii*, p. 10.)

98. Mark Vishniak, *Dan' proshlomu* (New York: Izdatel'stvo imeni Chekhova, 1954), pp. 13–16, 37. This volume of Vishniak's memoirs covers his life through the meeting of the Constituent Assembly.

99. Ibid., pp. 77–194, 255, 256.

100. See Vishniak's vivid account of the meeting in *Dan' proshlomu*, pp. 360–381, and Malchevskii, *Vserossiiskoe uchreditel'noe sobranie*, pp. 24, 25.

101. Vishniak, *Dan' proshlomu*, p. 6.

102. M. V. Vishniak, *"Sovremennye zapiski": Vospominaniia redaktora* (n.p.: Indiana University Publications, 1957), pp. 22–32, 42–51, 78–88. On the Kadets' Crimean government, see William G. Rosenberg, *Liberals in the Russian Revolution: The Constitutional Democratic Party, 1917–1921* (Princeton: Princeton University Press, 1974), pp. 357–381.

103. Vishniak, *Gody emigratsii*, p. 48. Vishniak here describes his political work in the 1920s as "insignificant."

104. *Bol'shevizm i demokratiia* (New York: Narodopravtsvo, 1919). "Narodopravstvo" in New York also published Axelrod's *Who Betrayed Bolshevism?*

105. *Bol'shevizm i demokratiia*, pp. 6, 7.

106. For the April theses, see V. I. Lenin, *Polnoe sobranie sochinenii*, 31:113–118.

107. Vishniak, *Bol'shevizm i demokratiia*, pp. 1–3.

108. Ibid., pp. 3–4.

109. Ibid., pp. 4–5.

110. Ibid., pp. 5–6. Vishniak is referring to the Bolsheviks' Seventh Party Congress, which he, evidently using the Old Style calendar, describes as taking place in February 1918. For excerpts from the program to which he refers see James Bunyan and H. H. Fisher, *The Bolshevik Revolution, 1917–1918: Documents and Materials* (Stanford: Stanford University Press, 1934), pp. 547–550.

111. Vishniak, *Bol'shevizm*, p. 9.

112. Ibid., pp. 12–21, 24.

113. See Vishniak's defense of democracy as essential to socialism in *Bol'shevizm i demokratiia*, pp. 29–32.

114. M. V. Vishniak, "Ideia uchreditel'nogo sobraniia," *Griadushchaia Rossiia*, 1920, no. 1, pp. 170–192; no. 2, pp. 182–216. *Griadushchaia Rossiia* united both literary and political figures. Its editors were N. V. Chaikovskii, V. A. Anri, M. A. Aldanov, and A. N. Tolstoy; Amari, Teffi, Nol'de, Bunakov, Dioneo, Minskii, and V. V. Nabokov were among the contributors.

115. M. V. Vishniak, "Ideia uchreditel'nogo sobraniia," no. 1, pp. 270–292. Vishniak noted that a liberal, Petrunkevich, had first proposed the Constituent Assembly: "Ideia," no. 1, pp. 278–279.

116. M. V. Vishniak, "Ideia uchreditel'naia sobraniia," no. 2, p. 185.

117. Vishniak, "Ideia," no. 2, pp. 186–187. Vishniak noted that Plekhanov had continued to defend this stand even after the dismissal of Constituent Assembly, see pp. 36 and 37, above.

118. Ibid., pp. 189–193.

119. Ibid., p. 215. Vishniak's argument in this article recalls that of B. A. Kistiakovskii in *Vekhi: Vekhi* (Moscow, 1909), pp. 139–141.

120. Marc Vichniac, *Le régime soviétiste* (Paris: Imprimerie Union, 1920).

121. On the SRs' activity at the Stockholm Peace Conference and at the Berne Conference of the International, see Vishniak, *Gody emigratsii*, pp. 27–30.

122. Vishniak, *Le régime*, p. 9. Many of Vishniak's arguments in this work were presented first in *Bol'shevizm i demokratiia*.
123. Vishniak, pp. 18–19, 21. The Constituent Assembly was to be convened on November 28, but was postponed by the government until January. Avksent'ev, Argunov, Gukovskii, and Pitirim Sorokin were among the SR delegates arrested a few days before the meeting on January 5–6: ibid., p. 21.
124. As in his earlier work, Vishniak refers to the congress as having taken place in February.
125. Vishniak, *Le régime*, pp. 22–23.
126. Ibid., pp. 22–27.
127. Ibid., pp. 24–26.
128. Ibid., pp. 29, 31, 32.
129. Ibid., p. 33.
130. Ibid., pp. 32, 38–39. The electoral law resembled that of the imperial Duma, something Vishniak did not point out but that is consistent with his argument.
131. Ibid., p. 39.
132. Ibid., pp. 29, 31, 40–48.
133. Ibid., pp. 42–43.
134. Ibid., pp. 43–45.
135. Ibid., pp. 47–56.
136. Ibid., p. 49.
137. Ibid., pp. 58–59.
138. Ibid., pp. 59–60.
139. Ibid., pp. 48, 62–63.
140. Ibid., pp. 63–64.
141. Ibid., p. 65.
142. Ibid., p. 65.
143. Ibid., p. 64.
144. Ibid., pp. 66, 77–78.
145. Ibid., pp. 89–90, 98.
146. Ibid., p. 90.
147. Ibid., p. 5.
148. Ibid., pp. 90, 99.
149. Vishniak, *"Sovremennye zapiski": Vospominaniia redaktora*, pp. 93–94. For the history of the journal see this memoir by Vishniak, an editor for its twenty years of publication.
150. "Ot redaktsii," *Sovremennye zapiski*, 1 (November 1920).
151. Chernov to the Central Committee of the PSR, 2 June 1921 [date attributed by archive], Nicolaevsky Collection, no. 7, box 1, folio 20. Eventually, Chernov took his case against *Sovremennye zapiski* to the Executive Committee of the Socialist International: Vishniak, *"Sovremennye zapiski,"* pp. 269–270. Martov regarded St. Ivanovich's participation in *Sovremennye zapiski* as a sign of a dangerous "current" on the left; see his "Liberal'nyi sotsializm," *Sotsialisticheskii vestnik*, no. 1(47) (1 January 1923), p. 7.
152. Mark Vishniak, *Chernyi god* (Paris: Franko-russkaia pechat', 1922), p. [i]. This volume is a collection of Vishniak's articles in *Sovremennye zapiski* from 1920 and 1921.
153. On the rebellion, see Paul Avrich, *Kronstadt 1921* (New York: Norton, 1970) and

Israel Getzler, *Kronstadt 1917–1921: The Fate of a Soviet Democracy* (Cambridge: Cambridge University Press, 1983).

154. M. V. Vishniak, "Na rodine (Kronshtadt)," *Sovremennye zapiski*, 4 (April 1921), 362.

155. Ibid., p. 349. Vishniak cited the Kronstadt sailors' *Izvestiia*. For this and other declarations of the rebellion, see Avrich, *Kronstadt*, pp. 241–246.

156. Vishniak, "Na rodine (Kronshtadt)," p. 349.

157. Ibid., p. 350–352.

158. Ibid., pp. 354–356.

159. Ibid., p. 359.

160. Ibid., pp. 356–357.

161. Ibid., p. 356.

162. M. Vishniak, "Na rodine (Ekonomicheskii realizm ili politicheskii tupik?)" *Sovremennye zapiski*, 8 (December 1921), 348–352.

163. Ibid., p. 353.

164. On Kropotkin's funeral, see Emma Goldman, *My Disillusionment in Russia* (New York: Thomas Y. Crowell, n.d.; reprint ed., n.p.: Apollo, 1970), pp. 189–192; Paul Avrich, *The Russian Anarchists* (Princeton: Princeton University Press, 1967), pp. 227–228; N. Lebedev, "Skorbnyi den'," in *Pamiati Petra Alekseevicha Kropotkina* (Petrograd and Moscow: Vserossisskii obshchestvennyi komitet po uvekovecheniiu pamiati P. A. Kropotkina, 1921), pp. 5–10. Several of the essays in this last source were written from the Butyrki prison. The principal scholarly biography of Kropotkin is Martin A. Miller, *Kropotkin* (Chicago: University of Chicago Press, 1976).

165. Avrich, *The Russian Anarchists*, pp. 152–254. This is the major history of the anarchists in the revolutionary period. See also Avrich's outstanding collection of documents: Paul Avrich, ed., *The Anarchists in the Russian Revolution* (Ithaca: Cornell University Press, 1973).

166. For an account of Kropotkin's last years in Russia, see Miller, *Kropotkin*, pp. 234–247.

167. Emma Goldman, in *Pamiati*, p. 120; N. M. Pirumova, *Petr Alekseevich Kropotkin* (Moscow: Nauka, 1972), pp. 190–192. This is a very informative biography.

168. Citing England's example, Kropotkin insisted that "social control" over production and supply were necessary to win the war: P. A. Kropotkin, *Pis'ma o tekushchikh sobytiakh* (Moscow: Zadruga, 1917 [cover: 1918]), pp. 92–111.

169. See Kropotkin's speech at the Moscow State Conference; excerpts are quoted in Pirumova, *Kropotkin*, pp. 192–194, and in Miller, *Kropotkin*, p. 236.

170. Pirumova, *Kropotkin*, p. 195. Pirumova quotes extensively from Kropotkin's diaries and letters. On Kropotkin's first, despairing, response to the coup, see Miller, *Kropotkin*, p. 238.

171. Miller, *Kropotkin*, p. 239; Pirumova, *Kropotkin*, p. 195; Goldman, *My Disillusionment*, p. 187.

172. Pirumova, *Kropotkin*, pp. 195–196; V. Ryzhkov, in *Pamiati*, p. 101.

173. For Kropotkin's life in Dmitrov, see Goldman, *My Disillusionment*, pp. 97–100, 186–189, and Miller, *Kropotkin*, pp. 239–243.

174. "Just like a saint [*nu priamo vot kak sviatoi*]," said one woman of Kropotkin: A. Shakhovskaia, in *Pamiati*, p. 105.

175. On the Dmitrov cooperative, see V. Sazonov and A. Shakovskaia in *Pamiati*, pp. 100–105; Pirumova, *Kropotkin*, pp. 204–207; and Miller, *Kropotkin*, pp. 242–243.

176. "The animal species in which individual struggle has been reduced to its narrowest limits and the practice of mutual aid has attained the greatest development are invariably the most numerous, the most prosperous, and the most open to further progress": Peter Kropotkin, *Mutual Aid: A Factory of Evolution*, ed. Paul Avrich (New York: New York University Press, 1972), p. 246. See Avrich's introduction in this volume for a discussion of the development of Kropotkin's theory.

177. Kropotkin, *Mutual Aid*, pp. 194–245.

178. Peter Kropotkin, "Message to the Workers of the West," in Avrich, *The Anarchists in the Russian Revolution*, p. 151.

179. *Kommunizm i anarkhiia* (Moscow: Izdanie gruppy osvobozhdennykh politicheskikh, 1917).

180. Ibid., pp. 21–28.

181. Kropotkin, "Message," pp. 150–152.

182. One meeting with Lenin is reported in V. D. Bonch-Bruevich, *Vospominaniia o Lenine* (Moscow: Nauka, 1969), pp. 442–447. It is not clear that the 1920 meeting took place, after Kropotkin's efforts to arrange it: see E. V. Starostin, "O strechakh V. I. Lenina i P. A. Kropotkina (K voprosu o datirovke)," in *Arkheograficheskii ezhegodnik za 1968 god* (Moscow: Nauka, 1970), pp. 225–229. See also Miller, *Kropotkin*, pp. 241–242.

183. V. A. Tvardovskaia writes that Kropotkin sent Lenin "about twenty letters": V. A. Tvardovskaia, "Predislovie," in P. A. Kropotkin, *Zapiski revoliutsionera* (Moscow: Mysl', 1966), p. 31. I wish to thank Paul Avrich for bringing this to my attention. Two of these were published in V. D. Bonch-Bruevich, "Moi vospominaniia o Petre Alekseeviche Kropotkine," *Zvezda* (Leningrad), no. 6 (1930), pp. 182–211, and are now available in Avrich, *The Anarchists in the Russian Revolution*, pp. 146–149. The remainder have not been made public by the Soviet government. Emma Goldman mentions two protests made by Kropotkin to the authorities: Goldman, *My Disillusionment*, pp. 188–189.

184. Kropotkin to Lenin, 4 March 1920, in Avrich, *The Anarchists in the Russian Revolution*, p. 146. Translations from this letter are from this source.

185. Ibid.

186. Ibid., pp. 146–148.

187. Kropotkin to Lenin, 21 December 1921, in Avrich, *The Anarchists in the Russian Revolution*, pp. 148–149.

188. P. A. Kropotkin, "Ideal v revoliutsii," in *Pamiati*, pp. 58–69.

189. Ibid., pp. 58–59.

190. This project was worthy of notice to the broader intelligentsia. When the Mensheviks were allowed to publish their newspaper in the beginning of 1919, Kropotkin's work on ethics was mentioned: *Vsegda vpered*, no. 13, 22 February 1919.

191. Kropotkin to Alexander Berkman, in *Pamiati*, p. 121.

192. Ibid.

193. P. A. Kropotkin, *Etika*, Vol. 1, *Proiskhozhdenie i razvitie nravstvennosti* (Peterburg-Moskva: Golos truda, 1922), p. 251.

194. Kropotkin to Berkman, in *Pamiati*, p. 121.

195. V. A. Tvardovskaia, "Predislovie," p. 31.

196. As Viktor Shklovskii pointed out in his *Sentimental Journey*, "During the first years of the revolution there wasn't a man alive who didn't experience periods of belief. . . . For whole minutes, you would believe in Bolshevism" (trans. Richard Sheldon [Ithaca: Cornell University Press, 1970], p. 240).

197. Goldman, *My Disillusionment*, pp. 36, 98.

198. Peter Kropotkin, "What to Do," in *Kropotkin's Revolutionary Pamphlets*, ed. Roger N. Baldwin (New York: Vanguard Press, 1927; reprint, New York: Dover Publications, 1970), pp. 256–259. This is an excellent collection of Kropotkin's works.

199. His visitors all testify that he never complained; see Goldman, *My Disillusionment*, pp. 97–100; N. A. Kropotkin, "Vospominaniia N. A. Kropotkina," in *Biulleten' Vserossiiskogo obshchestvennogo komiteta po uvekovecheniiu pamiati P. A. Kropotkina*, no. 2 (9 December 1924), pp. 19–20; *Pamiati*, pp. 100–105. His wife, Sofia Grigor'evna, who did most of the heavy labor, deserves credit as well; see I'lia Ginzburg, "Moe poslednee svidanie s P. A. Kropotkin," in *Pamiati*, p. 96; V. Ryzhkov, in *Pamiati*, pp. 103–104; Goldman, *My Disillusionment*, p. 97.

200. "Kronshtadt i demokratiia," *Revoliutsionnaia Rossiia*, no. 5 (April 1921), pp. 4–6.

201. Ibid.

202. Ibid.

203. "Uroki Kronshtadt," *Revoliutsionnaia Rossia*, no. 5 (April 1921), pp. 1–2.

204. Viktor Chernov, "Desiatyi sovet PSR," *Revoliutsionnaia Rossiia*, no. 11 (August 1921), p. 2.

205. See the call to correspondents to submit material in *Revoliutsionnaia Rossiia*, no. 2 (January 1921).

206. See Chernov's letter to *Sotsialisticheskii vestnik*, "Pis'mo v redaktsiiu," *Sotsialisticheskii vestnik*, no. 17(39) (8 September 1922), p. 14, and for Martov's side, see his "Neosnovatel'nye pretenzii," *Sotsialisticheskii vestnik*, no. 10(32) (16 May 1922), pp. 9–10, and his analysis of the SRs in the revolution, "Nekotorye itogi," *Sotsialisticheskii vestnik*, no. 17(34) (8 September 1922), pp. 1–4.

207. See, among many other articles, "Stikhiia revoliutsii i politicheskie trezvenniki," *Revoliutsionnaia Rossiia*, no. 12–13 (September–October 1921), pp. 3–10; "Iz itogov proshlogo opyta," *Revoliutsionnaia Rossiia*, no. 23 (December 1922), pp. 3–12; "Tezisy V. M. Chernova po obshche-politicheskim voprosam," *Revoliutsionnaia Rossiia*, no. 24–25 (January–February 1923), pp. 24–25.

208. "Fazy sotsializma," *Revoliutsionnaia Rossiia*, no. 1 (25 December 1920), pp. 11–15.

209. "Osnovnye motivy 'gil'deiskogo sotsializma'," *Revoliutsionnaia Rossiia*, no. 6 (April 1921), pp. 11–14.

210. "Vosstanovlenie internatsionala," *Revoliutsionnaia Rossiia*, no. 2 (January 1921), pp. 10–11.

211. "Osnovnye motivy 'gil'deiskogo sotsializma'," *Revoliutsionnaia Rossiia*, no. 6 (April 1921), p. 14.

212. This version of Chernov's "synthesis" differed from his prerevolutionary program in that he no longer regarded Russia's revolutionary movement as funda-

mentally different from the struggle based on advanced capitalism in the countries of the West. He was now concerned with a universal socialist order that would unite agrarian and industrial nations. In other words, Chernov's prerevolutionary idea of the united struggle of peasants and industrial workers in Russia was extended to the world, and the orthodox idea of an industrial path to socialism was dropped.

213. On the peasant rebellions, see Oliver H. Radkey's study, *The Unknown Civil War in Soviet Russia* (Stanford: Hoover Institution Press, 1976). A list of peasant uprisings from 1918 through 1921 is provided in Jan M. Meijer, "Town and Country in the Civil War," in Richard Pipes, ed., *Revolutionary Russia* (Cambridge, Mass.: Harvard University Press, 1968), pp. 276–277.

214. Lenin, *Polnoe sobranie sochinenii*, 45:282.

215. See Radkey's careful examination of the SRs' role in the rebellion in his *Unknown Civil War*, pp. 111–127.

216. "Zadachi i metody raboty P.S.R. v derevne," Nicolaevsky Collection, no. 7, box 1, folio 8.

217. "Beseda s V. M. Chernovym," *Poslednie novosti*, no. 320, 8 June 1921.

218. Lazar Volin, *A Century of Russian Agriculture* (Cambridge, Mass.: Harvard University Press, 1970), p. 173.

219. Benjamin Weissman, *Herbert Hoover and Famine Relief to Soviet Russia: 1921–1923* (Stanford: Hoover Institution Press, 1974), p. 6. The estimates of the number of people affected vary; see Weissman, *Hoover*, pp. 3–7, and Volin, *Century*, p. 174.

220. "Ko vsem grazhdanam" and "K demokratii Evropy i Ameriki," both in *Revoliutsionnaia Rossiia*, no. 10 (July 1921).

221. He quoted *Novyi mir*'s description of the impressions of visiting Comintern delegates: Viktor Chernov, "Vokrug goloda," *Revoliutsionnaia Rossiia*, no. 11 (August 1921), p. 14.

222. Ibid., pp. 14–20. For the PSR's analysis of NEP, see "Ko vsem chlenam partii," *Revoliutsionnaia Rossiia*, no. 10 (July 1921), pp. 10–13. On the All-Russian Famine Relief Committee, see Weissman, *Hoover*, pp. 12–16, 75–77, 92–93.

223. This was at Lenin's orders; see his letter to Stalin, cited in Weissman, pp. 75–76; Mark Vishniak, "Na rodine (Tikhaia smert')," *Sovremennye zapiski*, 7 (5 October 1921), p. 384.

224. "Na rodine (Tikhaia smert')," *Sovremennye zapiski*, 7 (5 October 1921), pp. 368–373.

225. Ibid., pp. 386–391. Despite Vishniak's scepticism, Western aid—in particular Herbert Hoover's American Relief Administration—did play a critical role in famine relief. The Soviet government credited the ARA with saving ten million lives: Weissman, *Hoover*, p. 199.

226. "Na rodine (Ekonomicheskii realizm)," *Sovremennye zapiski*, 8 (December 1921), p. 347.

227. Lenin, *Polnoe sobranie sochinenii*, 43:241, 242. See above, p. 61.

228. See the letter of the Central Organizational Bureau of the PSR, 8 June 1921 on the destruction of the central party organs, Nicolaevsky Collection, no. 7, box 1, folio 12.

229. Jansen, *Show Trial*, pp. 23, 27.

230. Ibid., pp. 54–55, 83–104.

231. Ibid., pp. 47–50, 60–62; *The Twelve Who Are To Die: The Trial of the Socialist Revolutionaries in Moscow* (Berlin: The Delegation of the Party of Socialist-Revolutionaries, 1922), pp. 50–52.

232. Lenin, *Polnoe sobranie sochinenii*, 44:399; see also Jansen, *Show Trial*, p. 27.

233. Lenin, *Polnoe sobranie sochinenii*, 44:396; also cited in Jansen, *Show Trial*, p. 27.

234. *The Twelve*, pp. 42–50; Jansen provides a detailed description of the propaganda campaign: Jansen, *Show Trial*, pp. 66–70, 141–155.

235. *The Twelve*, pp. 57–60; Jansen, *Show Trial*, pp. 70–75.

236. The SRs abroad were instrumental in bringing the trial to the attention of Western socialists; see Jansen, *Show Trial*, pp. 30–39.

237. This was the title of his article on Radek's and Bukharin's "mistakes": Lenin, *Polnoe sobranie sochinenii*, 45:140–144.

238. He led the hostile demonstration with which the socialists were met when they arrived in Moscow: see *The Twelve*, p. 42, and Jansen, *Show Trial*, p. 56. In the propaganda campaign associated with the trial, European socialism, Menshevism, the PSR, and Russian liberals were all identified as one, allied, enemy: see Jansen, *Show Trial*, pp. 152–155.

239. *The Twelve*, pp. 52–56; Jansen, *Show Trial*, pp. 64–66.

240. Jansen, *Show Trial*, pp. 135–139; Julius Braunthal, *Geschichte der Internationale*, 3 vols. (Hannover: J. H. W. Dietz, 1963), 2:269, note 2.

241. See Jansen, *Show Trial*, pp. 173–185, for an account of the fate of the individual defendants and of others connected with the trial.

242. The PSR also withdrew from the Second International; see *Revoliutsionnaia Rossiia*, no. 8 (May 1921).

243. *Revoliutsionnaia Rossiia* lasted until 1931. In the last number, Chernov memorialized the thirtieth year since its first appearance in the struggle against the autocracy: Viktor Chernov, "Vmesto iubileia," *Revoliutsionnaia Rossiia*, no. 77–78 (February–March 1931), p. 32.

244. "Tezisy V. M. Chernova. Po obshche-politicheskim voprosam," *Revoliutsionnaia Rossiia*, no. 24–25 (January–February 1923), pp. 24–25. See also Chernov's summary of the PSR's experience in the revolution in "Voprosy taktiki: Iz itogov proshlogo opyta," *Revoliutsionnaia Rossiia*, no. 23 (December 1922), pp. 3–12.

245. Maiskii, *Demokraticheskaia kontr-revoliutsiia*, p. 113.

246. Kropotkin, *Kommunizm i anarkhiia*, frontispiece. Kropotkin's Russian version of John Henry McKay's poem was a free translation: "Why am I an anarchist? I do not covet lordship for myself, nor slavery do I want." I thank Paul Avrich for identifying the original poem.

247. Cited in M. Vishniak, "Na rodine," *Sovremennye zapiski*, 11 (July 1922), pp. 366–367.

Chapter 3

1. Marc Ferro, *La révolution de 1917*, 2 vols. (Paris: Auber, 1967–1976), 2:423. The papers were shut down even before the formation of the Bolshevik government. See also *Novaia zhizn'*, no. 164(158), 27 October (9 November) 1917, and no. 185(179), 19 November (2 December) 1917.

2. William G. Rosenberg, *Liberals in the Russian Revolution: The Constitutional*

Democratic Party, 1917–1921 (Princeton: Princeton University Press, 1974), pp. 275–281. Rosenberg's study provides a comprehensive and thoughtful account of the Kadet party during the revolution and the civil war. The arrests of the Kadet leaders were part of a general campaign against the Bolsheviks' political opponents, especially those involved in the organization of the Constituent Assembly; see Mark Vishniak, *Dan' proshlomu* (New York: Izdatel'stvo imeni Chekhova, 1954), pp. 323–334.

3. Panina was convicted, but the trial was a political flop. Workers and many social organizations came to her defense and effectively refuted the charge of "class enemy"; see Rosenberg, *Liberals*, pp. 279–281.

4. An account of the murder, by Shingarev's sister Aleksandra Ivanovna Shingareva who was in the hospital shortly before the killings, is in A. I. Shingarev, *Kak eto bylo: Dnevnik A. I. Shingareva* (Moscow: Izdatel'stvo Komiteta po uvekovecheniiu pamiati F. F. Kokoshkina i A. I. Shingareva, 1918; reprint ed., Royal Oak, Mi.: Strathcona Publishing Co., 1978), pp. 61–68.

5. Shingarev, who had been a country doctor, was a minister in the Provisional Government until July and a member of the Kadet Central Committee. His wife had died in the fall of 1917, distraught after a peasant raid upon their home. See Rosenberg, *Liberals*, p. 234.

6. On various aspects of liberalism in Russia, see the articles in Charles E. Timberlake, ed., *Essays on Russian Liberalism* (Columbia, Mo.: University of Missouri Press, 1972). The origins of Russian liberalism are the subjects of George Fischer, *Russian Liberalism: From Gentry to Intelligentsia* (Cambridge, Mass.: Harvard University Press, 1958); Shmuel Galai, *The Liberation Movement in Russia: 1900–1905* (Cambridge: At the University Press, 1973); and Victor Leontovitsch, *Geschichte des Liberalismus in Russland* (Frankfurt am Main: Vittorio Klostermann, 1957). Raymond Pearson's *The Russian Moderates and the Crisis of Tsarism: 1914–1917* (London, Macmillan & Co., 1977) examines Kadet politics during the war. For an excellent sketch of Kadet attitudes after the February revolution, see Thomas Riha's "1917—A Year of Illusions," *Soviet Studies*, 19, no. 1 (July 1967), 115–121.

7. See Rosenberg, *Liberals*, pp. 32–44, for the party's various disputes before the revolution. The Kadet's lack of "discipline" is a theme of this study.

8. The history of these committees and of individual Kadets in this period is in Rosenberg, *Liberals*, pp. 263–445.

9. Rosenberg, *Liberals*, p. 430, and Richard Pipes, *Struve: Liberal on the Right, 1905–1944* (Cambridge, Mass.: Harvard University Press, 1980), p. 265. See the report of the executions in *Russkaia zhizn'* (Helsinki), no. 181, 8 October 1919.

10. For Struve's life and thought, see Richard Pipes's two-volume study: *Struve: Liberal on the Left, 1870–1905* (Cambridge, Mass.: Harvard University Press, 1970) and *Struve: Liberal on the Right, 1905–1944* (Cambridge, Mass.: Harvard University Press, 1980). Miliukov is the subject of his autobiography: P. N. Miliukov, *Vospominaniia (1859–1917)*, ed. M. M. Karpovich and B. I. El'kin, 2 vols. (New York: Izdatel'stvo imeni Chekhova, 1955), and of Thomas Riha, *A Russian European: Paul Miliukov in Russian Politics* (Notre Dame: University of Notre Dame Press, 1969). A comprehensive bibliography of Struve's writings is in Pipes, *Struve: Liberal on the Right*, pp. 470–508, and a list of Miliukov's publications through 1930 is in S. A. Smirnov et al., eds., *P. N. Miliukov: Sbornik*

materialov po chestvovaniu ego semidesiatiletiia, 1859–1929 (Paris, 1929), pp. 313–351.

11. Their disputes—over the breadth of the liberation movement, policy toward the army during the Russo-Japanese War, and the nationalities problem—presaged their positions after the revolution; see Pipes, *Struve: Liberal on the Left*, pp. 317–318, 342, 365.

12. "Intelligentsiia i revoliutsiia," *Vekhi: Sbornik statei o russkoi intelligentsii* (Moscow, 1909; reprint ed., Frankfurt a.M.: Posev, 1967), pp. 156–174.

13. Pipes, *Struve: Liberal on the Right*, pp. 218–219.

14. S. L. Frank, *Biografiia P. B. Struve* (New York: Izdatel'stvo imeni Chekhova, 1956), pp. 112–113; Riha, *Russian European*, pp. 287–289.

15. For the history of this work, see Miliukov's introduction: P. N. Miliukov, *Istoriia vtoroi russkoi revoliutsii*, 3 vols. (Sofia: Rossiisko-bolgarskoe knigoizdatel'stvo, 1921–1924), 1:3, and "M. Miliukov's Statements," *The Russian Commonwealth*, 1, no. 5–6 (20 January 1919), 140. All three volumes were labeled "issues" (*vypuski*) of a "first volume," but Miliukov did not publish any continuation. The first "*vypusk*" has been translated into English: Paul N. Miliukov, *The Russian Revolution*, ed. Richard Stites, trans. Tatyana and Richard Stites (Gulf Breeze, Fla.: Academic International Press, 1978).

16. The first revolution was that of 1905.

17. Miliukov, *Istoriia*, 1:4.

18. Ibid. Here Miliukov, as was his habit, referred to himself in the third person.

19. Ibid., 1:22.

20. Ibid., 1:117.

21. Ibid., 1:57.

22. Ibid., 1:59, 66–70, 122.

23. Ibid., 1:122.

24. Ibid., 1:117, 122.

25. Ibid., 2:9; 3:3–7.

26. Ibid., 2:9–10.

27. Ibid., 2:9.

28. Ibid., 3:184, 187.

29. Ibid., 1:122.

30. Ibid.

31. Ibid., 1:119.

32. Ibid., 1:12.

33. Ibid., 1:11–20.

34. Ibid., 3:256.

35. Ibid., 1:211.

36. Ibid., 1:16.

37. Ibid., 2:8.

38. Ibid., 1:248.

39. Ibid., 2:10.

40. See Miliukov's memoirs for his estimation of Comte: *Vospominaniia*, 1:86–89.

41. Miliukov, *Istoriia*, 3:186.

42. On November 17, before the Kadets were outlawed, sailors came to Miliukov's apartment to arrest him: Rosenberg, *Liberals*, p. 275. Miliukov's career after the

Bolshevik seizure of power is described in this study; see especially pp. 275, 277, 308–321.

43. On the Volunteer Army and Miliukov's relations with it, see Peter Kenez, *Civil War in South Russia, 1918* (Berkeley: University of California Press, 1971), especially pp. 76, 162–164.
44. On the "Ice March," see Kenez, *Civil War, 1918*, pp. 96–132.
45. See Rosenberg, *Liberals*, pp. 313–315, and Miliukov's careful accounting in an interview with the foreign press: "M. Miliukov's Statements," p. 140.
46. P. N. Miliukov, "Dnevnik," 29 May (10 June)–11 (24) July, 1918, Miliukov Collection, Bakhmeteff Archive, Columbia University, New York. The "diary" is a text transcribed from Miliukov's notebooks by A. Vel'min. I am grateful to Stephen Corrsin, former curator of the Bakhmeteff Archive, for this information.
47. Among other fallings out, Miliukov's German strategy precipitated a break with M. M. Vinaver, his long-time partner in party politics; see Rosenberg, *Liberals*, pp. 319, 320.
48. See Kenez, *Civil War, 1918*, p. 162, and "M. Miliukov's Statements," pp. 138–140.
49. Miliukov, "Dnevnik," 4 (17) June 1918; "M. Miliukov's Statements," pp. 138–140.
50. See his comments to Astrov and Panina in "Dnevnik," 9 (22) September 1918.
51. See Rosenberg, *Liberals*, pp. 328, 350.
52. Miliukov, *Istoriia*, 1:3.
53. Pavel Dmitrievich Dolgorukov, *Velikaia razrukha* (Madrid, 1964), p. 119.
54. See Miliukov, "Dnevnik," from September through November 1918.
55. Miliukov, "Dnevnik," 8, 9 September 1918.
56. Ibid., 21 October (3 November) 1918.
57. Ibid., 31 August (13 September) 1918, 16 (29) October 1918. On the Kadets' politics in the Ukraine, and Miliukov's activities there, see Rosenberg, *Liberals*, pp. 314–332.
58. Rosenberg, *Liberals*, pp. 351–352. On the conference, see Robert H. McNeal, "The Conference of Jassy: An Early Fiasco of the Anti-Bolshevik Movement," in John Shelton Curtiss, ed., *Essays in Russian and Soviet History* (New York: Columbia University Press, 1962), pp. 221–236.
59. Miliukov's pro-German stance caused him difficulties in his early dealings with the Allies; see his justification in "M. Miliukov's Statements," pp. 138–140.
60. Riha, *Russian European*, p. 347.
61. See his appointment book and collection of clippings in the Miliukov Collection, Bakhmeteff Archive.
62. A partial bibliography for this period is in S. A. Smirnov et al., eds., *P. N. Miliukov: Sbornik materialov*, pp. 335–339.
63. See the committee's pamphlets, for example, Dioneo (I. V. Shklovskii), *Russia under the Bolsheviks* (London: Russian Liberation Committee, [1919]), cover.
64. See the advertisement for the committee's pamphlets in the *Supplement* to the *Bulletin of the Russian Liberation Committee*, no. 19 (30 June 1919).
65. At the encouragement of D. Dickinson, the Russian Liberation Committee's contact in the Foreign Office, a few copies of the committee's pamphlets were ordered by the War Office for propaganda purposes; see the correspondence in the Records of the Foreign Office: F.O.395/276: files 9/1678, 1746, 1782, 2059,

2347, 3214; 118/2363, Public Record Office, Kew. On the basis of its role as a "non-profit making anti-Bolshevik propaganda society," the Russian Liberation Committee claimed an exemption from income taxes in 1920 and was, apparently, turned down: F.O. 371/4057, file 203659.

66. London: George Allen & Unwin, 1920.
67. Miliukov, *Bolshevism*, pp. 19–22.
68. Ibid., pp. 22–30.
69. Ibid., pp. 28–30.
70. Ibid., pp. 19, 31–33.
71. Ibid., pp. 6–7.
72. Ibid., pp. 9–10.
73. Ibid., pp. 56–59, 63, 83, 99–105.
74. Ibid., p. 159.
75. Ibid., p. 126.
76. Ibid., pp. 101, 115, 116, 176.
77. Ibid., pp. 81–82.
78. Ibid., p. 189.
79. Ibid., pp. 295–298.
80. Ibid., p. 297.
81. Ibid., p. 299.
82. Ibid., p. 303.
83. Ibid.
84. Struve to Denikin, 11 November 1919, Denikin Collection, Bakhmeteff Archive.
85. For an elaboration of Struve's conception of patriotism, see his "Natsional'nyi eros i ideia gosudarstvo, *Russkaia mysl'* (January 1917), pp. 99–104 (*Col. Works*, no. 517). Struve's writings have been published in P. B. Struve *Collected Works in Fifteen Volumes*, ed. Richard Pipes (Ann Arbor: University Microfilms, 1970). The pagination of this photographically reproduced collection conforms to that of the original works. My citations are to the original editions, with the volume and item number in the *Collected Works* included in each first reference.
86. "V chem revoliutsiia i kontr-revoliutsiia?," *Russkaia mysl'* (November–December 1917), part 2, pp. 57–58 (*Col. Works*, 11, no. 532).
87. Ibid., pp. 58–60.
88. Ibid., p. 60.
89. Ibid., pp. 60–61.
90. Ibid., p. 60.
91. See Pipes, *Struve: Liberal on the Left*, especially pp. 208–233, for the history of Struve's intellectual accomplishments and transformation before 1905.
92. See Pipes, *Struve: Liberal on the Right*, pp. 66–114, 169–198.
93. Struve, "Nasha zadacha," *Russkaia svoboda*, no. 1 (March–April 1917), pp. 4–5 (*Col. Works*, 11, no. 519). Struve's articles in *Russkaia svoboda* anticipated many of his writings after October; see especially "Illiuzii russkikh sotsialistov," *Russkaia svoboda*, no. 7 (7 June 1917), pp. 3–6 (*Col. Works*, 11, no. 526), and "Rossii nuzhno organizovannoe patrioticheskoe dvizhenie," *Russkaia svoboda*, no. 9 (21 June 1917), pp. 26–29 (*Col. Works*, 11, no. 529).
94. See Struve's speech on the league: Petr Struve, "Neskol'ko slov o Lige russkoi kul'tury," *Russkaia svoboda*, no. 9 (21 June 1917), pp. 24–26 (*Col. Works*, 11, no. 528).

95. Pipes, *Struve: Liberal on the Right*, pp. 245–257. The last number of *Russkaia svoboda* was printed in October 1917: *Russkaia svoboda*, no. 24–25 (October 1917).

96. S. L. Frank, *Biografiia P. B. Struve* (New York: Izdatel'stvo imeni Chekhova, 1956), p. 120.

97. S. A. Askol'dov et al., *Iz glubiny: Sbornik statei o russkoi intelligentsii*, 2nd ed. (Paris: YMCA Press, 1967).

98. Frank, *Biografiia Struve*, pp. 120–121.

99. Nicholas Berdiaev brought one copy with him to Europe; another was obtained by a Dutch scholar: Frank, *Biografiia Struve*, p. 121. A "second" edition was printed by the YMCA Press in Paris in 1967 and has been widely circulated. For *Iz glubiny*'s checkered history, see Pipes, *Struve: Liberal on the Right*, pp. 257–258.

100. Frank's account suggests that it was the authors, or some of them, who decided not to distribute the book in 1918. When Frank learned in 1921 that the book had been made available in Moscow by the printers of the Kushnarev firm—"*izvestie dovol'no zhutkoe po tomu vremeni*"—he feared for the safety of the contributors who were still in Russia: Frank, *Biografiia Struve*, pp. 120–121.

101. Petr Struve, "Istoricheskii smysl russkoi revoliutsii i natsional'nye zadachi," in Askol'dov, *Iz glubiny*, pp. 290–291 (*Col. Works* 11, no 539.)

102. Ibid., p. 291.

103. Ibid.

104. Ibid., pp. 291–292.

105. Ibid., pp. 293–295.

106. Ibid.

107. See his article "Intelligentsiia i revoliutsiia," in *Vekhi*, pp. 156–174.

108. Struve, "Istoricheskii smysl," p. 297.

109. Ibid., p. 298.

110. Ibid., p. 299.

111. Ibid.

112. Ibid., pp. 301–302.

113. On these brilliant investigations, see Pipes, *Struve: Liberal on the Left*, pp. 156–163.

114. Struve, "Istoricheskii smysl," p. 300.

115. Ibid., pp. 300–301.

116. Ibid., pp. 301–303.

117. Ibid., p. 303.

118. Ibid., pp. 303–305.

119. Ibid., p. 305.

120. For Struve's activities, see Pipes, *Struve: Liberal on the Right*, pp. 259–278.

121. Struve was influential in convincing Denikin to recognize Kolchak as supreme commander of the White forces, in the interest of gaining Allied support for the anti-Bolshevik military: Pipes, *Struve: Liberal on the Right*, pp. 277–278.

122. See, for example, his "Natsionalizm," *Velikaia Rossia*, no. 335, 1 (14) November 1919.

123. Razmyshleniia o russkoi revoliutsii," *Russkaia mysl'* (January–February 1921), pp. 6–37 (*Col. Works*, 11, no. 541.)

124. Ibid., pp. 9–12.

125. Ibid., pp. 13, 14.

126. Ibid., pp. 17–19.
127. Ibid., p. 14.
128. Ibid., pp. 14, 15.
129. Ibid., p. 19.
130. Ibid.
131. Ibid.
132. Ibid., pp. 19–20.
133. The Russian socialists generally excoriated Struve as a reactionary and dismissed his ideas on this basis. But Potresov belatedly recognized Struve's personal and intellectual qualities: Pipes, *Struve: Liberal on the Right*, pp. 429–430.
134. Struve, "Razmyshleniia," pp. 28–33.
135. Ibid., pp. 33, 34.
136. Ibid., p. 20.
137. Ibid., pp. 22, 35, 36.
138. Ibid., p. 36.
139. Ibid., pp. 23–27.
140. Prince Dmitrii Pozharskii and Kuz'ma Minin are heroic figures in the history of the seventeenth-century "national movement."
141. "Smysl proisshedshogo na iuge Rossii," Miliukov Collection, Bakhmeteff Archive, pp. 1–2.
142. Ibid.
143. Ibid.
144. "Istoriko-politicheskie zametki o sovremennosti," *Russkaia mysl'* (May–June 1921), p. 213 (*Col. Works*, 12, no. 548).
145. Struve, "Smysl," pp. 3, 4.
146. For Struve's role in Wrangel's service, see Pipes, *Struve: Liberal on the Right*, pp. 280–296.
147. Pipes, *Struve: Liberal on the Right*, p. 335.
148. "K starym i novym chitateliam 'Russkoi mysli'," *Russkaia mysl'* (January–February 1921), pp. 3–4 (*Col. Works*, 12, no. 544).
149. Ibid., pp. 4–5.
150. "Itogi i sushchestvo kommunisticheskogo khoziaistva," (n.p., n.d.) ["Rech', proiznesennaia na obshchem s"ezde predstavitelei russkoi promyshlennosti i torgovli v Parizhe 17 maia 1921 goda"], pp. 13–15 (*Col. Works*, 12, no. 549). To those who objected that Russian conditions, and not socialism, were on trial, Struve responded that the attempt to establish socialism in Russia had been far "too serious and too profound" to be seen as a historical exception. The results of the experiment, as well, were too overwhelming to be blamed on the Russian peasant, the backward worker, the blockade, or other such factors (*op. cit.*, pp. 15–16).
151. Struve, "Itogi," pp. 16–17.
152. Ibid., p. 17.
153. Ibid., pp. 12, 18, 24–27.
154. Ibid., p. 27.
155. Ibid., pp. 4–6.
156. Petr Struve, "Golod," *Russkaia mysl'* (August–September 1921), p. 279 (*Col. Works*, 12, no. 550).
157. Struve, "Itogi," pp. 6–10.

158. Ibid., pp. 7–9.
159. Ibid., pp. 10–13.
160. Ibid., pp. 12, 13.
161. Ibid., pp. 19–23.
162. "Istoriko-politicheskie zametki o sovremennosti," *Russkaia mysl'* (October–December 1921), p. 319 (*Col. Works*, 12, no. 548).
163. "Istoriko-politicheskie zametki," pp. 318–320. In this article, Struve cited Walther Rathenau's ideas on socialism as the most significant development in Marxist theory and noted that they corresponded to the ideology that Marx had labeled "utopian socialism."
164. "Itogi," pp. 28–30.
165. Ibid., pp. 30–31.
166. "Smysl," p. 3.
167. Petr Struve, "Rossiia," *Russkaia mysl'* (March 1922), pp. 109, 110 (*Col. Works*, 12, no. 558).
168. See Pipes, *Liberal on the Left*, pp. 223–233, for Struve's break with Marxist orthodoxy.
169. Petr Struve, "Sotsializm," *Russkaia mysl'* (June–July 1922), pp. 286–288 (*Col. Works*, 12, no. 565).
170. Struve, "Rossiia," p. 108.
171. "[One's] attitude to the Russian revolution is a particular case of [one's] attitude to sin and depravity in general," Struve asserted in "Dvenadtsat' Aleksandra Bloka," *Russkaia mysl'* (January–February 1921), p. 233 (*Col. Works*, 12, no. 547).
172. Petr Struve, "Proshloe, nastoiashchee, budushchee: Mysli o natsional'nom vozrozhdenii Rossii," *Russkaia mysl'* (January–February 1922), p. 223 (*Col. Works*, 12, no. 556).
173. Ibid.
174. Petr Struve, "Oshibki i sofizmy 'istoricheskogo' vzgliada na revoliutsiiu: Po povodu stat'i K. I. Zaitseva," *Russkaia mysl'* (March 1922), p. 162 (*Col. Works*, 12, no. 559.).
175. Struve, "Proshloe," p. 223.
176. Ibid., p. 226.
177. Petr Struve, "Le bolchevisme et Lénine," in M. G. Kliuchnikov, ed., *La Russie d'aujourd'hui et de demain* (Paris: Attinger Frères, 1920), pp. 123–127 (*Col. Works*, 11, no. 543).
178. Struve, "Proshloe,", pp. 226–227.
179. See Pipes, *Struve: Liberal on the Left*, pp. 53, 54, 185–189, 295, and Pipes, Struve: Liberal on the Right, pp. 446, 447.
180. Struve, "Proshloe," pp. 224, 227.
181. Ibid., pp. 224, 225.
182. Struve, "Rossiia," pp. 102–104.
183. See, for example, his analysis of the *Smena vekh* movement and Eurasianism in "Proshloe," pp. 227–229, and in "Rossiia," pp. 104–106.
184. *Struve: Liberal on the Right*, p. 298. See this work, pp. 445–456, for a sympathetic discussion of Struve's life and work.
185. Struve, "Proshloe," pp. 226, 227.
186. Ibid., p. 224.

187. Struve, "Sotsializm," pp. 292–293.
188. Ibid., pp. 296–297, 300–301.
189. See, for example, his "Review of the Week," *The New Russia*, 2, no. 14 (6 May 1920), pp. 1–4.
190. "To Our Readers," *The New Russia*, 1, no. 1 (5 February 1920), p. 1. On the decision to expand the *Bulletin* into a journal, see the *Bulletin of the Russian Liberation Committee*, Supplement to no. 52 (21 February 1920). "We presumed," Miliukov wrote here, "that the reader, by attentively studying the facts and figures put before him, would come to the logical conclusion that Bolshevism leads to the complete destruction of democracy, to the destruction of the foundations of social and economic life, and that it is accompanied by unheard of brutality and tyranny on the part of a group of fanatical demagogues, intoxicated with power. . . . [But] mere information has proved to be insufficient. It is now necessary to state the Russian problem in full, and to illuminate it from every point of view, and likewise to discover the principal objects of the Allies' Russian policy."
191. Miliukov, "To Our Readers," pp. 1–2.
192. Published in *The New Russia*, 1, nos. 7–9 (18 March, 25 March, 1 April 1920).
193. A year later Miliukov wrote that Struve's "letter to General Wrangel of January 1920" [the memorandum entitled "Smysl proisshedshego na iuge Rossii"] had changed his opinion of the Volunteer Army ("Ne po sushchestvu: Otvet P. B. Struve," *Poslednie novosti*, no. 312, 26 April 1921); see Pipes, *Struve: Liberal on the Right*, p. 330.
194. "Review of the Week," *The New Russia*, 1, no. 10 (8 April 1920), pp. 290–293.
195. Ibid., p. 292.
196. Ibid., pp. 293–294.
197. Ibid., p. 294. Citations from *The New Russia* are not translated; English was one of Miliukov's dozen (or so) languages: Andrei Sedykh, *Dalekie, blizkie*, 3rd ed. (New York: Izdanie "Novogo russkogo slova," 1979), p. 154; M. Aldanov, "Pamiati P. N. Miliukova," *Novyi zhurnal*, 5 (1943), 341.
198. "Review of the Week," *The New Russia*, 2, no. 14 (6 May 1920), pp. 2–3.
199. "Review of the Week," *The New Russia*, 2, no. 24 (15 July 1920), p. 327. Poland was always a sore point for Miliukov. He argued consistently for a Great Russian solution to boundary questions after the war. See "Consideration of the Russian Political Conference in Paris upon the Eastern Frontiers of Poland and Peace in Europe," *Bulletin of the Russian Liberation Committee*, no. 6 (31 March 1919); Paul Miliukov, *The Case for Bessarabia* (London: Russian Liberation Committee, no. 8 [1919]); *Memorandum on the Finnish Question* ([London: Russian Liberation Committee, no. 2], n.d.), probably written by Miliukov; *Memorandum on the Baltic Provinces Question* (London: Russian Liberation Committee, no. 10, n.d.), "by the author of 'The Finnish Question'."
200. "Review of the Week," *The New Russia*, 2, no. 24 (15 July 1920), pp. 326–327.
201. "Review of the Week," *The New Russia*, 1, no. 10 (8 April 1920), p. 295.
202. Ibid., pp. 295–296.
203. The French government's recognition of Wrangel in August 1920 was, from Miliukov's point of view, the one bright spot on the Allies' reputation that year; see "Review of the Week," *The New Russia*, 2, no. 29 (19 August 1920), pp. 481–483. Miliukov's comments on France and the United States became more positive as his confidence in Great Britain eroded.

204. For Miliukov's first trip to Paris in 1920, see Miliukov, "Dnevnik," 14–25 April 1920.
205. "Facts and Documents," *The New Russia*, 2, no. 17 (27 May 1920), pp. 123–124.
206. Ibid.
207. "Review of the Week," *The New Russia*, 2, no. 23 (8 July 1920), p. 293.
208. *The New Russia* ceased publication with the 16 December 1920 issue; see the declaration of the Russian Liberation Committee in this issue, 3 no. 46, pp. 1–2. Miliukov traveled back and forth between London and Paris until 1921, when he settled in Paris. He lived in France for the rest of his life.
209. The text of the program is published as "Chto delat' posle krymskoi katastrofy," in P. N. Miliukov, *Emigratsiia po pereput'e* (Paris: Izdanie Resp.-Dem. Ob''ed., 1926), The date of the speech indicated in this publication—27 December 1920—is incorrect; see the text in *Poslednie novosti*, no. 374, 7 July 1921, and Miliukov, *Istoriia*, 1:7, suggesting that Miliukov was in London on December 27.
210. "Chto delat'," pp. 132–136.
211. See "Facts and Documents," *The New Russia*, 2, no. 17 (27 May 1920), pp. 123–124.
212. "Review of the Week," *The New Russia*, 1, no. 10 (8 April 1920), p. 296.
213. "Chto delat'," pp. 132–134.
214. "Chto delat'," p. 136.
215. Miliukov, *Istoriia*, 1:6.
216. Ibid., pp. 6–7.
217. Paul Miliukov, "Leo Tolstoy and the Russian People," *The New Russia*, 3, no. 45 (9 December 1920), p. 461. The "signs" were not specified.
218. "Chto delat'," p. 136.
219. See "Review of the Week," *The New Russia*, 1, no. 10 (8 April 1920), pp. 296–297. On Miliukov's association with the SRs, see Rosenberg, *Liberals*, pp. 446–454.
220. See Rosenberg, *Liberals*, pp. 450–451, and above, pp. 57–58, 84.
221. On the editorial board with Miliukov were M. M. Vinaver, A. I. Konovalov, and I. A. Kharlamov. *Poslednie novosti* was the leading émigré newspaper until its demise during World War II. On the end of *Poslednie novosti*, see "N. P. Vakar's unedited account of his flight from Paris," a manuscript lent to me by his daughter Catherine Chvany.
222. On *Rech'*, see T. Riha, "*Riech'*: A Portrait of a Russian Newspaper," *Slavic Review*, 22 (1963), 663–682.
223. "Nashi zadachi," *Poslednie novosti*, no. 264, 1 March 1921, p. 1.
224. "Germanskie den'gi u Lenina," *Poslednie novosti*, no. 293, 3 April 1921.
225. "Nashi raznoglasiia," *Poslednie novosti*, no. 270, 8 March 1921, p. 2.
226. "Chto delat'," p. 132.
227. On the disintegration of the Kadet party, see Rosenberg, *Liberals*, pp. 445–461; Robert C. Williams, *Culture in Exile: Russian Emigrés in Germany, 1881–1941* (Ithaca: Cornell University Press, 1972), pp. 222–225; Dolgorukov, *Velikaia razrukha*, pp. 212–215.
228. On the National Congress, see Pipes, *Struve: Liberal on the Right*, pp. 340–344.
229. Paul N. Miliukov, *Russia To-day and To-morrow* (New York: Macmillan Company, 1922), pp. vii, ix–x.

230. Miliukov, *Russia To-Day*, p. vii.
231. Ibid., pp. viii, ix.
232. Miliukov, *Istoriia*, 1:16.
233. Miliukov, *Russia To-day*, pp. 11, 17.
234. Ibid., p. 43.
235. Ibid., p. 17.
236. Ibid., p. 153.
237. Ibid., p. 141.
238. Miliukov, "Dnevnik," 17(30) October 1918.
239. Miliukov, *Istoriia*, 1:11.
240. Miliukov, *Russia To-day*, p. 7.
241. Ibid., pp. 24–25, 29, 37, 53.
242. Ibid., pp. 60–62, 70.
243. Ibid., p. 52.
244. Ibid., pp. 117–120.
245. Ibid., p. 189.
246. Ibid.
247. Ibid., pp. 189–227.
248. Ibid., pp. 228–230.
249. Ibid., p. 230.
250. Ibid., pp. 230, 237, 250.
251. Ibid., pp. 230, 262.
252. Ibid., pp. 263–264, 290.
253. Ibid., pp. 292–293.
254. Ibid., p. 276.
255. Ibid., pp. 295–296.
256. Struve, "Istoriko-politicheskie zametki," pp. 215–216.
257. "*Shestidesiatnik*"—a person with the values of the 1860s, an appellation used in intelligentsia debates over its traditions.
258. P. N. Miliukov, "Nasha pozitsiia," *Golos Rossii*, no. 728, 5 August 1921.

Chapter 4

1. See Karamzin's *Zapiski o drevnei i novoi Rossii*, published in 1810–1811 and translated by Richard Pipes in his *Karamzin's Memoir on Ancient and Modern Russia* (Cambridge, Mass.: Harvard University Press, 1959; reprint ed., New York: Atheneum, 1966). For Pobedonostsev's views see Konstantin P. Pobedonostsev, *Reflections of a Russian Statesman* (Ann Arbor: University of Michigan Press, 1965). These essays were first published in Russia in 1896.
2. Struve's turn toward cultural nationalism in 1907 is indicative of the dilemma faced by intellectual conservatives at this time; see Richard Pipes, *Struve: Liberal on the Right, 1905–1944* (Cambridge, Mass.: Harvard University Press, 1980), pp. 66–70. As Mark Aldanov noted in 1921, not one monarchist entered the elections to the Constituent Assembly, an indication of the extreme weakness of the monarchy in 1917: M.-A. Landau-Aldanov, *Deux revolutions: La révolution française et la révolution russe* (Paris: Imprimerie Union, 1921), pp. 13–14.
3. On monarchism in the emigration, see Robert C. Williams, *Culture in Exile: Russian Emigrés in Germany, 1881–1941* (Ithaca: Cornell University Press,

1972), pp. 160–181, 202–222; Hans von Rimscha, *Russland jenseits der Grenzen, 1921–1926: Ein Beitrag zur russischen Nachkriegsgeschichte* (Jena: Verlag der Fromannschen Buchhandlung Walter Biedermann, 1927), pp. 59–82; and Hans-Erich Volkmann, *Die russische Emigration in Deutschland: 1919–1929* (Würzburg: Holzner-Verlag, 1966), pp. 74–120.

4. P. N. Miliukov, *Vospominaniia (1859–1917)*, 2 vols. (New York: Izdatel'stvo imeni Chekhova, 1955), 2:316.

5. G. V. Nemirovich-Danchenko was Wrangel's press secretary: Williams, *Culture*, p. 165.

6. Extremists who wanted to fight the Bolsheviks did so in alliance with the German forces, especially in the Baltic territories. An account of the various plots and campaigns launched from Germany into the Baltic area by Russian, Baltic German, and German army officers is in Williams, *Culture*, pp. 87–95.

7. Williams, *Culture*, p. 160.

8. Robert Williams's book *Culture in Exile* follows the Russian emigration in Germany from the 1880s to 1941. For biographies of Rosenberg and Scheubner-Richter and a discussion of their role as intermediaries between Russian and German extremists, see Walter Laqueur, *Russia and Germany: A Century of Conflict* (Boston: Little, Brown and Company, 1965), pp. 57–78.

9. F. V. Vinberg, *V plenu u obez'ian (Zametki "kontra-revoliutsionera")* (Kiev: Tipografiia Gubernskogo pravleniia, 1918), pp. 14–15, 29, 31. For his biography, see Laqueur, *Russia*, pp. 114–117, and Norman Cohn, *Warrant for Genocide* (London: Eyre & Spottiswoode, 1967), p. 128.

10. Vinberg, *V plenu*, pp. 8, 15–18, 99–107.

11. According to Purishkevich, who had participated in the assassination of Rasputin, Nicholas II and his immediate family were not suitable candidates for the throne: Vinberg, *V plenu*, pp. 31–32, 59–82. The "proletarian judges" dismissed the charge of conspiracy, but incarcerated the monarchists for their counterrevolutionary goals. Purishkevich died in the Ukraine in 1920. See the account of the trial in D. L. Golikov, *Krushenie antisovetskogo podpol'ia v SSSR*, 2 vols. (Moscow: Izdatel'stvo politicheskoi literatury, 1978), 1:94–99.

12. Petr Nikolaevich's godmother, Elizabeta Aleksandrovna Shabel'skaia-Bork, was the author of a slanderous novel about the revolution of 1905. Vinberg's friend, whom he identifies as Petr Nikolaevich Popov, apparently adopted her last name. See Vinberg, *V plenu*, pp. 36–37, 135.

13. Kiev: Tipografiia Gubernskogo pravleniia, 1918.

14. Williams, *Culture*, p. 86.

15. "We see in our revolution darkness, and, besides, the deepest triumph of evil, a great day for the forces of hell," *Luch sveta*, no. 1 (1919), p. 12.

16. Ibid., pp. 8, 12.

17. "Pered razsvetom," *Luch sveta*, no. 1 (1919), p. 12.

18. Ibid., pp. 9–12.

19. On the origins of the *Protocols of the Elders of Zion*, see Cohn, *Warrant for Genocide*, pp. 60–107.

20. Ibid., pp. 65–67, 292.

21. Ibid., pp. 114–115.

22. Purishkevich was active in this propaganda effort: Cohn, *Warrant*, p. 118. The murder of the imperial family lent the *Protocols* additional mystique—a copy was

discovered among the empress's possessions. According to one source, Shabel'skii-Bork was in Ekaterinburg after the murder of the imperial family; see the account in Henri Rollin, *L'apocalyse de notre temps* (Paris: Gallimard, 1939), pp. 480–481.

23. Cohn, *Warrant*, p. 119.
24. See Cohn, *Warrant*, pp. 132–138, 149–168, 292–296 on the propagation of the *Protocols*.
25. Laqueur, *Russia*, pp. 68–78, 116, 125.
26. Williams, *Culture*, p. 208. My citations are to the second Russian edition: *Krestnyi put'* (Munich: Tipografiia R. Ol'denburg, 1922).
27. Vinberg, *Krestnyi put'*, p. [VII].
28. Ibid., p. 240.
29. Ibid., pp. 16–18.
30. Ibid., p. 22; ellipses in the original.
31. Ibid., p. 57.
32. Ibid., p. 251.
33. Ibid., pp. 39, 49, 50.
34. Ibid., p. 161.
35. Ibid., pp. 359–372.
36. Ibid., pp. 31–35. Among these "documents" was the so-called "Zunder letter," a post-revolutionary forgery that called on Jews to guard their victory by destroying the "best and leading elements" in Russia in order that the people might have no other leaders than themselves; see *Krestnyi put'*, pp. 35–36, and, on the forgery, Cohn, *Warrant*, pp. 119–121.
37. Vinberg, *Krestnyi put'*, pp. 162–165.
38. Ibid., pp. 202–204.
39. Ibid., pp. 204–206.
40. Ibid., pp. 209–215.
41. Ibid., p. 40.
42. Ibid., p. 345.
43. There was only one slogan that could serve this function, Vinberg announced: "*Da zhivet na mnogi veki / Pravoslavnyi Russkii Tsar', / I da pravit cheloveki / Tak, kak pravil imi v star'* ": *Krestnyi put'*, p. 338.
44. Ibid., pp. 349–352, 357–358.
45. See the transition in *Krestnyi put'*, chapter 6, "Slander," pp. 151–155.
46. *Krestnyi put'*, p. 155.
47. On the exposé, see Cohn, *Warrant*, pp. 153–156. Miliukov published a Russian translation of the *Times*'s analysis in Paris in 1922: P. N. Miliukov, ed., *Pravda o "Sionskikh protokolakh"* (Paris: Franko-russkaia pechat', 1922).
48. See his revolting preface to a Russian translation of L. Fry's article in *La vieille France*, "Achad ha-Am et le Sionisme": "Podlinnost' 'Sionskikh Protokolov'," in *Akhad-Kham (Asher Gintsberg) Tainyi vozhd' iudeiskii* (Berlin: 1922), pp. 3–4.
49. For Vinberg's notion of honesty, see his declarations in *Krestnyi put'*, pp. 336–337. He admitted that there might be some inaccuracies and distortions in the text, but insisted that "on every page. . . . I told the truth as I felt and understood it."
50. For examples, see *Krestnyi put'*, pp. 179–192.
51. *Gosudar' Imperator Nikolai II Aleksandrovich* (Berlin: Stiag i Fond po izdaniiu tsarskikh portretov, 1922). This short work was the forerunner of Ol'denburg's

later, major history of Nicholas II and his reign: *Tsarstvovanie Imperatora Nikolaia II*, 2 vols. (Belgrad, Munich: Izdanie Obshchestva rasprostraneniia russkoi natsional'noi i patrioticheskoi literatury, 1939, 1949).

52. S. F. Ol'denburg was one of the few Kadet leaders who favored preserving the monarchy in 1917: William G. Rosenberg, *Liberals in the Russian Revolution: The Constitutional Democratic Party, 1917–1921* (Princeton: Princeton University Press, 1974), p. 53.

53. Beginning in 1921, Ol'denburg wrote a survey of political affairs for this journal.

54. Struve was more tolerant than most, but even he could not absolve the tsar from responsibility for the government's failures; see Pipes, *Struve: Liberal on the Right*, pp. 308–309.

55. "Russkie obrazovannogo, intelligentskogo klassa" (Ol'denburg, *Gosudar'*, p. 5).

56. Ol'denburg, *Gosudar'*, pp. 5–6.

57. Ibid., pp. 6–7.

58. Ibid., p. 6.

59. Ibid., pp. 6–7.

60. Ibid., p. 7.

61. Ibid., pp. 7–11.

62. Ibid., p. 11.

63. Ibid., pp. 11–12.

64. Ibid.

65. Ibid., p. 14.

66. Ibid., pp. 14–16.

67. Ibid., pp. 16, 54–58.

68. Ibid., pp. 16–17, 59–61.

69. Ibid., pp. 17–26.

70. Ibid., pp. 29–31.

71. Ibid., pp. 31, 70.

72. Ibid., p. 32.

73. Ibid., p. 23.

74. Rimscha, *Russland jenseits der Grenzen*, pp. 33, 48–49. On the Nationalists, see Robert Edelman, *Gentry Politics on the Eve of the Russian Revolution: The Nationalist Party 1907–1917* (New Brunswick: Rutgers University Press, 1980), pp. 217–234.

75. See Pipes, *Struve: Liberal on the Right*, pp. 340–341.

76. On the Reichenhall Congress and its organizers, see Laqueur, *Russia*, p. 64; Williams, *Culture*, pp. 174–181; Evgenii Efimovskii, "Sorokaletie Reikhengall'skogo obshchemonarkhicheskogo s''ezda," *Vozrozhdenie*, no. 130 (October 1962), pp. 104–111; and Iv. Nazhivin, *Sredi potukhshikh maiakov* (Berlin: Ikar', 1922), pp. 184–194.

77. Efimovskii, "Sorokoletie," p. 107.

78. Nazhivin's account captures the atmospherics: Nazhivin, *Sredi potukhshikh*, pp. 185–193.

79. Efimovskii, "Sorokaletie," p. 108. In Efimovskii, the organizers of the congress found an ideal spokesman. Forty years later he was still under the spell of the various favors and positions granted him by the meeting's leaders; see his "Sorokaletie," pp. 106–111.

80. Reports were approved before the meeting in Berlin; see Nazhivin's account in *Sredi potukhshikh*, p. 186.

81. Efimovskii, "Sorokaletie," p. 111. For Maslennikov's views, see his article "Evreiskii vopros v Rossii v proshlom, nastoiashchem i budushchem," *Griadushchaia Rossiia* (Berlin), no. 5, 29 September 1921.

82. Efimovskii, "Sorokaletie,", p. 111.

83. Ibid., p. 109; Williams, *Culture*, pp. 177–178.

84. Nazhivin, *Sredi potukhshikh*, pp. 188–189.

85. Evgenii Efimovskii, "Radi Rossii," *Griadushchaia Rossiia*, no. 4, 22 September 1921.

86. Ol'denburg wrote for *Griadushchaia Rossiia*, as did Prince Obolenskii and General Krasnov.

87. Commenting on the dismal quality of right-wing journalism, the novelist Nazhivin noted that although the extremists hated the liberal Berlin daily *Rul'*, they all read it as the only decent Russian newspaper available: "These people can only splutter, and intrigue, and throw mud at each other, and grieve over the irretrievable, and bluster in vain, but all the same, it's the Jews who have established a good Russian paper" (*Sredi potukhshikh*, p. 200).

88. See Struve's note in *Russkaia mysl'* (January–February 1922), p. 308.

89. Williams, *Culture*, pp. 199–202. Some German rightists realized that what they wanted was Bolshevik techniques, not monarchist ideology; see Louis Dupeux, *National bolshevisme, stratégie communiste et dynamique conservatrice*, 2 vols., (Paris: Librairie Honoré Champion, 1979), 1:71–83, 244–363.

90. On the claimants to the throne, see S. S. Ol'denburg, "Politicheskii obzor," *Russkaia mysl'* (1922), no. 8–12, pp. 197–198.

91. See Williams, *Culture*, pp. 295–296, on the Anastasia case and Nazhivin, *Sredi potukhshikh*, p. 200, on the hysterical mysticism that thrived in the emigration.

92. Williams, *Culture*, p. 206.

93. Nazhivin, *Sredi potukhshikh*, pp. 218–219.

94. The last number of *Luch sveta* provided a list of "Russian Masons" with their addresses. All the leaders of the liberal intelligentsia were included in the "great conspiracy" ("Velikii zagovor," *Luch sveta*, no. 4 [1922]).

95. See the account of the murder in *Rul'*, no. 417, 30(17) March 1922, p. 3.

96. On Nabokov's role in the emigration, see Williams, *Culture*, pp. 182–186, 210, 225.

97. Nazhivin, *Sredi potukhshikh*, pp. 223–224.

98. Rimscha, *Russland*, p. 95.

99. Laqueur, *Russia*, p. 110.

100. See the program of the National Congress in Paris: Pipes, *Struve: Liberal on the Right*, p. 343.

101. In Russia, the poet Gumilev participated in a conspiracy against the Soviet government for the sake of his monarchist convictions. This hopeless activity, for which Gumilev was shot in 1921, also had the quality of sacrificial symbolism; see Leonid I. Strakhovsky, *Three Poets of Modern Russia* (Cambridge, Mass.: Harvard University Press, 1949), pp. 51–52.

102. Shipov's autobiography, for example, concentrates on the heroic period of the zemstvo: D. N. Shipov, *Vospominaniia i dumy o perezhitom* (Moscow: M. i S. Sabashnikovy, 1918). Maklakov, who wrote only much later, focused on the

failure of reform after 1905; see V. A. Maklakov, *Vlast' i obshchestvennost' na zakate staroi Rossii (Vospominaniia sovremennika)*, 3 vols. (n.p.: Illiustrirovannaia Rossiia, n.d.), and its successor volumes: *Pervaia gosudarstvennaia duma* (Paris, [Imp. L. Beresniak, c. 1939]) and *Iz vospominanii* (New York: Izdatel'stvo imeni Chekhova, 1954).

103. Nazhivin, *Sredi potukhshikh*, p. 190.
104. Ibid., p. 217.

Chapter 5

1. See Pierre Pascal, "Les grands courants de la pensée russe contemporaine," *Cahiers du monde russe et soviétique*, 3, no. 1 (January–March 1962), 6, 13–50, for a discussion of the significance of the "renaissance" in Russian cultural history.

2. On the role of these individuals, see N. Poltoratskii, "Sbornik 'Iz glubiny' i ego znachenie," in S. A. Askol'dov et al., *Iz glubiny: Sbornik statei o russkoi revoliutsii*, 2nd ed. (Paris: YMCA Press, 1967), pp. XV–XVI. Other figures prominent in the idealist movement include P. I. Novgorodtsev, S. N. and E. N. Trubetskoi, and S. A. Askol'dov.

3. On the Russian "Silver Age" and its cultural achievements, see Pascal, "Les grands courants," pp. 13–49; Bernice Glatzer Rosenthal, *Dmitrii Sergeevich Merezhkovsky and the Silver Age* (The Hague: Martinus Nijhoff, 1975); Gleb Struve, "The Cultural Renaissance," in Theofanis George Stavrou, ed., *Russia under the Last Tsar* (Minneapolis: University of Minnesota Press, 1969), pp. 179–202.

4. P. I. Novgorodtsev, ed., *Problemy idealizma* (Moscow: Izdanie Moskovskogo psikhologicheskogo obshchestva, 1903); *Vekhi: Sbornik statei o russkoi intelligentsii* (Moscow, 1909; reprint ed., Frankfurt a.M.: Posev, 1967).

5. The debate over *Vekhi* is the subject of Christopher Read's excellent monograph, *Religion, Revolution and the Russian Intelligentsia 1900–1912* (London: Macmillan, 1979).

6. S. A. Askol'dov et al., *Iz glubiny: Sbornik statei o russkoi revoliutsii*, 2nd ed. (Paris: YMCA Press, 1967).

7. S. A. Askol'dov, "Religioznyi smysl russkoi revoliutsii," in Askol'dov et al., *Iz glubiny*, pp. 44–46.

8. See Sergei Bulgakov's "dialogues" on the revolution, "Na piru bogov," pp. 111–169, and S. L. Frank, "*De profundis*," pp. 311–330, both in Askol'dov et al., *Iz glubiny*.

9. Askol'dov, "Religioznyi smysl," p. 61; Frank, "*De profundis*," p. 321; S. A. Kotliarevskii, "Ozdorovlenie," p. 213, in Askol'dov et al., *Iz glubiny*.

10. Frank, "*De profundis*," p. 322.

11. P. I. Novgorodtsev, "O putiakh i zadachakh russkoi intelligentsii," in Askol'dov et al., *Iz glubiny*, p. 264.

12. Frank likened the reactionaries to the radicals in their ignorance of the spiritual aspects of social life, their preference for the use of force, their combination of the "hatred of living people with the romantic idealization of abstract political forms and parties" ("*De profundis*," p. 323).

13. Although the *Vekhi* group had intended in 1910 to produce another collection of

articles, expressing the positive, constructive aspect of their ideas, this project was never accomplished: Poltoratskii, "Sbornik 'Iz glubiny'," p. XX.

14. See, for example, S. L. Frank: "If our social thought, our moral will, is able to comprehend all that has happened, if the Lord's punishment has struck us not to destroy but to amend, then this healing frame of mind absolutely must mature in our church-religious and national-state consciousness" (*"De profundis,"* p. 330).

15. Except Ivanov's attack on the Provisional Government's orthographic reform!: Viacheslav Ivanov, "Nash iazyk," in Askol'dov et al., *Iz glubiny,* pp. 175–180.

16. Nikolai Berdiaev, "Dukhi russkoi revoliutsii," in Askol'dov et al., *Iz glubiny,* pp. 80–81, 96, 106.

17. The Western literature on Berdiaev is profuse. Two useful studies of his ideas are N. Poltoratskii, *Berdiaev i Rossiia (Filosofiia istorii Rossii u N. A. Berdiaeva* (New York: Obshchestvo druzei russkoi kul'tury, 1967), and Marko Markovic, *La philosophie de l'inégalité et les idées politiques de Nikolas Berdiaev* (Paris: Nouvelles éditions latines, 1968). The major biography of Berdiaev is Donald Lowrie's devotional *Rebelliousness Prophet: A Life of Nicolai Berdyaev* (1960; reprint ed., Westport, Conn.: Greenwood Press, 1974). Tamara Klépinine has produced a very informative bibliography: Tamara Klépinine, *Bibliographie des oeuvres de Nicolas Berdiaev* (Paris: YMCA Press, 1978).

18. Nikolai Berdiaev, *Filosofiia neravenstva: Pis'ma k nedrugam po sotsial'noi filosofii,* 2nd ed., rev. (Paris: YMCA Press, 1970), p. 14; first published in Berlin by Obelisk, 1923.

19. "Byla li v Rossii revoliutsiia?" *Narodopravstvo,* no. 15 (November 1917), p. 4.

20. Ibid.

21. Ibid., pp. 4–6.

22. "Dukhovnyi i material'nyi trud v russkoi revoliutsii," *Narodopravstvo,* no. 21–22 (January 1918), p. 3.

23. Berdiaev, "Dukhi russkoi revoliutsii," p. 72.

24. Ibid.

25. Ibid., pp. 73–75.

26. Ibid., pp. 77–78.

27. Ibid.

28. Ibid., p. 79.

29. Ibid., pp. 84–87.

30. Ibid., p. 91.

31. Ibid., pp. 81–84.

32. Ibid., p. 90.

33. Ibid., p. 85.

34. Ibid., p. 94.

35. Ibid., p. 95.

36. Ibid., pp. 84–85, 87–88, 95.

37. Ibid., pp. 96–97.

38. Ibid., p. 96.

39. Ibid.

40. Ibid., pp. 97–100.

41. Ibid., pp. 102–106.

42. My citations are from the second edition: *Filosofiia neravenstva: Pis'ma k nedrugam po sotsial'noi filosofii,* 2nd ed., rev. (Paris: YMCA Press, 1970). Later,

Berdiaev renounced this book; see his autobiography, *Samopoznanie (Opyt filosofskoi avtobiografii)* (Paris: YMCA Press, 1949), p. 248. Marko Markovic has based his study of Berdiaev's political thought on this work: Marko Markovich, *La philosophie de l'inégalité* (Paris: Nouvelles éditions latines, 1978).

43. Berdiaev, *Filosofiia neravenstva*, p. 14.
44. Ibid., p. 7.
45. Ibid., pp. 15–17.
46. Ibid., p. 16.
47. Ibid., p. 17.
48. Ibid., pp. 19–20.
49. Ibid., pp. 29–33.
50. Ibid., p. 81.
51. Ibid., p. 165.
52. Ibid., pp. 105–106, 111–116.
53. Berdiaev, *Samopoznanie*, pp. 58–60. The autobiography has been translated as *Dream and Reality: An Essay in Autobiography* (London: Geoffrey Bles, 1950).
54. Berdiaev, *Filosofiia neravenstva*, pp. 136, 145.
55. "Pure, abstract, autocratic democracy is the most terrible tyranny" (Berdiaev, *Filosofiia neravenstva*, p. 142).
56. Berdiaev, *Filosofiia neravenstva*, pp. 35–37.
57. Ibid., p. 152.
58. Ibid., p. 136.
59. Ibid., pp. 157–159.
60. Ibid., pp. 161, 167.
61. Ibid., pp. 155–156.
62. Ibid., pp. 84–87, 156, 157. This argument, like many of Berdiaev's comments on apocalyptic ideas, anticipates later studies of Jewish messianism; see especially Gershom Scholem, "Toward an Understanding of the Messianic Idea," in his *The Messianic Idea in Judaism* (New York: Schocken Books, 1971). On the role of Jewish expectations in the revolution, see the provocative observations of Rozanov in *The Apocalypse of Our Time*: V. Rozanov, *Apokalipsis nashego vremeni* (Sergei posad, 1917, 1918; reprint ed., Berlin-Paris: Moskva, n.d.), especially pp. 76–96. Rozanov probably influenced Berdiaev on this question, but as with many of Berdiaev's borrowings and elaborations, the extent of this connection is difficult to estimate. Berdiaev never acknowledged the ideas of others.
63. Berdiaev, *Filosofiia neravenstva*, pp. 84–86.
64. Ibid., p. 3.
65. Berdiaev, *Samopoznanie*, p. 10.
66. On Berdiaev's writing habits, see Lowrie, *Rebellious Prophet*, pp. 187–191.
67. "I must declare that I am not much interested in the product of my creativity, with its perfection. I am interested in expressing myself and shouting to the world what my inner voice reveals to me as the truth," he commented in his autobiography: Berdiaev, *Samopoznanie*, p. 92.
68. Berdiaev, *Filosofiia neravenstva*, p. 19.
69. Ibid., p. 18.
70. Berdiaev, *Samopoznanie*, p. 252.

71. Ibid.; Lowrie, *Rebellious Prophet*, pp. 153, 159.

72. Berdiaev, *Samopoznanie*, pp. 252–253, 260–263.

73. These were *Filosofiia neravenstva, Sud'ba Rossii, Mirosozertsanie Dostoevskogo*, and *Smysl istorii*. *Sud'ba Rossii* was also published in Moscow in 1918; see Klépinine, *Bibliographie*, pp. 30–35, for the publishing record.

74. For a general discussion of church-state relations at this time, see John Shelton Curtiss, *The Russian Church and the Soviet State: 1917–1950* (Boston: Little, Brown and Company, 1953), pp. 44–174.

75. Berdiaev, *Samopoznanie*, p. 255.

76. "Vol'naia akademiia dukhovnoi kul'tury v Moskve," in N. A. Berdiaev, ed., *Sofiia: Problemy dukhovnoi kul'tury i religioznoi filosofii* (Berlin: Obelisk, 1923), pp. 135–136.

77. Berdiaev, *Samopoznanie*, p. 259.

78. Nikolai Berdiaev, *Smysl istorii* (Berlin: Obelisk, 1923), p. 6; Nikolai Berdiaev, *Mirosozertsanie Dostoevskogo* (Prague: YMCA Press, Ltd., 1923), pp. 3–4.

79. "Vol'naia akademiia," p. 135.

80. Ibid., p. 136.

81. Among the other exiles were A. A. Kizevetter, V. A. Miakotin, N. A. Ossorgin, A. V. Peshekhonov, and Pitirim Sorokin: Lowrie, *Rebellious Prophet*, p. 294, note 24.

82. Berdiaev, *Samopoznanie*, p. 263.

83. "Vol'naia akademiia," p. 136.

84. N. A. Berdiaev, "Konets renessansa (K sovremennomu krizisu kul'tury)," in N. A. Berdiaev, ed., *Sofiia* (Berlin: Obelisk, 1923), pp. 21–46.

85. Ibid., pp. 27–33, 45.

86. Ibid., pp. 45–46.

87. Berdiaev, *Smysl istorii*, p. 266.

88. Ibid., p. 221.

89. "Religiozno-filosofskaia akademiia v Berline," in N. A. Berdiaev, *Sofiia*, pp. 136–138.

90. Ibid., p. 136.

91. See Lowrie, *Rebellious Prophet*, p. 165.

92. Berdiaev, *Samopoznanie*, pp. 250–269, 290.

93. This was the case in his complex domestic arrangements as well; see Lowrie, *Rebellious Prophet*, pp. 172–178, and the chapter on Berdiaev's "broken friendships," pp. 203–214.

94. "Predsmertnye mysli Fausta," in N. A. Berdiaev et al., *Osval'd Shpengler i zakat Evropy* (Moscow: Bereg, 1922), p. 72.

95. Ibid., pp. 56, 63–66, 68–70.

96. Ibid., pp. 71–72.

97. See, among other works, his *Christianity and Class War, The Destiny of Man, The Origin of Russian Communism, The Realm of the Spirit and the Realm of Caesar, The Russian Idea, The Fate of Man in the Modern World*.

98. On the Eurasian movement see Nicholas V. Riasanovsky, "The Emergence of Eurasianism," *California Slavic Studies*, 4 (1967), 39–72; Otto Böss, *Die Lehre der Eurasier: Ein Beitrag zur russischen Ideengeschichte des 20. Jahrhunderts* (Wiesbaden: Otto Harrasowitz, 1961); and Gleb Struve, *Russkaia literatura v izgnanii* (New York: Izdatel'stvo imeni Chekhova, 1956), pp. 40–49.

99. For the cultural background of Eurasianism, see George Nivat, "Du 'Panmongolisme' au 'mouvement Eurasien'," *Cahiers du monde russe et soviétique*, 7, no. 3 (July–September 1966), 460–478; on the history of Oriental studies in Russia, see V. Bartol'd, *Istoriia izucheniia vostoka v Evrope i Rossii*, 2nd ed. (Leningrad: Leningradskii institut zhivykh vostochnykh iazykov, 1925), pp. 233–298.

100. On Trubetskoi, see Roman Jakobson, "Necrologie Nikolaj Sergejevic Trubetzkoy (16. April 1890–25. Juni 1938)," *Acta linguistica*, 1 (139), 64–76, and "Autobiographical Notes on N. S. Trubetskoy," in N. S. Trubetskoy, *Principles of Phonology*, trans. Christiane A. M. Baltaxe (Berkeley: University of California Press, 1969), pp. 309–323.

101. Trubetskoi *père* is the subject of a biography by Martha Bohachevsky-Chomiak: *Sergei N. Trubetskoi: An Intellectual Among the Intelligentsia in Prerevolutionary Russia* (Belmont, Mass.: Nordland Publishing Company, 1976).

102. "Autobiographical Notes," pp. 309–310, 313–315; *N. S. Trubetzkoy's Letters and Notes*, ed. Roman Jakobson (The Hague: Mouton, 1975), pp. 1–4, 445–448 (hereafter cited as *Letters and Notes*).

103. N. S. Trubetskoi, *Evropa i chelovechestvo* (Sofia: Rossiisko-Bolgarskoe izdatel'stvo, 1920).

104. See Trubetskoi's letter to Roman Jakobson of 7 March 1921, *Letters and Notes*, p. 12.

105. Trubetskoi, *Evropa*, pp. III, IV.

106. Ibid., p. V.

107. Trubetskoi, *Evropa*, pp. V, VI.

108. See Nicholas Riasanovsky's "Prince N. S. Trubetskoi's 'Europe and Mankind,'" *Jahrbücher für Geschichte Osteuropas*, NF 12 (1964), 207–220, for a very informative discussion of *Europe and Humanity*.

109. Trubetskoi's father, the philosopher S. N. Trubetskoi, was also interested in the problem of ethical relativism; see his essay, "Chemu uchit istoriia filosofii," in S. N. Bulgakov et al., *Problemy idealizma* (Moscow: Izdanie Moskovskogo psikhologicheskogo obshchestva, [1902]), pp. 216–235, and the discussion in Read, *Religion*, p. 16.

110. Trubetskoi, *Evropa*, pp. 2–3, 5–6.

111. Ibid., p. 9.

112. Ibid., pp. 13–15.

113. This argument displayed Trubetskoi's positivist assumptions; he suggested that if we knew the course of history and the "end" of "world progress," we would be able to judge each culture according to its place along this path: Trubetskoi, *Evropa*, p. 17.

114. For an elaboration of this argument, see Riasanovsky, "Trubetskoi's 'Europe and Mankind,'" pp. 208–209.

115. Trubetskoi, *Evropa*, pp. 17–43.

116. He followed, generally, the theories of Gabriel Tarde; see Trubetskoi, *Evropa*, pp. 45–48, and Riasanovsky, "Trubetskoi's 'Europe and Mankind,'" pp. 209–210.

117. Trubetskoi, *Evropa*, pp. 46–50.

118. Ibid., pp. 50–53.

119. Ibid., p. 65.

120. Ibid.

121. Ibid., pp. 62–64.
122. Ibid., pp. 68–69.
123. Ibid., pp. 71–73.
124. Ibid., p. 75.
125. Ibid., pp. 72–73.
126. Ibid., p. 73. Trubetskoi could not conceive of the non-"Romano-Germans" as leaders of international socialism. If the Red Army had reached Berlin and a Communist revolution had taken place there, he commented in a letter to Roman Jakobson, the result would have been Russian "slavery" to the socialism of the more advanced Germans: *Letters and Notes*, p. 15.
127. Trubetskoi, *Evropa*, pp. 67–68.
128. Ibid., pp. 76, 79, 82.
129. *Letters and Notes*, p. 13.
130. Trubetskoi, *Evropa*, p. 9.
131. Ibid.
132. See, for example, Trubetskoi, *Evropa*, pp. 9, 71.
133. Trubetskoi expressed a milder, more judicious vision in his private correspondence: "If sometime my cherished dreams could come true, then I would imagine that in the world there would be several large cultures with 'dialectical' variants. . . . The most important thing would be that, with the possibility of true nationalism based on self-knowledge and the absence of exocentrism, each people will belong to the given culture not accidentally, but because it harmonizes with their internal essence and because this internal essence can find its fullest and clearest expression precisely in that culture" (Trubetskoi to Jakobson, 7 March 1921, *Letters and Notes*, p. 16).
134. *Letters and Notes*, pp. 12–13.
135. *Iskhod k vostoku: Predchuvstviia i sverzheniia; Utverzhdenie evraziitsev* (Sofiia, 1921), p. IV.
136. Brief biographies of Florovskii and Savitskii can be found in Böss, *Lehre*, p. 7.
137. *Iskhod k vostoku*, cover and title page.
138. Ibid., pp. III–VI.
139. Ibid., p. VI.
140. Ibid., p. VII.
141. Ibid.
142. Ibid.
143. Trubetskoi, *Evropa*, pp. 35–37.
144. The title of Savitskii's introductory article, *Iskhod*, p. 1.
145. Georgii V. Florovskii, "O narodakh ne-istoricheskikh," *Iskhod*, p. 60.
146. Petr Savitskii, "Kontinent-okean," *Iskhod*, pp. 104–125.
147. Petr Savitskii, "Povorot k vostoku," *Iskhod*, pp. 1–2.
148. Petr Savitskii, "Migratsiia kul'tury," *Iskhod*, pp. 40–51.
149. See his comments to Jakobson, *Letters and Notes*, p. 21.
150. Trubetskoi, "Ob istinnom i lozhnom natsionalizme," *Iskhod*, pp. 71–75, 83–84.
151. Ibid., pp. 75–79.
152. Trubetskoi, "Verkhi i nizy russkoi kul'tury," *Iskhod*, pp. 88–92.
153. Ibid., p. 94.
154. Ibid., pp. 94–96.
155. Ibid., pp. 95–101.

156. Ibid., p. 103.

157. *Na putiakh; Utverzhdenie evraziitsev*, kniga 2 (Moscow-Berlin: Gelikon, 1922). The book was printed in Germany.

158. Trubetskoi, "Religii Indii i khristianstvo," *Na putiakh*, pp. 226–227.

159. N. S. Trubetskoi, "'Russkaia problema'," *Na putiakh*, pp. 297–298, 303–304.

160. Trubetskoi, "'Russkaia problema'," *Na putiakh*, pp. 303–304.

161. Ibid., p. 305.

162. Ibid., pp. 305–306.

163. Ibid., p. 314.

164. Ibid., pp. 315–316.

165. See the list of Eurasian publications, in Böss, *Lehre*, pp. 125–127.

166. See, for example, Jakobson's "O fonologicheskikh iazykovykh soiuzakh," in *Evraziia v svete iazykoznaniia* ([Prague]: Izdanie evraziitsev, 1931), and George Vernadsky, *A History of Russia*, 5th rev. ed. (New Haven: Yale University Press, 1961), pp. 4–23.

167. N. S. Trubetskoi, "Predislovie," in G. D. Uel's, *Rossiia v mgle* (Sofiia: Rossiisko-bolgarskoe knigoizdatel'stvo, 1921), pp. XV–XVI.

168. The original Eurasians were in their late twenties or early thirties at this time.

169. *Letters and Notes*, p. 14.

170. Letter to I. Shishmanov, 27 April–10 May 1920, *Letters and Notes*, p. 445.

171. On the *Smena vekh* movement, see Erwin Oberländer, "National-bolschewistische Tendenzen in der russische Intelligenz: Die 'Smena Vech' Diskussion 1921–1922," *Jahrbücher für Geschichte Osteuropas*, NF 16, no. 2 (June 1968), 194–211; Gleb Struve, *Russkaia literatura v izgnanii* (New York: Izdatel'stvo imeni Chekhova, 1956), pp. 30–35, 39; Robert C. Williams, "'Changing Landmarks' in Russian Berlin, 1922–1924," *Slavic Review*, 27, no. 4 (December 1968), 581–593; and I. Ia. Trifonov, "Iz istorii bor'by kommunisticheskoi partii protiv smenovekhovstva," *Istoriia SSSR*, 3, no. 3 (May–June 1959), 64–82.

172. *Bol'shaia sovetskaia entsiklopediia*, 3rd ed., s.v. "Ustrialov, Nikolai Vasil'evich." Ustrialov is the central subject of M. Agurskii's *Ideologiia natsional-bol'shevizma* (Paris: YMCA Press, 1980).

173. Ustrialov was teaching at the Commercial Institute in Moscow in the first part of 1918; in the fall he taught at the university in Perm; he was the chairman of the Kadet committee of Kaluga province: N. Ustrialov, *Pod znakom revoliutsii (Sbornik statei)* (Harbin: Izdatel'stvo "Russkaia zhizn' "), 1925), pp. 204–205; Agurskii, *Ideologiia*, p. 66.

174. Ustrialov, *Pod znakom*, pp. 196–206; L. A. Krol', *Za tri goda (Vospominaniia, vpechatleniia i vstrechi)* (Vladivostock, "Svobodnaia Rossiia", 1921), p. 46; Vishniak, *Vserossiiskoe uchreditel'noe sobranie* (Paris: Sovremennye zapiski, 1932), p. 135.

175. Ustrialov, *Pod znakom*, pp. 220–224; William G. Rosenberg, *Liberals in the Russian Revolution* (Princeton: Princeton University Press, 1974), p. 397. For Ustrialov's career during this period, see Agurskii, *Ideologiia*, pp. 66–67.

176. "Perelom," in N. Ustrialov, *V bor'be za Rossiiu* (Harbin: Okno, 1920), pp. 3–5.

177. Ustrialov, "Perelom," pp. 3–5.

178. For the complex relations between the Russians, the Czech Legion, and Allied

advisors, see J. F. N. Bradley, *Civil War in Russia 1917–1920* (London: B. T. Batsford Ltd, 1975), pp. 82–116.

179. Ustrialov, "Perelom," p. 5.
180. Ibid.
181. Ibid.
182. In a letter to Struve, dated 15 October 1920, Ustrialov noted that he "had taken a position . . . of national Bolshevism (the use of Bolshevism for national ends— it seems that some people in contemporary Germany are also expressing this point of view)": Petr Struve, "Istoriko-politicheskie zametki o sovremennosti," *Russkaia mysl'*, (May–July 1921), p. 216 (*Col. Works*, 12, no. 548). While Struve used the term "national Bolshevism" to describe Ustrialov's views and while Ustrialov himself employed the term in 1921 and later, Ustrialov's followers preferred the *Smena vekh* label. For propaganda purposes in the emigration, national Bolshevism was inferior to the more historically resonant *Smena vekh*. On the German movements, which appear to have no connection with the Russian emigration, see Louis Dupeux, *National bolchevisme: Stratégie communiste et dynamique conservatrice*, 2 vols. (Paris: Librarie Honoŕe Champion, 1979), and for a discussion of national Bolshevist ideology in Russia, see Agurskii, *Ideologiia natsional-bol'shevizma*.
183. See his diary for 5 January 1921, "Moia perepiska so smenovekhovtsami," no. 2, Ustrialov Collection, Hoover Institution on War, Revolution and Peace, Stanford, California.
184. "Interventsiia," in Ustrialov, *V bor'be*, p. 6.
185. "Patriotica," in Ustrialov, *V bor'be*, pp. 34–35.
186. "Perspektivy," in Ustrialov, *V bor'be*, pp. 9–10.
187. Ibid., pp. 10–11.
188. Ibid.
189. Ibid., pp. 11.
190. "Staryi spor," in Ustrialov, *V bor'be*, p. 24.
191. "Patriotica," p. 34.
192. "Zelenyi shum," in Ustrialov, *V bor'be*, p. 65.
193. Ibid., pp. 66–67.
194. Ibid., p. 67.
195. Ibid., pp. 68–69.
196. "Logika natsionalizma," in *V bor'be*, p. 50.
197. Ibid.
198. Ibid., pp. 51–52.
199. Ibid., p. 52.
200. Ibid.
201. Ibid., pp. 53–54.
202. "Perspektivy," pp. 12–13.
203. Ustrialov, "Admiral Kolchak," in *V bor'be*, p. 76. The article was first published in March 1920, but Ustrialov placed it out of chronological order at the end of the collection.
204. Ustrialov, *V bor'be*, pp. 62–63.
205. See Ustrialov's afterword from October 26, 1920, in *V bor'be*, pp. 79–80.
206. Iu. V. Kliuchnikov to N. V. Ustrialov, end of March, 1921, "Perepiska," no. 7, Ustrialov Collection.

207. Kliuchnikov to Ustrialov, 13 July 1921, "Perepiska," no. 8, Ustrialov Collection.
208. Potekhin to Ustrialov, 1 September 1921, "Perepiska," no. 10, Ustrialov Collection.
209. *Smena vekh: Sbornik statei* (Prague, 1921). Ustrialov noted the "need for a new *'Vekhi'* in his diary on September 27, 1921; see "Perepiska," no. 9, Ustrialov Collection.
210. Iu. V. Kliuchnikov, "Smena vekh," in *Smena vekh*, p. 18.
211. S. S. Lukianov, "Revoliutsiia i vlast'," in *Smena vekh*, p. 65.
212. Kliuchnikov, "Smena vekh," pp. 4–43.
213. Iu. N. Potekhin, "Fizika i metafizika russkoi revoliutsii," in *Smena vekh*, p. 170.
214. A. V. Bobrishchev-Pushkin, "Novaia vera," in *Smena vekh*, pp. 96–100.
215. His study was based on "Patriotica," dated 17 June 1920, *V bor'be*, pp. 30–36, and "Put' Termidora," from June 1921, *Pod znakom*, pp. 20–24.
216. P. B. Struve, *Patriotica: politika, kul'tura, religiia, sotsializm. Sbornik statei za piat' let (1905–1910 gg)* (St. Petersburg: Izd. D. E. Zhukovskogo, 1911).
217. "We must paralyze the emigration and reconcile the intelligentsia with Soviet power," he wrote to Potekhin in February 1922, after he had received the *Smena vekh* collection and discovered to his dismay that he and his colleagues did not see eye to eye. He feared that the others' pro-Bolshevik enthusiasms would alienate many of the émigrés. See Ustrialov to Potekhin, 14 February 1922, "Perepiska," no. 22, Ustrialov Collection.
218. "Patriotica," in *Smena vekh*, pp. 54–55.
219. Ibid., pp. 52–53.
220. Ibid., pp. 54–56.
221. Potekhin, in his "Physics and Metaphysics of the Russian Revolution," argued similarly: "We know that the depth of the moral decline, which is easy to perceive in a great number of episodes of the revolution, is only the other side of the lack of satisfaction of the highest moral demands, [demands] that not one other nation of Europe has tried to resolve or even set for themselves" (Potekhin, "Fizika," p. 174).
222. Ustrialov, "Patriotica," p. 63.
223. "Pererozhdenie bol'shevizma," in Ustrialov, *Pod znakom*, p. 9.
224. "Rediska," in Ustrialov, *Pod znakom*, pp. 15–19.
225. Ustrialov to Kliuchnikov, 30 January 1920, "Perepiska," no. 21, Ustrialov Collection. On the *Smena vekh* group in Berlin, see Williams, "Changing Landmarks," pp. 506–509. Both articles were published later in Ustrialov, *Pod znakom*, pp. 233–247.
226. "Intelligentsiia i narod v russkoi revoliutsii," in Ustrialov, *Pod znakom*, pp. 233, 235.
227. Ibid., pp. 234, 238–239.
228. Ibid., pp. 242–243.
229. Ibid., p. 244.
230. Ibid., pp. 244–247.
231. For Struve's assessment of Ustrialov and *Smena vekh*, see Richard Pipes, *Struve: Liberal on the Right* (Cambridge, Mass.: Harvard University Press, 1980), pp. 352–356.
232. "Intelligentsiia i narod," in Ustrialov, *Pod znakom*, p. 242.
233. "O 'budushchei Rossii,'" ibid., pp. 108–109.
234. "Chrezvychaika," ibid., p. 80.

235. "Obmirshchenie," ibid., pp. 115–116.

236. Ibid., pp. 117–119. The intelligentsia wanted its "Scythian" to have "all the good qualities of the savage, without his defects," Ustrialov commented: "Like those Zulus that were decorously exhibited in the zoos of Paris and London, he was obliged only to make terrible faces, but not allowed obscene gestures (*op. cit.*, p. 118)."

237. Ibid., pp. 117–118.

238. "Problema vozvrashcheniia," ibid., p. 40. For Ustrialov's predictions of a Russian Thermidor, see his "Put' Termidora," pp. 20–24.

239. S. S. Chakhotin, "V Kanossu!," in *Smena vekh*, pp. 162–165.

240. Ustrialov to Kliuchnikov, 3 January 1921, "Perepiska," no. 18, Ustrialov Collection.

241. V. I. Lenin, *Polnoe sobranie sochinenii*, 5th ed. (Moscow: Gospolitizdat, 1958–1965) 45:93–95.

242. Williams, "'Changing Landmarks,'" p. 588.

243. The first *smena vekh* publication to appear in Russia was *Letopis' Doma literatorov*, a biweekly that appeared at the end of 1921. Among the publications connected with the movement were *Ekonomist, Ekonomicheskoe vozrozhdenie*, and *Novaia Rossiia* (issued as *Rossiia* from 1922 to 1925). Ustrialov's "Obmirshchenie" was published in *Rossiia*: Ustrialov, *Pod znakom*, p. 114. On these publications, see Agurskii, *Ideologiia*, pp. 133–134.

244. See his diary for 24 October 1921, "Perepiska," no. 11, Ustrialov Collection, and his letter to Kliuchnikov from 3 January 1922, "Perepiska," no. 18, Ustrialov Collection.

245. Bobrishchev-Pushkin to Ustrialov, 10 June 1922, "Perepiska," no. 32a, Ustrialov Collection. See also Marc Jansen, *A Show Trial under Lenin* (The Hague: Martinus Nijhoff, 1982), pp. 160–161.

246. See *Nakanune* for June 1922.

247. 1 July 1922, "Perepiska," no. 33, Ustrialov Collection.

248. Ustrialov to Bobrishchev-Pushkin, 22 October 1922, "Perepiska," no. 42, Ustrialov Collection.

249. See I. Ia. Trifonov, "Iz istorii bor'by kommunisticheskoi partii protiv smenovekhovstva," *Istoriia SSSR*, 3, no. 3 (May–June 1959), 70–71.

250. See Trifonov, "Iz istorii," p. 80, and Agurskii, *Ideologiia*, pp. 133–134, 215–216.

251. Agurskii, *Ideologiia*, pp. 220–221.

252. *Bol'shaia sovetskaia entsiklopediia*, 3rd ed., s.v. "Ustrialov, Nikolai Vasil'evich"; Agurskii, *Ideologiia*, p. 237. For a discussion of Ustrialov's place in the party debates of the 1920s and 1930s, see Agurskii's *Ideologiia*. This work attempts to show that Stalin was influenced by National Bolshevism.

253. Potekhin, "Fizika," in *Smena vekh*, p. 174.

254. N. Ustrialov, "Smysl vstrechi," *Nakanune*, no. 34, 7 May 1922.

Chapter 6

1. N. Ustrialov, *Pod znakom revoliutsii* (Harbin: Russkaia mysl', 1925), p. 117.

2. On the Menshevik arrests, see Leonard Schapiro, *The Origin of the Communist Autocracy* (Cambridge, Mass.: Harvard University Press, 1977), pp. 205–206.

For the beginning of the prison camps, consult Aleksandr I. Solzhenitsyn, *The Gulag Archipelago* (New York: Harper & Row, 1973), 1:24–47.

3. For a discussion of the role and definition of the Soviet intelligentsia, see Leopold Labedz, "The Structure of the Soviet Intelligentsia," in Richard Pipes, ed., *The Russian Intelligentsia* (New York: Columbia University Press, 1961), pp. 63–79, and on the relationship between prerevolutionary and Soviet categories, see Richard Pipes, "The Historical Evolution of the Russian Intelligentsia," pp. 47–62, in the same collection.

4. *Novyi luch*, no. 4(28), 6 January 1918.

5. "1-e maia 1919 goda," Portugeis Collection, International Institute of Social History (I.I.S.H.), Amsterdam.

6. Mark Vishniak, *Le régime soviétiste* (Paris: Union, 1920), pp. 33–39.

7. S. S. Chakhotin, "V Kanossu!" in *Smena vekh* (Prague, 1921).

8. "Tov. P. B. Aksel'rod o bol'shevizme i bor'be s nim," *Sotsialisticheskii vestnik*, no. 6 (20 April 1921), p. 6.

9. Martov to N. S. Kristi, in *Martov i ego blizkie* (New York, 1959), p. 49.

10. Petr Struve, "Istoriko-politicheskie zametki o sovremennosti," *Russkaia mysl'* (May–June 1921), p. 213 (P. B. Struve, *Collected Works in Fifteen Volumes*, ed. Richard Pipes [Ann Arbor: University Microfilms, 1970] [hereafter cited as *Col. Works*], 12, no. 548).

11. "Byla li v Rossii revoliutsiia?," *Narodopravstvo*, no. 15 (November 1917), p. 4.

12. "Razmyshleniia o russkoi revoliutsii," *Russkaia mysl'* (January–February 1921), p. 13 (*Col. Works*, 11, no. 541.).

13. Iu. Martov, *Mirovoi bol'shevizm* (Berlin: Iskra, 1923), pp. 15–17.

14. *Pervyi Vserossiiskii s''ezd professional'nykh soiuzov* (Moscow: Izdanie Vserossiiskogo tsentral'nogo soveta professional'nykh soiuzov, 1918), pp. 79–82.

15. 4 March 1920, in Paul Avrich, ed., *The Anarchists in the Russian Revolution* (Ithaca: Cornell University Press, 1973), p. 147.

16. See Martov's description of socialism as the "highest embodiment" of "individual liberty and individualism": Martov to N. S. Kristi, in *Martov i ego blizkie* (New York, 1959), p. 48.

17. Nikolai Berdiaev, "Dukhi russkoi revoliutsii," in *Iz glubiny*, 2nd ed. (Paris: YMCA Press, 1967), p. 96.

18. Ibid., p. 91. Berdiaev was quoting from Dostoevsky's novel *The Possessed*.

19. Ustrialov, *Pod znakom*, p. 242.

20. Ibid., pp. 108, 242.

21. N. Ustrialov, *V bor'be za Rossiiu* (Harbin: Okno, 1920), p. 5.

22. Vera Zasulich, "Sotsializm Smol'nogo," *Nachalo*, no. 2, 2(15) February 1918.

23. N. S. Trubetskoi, *Evropa i chelovechestvo* (Sofia: Rossiisko-Bolgarskoe izdatel'stvo, 1920), pp. 72–73.

24. Ustrialov, *V bor'be*, p. 5.

25. Ustrialov, *Pod znakom*, p. 103.

26. N. S. Trubetskoi, "'Russkaia problema'," *Na putiakh: Utverzhdenie evraziitsev*, Kniga 2 (Moscow-Berlin: Gelikon, 1922), pp. 305–306, 314.

27. Ibid., pp. 304–305.

28. Ustrialov, *V bor'be*, p. 67.

29. Ustrialov, *Pod znakom*, p. 244.

30. *Vpered*, no. 63(309), 14(1) April 1918.

31. See the quotation from Tiutchev in *Pod znakom*, p. 277.

32. Ustrialov, *V bor'be*, pp. 44–45.

33. Ustrialov, *Pod znakom*, p. 247.

34. He returned to the Soviet Union in 1935: *Bol'shaia sovetskaia entsiklopediia*, 3rd ed., s.v."Ustrialov, Nikolai Vasil'evich"; see above, p. 234.

35. A. N. Potresov, "Privet 'Russkomu bogatstvu'," in A. N. Potresov, *Posmertnyi sbornik proizvedenii* (Paris, 1937), p. 281; from *Novyi den'*, 15(2) February 1918.

36. Ustrialov to N. N. Alekseev, 4 November 1922, "Moia perepiska so smenovekhovtsami," no. 44, Ustrialov Collection, Hoover Institution on War, Revolution and Peace, Stanford, California.

Selected Bibliography

This study is based upon the rich, but widely scattered collections of Russian sources in the United States and Western Europe. Of the archival depositories listed here, three—the International Institute of Social History in Amsterdam, the archives of the Hoover Institution on War, Revolution and Peace, and the Bakhmeteff Archive at Columbia University—are indispensable for research on the intelligentsia in the revolutionary period. In addition to personal correspondence and manuscripts, their files contain extensive collections of pamphlets, party records, and newspaper clippings—ephemera of the revolution, carefully preserved and easily accessible. For the intelligentsia's newspapers and journals in 1917 and after, both in Russia and abroad, and for other published contemporary sources, I found the following libraries particularly helpful: the Bibliothèque de documentation internationale contemporaine at Nanterre, the library of the Hoover Institution, the Bayerische Staatsbibliothek in Munich, the library of the Eberhard-Karls-Universität in Tübingen, and Widener Library at Harvard University. The Bibliothèque de documentation internationale contemporaine, the International Institute of Social History, and the Osteuropa-Institut in Munich have useful analytic catalogs.

This bibliography indicates my principal sources—newspapers, journals, books, pamphlets, correspondence, broadsides, and other political records from the revolutionary period. I have included a number of books and essays that, while not central to this study, were written by Russians in response to the revolution and may be of interest to scholars who pursue this topic. The list of secondary works is limited to sources bearing directly on the politics and ideas of the non-Bolshevik intelligentsia from 1917 to 1922 and to a few of the most relevant monographs on the revolution.

I. Archives

Amsterdam. International Instituut voor Sociale Geschiedenis:
1. Akselrod Archive.
2. Lydia Dan Archive.
3. Plekhanov Archive.
4. Portugeis Archive.

Kew. Public Record Office. Records of the Foreign Office on Russia, 1919–1920:
1. F.O. 371.
2. F.O. 395.

New York. Bakhmeteff Archive, Columbia University:
1. Denikin Collection.
2. Miliukov Collection.

Paris. Archives nationales. Fonds Albert Thomas.

Stanford. Hoover Institution on War, Revolution and Peace:
1. Nicolaevsky Collection.
2. Ustrialov Collection.

II. Newspapers and Journals

Arkhiv russkoi revoliutsii, Berlin, 1921–1937.
Le Bulletin de la Ligue russe pour la défense révolutionnaire, Paris, 1918.
Bulletin d'information "Pour la Russie," Paris, 1920–1921.
Bulletin of the Russian Liberation Committee, London, 1919–1920.
Delo, Petrograd, Moscow, 1918.
Delo naroda, Petrograd, 1917.
Den', Petrograd, 1917–1918.
Dni, Berlin, 1922.
Dvuglavyi orel, Berlin, Munich, 1920–1922.
Les Echos de Russie, Stockholm, 1918.
Edinstvo, 1917–1918.
Golos Rossii, Berlin, 1919–1922.
Golos truda, Petrograd, 1917–1918.
Griadushchaia Rossiia, Berlin, 1921–1922.
Griadushchaia Rossiia, Paris, 1920.
Iskra, Petrograd, Moscow, 1917–1918.
Luch, Petrograd, 1917.
Luch sveta, Berlin, Munich, 1919–1922.
Mysl', Kharkov, 1919.
Nachalo, Petrograd, 1918.
Nakanune, Berlin, 1922.
Narodnoe delo, Moscow, 1918.
Narodnoe delo, Tallinn, 1920–1921.
Narodopravstvo, Moscow, 1917–1918.
Nasha zhizn', [Moscow], 1922–1923.
The New Russia, London, 1920.
Novaia zaria, Moscow, 1918.
Novyi luch, Petrograd, 1917–1918.

Poslednie novosti, Paris, 1920–1922.
Pour la Russie, Paris, 1919–1920.
Pravda, Petrograd, Moscow, 1917–1922.
Rabochaia gazeta, Petrograd, 1917.
La République russe, Paris, 1919–1921.
Revoliutsionnaia Rossiia, Tallinn, Berlin, 1920–1931.
Rodina, Lausanne, 1920.
Rul', Berlin, 1920–1922.
The Russian Commonwealth, London, 1918–1920.
La Russie démocratique, Paris, 1919.
Russkaia mysl', Moscow, Sofia, 1917–1918, 1921–1922.
Russkaia svoboda, Petrograd-Moscow, 1917.
Russkaia zhizn', Helsinki, 1919.
Russkoe delo, Prague, 1919–1920.
Slavianskaia zaria, Prague, 1920.
Sotsialisticheskii vestnik, Berlin, Paris, New York, 1921–1963.
Sovremennye zapiski, Paris, 1920–1940.
Velikaia Rossiia, Rostov na Donu, 1919.
Volia Rossii, Prague, 1920.
Voskresen'e, Berlin, 1921.
Vpered, Moscow, 1917–1918.
Vremia, Berlin, 1919–1921.
Vsegda vpered, Moscow, 1919.
Zaria, Berlin, 1922.
Zhizn', Berlin, 1920

III. Other Primary Sources

Abramovich, Rafael Abramovich (Rein). *Men'sheviki i sotsialisticheskii internatsional (1918–1940)*. N.p., n.d.
Aldanov, Mark Aleksandrovich. *Deux révolutions: La révolution française et la révolution russe*. Paris: Imprimerie Union, 1921.
_____. *Ogon' i dym*. Paris: Franko-russkaia pechat', 1922.
Andreyev, Olga Chernov. *Cold Spring in Russia*. Ann Arbor: Ardis, 1978.
Aksel'rod, Pavel Borisovich. *Kto izmenil sotsializmu (Bol'shevizm i sotsial'naia demokratiia v Rossii)*. New York: Narodopravstvo, 1919.
_____. *Perezhitoe i peredumannoe*. Berlin: Grzhebin, 1923.
Aronson, Grigorii Ia. *Dvizhenie upolnomochennykh ot rabochikh fabrik i zavodov v 1918 godu*. Inter-University Project on the History of the Menshevik Movement. New York, 1960.
_____. *K istorii pravogo techeniia sredi men'shevikov*. Inter-University Project on the History of the Menshevik Movement, Paper no. 4. New York, 1960.
_____. "Stranitsy proshlogo." In *Protiv techeniia: Sbornik*, edited by V. Dvinov. New York, 1952.
Ascher, Abraham, ed. *The Mensheviks in the Russian Revolution*. London: Thames and Hudson, 1976.
Avrich, Paul, ed. *The Anarchists in the Russian Revolution*. Ithaca: Cornell University Press, 1973.

Berdiaev, Nikolai Aleksandrovich. *Filosofiia neravenstva: Pis'ma k nedrugam po sotsial'noi filosofii.* 2nd ed., rev. Paris: YMCA Press, 1970.

———. *The Meaning of History.* London: Geoffrey Bles: The Centenary Press, 1936.

———. *Mirosozertsanie Dostoevskogo.* Prague: YMCA Press, 1923.

———. *Samopoznanie (Opyt filosofskoi avtobiografii).* Paris, YMCA Press, 1949.

———, et al. *Osval'd Shpengler i zakat Evropy.* Moscow: Bereg, 1922.

———, ed. *Sofiia: Problemy dukhovnoi kul'tury i religioznoi filosofii.* Berlin: Obelisk, 1922.

Bernshtam, M. S., ed. *Nezavisimoe rabochee dvizhenie v 1918 godu: Dokumenty i materialy.* Issledovaniia noveishei russkoi istorii, no. 2. Paris: YMCA Press, 1981.

———, ed. *Ural i prikam'e noiabr' 1917–ianvar' 1919: Dokumenty i materialy.* Issledovaniia noveishei russkoi istorii, no. 3. Paris: YMCA Press, 1982.

Biulleten' Vserossiiskogo obshchestvennogo komiteta po uvekovecheniiu pamiati P. A. Kropotkina. No. 2. Moscow: Vserossiiskii komitet po uvekovecheniiu pamiati P. A. Kropotkina, 1924.

Blok, Aleksandr. *Sobranie sochinenii v vos'mi tomakh.* Moscow: Gos. izd. khudozhestvennoi literatury, 1960–1965.

Broido, Eva. *Memoirs of a Revolutionary.* London: Oxford University Press, 1967.

Bunyan, James, and H. H. Fisher. *The Bolshevik Revolution 1917–1918: Documents and Materials.* Stanford: Stanford University Press, 1934.

Che-ka: Materialy po deiatel'nosti chrezvychainykh komissii. Berlin: Tsentral'nyi biuro Partii sotsialistov-revoliutsionerov, 1922.

Chernov, Viktor Mikhailovich. *Marksizm i slavianstvo (K voprosu o vneshnei politike sotsializma).* Petrograd: Ts. Kom. P.-SR, 1917.

———. *Mes tribulations en Russie soviétique.* Paris: Povolozky, 1921.

———. *Pered burei: Vospominaniia.* New York: Izdatal'stvo imeni Chekhova, 1953.

———. *Voina i "tret'ia sila": Sbornik statei.* 2nd ed. Petrograd 1917.

———. *Zapiski sotsialista revoliutsionera.* Berlin: Izdatel'stvo S. I. Grzhebina, 1922.

———. *Zemlia i pravo: Sbornik statei.* Petrograd, 1919.

Chetvertyi Vserossiiskii s"ezd sovetov rabochikh, krest'ianskikh, soldatskikh i kazakh'ikh deputatov: Stenograficheskii otchet. Moscow: Gosudarstvennoe izdatel'stvo, 1919.

Dalin, David. *Posle voin i revoliutsii.* Berlin: Grani, 1922.

Denikin, Anton Ivanovich. *The Russian Turmoil.* London: Hutchinson and Co., 1920. Reprint. Westport, Conn.: Hyperion Press, 1973.

Dolgorukov, Pavel Dmitrievich. *Velikaia razrukha.* Madrid, 1964.

Dvinov, Boris. *From Legality to the Underground (1921–1922)* (in Russian). Stanford: The Hoover Institution on War, Revolution and Peace, 1968.

Efimovskii, Evgenii. "Sorokaletie Reikhengall'skogo obshchemonarkhicheskogo s"ezda." *Vozrozhdenie*, no. 130 (October 1962), pp. 104–111.

Five Sisters: Women Against the Tsar. Edited and translated by Barbara Alpern Engel and Clifford N. Rosenthal. New York: Knopf, 1975.

Fleishman, L., et al. *Russkii Berlin 1921–1923: Po materialam arkhiva B. I. Nikolaevskogo v Guverovskom institute.* Paris: YMCA Press, 1983.

Frank, Semen Liudvigovich. *Biografiia P. B. Struve.* New York: Izdatel'stvo imeni Chekhova, 1956.

Garvi, Petr Abramovich. *Professional'nye soiuzy v Rossii v pervye gody revoliutsii.* Edited by G. A. Aronson. New York: 1958.

_____. *Vospominaniia sotsial-demokrata.* New York: Fond . . . P. A. Garvi, 1946.

Goldman, Emma. *My Disillusionment in Russia.* New York: Thomas Y. Crowell, n.d.

Iskhod k vostoku: Predchuvstviia i sverzheniia: Utverzhdenie evraziitsev. Sofia, 1921.

Ivanov, Viacheslav and M. O. Gershenzon. *Perepiska iz dvukh uglov.* Peterburg: Alkonost, 1921. Reprint. Ann Arbor: Ardis, 1980.

Ivanov-Razumnik, R. V. *Chto takoe intelligentsiia.* Berlin: Skify, 1920.

_____. *Istoriia russkoi obshchestvennoi mysli.* 2 vols. 3rd ed. St. Petersburg: Tipografiia M. M. Stasiulevicha, 1911. Reprint. The Hague: Mouton, 1969.

Ivanovich, Stepan (Simen Osipovich Portugeis). *A. N. Potresov: Opyt kul'turno-psikhologicheskogo portreta.* Paris, 1938.

Iz glubiny: Sbornik statei o russkoi revoliutsii. 2nd ed. Paris: YMCA Press, 1967.

The Jewish Peril: Protocols of the Learned Elders of Zion. London: Eyre & Spottiswoode, 1920.

Keep, John L. H., ed. and trans. *The Debate on Soviet Power: Minutes of the All-Russian Central Executive Committee of Soviets.* Oxford: Clarendon Press, 1979.

Kerenskii, Aleksandr Fedorovich. *La Russie des soviets d'après les bolcheviks eux-mêmes.* Paris: Pour la Russie, 1920.

Kliuchnikov, M. G., ed. *La Russie d'aujourd'hui et de demain.* Paris: Attinger Frères, 1920.

Krol', L. A. *Za tri goda (Vospominaniia, vpechatleniia i vstrechi).* Vladivostok: Svobodnaia Rossiia, 1921.

Kropotkin, Petr Alekseevich. *Etika.* Petersburg and Moscow: Golos trudy, 1922.

_____.*Kommunizm i anarkhiia.* Moscow: Izdanie gruppy osvobozhdennykh politicheskikh, 1917.

_____.*Kropotkin's Revolutionary Pamphlets.* Edited by Roger N. Baldwin. New York: Vanguard Press, 1927.

_____. *Mutual Aid: A Factor of Evolution.* Edited by Paul Avrich. New York: New York University Press, 1972.

_____. *Pis'ma o tekushchikh sobytiakh.* Moscow: Zadruga, 1917.

_____. *Zapiski revoliutsionera.* Moscow: Mysl', 1966.

Lenin, Vladimir Il'ich. *Polnoe sobranie sochinenii.* 55 vols. 5th ed. Moscow: Izdatel'stvo politicheskoi literatury, 1958–1965.

Luxemburg, Rosa. *The Russian Revolution and Leninism or Marxism.* Ann Arbor: University of Michigan Press, 1961.

Maiskii, I. *Demokraticheskaia kontr-revoliutsiia.* Moscow: Gos. Izd., 1923.

Malchevskii, I. S., ed. *Vserossiiskoe uchreditel'noe sobranie.* Moscow: Gosudarstven-noe izdatel'stvo, 1930.

Martov, Iulii Osipovich. *Bol'shevizm v Rossii i v internatsionale.* Berlin: Sotsia-listicheskii vestnik, 1923.

_____. *Mirovoi bol'shevizm.* Berlin: Iskra, 1923.

_____. *Obshchestvennye i umstvennye techeniia v Rossii 1870–1905 g.g.* Leningrad-Moscow, 1924.

_____. *The State and the Socialist Revolution.* New York: International Review, 1938.

_____. *V bor'be za internatsional.* Berlin: Iskra, 1924.

_____. *Zapiski sotsial-demokrata.* Berlin, Petersburg, Moscow: Grzhebin, 1922.

———, ed. *Oborona revoliutsii i sotsial-demokratiia*. Petrograd: Kniga, 1920.

Martov i ego blizkie. New York, 1959.

Mel'gunov, Sergei Petrovich. *Kak bol'sheviki zakhvatili vlast'*. Paris: La Renaissance, 1953.

Miliukov, Pavel Nikolaevich. *Bolshevism: An International Danger*. London: George Allen & Unwin, 1920.

———. *The Case for Bessarabia*. Russian Liberation Committee Publications, no. 8. London: Russian Liberation Committee, [1919].

———. Emigratsiia na pereput'e. Paris: Izdanie Resp.-Dem. Ob''ed., 1926.

———. Istoriia vtoroi russkoi revoliutsii. 3 vols. Sofia: Rossiisko-bolgarskoe knigoizdatel'stvo, 1921–1924.

———. *Iz istorii russkoi intelligentsii*. 2nd ed. St. Petersburg: Znanie, 1903.

———. *Russia and England*. Russian Liberation Committee Publications, no. 13. London: Russian Liberation Committee, [1919].

———. *Russia To-day and To-morrow*. New York: Macmillan Co., 1922.

———. *Tri popytki (K istorii russkogo lzhe-konstitutsionalizma)*. Paris: Franko-russkaia pechat', [1921].

———. *Vospominaniia (1859–1917)*. Edited by M. M. Karpovich and B. I. Elkin. 2 vols. New York: Izdatel'stvo imeni Chekhova, 1955.

———, ed. *Pravda o "Sionskikh protokolakh."* Paris: Franko-russkaia pechat', 1922.

Na putiakh: Utverzhdenie evraziitsev: Kniga vtoraia. Moscow-Berlin: Gelikon, 1922.

Nazhivin, Ivan Fedorovich. *Sredi potukhshikh maiakov*. Berlin: Ikar', 1922.

Nikolaevskii, B. I. *Men'sheviki v dni oktiabr'skogo perevorota*. Inter-University Project on the History of the Menshevik Movement, Paper No. 8. New York, 1962.

Ol'denburg, Sergei Sergeevich. *Gosudar' Imperator Nikolai II Aleksandrovich*. Berlin: Stiag i Fond po izdaniiu tsarskikh portretov, 1922.

Pamiati Petra Alekseevicha Kropotkina. Petrograd and Moscow: Vserossiiskii obshchestvennyi komitet po uvekovecheniiu pamiati P. A. Kropotkina, 1921.

Pervyi Vserossiiskii s''ezd professional'nykh soiuzov. Moscow: Izdanie Vserossiiskogo tsentral'nogo soveta professional'nykh soiuzov, 1918.

Plekhanov, Georgii Valentinovich. *God na rodine*. 2 vols. Paris: J. Povolozky, 1921.

Potresov, Aleksandr Nikolaevich. *Posmertnyi sbornik proizvedenii*. Paris, 1937.

———. *V plenu u illiuzii (Moi spor s ofitsial'nym men'shevizmom)*. Paris, 1927.

Protokoly zasedanii Vserossisskogo ispolnitel'nogo komiteta chetvertogo sozyva. Moscow: Gosizdat, 1920.

Rozanov, Vasilii Vasil'evich. *Apokalipsis nashego vremeni*. Sergiev posad, 1917, 1918. Reprint. Berlin-Paris: Moskva, n.d.

Shestov, Lev. "Qu'est-ce que le bolshevisme?" *Mercure de France*, 132, no. 533 (1 September 1920), 257–290.

Shingarev, Andrei Ivanovich. *Kak eto bylo: Dnevnik A. I. Shingareva*. Moscow: Izdanie Komiteta po uvekovecheniiu pamiati F. F. Kokoshkina i A. I. Shingareva, 1918. Reprint. Royal Oak, Mi.: Strathcona Publishing Co., 1978.

Smena vekh: Sbornik statei. Prague, 1921.

Smirnov, A. A., et al., eds. *P. N. Miliukov: Sbornik materialov po chestvovaniiu ego semidesiatiletiia*. Paris, n.d.

Sovremennyi moment v otsenki Partii Sots.-Revoliutsionerov (Fevral'-mart 1919 g.). New York: N'iu Iorkskaia gruppa Partii Sotsialistov-Revoliutsionerov, 1919.

Struve, Petr Berngardovich. *Collected Works in Fifteen Volumes.* Edited by Richard Pipes. Ann Arbor: University Microfilms. 1970.

Sukhanov, N. N. *Zapiski o revoliutsii.* 7 vols. Berlin: Grzhebin, 1922–1923.

Trubetskoi, Nikolai Sergeevich. *Evropa i chelovechestvo.* Sofia: Rossiisko-bolgarskoe izdatel'stvo, 1920.

———. *N. S. Trubetskoy's Letters and Notes.* Edited by Roman Jakobson. The Hague: Mouton, 1975.

———. *Principles of Phonology.* Translated by Christiane A. M. Baltaxe. Berkeley: University of California Press, 1969.

The Twelve Who Are to Die: The Trial of the Socialist Revolutionists in Moscow. Berlin: The Delegation of the Party of Socialist-Revolutionists, 1922.

Ustrialov, Nikolai Vasil'evich. *Pod znakom revoliutsii.* Harbin: Russkaia mysl', 1925.

———. *V bor'be za Rossiiu.* Harbin, Okno, 1920.

Vekhi. Moscow, 1909. Reprint. Frankfurt a.M.: Posev, 1967.

Vetlugin, A. *Tret'ia Rus'.* Paris: Franko-russkaia pechat', 1922.

Vinberg, Fedor Viktorovich. *Krestnyi put'.* 2nd ed. Munich: Tipografiia R. Ol'denburg, 1922.

———. "Podlinnost' 'Sionskikh protokolov'." In *Akhad-Kham: Tainyi vozhd' iudeiskii.* Berlin: 1922.

———. *V plenu u obez'ian (Zapiski "kontr-revoliutsionera").* Kiev: Tipografiia Gubernskogo pravleniia, 1918.

Vishniak, Mark Veniaminovich. *Bol'shevizm i demokratiia.* New York: Narodo-pravstvo, 1919.

———. *Chernyi god.* Paris: Franko-russkaia pechat', 1922.

———. *Dan' proshlomu.* New York: Izdatel'stvo imeni Chekhova, 1954.

———. *Le régime soviétiste.* Paris: Union, 1920.

———. *"Sovremennye zapiski": Vospominaniia redaktora.* N.p.: Indiana University Publications, 1957.

———. *Vserossiiskoe uchreditel'noe sobranie.* Paris: Sovremennye zapiski, 1932.

———. *Years of Emigration 1919–1969: Paris–New York* (in Russian): *Gody emigratsii: 1919–1969.* Stanford: Hoover Institution Press, 1970.

Volin, Simon. *Men'shevizm v pervye gody NEP'a.* Inter-University Project on the History of the Menshevik Movement. New York, 1961.

Zenzinov, Vladimir Mikhailovich. *Iz zhizni revoliutsionera.* Paris, 1919.

Zinov'ev, Grigorii Evseevich. *Kontr-revoliutsiia i zadachi rabochikh: Rech' na zasedanii petrogradskogo soveta 15 iiunia 1918 g.* Moscow: Izdatel'stvo Vserossiiskogo tsentral'nogo ispolnitel'nogo komiteta Sovetov r., s., i k. deputatov, 1918.

IV. Secondary Sources

Agurskii, Mikhail. *Ideologiia natsional-bol'shevizm.* Paris: YMCA Press, 1980.

Ascher, Abraham. "Axelrod and Kautsky." *Slavic Review,* 26 (March 1967), 94–112.

———. *Pavel Axelrod and the Development of Menshevism.* Cambridge, Mass.: Harvard University Press, 1972.

Avrich, Paul. "The Bolshevik Revolution and Workers' Control in Russian Industry." *Slavic Review,* 22, no. 1 (March 1963), 47–63.

———. *Kronstadt 1921.* New York: Norton, 1970.

———. *The Russian Anarchists*. Princeton: Princeton University Press, 1967.

Baron, Samuel H. *Plekhanov: The Father of Russian Marxism*. Stanford: Stanford University Press, 1963.

Basil, John D. *The Mensheviks in the Revolution of 1917*. Columbus, Ohio: Slavica, 1984.

Baynac, Jacques. *Les socialistes-révolutionnaires*. Paris: Robert Laffont, 1979.

Bergman, Jay. *Vera Zasulich*. Stanford: Stanford University Press, 1983.

Böss, Otto. *Die Lehre der Eurasier: Ein Beitrag zur russischen Ideengeschichte des 20. Jahrhunderts*. Wiesbaden: Otto Harrossowitz, 1961.

Bourgina, Anna. *Russian Social Democracy: The Menshevik Movement* (in Russian). Stanford: The Hoover Institution, 1968.

Bradley, J. F. N. Civil War in Russia 1917–1920. London: B. T. Batsford, 1975.

Braunthal, Julius. *Geschichte der Internationale*. 3 vols. Hannover: J. H. W. Dietz, 1963.

Brovkin, Vladimir. "The Mensheviks' Political Comeback: The Elections to the Provincial City Soviets in Spring 1918." *Russian Review*, 42, no. 1 (January 1983), 1–50.

Brym, Robert J. *The Jewish Intelligentsia and Russian Marxism: A Sociological Study of Intellectual Radicalism and Ideological Divergence*. New York: Schocken Books, 1978.

Burbank, Jane. "Waiting for the People's Revolution: Martov and Chernov in Revolutionary Russia, 1917–1923." *Cahiers du monde russe et soviétique*, 26, nos. 3–4 (1985), 375–394.

Carr, Edward Hallett. *The Bolshevik Revolution: 1917–1923*. 3 vols. London: Macmillan, 1951–1953.

Chamberlin, William Henry. *The Russian Revolution*. 2 vols. New York: Grosset and Dunlap, 1965.

Chernov, Victor. *The Great Russian Revolution*. Translated by Philip E. Mosely. New Haven: Yale University Press, 1936.

Cohen, Stephen F. *Bukharin and the Bolshevik Revolution: A Political Biography, 1888–1938*. New York: Alfred A. Knopf, 1973.

Cohn, Norman. *Warrant for Genocide*. London: Eyre & Spottiswoode, 1967.

Confino, Michael. "On Intellectuals and Intellectual Traditions in Eighteenth- and Nineteenth-Century Russia." *Daedalus*, 101, no. 2 (Spring 1972), 117–149.

Curtiss, John Shelton. *The Russian Church and the Soviet State, 1917–1950*. Boston: Little, Brown, 1953.

Daniels, Robert Vincent. *The Conscience of the Revolution: Communist Opposition in Soviet Russia*. Cambridge, Mass.: Harvard University Press, 1960.

Dupeux, Louis. *National bolchevisme: Stratégie communiste and dynamique conservatrice*. 2 vols. Paris: Librairie Honoré Champion, 1979.

Edelman, Robert. *Gentry Politics on the Eve of the Russian Revolution: The Nationalist Party, 1907–1917*. New Brunswick: Rutgers University Press, 1980.

Emmons, Terence and Wayne S. Vucinich, eds. *The Zemstvo in Russia: An Experiment in Local Self-Government*. Cambridge: Cambridge University Press, 1982.

Ferro, Marc. *La révolution de 1917*. 2 vols. Paris: Aubier, 1967, 1976.

Fitzpatrick, Sheila. *The Commissariat of Enlightenment: Soviet Organization of Education and the Arts under Lunacharsky October 1917–1921*. Cambridge: At the University Press, 1970.

_____. *The Russian Revolution: 1917–1932*. Oxford: Oxford University Press, 1984.

Frankel, Jonathan. *Prophecy and Politics: Socialism, Nationalism, and the Russian Jews, 1862–1917*. Cambridge: Cambridge University Press, 1981.

Florinsky, Michael T. *The End of the Russian Empire*. New York: Collier Books, 1961.

Galili y Garcia, Ziva. "The Origins of Revolutionary Defensism." *Slavic Review*, 41, no. 3 (Fall 1982), 454–476.

Getzler, Israel. *Kronstadt 1917–1921: The Fate of a Soviet Democracy*. Cambridge: Cambridge University Press, 1983.

_____. *Martov: A Political Biography of a Russian Social Democrat*. Cambridge: At the University Press, 1967.

Golikov, D. L. *Krushenie antisovetskogo podpol'ia v SSSR*. 2 vols. Moscow: Izdatel'stvo politicheskoi literatury, 1978.

Gusev, K. V. *Partiia eserov: Ot melko-burzhuaznogo revoliutsionarizma k kontr-revoliutsii*. Moscow: Mysl', 1975.

Haimson, Leopold H. "The Mensheviks After the October Revolution." Parts 1,2. *Russian Review*, 38, no. 4 (October 1979), 456–473; 39, no. 2 (April 1980), 181–207.

_____. *The Russian Marxists and the Origins of Bolshevism*. Cambridge, Mass.: Harvard University Press, 1955.

_____, ed. *The Mensheviks*. Chicago: University of Chicago Press, 1974.

Hasegawa, Tsuyoshi. *The February Revolution: Petrograd 1917*. Seattle: University of Washington Press, 1981.

Hildermeier, Manfred. *Die Sozialrevolutionäre Partei Russlands: Agrarsozialismus und Modernisierung im Zarenreich (1900–1914)*. Cologne: Bohlau Verlag, 1978.

Ioffe, G. Z. *Krakh rossiiskoi monarkhicheskoi kontrrevoliutsii*. Moscow: Nauka, 1977.

Jakobson, Roman. "Nécrologie Nikolaj Sergejevic Trubetzkoy (16. April 1890–25. Juni 1938)." *Acta linguistica*, 1 (1939), 64–76.

Jansen, Marc. *A Show Trial under Lenin: The Trial of the Socialist Revolutionaries, Moscow 1922*. The Hague: Martinus Nijhoff, 1982.

Katkov, George. *Russia 1917: The February Revolution*. London: Longmans, 1967.

Keenan, Edward L. "Russian Political Culture." Photocopied. Cambridge, Mass.: Russian Research Center, Harvard University, July 1976.

Keep, John L. H. *The Rise of Social Democracy in Russia*. Oxford: Clarendon Press, 1963.

_____. *The Russian Revolution: A Study in Mass Mobilization*. New York: Norton, 1976.

Kenez, Peter. *Civil War in South Russia, 1918*. Berkeley: University of California Press, 1971.

_____. *Civil War in South Russia, 1919–1920*. Berkeley: University of California Press, 1977.

Kindersley, Richard. *The First Russian Revisionists: A Study of 'Legal Marxism' in Russia*. Oxford: Clarendon Press, 1962.

Kingston-Mann, Esther. *Lenin and the Problem of Marxist Peasant Revolution*. New York: Oxford University Press, 1983.

Klépinine, Tamara. *Bibliographie des oeuvres de Nicolas Berdiaev*. Paris: YMCA Press, 1978.

Laqueur, Walter. *Russia and Germany: A Century of Conflict*. London: Weidenfeld and Nicolson, 1965.

Leikina-Svirskaia, V. R. *Russkaia intelligentsiia v 1900–1917 godakh*. Moscow: Mysl', 1981.

Liebich, André. *Les Mencheviks en exil face à l'Union soviétique*. Cahier de recherche du CIEE, no. 4. Montreal: Centre interuniversitaire d'Etudes européennes, 1982.

Lowrie, Donald. *Rebellious Prophet: A Life of Nicolai Berdyaev*. 1960. Reprint. Westport, Conn.: Greenwood Press, 1974.

Manning, Roberta Thompson. *The Crisis of the Old Order in Russia: Gentry and Government*. Princeton: Princeton University Press, 1982.

Marcovic, Marko. *La philosophie de l'inégalité et les idées politiques de Nicolas Berdiaev*. Paris: Nouvelles éditions latines, 1968.

Mendel, Arthur P. *Dilemmas of Progress in Tsarist Russia: Legal Marxism and Legal Populism*. Cambridge, Mass.: Harvard University Press, 1961.

Miller, Martin A. *Kropotkin*. Chicago: Chicago University Press, 1976.

Nivat, George. "Du 'Panmongolisme' au 'mouvement Eurasien.' " *Cahiers du monde russe et soviétique*, 7, no. 3 (July–September 1966), 460–478.

Oberländer, Erwin. "Nationalbolschewistische Tendenzen in der russische Intelligenz: Die 'Smena Vech' Diskussion 1921–1922." *Jahrbücher für Geschichte Osteuropas*, NF 16, no. 2 (June 1968), 194–211.

Ol'denburg, Sergei Sergeevich. *Last Tsar: Nicholas II, His Reign & His Russia*. Translated by Leonid I. Mihalap and Patrick J. Rollins; edited by Patrick J. Rollins. 4 vols. Gulf Breeze: Academic International Press, 1975–1978; Russian edition published 1939–1949.

Pascal, Pierre. "Les grands courants de la pensée russe contemporaine." *Cahiers du monde russe et soviétique*, 3, no. 1 (January–March 1962), 5–89.

Pearson, Raymond. *The Russian Moderates and the Crisis of Tsarism: 1914–1917*. London: Macmillan & Co., 1977.

Perrie, Maureen. *The Agrarian Policy of the Russian Socialist-Revolutionary Party*. Cambridge: Cambridge University Press, 1976.

Pipes, Richard. *The Formation of the Soviet Union*. Cambridge, Mass.: Harvard University Press, 1964.

————. *Struve: Liberal on the Left, 1870–1905*. Cambridge, Mass.: Harvard University Press, 1970.

————. *Struve: Liberal on the Right, 1905–1944*. Cambridge, Mass.: Harvard University Press, 1980.

————, ed. *Revolutionary Russia*. Cambridge, Mass.: Harvard University Press, 1968.

————, ed. *The Russian Intelligentsia*. New York: Columbia University Press, 1961.

Pirumova, N. M. *Petr Alekseevich Kropotkin*. Moscow: Nauka, 1972.

Poltoratskii, N. *Berdiaev i Rossiia (Filosofiia istorii Rossii u N. A. Berdiaeva*. New York: Obshchestvo druzei russkoi kul'tury, 1967.

Rabinowitch, Alexander. *The Bolsheviks Come to Power: The Revolution of 1917 in Petrograd*. New York: Norton, 1976.

Radkey, Oliver Henry. *The Agrarian Foes of Bolshevism*. New York: Columbia University Press, 1958.

————. *The Election to the Russian Constituent Assembly of 1917*. Cambridge, Mass.: Harvard University Press, 1950.

_____.*The Sickle under the Hammer: The Russian Socialist Revolutionaries in the Early Months of Soviet Rule.* New York: Columbia University Press, 1963.

_____.*The Unknown Civil War in Soviet Russia.* Stanford: Hoover Institution Press, 1976.

Read, Christopher. *Religion, Revolution and the Russian Intelligentsia 1900–1912: The "Vekhi" Debate and Its Intellectual Background.* London: Macmillan Press, 1979.

Riasanovsky, Nicholas V. "The Emergence of Eurasianism." *California Slavic Studies*, 4 (1967), 39–72.

_____. "Prince N. S. Trubetskoy's 'Europe and Mankind.'" *Jahrbücher für Geschichte Osteuropas*, NF 12 (1964), 207–220.

Riha, Thomas. *A Russian European: Paul Miliukov in Russian Politics.* Notre Dame: University of Notre Dame Press, 1969.

Rimscha, Hans von. *Der russische Bürgerkrieg und die russische Emigration: 1917–1921.* Jena: Verlag der Frommannsche Buchhandlung, 1924.

_____.*Russland jenseits der Grenzen, 1921–1926: Ein Beitrag zur russischen Nachkriegsgeschichte.* Jena: Verlag der Frommannschen Buchhandlung (Walter Biedermann), 1927.

Rollin, Henri. *L'Apocalypse de notre temps.* Paris: Gallimard, 1939.

Rosenberg, William G. *Liberals in the Russian Revolution: The Constitutional Democratic Party, 1917–1921.* Princeton: Princeton University Press, 1974.

_____. "Russian Labor and Bolshevik Power after October." *Slavic Review*, 44, no. 2 (Summer 1985), 213–238.

_____, ed. *Bolshevik Visions: First Phase of the Cultural Revolution in Soviet Russia.* Ann Arbor: Ardis, 1984.

Rosenthal, Bernice Glatzer. *Dmitri Sergeevich Merezhkovsky and the Silver Age.* The Hague: Nijhoff, 1975.

Russia Enters the Twentieth Century: 1894–1917. Edited by Erwin Oberländer et al., London: Methuen and Co., 1973.

Schapiro, Leonard. *The Origin of the Communist Autocracy.* 2nd ed. Cambridge, Mass.: Harvard University Press, 1977.

_____. *Rationalism and Nationalism in Russian Nineteenth-Century Thought.* New Haven: Yale University Press, 1967.

Scherrer, Jutta. "Intelligentsia, religion, révolution: Premières manifestations d'un socialisme chrétien en Russie, 1905–1907." *Cahiers du monde russe et soviétique*, 17, no. 4 (1976), 427–466; 18, no. 1–2 (1977), 5–32.

_____. *Die Petersbürger religios-philosophischen Vereinigungen.* Forschungen zur Osteuropeischen Geschichte, no. 19. Berlin: Otto Harrassowitz, 1973.

Shub, David. *Lenin, A Biography.* Rev. ed. Harmondsworth: Penguin, 1966.

_____. *Politicheskie deiateli Rossii (1850-ykh-1920-ykh gg.)* New York: Izdanie "Novogo zhurnala," 1969.

Sirianni, Carmen. *Workers' Control and Socialist Democracy: The Soviet Experience.* London: Verso Editions and NLB, 1982.

Smith, S. A. *Red Petrograd: Revolution in the Factories 1917–1918.* Cambridge: Cambridge University Press, 1983.

Stavrou, George, ed. *Russia under the Last Tsar.* Minneapolis: University of Minnesota Press, 1969.

Struve, Gleb. *Russkaia literatura v izgnanii*. New York: Izdatel'stvo imeni Chekhova, 1956.

Suny, Ronald Grigor. *The Baku Commune 1917–1918: Class and Nationality in the Russian Revolution*. Princeton: Princeton University Press, 1972.

Timberlake, Charles E., ed. *Essays on Russian Liberalism*. Columbia, Mo.: University of Missouri Press, 1972.

Treadgold, Donald W. *Lenin and His Rivals*. New York: Praeger, 1955.

Trifonov, I. Ia. "Iz istorii bor'by kommunisticheskoi partii protiv smenovekhovstva." *Istoriia SSSR*, 3, no. 3 (May–June 1959), 64–82.

Trotsky, Leon. *The History of the Russian Revolution*. 1932. New York: Monad, 1980.

Ulam, Adam B. *The Bolsheviks*. N.p.: Collier, 1965.

———. *Ideologies and Illusions: Revolutionary Thought from Herzen to Solzhenitsyn*. Cambridge, Mass.: Harvard University Press, 1976.

Volkmann, Hans-Erich. *Die russische Emigration in Deutschland: 1919–1929*. Würzburg: Holzner-Verlag, 1966.

Weidlé, Wladimir. *Russia: Absent and Present*. New York: Vintage Books, 1961.

Weissman, Benjamin. *Herbert Hoover and Famine Relief to Soviet Russia*. Stanford: Hoover Institution Press, 1974.

Williams, Robert C. " 'Changing Landmarks' in Russian Berlin, 1922–1924." *Slavic Review*, 27, no. 4 (December 1968), 581–593.

———. *Culture in Exile: Russian Emigrés in Germany, 1881–1941*. Ithaca: Cornell University Press, 1972.

Index